Exposition of the
Divine Principle

Exposition of the Divine Principle

The Holy Spirit Association for the
Unification of World Christianity

The Holy Spirit Association for the Unification of Christianity
4 West 43rd Street, New York, NY 10036

Copyright © H.S.A.-U.W.C., 1996

Revised edition copyright © H.S.A.-U.W.C., 2006

First Printing 1996, reprinted 1998, 2006

All rights reserved. No part of this publication may be reproduced, stored in a retrieval system or transmitted in any form or by any means electronic, mechanical, photocopying, recording or otherwise without the prior written permission of the publisher.

ISBN 0-910621-80-2

Library of Congress Catalog Number 73-86259

Printed in the United States of America

Unless otherwise noted, the Scriptural quotations in this edition are from the
Revised Standard Version of the Holy Bible, copyright 1946, 1952 and 1971 by the Division of Christian Education, National Council of Churches of Christ in the USA. Used by permission.

Sun Myung Moon

Overview

PREFACE XXI

INTRODUCTION 1

PART I

CHAPTER 1   THE PRINCIPLE OF CREATION 15
CHAPTER 2   THE HUMAN FALL 53
CHAPTER 3   ESCHATOLOGY AND HUMAN HISTORY 79
CHAPTER 4   THE MESSIAH: HIS ADVENT AND THE PURPOSE
            OF HIS SECOND COMING 111
CHAPTER 5   RESURRECTION 133
CHAPTER 6   PREDESTINATION 153
CHAPTER 7   CHRISTOLOGY 163

PART II

INTRODUCTION TO RESTORATION 175

CHAPTER 1   THE PROVIDENCE TO LAY THE FOUNDATION
            FOR RESTORATION 189
CHAPTER 2   MOSES AND JESUS IN THE PROVIDENCE
            OF RESTORATION 225
CHAPTER 3   THE PERIODS IN PROVIDENTIAL HISTORY AND THE
            DETERMINATION OF THEIR LENGTHS 289
CHAPTER 4   THE PARALLELS BETWEEN THE TWO AGES
            IN THE PROVIDENCE OF RESTORATION 313
CHAPTER 5   THE PERIOD OF PREPARATION FOR THE
            SECOND ADVENT OF THE MESSIAH 347
CHAPTER 6   THE SECOND ADVENT 381

Table of Contents

PREFACE xxiii
INTRODUCTION 1

PART I

CHAPTER 1

THE PRINCIPLE OF CREATION 15

SECTION 1
THE DUAL CHARACTERISTICS OF GOD AND THE CREATED UNIVERSE 15

1.1 The Dual Characteristics of God 15
1.2 The Relationship between God and the Universe 19

SECTION 2
UNIVERSAL PRIME ENERGY, GIVE AND TAKE ACTION AND
THE FOUR POSITION FOUNDATION 21

2.1 Universal Prime Energy 21
2.2 Give and Take Action 22
2.3 The Four Position Foundation Which Realizes the
    Three Object Purpose through Origin-Division-Union Action 24
    2.3.1 Origin-Division-Union Action 24
    2.3.2 The Three Object Purpose 25
    2.3.3 The Four Position Foundation 25
    2.3.4 The Mode of Existence of the Four Position Foundation .. 25
2.4 The Omnipresence of God 31
2.5 The Multiplication of Life 31
2.6 The Reason All Beings Are Composed of
    Dual Characteristics 31

SECTION 3
THE PURPOSE OF CREATION 32

3.1 The Purpose of the Creation of the Universe 32
3.2 Good Object Partners for the Joy of God 33

SECTION 4
ORIGINAL VALUE 36

4.1 The Process and Standard for the Determination
    of Original Value 36

4.2 Original Emotion, Intellect and Will;
   and Original Beauty, Truth and Goodness 37
4.3 Love and Beauty, Good and Evil,
   Righteousness and Unrighteousness 38
   4.3.1 Love and Beauty 38
   4.3.2 Good and Evil 39
   4.3.3 Righteousness and Unrighteousness 40

SECTION 5
THE PROCESS OF THE CREATION OF THE UNIVERSE
AND ITS GROWING PERIOD 40

5.1 The Process of the Creation of the Universe 40
5.2 The Growing Period for the Creation 41
   5.2.1 The Three Ordered Stages of the Growing Period 41
   5.2.2 The Realm of Indirect Dominion 43
   5.2.3 The Realm of Direct Dominion 44

SECTION 6
THE INCORPOREAL WORLD AND THE CORPOREAL WORLD
WHOSE CENTER IS HUMAN BEINGS 45

6.1 The Incorporeal World and the Corporeal World
   as Substantial Realities 45
6.2 The Position of Human Beings in the Cosmos 46
6.3 The Reciprocal Relationship between the
   Physical Self and the Spirit Self 47
   6.3.1 The Structure and Functions of the Physical Self 47
   6.3.2 The Structure and Functions of the Spirit Self 48
   6.3.3 The Spirit Mind, the Physical Mind
       and Their Relationship in the Human Mind 50

CHAPTER 2

THE HUMAN FALL 53

SECTION 1
THE ROOT OF SIN 53

1.1 The Tree of Life and the Tree of the Knowledge
   of Good and Evil 54
   1.1.1 The Tree of Life 55
   1.1.2 The Tree of the Knowledge of Good and Evil 56
1.2 The Identity of the Serpent 57
1.3 The Fall of the Angel and the Fall of Human Beings 58
   1.3.1 The Crime of the Angel 58
   1.3.2 The Crime of the Human Beings 59
   1.3.3 The Illicit Sexual Act between the Angel
       and the Human Beings 59
1.4 The Fruit of the Tree of the Knowledge of Good and Evil 60
1.5 The Root of Sin 61

Section 2
The Motivation and Process of the Fall 62

2.1 Angels, Their Missions and Their Relationship
    to Human Beings 62
2.2 The Spiritual Fall and the Physical Fall 63
    2.2.1 The Spiritual Fall 63
    2.2.2 The Physical Fall 64

Section 3
The Power of Love, the Power of the Principle
and God's Commandment 65

3.1 The Power of Love and the Power of the Principle
    in the Human Fall 65
3.2 Why God Set Up the Commandment as an Object of Faith 66
3.3 The Period During Which the Commandment Was Necessary 67

Section 4
The Consequences of the Human Fall 68

4.1 Satan and Fallen Humanity 68
4.2 Satan's Activities in Human Society 68
4.3 Good and Evil Seen from the Viewpoint of Purpose 69
4.4 The Works of Good Spirits and Evil Spirits 71
4.5 Sin 72
4.6 The Primary Characteristics of the Fallen Nature 72

Section 5
Freedom and the Human Fall 74

5.1 The Meaning of Freedom from the Viewpoint of the Principle 74
5.2 Freedom and the Human Fall 74
5.3 Freedom, the Fall and Restoration 75

Section 6
The Reasons God Did Not Intervene in the Fall
of the First Human Ancestors 76

6.1 To Maintain the Absoluteness and Perfection
    of the Principle of Creation 77
6.2 That God Alone Be the Creator 77
6.3 To Make Human Beings the Lords of Creation 78

Chapter 3

Eschatology and Human History 79

Section 1
The Completion of God's Purpose of Creation
and the Human Fall 80

1.1 The Completion of God's Purpose of Creation 80
1.2 Consequences of the Human Fall 81

Section 2
God's Work of Salvation 82

2.1 God's Work of Salvation is the Providence of Restoration 82
2.2 The Goal of the Providence of Restoration 83
2.3 Human History Is the History of the
   Providence of Restoration 84

Section 3
The Last Days 88

3.1 The Meaning of the Last Days 88
   3.1.1 Noah's Day was the Last Days 89
   3.1.2 Jesus' Day was the Last Days 89
   3.1.3 The Day of Christ's Second Advent is the Last Days 90
3.2 Bible Verses Concerning the Signs of the Last Days 90
   3.2.1 Heaven and Earth Destroyed,
      and a New Heaven and a New Earth Created 91
   3.2.2 Heaven and Earth Judged by Fire 91
   3.2.3 The Dead Rising from Their Tombs 93
   3.2.4 People on Earth Caught Up to
      Meet the Lord in the Air 94
   3.2.5 The Sun Darkened, the Moon
      Not Giving Light and the Stars Falling from Heaven 94

Section 4
The Last Days and the Present Days 96

4.1 Signs of the Restoration of the First Blessing 96
4.2 Signs of the Restoration of the Second Blessing 98
4.3 Signs of the Restoration of the Third Blessing 101

Section 5
The Last Days, the New Truth and Our Attitude 103

5.1 The Last Days and the New Truth 103
5.2 Our Attitude in the Last Days 106

Chart 1: The Unfolding Manifestation of God's Word in the Creation
of the Universe and the Providence of Restoration 109

Chapter 4

The Messiah: His Advent and the Purpose of His Second Coming 111

Section 1
Salvation through the Cross 112

1.1 The Purpose of Jesus' Coming as the Messiah 112
1.2 Was Salvation Completed through the Cross? 113
1.3 Jesus' Death on the Cross 114
1.4 The Limit of Salvation through Redemption
    by the Cross and the Purpose of Jesus' Second Advent 118
1.5 Two Kinds of Prophecies Concerning the Cross 119
1.6 Gospel Passages in Which Jesus Spoke
    of His Crucifixion as if It Were Necessary 121

Section 2
The Second Coming of Elijah and John the Baptist 122

2.1 The Jewish Belief in the Return of Elijah 123
2.2 The Direction the Jewish People Would Choose 124
2.3 The Faithlessness of John the Baptist 126
2.4 The Sense in Which John the Baptist Was Elijah 130
2.5 Our Attitude toward the Bible 130

Chapter 5
Resurrection 133

Section 1
Resurrection 133

1.1 The Biblical Concepts of Life and Death 133
1.2 The Death Caused by the Human Fall 135
1.3 The Meaning of Resurrection 136
1.4 What Changes Does Resurrection Cause in Human Beings? 137

Section 2
The Providence of Resurrection 138

2.1 How Does God Carry out His Work of Resurrection? 138
2.2 The Providence of Resurrection for People on Earth 139
    2.2.1 The Providence to Lay the Foundation for Resurrection 139
    2.2.2 The Providence of Formation-Stage Resurrection 139
    2.2.3 The Providence of Growth-Stage Resurrection 139
    2.2.4 The Providence of Completion-Stage Resurrection 140
    2.2.5 The Kingdom of Heaven and Paradise 140
    2.2.6 Spiritual Phenomena in the Last Days 141
    2.2.7 The First Resurrection 143
2.3 The Providence of Resurrection for Spirits 144
    2.3.1 The Purpose and the Way of Returning Resurrection 144

  2.3.2 The Returning Resurrection of the Spirits
    of Israelites and Christians 145
    2.3.2.1 Growth-Stage Returning Resurrection 145
    2.3.2.2 Completion-Stage Returning Resurrection 146
  2.3.3 The Returning Resurrection of Spirits
    Who Abide Outside of Paradise 147
2.4 The Theory of Reincarnation Examined
  in Light of the Principle of Returning Resurrection 149

SECTION 3
THE UNIFICATION OF RELIGIONS THROUGH RETURNING RESURRECTION 150

3.1 The Unification of Christianity through
  Returning Resurrection 150
3.2 The Unification of All Other Religions
  through Returning Resurrection 150
3.3 The Unification of Non-Religious People
  through Returning Resurrection 151

CHAPTER 6

PREDESTINATION 153

SECTION 1
THE PREDESTINATION OF GOD'S WILL 155

SECTION 2
THE PREDESTINATION OF THE WAY IN WHICH GOD'S WILL IS FULFILLED 156

SECTION 3
THE PREDESTINATION OF HUMAN BEINGS 158

SECTION 4
ELUCIDATION OF BIBLICAL VERSES WHICH SUPPORT
THE DOCTRINE OF ABSOLUTE PREDESTINATION 159

CHAPTER 7

CHRISTOLOGY 163

SECTION 1
THE VALUE OF A PERSON WHO HAS REALIZED
THE PURPOSE OF CREATION 163

SECTION 2
JESUS AND THE PERSON WHO HAS REALIZED
THE PURPOSE OF CREATION 165

2.1 Perfected Adam, Jesus and the Restoration
  of the Tree of Life 165

2.2 Jesus, Human Beings and the Fulfillment
of the Purpose of Creation 166
2.3 Is Jesus God Himself? 167

SECTION 3
JESUS AND FALLEN PEOPLE 168

SECTION 4
REBIRTH AND TRINITY 169
4.1 Rebirth 169
    4.1.1 Jesus and the Holy Spirit and
        Their Mission to Give Rebirth 169
    4.1.2 Jesus and the Holy Spirit and
        the Dual Characteristics of the Logos 170
    4.1.3 Spiritual Rebirth through Jesus and the Holy Spirit 171
4.2 The Trinity 171

PART II

INTRODUCTION TO RESTORATION 175

SECTION 1 ....
THE PRINCIPLE OF RESTORATION THROUGH INDEMNITY 176

1.1 Restoration through Indemnity 176
1.2 The Foundation for the Messiah 179
    1.2.1 The Foundation of Faith 180
    1.2.2 The Foundation of Substance 181

SECTION 2 181
THE COURSE OF THE PROVIDENCE OF RESTORATION 181

2.1 The Ages in the Course of the Providence of Restoration 181
2.2 Categorization of the Ages in the Course
    of the Providence of Restoration 183
    2.2.1 The Ages Categorized with Reference to God's Word 183
    2.2.2 The Ages Categorized with Reference
        to God's Work of Resurrection 184
    2.2.3 The Ages Categorized with Reference to the Providence
        to Restore through Indemnity the Lost Periods of Faith 184
    2.2.4 The Ages Categorized with Reference to the
        Expanding Scope of the Foundation for the Messiah 185
    2.2.5 The Ages Categorized with Reference to Responsibility 186
    2.2.6 The Ages Categorized with Reference
        to the Parallels in the Providence 186

SECTION 3
THE HISTORY OF THE PROVIDENCE OF RESTORATION AND I 187

Chapter 1

The Providence to Lay the Foundation for Restoration 189

Section 1
The Providence of Restoration in Adam's Family 189

1.1 The Foundation of Faith 190
1.2 The Foundation of Substance 192
1.3 The Foundation for the Messiah in Adam's Family 195
1.4 Some Lessons from Adam's Family 197

Section 2
The Providence of Restoration in Noah's Family 198

2.1 The Foundation of Faith 199
    2.1.1 The Central Figure for the Foundation of Faith 199
    2.1.2 The Object for the Condition in
          Restoring the Foundation of Faith 199
2.2 The Foundation of Substance 203
2.3 Some Lessons from Noah's Family 205

Section 3
The Providence of Restoration in Abraham's Family 206

3.1 The Foundation of Faith 206
    3.1.1 The Central Figure for the Foundation of Faith 206
    3.1.2 The Objects for the Condition
          Offered for the Foundation of Faith 208
        3.1.2.1 Abraham's Symbolic Offering 208
        3.1.2.2 Abraham's Offering of Isaac 213
        3.1.2.3 Isaac's Position and His Symbolic Offering
            in the Sight of God 215
3.2 The Foundation of Substance 217
3.3 The Foundation for the Messiah 220
3.4 Some Lessons from Abraham's Course 222

Chapter 2

Moses and Jesus in the Providence of Restoration 225

Section 1
The Model Courses for Bringing Satan to Submission 225

1.1 Why Jacob's Course and Moses' Course
    Were Set Up as the Models for Jesus' Course 226
1.2 Jacob's Course as the Model for Moses' and Jesus' Courses 227

SECTION 2
THE PROVIDENCE OF RESTORATION UNDER THE LEADERSHIP OF MOSES 230

2.1 Overview of the Providence Led by Moses 230
   2.1.1 The Foundation of Faith 230
      2.1.1.1 The Central Figure to Restore
           the Foundation of Faith 230
      2.1.1.2 The Object for the Condition
           in Restoring the Foundation of Faith 232
   2.1.2 The Foundation of Substance 233
   2.1.3 The Foundation for the Messiah 233
2.2 The National Courses to Restore Canaan
under the Leadership of Moses 234
   2.2.1 The First National Course to Restore Canaan 234
      2.2.1.1 The Foundation of Faith 234
      2.2.1.2 The Foundation of Substance 235
      2.2.1.3 The Failure of the First National Course
           to Restore Canaan 236
   2.2.2 The Second National Course to Restore Canaan 237
      2.2.2.1 The Foundation of Faith 237
      2.2.2.2 The Foundation of Substance 237
      2.2.2.3 The Providence of Restoration and the Tabernacle 244
          2.2.2.3.1 The Significance and Purpose
               of the Tablets of Stone, the Tabernacle
               and the Ark of the Covenant 245
          2.2.2.3.2 The Foundation for the Tabernacle 248
      2.2.2.4 The Failure of the Second National Course
           to Restore Canaan 252
   2.2.3 The Third National Course to Restore Canaan .252
      2.2.3.1 The Foundation of Faith 252
      2.2.3.2 The Foundation of Substance 253
          2.2.3.2.1 The Foundation of Substance
               Centered on Moses 253
          2.2.3.2.2 The Foundation of Substance
               Centered on Joshua 259
      2.2.3.3 The Foundation for the Messiah 263
2.3 Some Lessons from Moses' Course 264

SECTION 3
THE PROVIDENCE OF RESTORATION UNDER THE LEADERSHIP OF JESUS 266

3.1 The First Worldwide Course to Restore Canaan 267
   3.1.1 The Foundation of Faith 267
   3.1.2 The Foundation of Substance 268
   3.1.3 The Failure of the First Worldwide Course
      to Restore Canaan 269
3.2 The Second Worldwide Course to Restore Canaan 270
   3.2.1 The Foundation of Faith 270
      3.2.1.1 Jesus Takes On the Mission of John the Baptist 270
      3.2.1.2 Jesus' Forty-Day Fast and Three Temptations
           in the Wilderness 271
      3.2.1.3 The Result of the Forty-Day Fast
           and the Three Temptations 275

    3.2.2 The Foundation of Substance 276
    3.2.3 The Failure of the Second Worldwide Course
         to Restore Canaan 277
3.3 The Third Worldwide Course to Restore Canaan 277
    3.3.1 The Spiritual Course to Restore Canaan
         under Jesus' Leadership 277
        3.3.1.1 The Spiritual Foundation of Faith 278
        3.3.1.2 The Spiritual Foundation of Substance 279
        3.3.1.3 The Spiritual Foundation for the Messiah 280
        3.3.1.4 The Restoration of Spiritual Canaan 281
    3.3.2 The Course to Restore Substantial Canaan
         under the Leadership of Christ at the Second Advent 281
3.4 Some Lessons from Jesus' Course 286

CHAPTER 3

THE PERIODS IN PROVIDENTIAL HISTORY AND
THE DETERMINATION OF THEIR LENGTHS 289

SECTION 1
PARALLEL PROVIDENTIAL PERIODS 289

SECTION 2
THE NUMBER OF GENERATIONS OR YEARS IN THE PERIODS OF THE AGE
OF THE PROVIDENCE TO LAY THE FOUNDATION FOR RESTORATION 291

2.1 Why and How the Providence of Restoration Is Prolonged 291
2.2 Vertical Indemnity Conditions and Horizontal Restoration
    through Indemnity 292
2.3 Horizontal Restoration through Indemnity
    Carried Out Vertically 294
2.4 Numerical Indemnity Periods for Restoring
    the Foundation of Faith 294
2.5 The Parallel Periods Determined by
    the Number of Generations 299
2.6 Providential Periods of Horizontal Restoration
    through Indemnity Carried Out Vertically 301

SECTION 3
THE PERIODS IN THE AGE OF THE PROVIDENCE
    OF RESTORATION AND THEIR LENGTHS 302

3.1 The Four-Hundred-Year Period of Slavery in Egypt 302
3.2 The Four-Hundred-Year Period of the Judges 303
3.3 The One-Hundred-and-Twenty-Year Period
    of the United Kingdom 303
3.4 The Four-Hundred-Year Period
    of the Divided Kingdoms of North and South 305
3.5 The Two-Hundred-and-Ten-Year Period
    of Israel's Exile and Return 305
3.6 The Four-Hundred-Year Period of Preparation
    for the Advent of the Messiah 306

Section 4
The Periods in the Age of the Prolongation
  of the Providence of Restoration and Their Lengths 307

4.1 The Four-Hundred-Year Period of Persecution
    in the Roman Empire 307
4.2 The Four-Hundred-Year Period
    of Regional Church Leadership 308
4.3 The One-Hundred-and-Twenty-Year Period
    of the Christian Empire 308
4.4 The Four-Hundred-Year Period of the Divided Kingdoms
    of East and West 308
4.5 The Two-Hundred-and-Ten-Year Period
    of Papal Exile and Return 309
4.6 The Four-Hundred-Year Period of Preparation
    for the Second Advent of the Messiah 309

Chart 2: Parallel Providential Periods 311

Chapter 4

The Parallels between the Two Ages
in the Providence of Restoration 313

Section 1
The Period of Slavery in Egypt and the Period
of Persecution in the Roman Empire 315

Section 2
The Period of the Judges and the Period
of Regional Church Leadership 317

Section 3
The Period of the United Kingdom and the Period
of the Christian Empire 318

Section 4
The Period of the Divided Kingdoms of North and South
and the Period of the Divided Kingdoms of East and West 321

Section 5
The Period of Israel's Exile and Return and the Period
of the Papal Exile and Return 323

Section 6
The Period of Preparation for the Advent of the Messiah and
the Period of Preparation for the Second Advent of the Messiah 325

Section 7
The Providence of Restoration and the Progress of History 328

7.1 The Progress of History in the Age of the Providence
    of Restoration 329

7.2 The Progress of History in the Age of the Prolongation
of the Providence of Restoration 332
    7.2.1 The Providence of Restoration and the History
of the West 332
    7.2.2 The Mutual Relations between Religious History,
Economic History and Political History 333
    7.2.3 Clan Society 335
    7.2.4 Feudalistic Society 336
    7.2.5 Monarchic Society and Imperialism 337
    7.2.6 Democracy and Socialism 340
    7.2.7 The Ideals of Interdependence, Mutual Prosperity and Universally Shared
Values versus Communism 342

CHART 3: THE PROGRESS OF HISTORY AS GUIDED BY
THE PROVIDENCE OF RESTORATION 345

CHAPTER 5

THE PERIOD OF PREPARATION FOR THE
SECOND ADVENT OF THE MESSIAH 347

SECTION 1
THE PERIOD OF THE REFORMATION (1517-1648) 347

1.1 The Renaissance 351
1.2 The Reformation 352

SECTION 2
THE PERIOD OF RELIGIOUS AND IDEOLOGICAL CONFLICTS (1648-1789) 353

2.1 The Cain-Type View of Life 354
2.2 The Abel-Type View of Life 356

SECTION 3
THE PERIOD OF MATURATION OF POLITICS, ECONOMY
AND IDEOLOGY (1789-1918) 357

3.1 Democracy 358
    3.1.1 Cain-Type Democracy 359
    3.1.2 Abel-Type Democracy 360
3.2 The Significance of the Separation of Powers 361
3.3 The Significance of the Industrial Revolution 363
3.4 The Rise of the Great Powers 364
3.5 Religious Reforms and Political and Industrial Revolutions
since the Renaissance 364

SECTION 4
THE WORLD WARS 365

4.1 The Providential Causes of the World Wars 365
4.2 The First World War 367
    4.2.1 Summary of the Providence in the First World War 367
    4.2.2 What Decides God's Side and Satan's Side? .368
    4.2.3 The Providential Causes behind the First World War 369
    4.2.4 The Providential Results of the First World War 370

4.3 The Second World War .... .371
    4.3.1 Summary of the Providence in the Second World War .... .371
    4.3.2 The Nature of Fascism .... .371
    4.3.3 The Nations on God's Side and the Nations
         on Satan's Side in the Second World War .... .372
    4.3.4 The Providential Roles of the Three Nations
         on God's Side and Satan's Side .... .372
    4.3.5 The Providential Causes behind the Second World War .... .374
    4.3.6 The Providential Results of the Second World War .... .375
4.4 The Third World War .... .376
    4.4.1 Is the Third World War Inevitable? .... .376
    4.4.2 Summary of the Providence in the Third World War .... .377
    4.4.3 The Providential Causes behind the Third World War .... .378
    4.4.4 The Providential Results of the Third World War .... .379

CHAPTER 6

THE SECOND ADVENT .... .381

SECTION 1
WHEN WILL CHRIST RETURN? .... .382

SECTION 2
IN WHAT MANNER WILL CHRIST RETURN? .... .383

2.1 Perspectives on the Bible .... .383
2.2 Christ Will Return as a Child on the Earth .... .385
2.3 What is the Meaning of the Verse that Christ Will Return
    on the Clouds? .... .393
2.4 Why Did Jesus Say that the Lord Will Come on the Clouds? .... .395

SECTION 3
WHERE WILL CHRIST RETURN? .... .396

3.1 Will Christ Return among the Jewish People? .... .396
3.2 Christ Will Return to a Nation in the East .... .398
3.3 The Nation in the East is Korea .... .399
    3.3.1 A National Condition of Indemnity .... .399
    3.3.2 God's Front Line and Satan's Front Line 401
    3.3.3 The Object Partner of God's Heart 402
    3.3.4 Messianic Prophecies 404
    3.3.5 The Culmination of All Civilizations 406

SECTION 4
PARALLELS BETWEEN JESUS' DAY AND TODAY 407

SECTION 5
THE CHAOTIC PROFUSION OF LANGUAGES AND
THE NECESSITY FOR THEIR UNIFICATION 410

INDEX 413

Preface

The text which you hold in your hands contains the Divine Principle, the teaching of the Reverend Sun Myung Moon. The earliest manuscript of the Divine Principle was lost in North Korea during the Korean War. Upon arriving as a refugee in Pusan, Reverend Moon wrote and dictated a manuscript called *Wŏlli Wŏnbon* (Original Text of the Divine Principle). He then guided Hyo Won Eu, the first president of the Unification Church of Korea, to prepare more systematic presentations of his teaching with biblical, historical and scientific illustrations. Reverend Moon gave President Eu special instruction regarding the content of these texts and then checked them over meticulously. These efforts resulted in *Wŏlli Hĕsŭl* (Explanation of the Divine Principle) published in 1957 and *Wŏlli Kangron* (Exposition of the Divine Principle) published in 1966. For the past thirty years, *Wŏlli Kangron* has been the text of Reverend Moon's basic teaching.

Exposition of the Divine Principle is the new authorized English translation of *Wŏlli Kangron*. The first English translation, *The Divine Principle,* was made in 1973 by Dr. Won Pok Choi. Dr. Choi labored with considerable erudition to select the proper terminology and convey the complex thought of this text. Aware of its sacred nature, she made a point of producing a literal translation. Through this work, she laid the foundation for the teaching of the Divine Principle in the Western world. In recognition of Dr. Choi's pioneering work, when Reverend Moon commissioned this new translation he requested that the translators seek out her advice. She gave constructive guidance and played an active role in improving the translation. In a real sense, her hands have guided this project.

For this version, the translators have sought, above all, to accurately render the meaning of the Korean text into clear English. The style of the Korean text, in keeping with the most erudite efforts of that generation, employs long and complicated sentences with numerous embedded clauses expressing complex relationships. It is simply not possible to express every nuance in the compact, linear structure of modern English. Whereas modern English wants to pin down every thought in an unequivocal proposition, the Korean of that time often renders thought loosely and dynamically, utilizing metaphor and context to convey meaning. Wherever a literal translation would not adequately express the thought and argumentation of the text, we have rearranged the order of thought in a manner more suitable to the Western mind. At times we used creative phraseology rather than dictionary definitions to evoke comparable understandings, feelings and cultural associations.

Furthermore, the Divine Principle employs some technical terminology and gives distinctive meanings to certain common words. Wherever possible, for this translation, we drew from common English vocabulary rather than invent new theological terms. Hence, ordinary words may be invested with distinctive meanings, for example: "indemnity," "condition" and "foundation." Proper understanding requires attention to their particular usage in the text.

The time and cultural context of this book was another issue for the translators. It was written in the 1960s, when communism was still a worldwide menace and Christianity was still confident of its cultural superiority and continuing expansion. Although these and other conditions of the time may have changed in the intervening decades, we have preserved the original perspective of the text. God's providence continues to advance precisely as explained in the Divine Principle.

In one sense, this new version seeks to accomplish more than a conventional translation. In the 1960s, when Korea was still recovering from the ravages of the Korean War, there was a paucity of historical and scientific texts available for study. This hindered President Eu in his efforts to accurately frame the scientific and historical examples which he employed to illustrate the operation of the Divine Principle in nature and in history. As authorized by Reverend Moon, and with Dr. Choi's guidance, the translators drew upon the knowledge of scholars in various fields and made minimal, necessary changes in certain scientific, historical and biblical illustrations. Nevertheless, throughout the translation, we adhered strictly to Reverend Moon's wishes that the integrity and purity of the text be maintained. Finally, the new translation has been carefully and extensively reviewed by church elders Rev. Young Whi Kim and Rev. Chung Hwan Kwak and has received their blessing.

In the deluxe color coded edition, the colors are based upon the 39th Korean edition of *Wŏlli Kangron* with colors prepared by Mrs. Gil Ja Sa Eu. The main ideas are shaded red, topics of second rank are shaded blue, and topics of third rank are shaded yellow. The reader can grasp the main thread of the teaching of the Divine Principle in a short time by reading only the red text. Reading the red and blue text together provides a richer framework; reading all three colors together gives a rather full exposition including many examples. To get the fullest meaning, the text must be studied in its entirety. Yet even when reading the full text, attention to the passages in red can help to clarify the thread of the argument.

Exposition of the Divine Principle expresses a truth which is universal. It inherits and builds upon the core truths which God revealed through the Jewish and Christian scriptures and encompasses the profound wisdom of the Orient. Through this translation, we hope the deep message of the Divine Principle may be better understood in the Western world.

The Divine Principle Translation Committee
March 1996

Exposition of the

Divine Principle

Introduction

Every human being is struggling to attain life-long happiness and overcome misfortune. From the commonplace affairs of individuals to the great events that shape the course of history, each is at root an expression of the human aspiration for ever greater happiness. How, then, does happiness arise?

People feel joy when their desires are fulfilled. The word "desire," however, is often not understood in its original sense, because in the present circumstances our desires tend to pursue evil rather than good. Desires which result in injustice do not emanate from a person's original mind. The original mind is well aware that such desires lead to misfortune. Therefore, it repels evil desires and strives to follow the good. Even at the cost of their lives, people seek for the joy that can enrapture the original mind. This is the human condition: we grope along exhausting paths to cast off the shadow of death and search for the light of life.

Has anyone realized the joy in which the original mind delights by pursuing evil desires? Whenever such desires are sated, we feel unrest in our conscience and agony in our heart. Would a parent ever instruct his child to be evil? Would a teacher deliberately instill unrighteousness in his students? The impulse of the original mind, which everyone possesses, is to abhor evil and exalt goodness.

In the lives of religious people one can see an intense struggle to realize goodness by single-mindedly following the desires of the original mind. Yet since the beginning of time, not even one person has abided strictly by his original mind. As St. Paul noted, "None is righteous, no, not one; no one understands, no one seeks for God."[1] Confronted with the human condition, he lamented, "For I delight in the law of God,

---

1. Rom. 3:10-11

in my inmost self, but I see in my members another law at war with the law of my mind and making me captive to the law of sin which dwells in my members. Wretched man that I am!"[2]

We find a great contradiction in every person. Within the self-same individual are two opposing inclinations: the original mind that desires goodness and the evil mind that desires wickedness. They are engaged in a fierce battle, striving to accomplish two conflicting purposes. Any being possessing such a contradiction within itself is doomed to perish. Human beings, having acquired this contradiction, live on the brink of destruction.

Can it be that human life originated with such a contradiction? How could beings with a self-contradictory nature come into existence? If burdened by such a contradiction from its inception, human life would not have been able to arise. The contradiction, therefore, must have developed after the birth of the human race. Christianity sees this state of destruction as the result of the human Fall.

Can anyone dispute that the human condition is fallen? When we realize the fact that, due to the Fall, we have arrived at the brink of self-destruction, we make desperate efforts to resolve the contradiction within. We repel the evil desires coming from our evil mind and embrace the good desires springing from our original mind.

Nevertheless, we have been unable to find the ultimate answer to the question: What is the nature of good and evil? We still do not have an absolute and definitive truth which can enable us to distinguish, for example, which of the two, theism or atheism, is good and which is evil. Furthermore, we remain entirely ignorant of the answers to such questions as: What is the original mind, the wellspring of good desires? What is the origin of the evil mind that incites evil desires in opposition to the original mind? What is the root cause of the contradiction that brings people to ruin? In order to ward off evil desires and follow good desires, we must overcome this ignorance and gain the ability to distinguish clearly between good and evil. Then we can take the path to the good life the original mind seeks.

Considered from the viewpoint of the intellect, the human Fall represents humanity's descent into ignorance. People are composed of two aspects: internal and external, or mind and body; likewise, the intellect consists of two aspects: internal and external. In the same way, there are two types of ignorance: internal ignorance and external ignorance.

---

2. Rom. 7:22-24

Internal ignorance, in religious terms, is spiritual ignorance. It is ignorance of such questions as: What is the origin of human beings? What is the purpose of life? What happens after death? Do God and the next world exist? What is the nature of good and evil? External ignorance refers to ignorance of the natural world, including the human body. It is ignorance of such issues as: What is the origin of the physical universe? What are the natural laws governing all phenomena?

From the dawn of history until today, human beings have ceaselessly searched for the truth with which to overcome both types of ignorance and attain knowledge. Humanity through religion has followed the path of searching for internal truth, and through science has followed the path of seeking external truth. Religion and science, each in their own spheres, have been the methods of searching for truth in order to conquer ignorance and attain knowledge. Eventually, the way of religion and the way of science should be integrated and their problems resolved in one united undertaking; the two aspects of truth, internal and external, should develop in full consonance. Only then, completely liberated from ignorance and living solely in goodness in accord with the desires of the original mind, will we enjoy eternal happiness.

We can discern two broad courses in the search for solutions to the fundamental questions of human life. In the first, people have searched within the resultant, material world. Those who walk this path, believing it to be the supreme way, kneel before the glories of highly developed science. They take pride in its omnipotence and the material comforts it provides. Nevertheless, can we enjoy full happiness founded only upon external conditions that satisfy the flesh? The advance of science may create a comfortable social environment in which we can enjoy abundant wealth and prosperity, but can that alone truly gratify the spiritual desires of the inner self?

The passing joys of those who delight in the pleasures of the flesh are nothing compared to the bliss experienced by those on the path of enlightenment, who find joy in the midst of simple poverty. Gautama Buddha, who abandoned the luxuries of the royal palace and became enraptured in the pursuit of the Way, was not the only one who wandered about homeless while searching for his heart's resting place. Just as a healthy body depends upon a sound mind, so also only when the mind is content does the body have complete satisfaction.

What of the sailor who voyages on the sea of the material world under the sail of science in search of physical comforts? Let him reach the coast for which he longs. He eventually will come to realize that it is nothing more than the very graveyard where his body will be buried.

Where is science heading? Until now, scientific research has not embraced the internal world of cause; it has limited itself to the external world. It has not embraced the world of essence, but has limited itself to the world of phenomena. However, science today is entering a new phase. It is compelled to elevate its gaze from the external and resultant world of phenomena to the internal and causal world of essence. The scientific world has begun to recognize that science cannot achieve its ultimate goals without a theoretical explanation of the causal, spiritual world.

When the sailor, who has completed his voyage in search of external truth under the sail of science, adds another sail, the sail of religion, and embarks on a new voyage in search of internal truth, he finally will be headed toward the destination for which his original mind yearns.

The second course of human endeavor is the attempt to answer the fundamental questions about human life by transcending the resultant world of phenomena and searching in the world of essence. Undeniably, philosophies and religions which have pursued this path have made many contributions. Philosophers, saints and sages set out to pave the way of goodness for the people of their times. Yet so many of their accomplishments have become added spiritual burdens for the people of today.

Consider this objectively. Has any philosopher ever arrived at the knowledge that could solve humanity's deepest anguish? Has any sage ever clearly illuminated the path by resolving all the fundamental questions of human life and the universe? Have not their teachings and philosophies raised more unsettled questions, thus giving rise to skepticism?

Furthermore, the lights of revival which religions of every age cast upon the many souls who were groping in the darkness have faded with the onward flow of history. They have left only dim, sputtering wicks glimmering in the falling darkness.

Examine the history of Christianity. Professing the salvation of humankind, Christianity has expanded through a tumultuous history of two thousand years, extending its influence throughout the world in the present era. Yet what has become of the Christian spirit that once cast flames of life so brilliant that, despite the most brutal persecution by the Roman empire, Roman citizens were brought to their knees before the crucified Jesus? Medieval feudal society buried Christianity alive. Even though the Reformation raised high the torch of new life, its flame could not turn back the sweeping tide of darkness.

When ecclesiastic love waned, when waves of capitalistic greed surged across Christian Europe, when starving masses cried out bitterly in the slums, the promise of their salvation came not from heaven but from the earth. Its name was communism. Christianity, though it professed the love of God, had degenerated into a dead body of clergy trailing empty slogans. It was then only natural that a banner of rebellion would be raised, arguing that a merciless God who would allow such suffering could not exist. Hence, modern materialism was born. Western society became a hotbed of materialism; it was the fertile soil in which communism flourished.

Christianity lost the ability to equal the successes of either communism or materialism and failed to present the truth that could conquer their theories. Christians watched helplessly as these ideologies budded and thrived in their midst and expanded their influence all over the world. What a pity this is! What is more, although Christian doctrine teaches that all humanity descended from the same parents, many citizens of Christian nations who profess this doctrine will not even sit together with their brothers and sisters of different skin colors. This illustrates the actual situation of today's Christianity, which has lost much of the power to put the words of Jesus into practice. It has become a house of lifeless rituals, a whitewashed tomb.

There may come a day when human efforts bring an end to such social evils, but there is one social vice that human efforts alone can never eradicate. That is sexual immorality. Christian doctrine regards this as a cardinal sin. What a tragedy that today's Christian society cannot block this path of ruin down which so many people are rushing blindly! Christianity today has fallen victim to confusion and division, and it can only watch helplessly while countless lives are sucked into the maelstrom of immorality. This is evidence that conventional Christianity stands powerless to carry on God's providence to save humanity in this present age.

What is the reason that religious people, though earnestly searching for internal truth, have been unable to accomplish their God-given mission? The relationship between the world of essence and the world of phenomena can be compared to that between mind and body. It is a relationship of cause and result, internal and external, subject partner and object partner.[3] Just as people attain perfection of character only when the mind and body are fully united, the two worlds of essence and phenomena must join in perfect harmony before the ideal world can be realized.

---

3. cf. Creation 1.1

As with the relationship between mind and body, so too the world of phenomena cannot exist apart from the world of essence, and the world of essence cannot exist apart from the world of phenomena. Accordingly, life after death is inseparably linked to life in this world. Spiritual joy is incomplete without physical well-being.

Religions have made strenuous efforts to deny life in this world in their quest for the life eternal. They have despised the pleasures of the body for the sake of spiritual bliss. Yet however hard they may try, people cannot cut themselves off from the reality of this world or annihilate the desire for physical pleasures, which follows them like a shadow and cannot be shaken off. This world and its desires tenaciously grab hold of religious people, driving them into the depths of agony. Such is the contradiction which plagues their devotional lives. Even many enlightened spiritual leaders, still torn by this contradiction, have met a sad end. Herein is a principal cause for the inactivity and weakness of today's religions: they have not overcome this self-contradiction.

Another factor has fated religions to decline. In step with the progress of science, the human intellect has become highly sophisticated, requiring a scientific approach to understanding reality. The traditional doctrines of religions, on the other hand, are largely devoid of scientific explanations. That is to say, the current interpretations of internal truth and external truth do not agree.

The ultimate purpose of religion can be attained only when one first believes it in one's heart and then puts it into practice. However, without first understanding, beliefs do not take hold. For example, it is in order to understand the truth and thereby solidify our beliefs that we study holy scriptures. Likewise, it was to help the people understand that he was the Messiah, and thereby lead them to believe in him, that Jesus performed miracles. Understanding is the starting point for knowledge. Today, however, people will not accept what is not demonstrable by the logic of science. Accordingly, since religions are now unable to guide people even to the level of understanding, much less to belief, they are unable to fulfill their purpose. Even internal truth demands logical and convincing explanations. Indeed, throughout the long course of history, religions have been moving toward the point when their teachings could be elucidated scientifically.

Religion and science, setting out with the missions of dispelling the two aspects of human ignorance, have seemed in the course of their development to take positions that were contradictory and irreconcilable.

However, for humankind to completely overcome the two aspects of ignorance and fully realize the goodness which the original mind desires, at some point in history there must emerge a new truth which can reconcile religion and science and resolve their problems in an integrated undertaking.

It may be displeasing to religious believers, especially to Christians, to learn that a new expression of truth must appear. They believe that the scriptures they have are already perfect and flawless. Certainly, truth itself is unique, eternal, immutable and absolute. Scriptures, however, are not the truth itself, but are textbooks teaching the truth. They were given at various times in history as humankind developed both spiritually and intellectually. The depth and extent of teaching and the method of expressing the truth naturally varied according to each age. Consequently, we must never regard such textbooks as absolute in every detail.[4]

People need religion in order to seek the Ultimate Reality and realize goodness in accordance with the inclination of the original mind. Thus, the purpose of every religion is identical. However, religions have appeared in different forms according to their various missions, the cultures in which they took root, and their particular historical period. Their scriptures have taken different forms for similar reasons. All scriptures have the same purpose: to illuminate their surroundings with the light of truth. Yet when a brighter lamp is lit, the old lamp is outshone and its mission fades. Because religions lack the power to guide modern people out of the dark valley of death into the full radiance of life, there must emerge a new expression of truth that can radiate a new and brighter light. Jesus indicated that God would someday reveal a new truth: "I have said this to you in figures; the hour is coming when I shall no longer speak to you in figures but tell you plainly of the Father."[5]

What missions must the new truth fulfill? The new truth should be able to unify knowledge by reconciling the internal truth pursued by religion and the external truth pursued by science. Consequently, it will enable all people to overcome the two types of ignorance, internal and external, and fully comprehend the two types of knowledge.

Next, the new truth should lead fallen people to block the ways of the evil mind and to pursue the goals of the original mind, enabling them to attain goodness. It should guide people to remove the double-mindedness that sometimes seeks good and sometimes evil. It should

---

4. cf. Eschatology 5
5. John 16:25

empower religious people to overcome the contradiction which they face in their struggle to live according to the Way. For fallen people, knowledge is the light of life holding the power of revival, while ignorance is the shadow of death and the cause of ruin. Ignorance cannot beget true sentiments, and in the absence of knowledge and emotion the will to act cannot arise. Without the proper functioning of emotion, intellect and will, one cannot live the life of a true human being.

If we are created in such a way that we cannot live apart from God, then surely our ignorance of God consigns us to walk miserable paths. Though we may diligently study the Bible, can we really say that we know clearly the reality of God? Can we ever grasp the *Heart of God?* The new expression of truth should be able to reveal the Heart of God: His heart of joy at the time of creation; the broken heart He felt when humankind, His children whom He could not abandon, rebelled against Him; and His heart of striving to save them throughout the long course of history.

Human history, woven of the lives of people who are inclined toward both good and evil, is filled with struggle. Today, external conflicts—battles over property, people and territory—are gradually diminishing. People are coming together transcending the differences between races. The victors of World War II liberated their colonies, gave them rights equal to those of the great powers and included them as members of the United Nations. Together, they are working toward a world order. Hostility and discord in international relations have been mitigated as economic concerns come to the forefront and nations are cooperating to construct common markets. Culture is freely circulating, the traditional isolation of nations is being overcome and the cultural distance between East and West is being bridged.

Nonetheless, one final and inescapable conflict remains before us, the war between democracy and communism. Although each side has equipped itself with fearsome weapons and is pitted against the other in readiness for battle, the core of their conflict is internal and ideological.

Which side will triumph in this final ideological conflict? Anyone who believes in the reality of God will surely answer that democracy will win. However, democracy does not possess any doctrine which can win over communism, nor does it have the power to do so. Therefore, in order for God's providence of salvation to be completely fulfilled, this new truth should first elevate the idealism of the democratic world to a new level, then use it to assimilate materialism, and finally bring humanity into a new world. This truth must be able to embrace all historical religions, ideologies and philosophies and bring complete unity among them.

Some people do, indeed, refuse to believe in religion. They disbelieve because they do not know the reality of God and life after death. Yet, however strongly they would like to deny these realities, it is human nature to accept and believe in them if they can be proven scientifically. Moreover, Heaven has implanted in human beings a nature such that those who place their ultimate purpose of life in the material world will eventually come to feel a great void and emptiness in their hearts. When people come to know God through the new truth and encounter the reality of the spirit world, they will realize that they should not set the ultimate purpose of life in the material world, but instead should look to the eternal world. They will walk the path of faith, and when they reach their final destination, they will meet as brothers and sisters.

If all people are to meet as brothers and sisters by virtue of this one truth, what will that world be like? Under the light of the new truth, all those who have struggled over the long course of history to dispel the darkness of ignorance will gather. They will form one great family. Since the purpose of truth is to realize goodness, and since God is the origin of goodness, God will be the center of the world founded upon this truth. Everyone will adore and serve God as their Parent and live in harmony with each other in brotherly love. It is human nature that when people wrong their neighbor for selfish ends, they suffer more from the pangs of conscience than they benefit from the enjoyment of unrighteous gains. Anyone realizing this will restrain himself from hurting his neighbor. But were genuine brotherly love to overflow from the depth of people's hearts, they would no longer wish to do anything that would cause pain to their neighbor. How much more would this be true in a society of people who actually feel that God, who transcends time and space and observes their every act, wants them to love each other? Therefore, once the sinful history of humanity has come to an end, a new historical era will begin wherein people simply will not commit sins.

The reason why people who believe in God continue to commit sins is because their faith in God has been merely conceptual. It has not touched their innermost feelings. Who among them would ever dare to commit sin if they experienced God in the depths of their being? Would they not tremble if they felt the reality of the heavenly law that those who commit crimes cannot escape the destiny of hell?

The world without sin which has just been described, this long-sought goal of humankind, may be called the *Kingdom of Heaven*.

Since this world is to be established on the earth, it may be called the Kingdom of Heaven on earth.

We can conclude that the ultimate purpose of God's work of salvation is to establish the Kingdom of Heaven on earth. It was explained above that human beings fell, and that this fall took place after the human race originated. If we accept the existence of God, then it is obvious what kind of world God originally wanted to realize before the fall of the first human ancestors. It suffices to say that this world was to be the Kingdom of Heaven on earth, wherein God's purpose of creation would bear fruit.[6]

Due to the Fall, human beings failed to establish this world. Instead, they fell into ignorance and built a sinful world. Since then, fallen human beings have unceasingly struggled to restore the Kingdom of Heaven on earth, the world God originally intended to create. Over the long course of history, they have sought for truth, both internal and external, and have strived to pursue goodness. Thus, behind human history is God's providence to restore a world where the purpose of God's creation is fulfilled. Accordingly, the new truth should guide fallen human beings to return to their original state. To do this, it must reveal the purpose for which God created humankind and the universe, and teach about the process of their restoration and its ultimate goal.

Did human beings fall by eating a fruit called the fruit of the tree of the knowledge of good and evil, as is written literally in the Bible? If not, then what was the cause of the Fall? The new truth must answer these and other questions which have pained and troubled the minds of profound thinkers throughout the ages: Why did the God of perfection and beauty create human beings with the potential to fall? Why did the omniscient and omnipotent God not prevent their fall, even though He was aware that they were falling? Why did God not save sinful humankind in an instant with His almighty power?

As we marvel at the scientific laws concealed in the natural world, we can deduce that God, its Creator, truly is the very origin of science. If human history is God's providence to restore the world wherein His purpose of creation is fulfilled, it must be that God, the Master of all laws, has led the long providence of restoration according to an orderly plan. It is our most urgent task to comprehend how the sinful history of humanity began, what formulas and laws have governed the course of the providence, how history will be consummated and, finally, into what kind of world humanity will enter. The new truth must offer answers to all of these deeper questions of life. When the answers are made clear, it will

---

6. cf. Creation 3.1

not be possible to deny the existence of God, the Ruler who plans and guides history. We will recognize in every historical event traces of the Heart of God as He has struggled to save fallen human beings.

In addition, the new truth should be able to elucidate many difficult issues in Christianity, which has been granted the mission to establish its sphere of culture worldwide. Educated people are not fully satisfied with the simple assertion that Jesus is the Son of God and the Savior of humanity. They have carried on many theological debates in their efforts to understand the deeper significance of Christian doctrines. The new truth should elucidate the relationships between God, Jesus and human beings; they will be explained in light of the Principle of Creation. Furthermore, it should clarify the difficult mysteries surrounding the Holy Trinity. It should show why God's salvation of humanity was possible only through shedding the blood of His only begotten Son on the cross.

Still, difficult issues remain. Christians believe that salvation is given through the atonement of the cross. Yet no one has ever given birth to a child who is sinless and in no need of redemption by the Savior. This demonstrates that, even after their rebirth in Christ, people continue to pass down the original sin to their children. This raises a crucial question: What is the extent of redemption by the cross? How many millions of Christians in the two-thousand-year history of Christianity have boasted that their sins were completely forgiven by virtue of the blood of the crucifixion? Yet in reality, a sinless individual, family or society has never appeared. Furthermore, the Christian spirit has been in gradual decline. How are we going to reconcile the discrepancy between the conventional belief in complete redemption through the crucifixion and the actual reality? These are only some of many dilemmas we face. The new truth, for which we long, should provide plain answers.

Many other difficult riddles are found in the Bible, couched in symbolism and metaphor, such as: Why must Jesus come again? When, where and how will his return take place? How will fallen people be resurrected at his coming? What is the meaning of the biblical prophecies that heaven and earth will be destroyed by fire and other calamities? The new truth should explain these puzzles, not in esoteric language but, as Jesus promised, in plain language that everyone can understand.[7] Divergent interpretations of such symbolic and metaphorical Bible verses have inevitably led to the division of Christianity into denominations. Only with the aid of the new truth, with its clear expla-

---

7. John 16:25
8. Rev. 10:11

nations, can we bring about Christian unity.

This ultimate life-giving truth, however, cannot be discovered through an exhaustive investigation of scriptures or scholarly texts; nor can it be invented by any human intellect. As is written in the Book of Revelation, "You must again prophesy about many peoples and nations and tongues and kings."[8] This truth must appear as a revelation from God.

With the fullness of time, God has sent one person to this earth to resolve the fundamental problems of human life and the universe. His name is Sun Myung Moon. For several decades he wandered through the spirit world so vast as to be beyond imagining. He trod a bloody path of suffering in search of the truth, passing through tribulations that God alone remembers. Since he understood that no one can find the ultimate truth to save humanity without first passing through the bitterest of trials, he fought alone against millions of devils, both in the spiritual and physical worlds, and triumphed over them all. Through intimate spiritual communion with God and by meeting with Jesus and many saints in Paradise, he brought to light all the secrets of Heaven.

The words proclaimed on these pages are only a portion of this truth. This volume is merely a compilation of what his disciples have hitherto heard and seen. We believe and hope that when the time is ripe, more profound portions of the truth will be published.

In every corner of the world, countless souls who had been groping in the darkness are receiving the light of this new truth and are being reborn. As we witness this, we cannot stop shedding tears of deepest inspiration. We desire from the bottom of our hearts that its light quickly fills the earth.

Part I

Chapter 1

The Principle of Creation

Throughout history, people have anguished over the fundamental questions of human life and the universe without arriving at satisfying answers. This is because no one has understood the root principle by which humanity and the universe were originally created. To approach this topic properly, it is not enough to examine resultant reality. The fundamental question is that of the causal reality. Problems concerning human life and the universe cannot be solved without first understanding the nature of God. This chapter deals extensively with these questions.

SECTION 1

THE DUAL CHARACTERISTICS OF GOD AND THE CREATED UNIVERSE

1.1 THE DUAL CHARACTERISTICS OF GOD

How can we know the divine nature of the invisible God? One way to fathom His deity is by observing the universe which He created. Thus, St. Paul said:

> Ever since the creation of the world his invisible nature, namely, his eternal power and deity, has been clearly perceived in the things that have been made. So they are without excuse. —*Rom. 1:20*

Just as a work of art displays the invisible nature of its maker in a concrete form, everything in the created universe is a substantial manifestation of some quality of the Creator's invisible, divine nature. As such, each stands in a relationship to God. Just as we can come to know the character of an artist through his works, so we can understand the nature of God by observing the diverse things of creation.

Let us begin by pointing out the common elements which are found universally throughout the natural world. Every entity possesses *dual characteristics* of *yang* (masculinity) and *yin* (feminity) and comes into existence only when these characteristics have formed reciprocal relationships, both within the entity and between it and other entities.

For example, subatomic particles, the basic building blocks of all matter, possess either a positive charge, a negative charge or a neutral charge formed by the neutralization of positive and negative constituents. When particles join with each other through the reciprocal relationships of their dual characteristics, they form an atom. Atoms, in turn, display either a positive or a negative valence. When the dual characteristics within one atom enter into reciprocal relationships with those in another atom, they form a molecule. Molecules formed in this manner engage in further reciprocal relationships between their dual characteristics to eventually become nourishment fit for consumption by plants and animals.

Plants propagate by means of stamen and pistil. Animals multiply and maintain their species through the relationship between males and females. According to the Bible, after God created Adam, He saw that it was not good for the man to live alone.[1] Only after God created Eve as Adam's female counterpart did He declare that His creations were "very good."[2]

Even though atoms become positive or negative ions after ionization, each still consists of a positive nucleus and negative electrons in stable unity. Similarly, each animal, whether male or female, maintains its life through the reciprocal relationships of yang and yin elements within itself. The same holds true for every plant. In people, a feminine nature is found latent in men and a masculine nature is found latent in women.

Moreover, every creation exists with correlative aspects: inside and outside, internal and external, front and rear, right and left, up and down, high and low, strong and weak, rising and falling, long and short, wide and narrow, east and west, north and south, etc. The rea-

---
1. Gen. 2:18
2. Gen. 1:31

son for this is that everything is created to exist through the reciprocal relationships of dual characteristics. Thus, we can understand that everything requires for its existence a reciprocal relationship between the dual characteristics of yang and yin.

However, there is another pair of dual characteristics in reciprocal relationship which are even more fundamental to existence than the dual characteristics of yang and yin. Every entity possesses both an outer form and an inner quality. The visible outer form resembles the invisible inner quality. The inner quality, though invisible, possesses a certain structure which is manifested visibly in the particular outer form. The inner quality is called *internal nature,* and the outer form or shape is called *external form*. Since internal nature and external form refer to corresponding inner and outer aspects of the same entity, the external form may also be understood as a second internal nature. Therefore, the internal nature and external form together constitute dual characteristics.

Let us take human beings as an example. A human being is composed of an outer form, the body, and an inner quality, the mind. The body is a visible reflection of the invisible mind. Because the mind possesses a certain structure, the body which reflects it also takes on a particular appearance. This is the idea behind a person's character and destiny being perceived through examining his outward appearance by such methods as physiognomy or palm reading. Here, mind is the internal nature and body is the external form. Mind and body are two correlative aspects of a human being; hence, the body may be understood as a second mind. Together, they constitute the dual characteristics of a human being. Similarly, all beings exist through the reciprocal relationships between their dual characteristics of internal nature and external form.

What is the relationship between internal nature and external form? The internal nature is intangible and causal, and stands in the position of a *subject partner* to the external form; the external form is tangible, resultant, and stands in the position of an *object partner* to the internal nature. The mutual relationships between these two aspects of an entity include: internal and external, cause and result, subject partner and object partner, vertical and horizontal. Let us again use the example of a human being, whose mind and body are his internal nature and external form, respectively. The body resembles the mind and moves according to its commands in such a way as to sustain life and pursue the mind's purposes. Mind and body thus have a mutual relationship of internal and external, cause and result, subject partner and object partner, vertical and horizontal.

Similarly, all created beings, regardless of their level of complexity, possess an intangible internal nature, which corresponds to the human mind, and a tangible external form, which corresponds to the human body. Within each being, the internal nature, which is causal and subject, commands the external form. This relationship allows the individual being to exist and function purposefully as a creation of God. Animals live and move because their bodies are directed by an internal faculty corresponding to the human mind, which endows them with a certain purpose. Plants maintain their organic functions by virtue of their internal nature, which also operates like the human mind in some respects.

The human mind imparts to every person a natural inclination to join with others in harmony. Likewise, positive ions and negative ions come together to form particular molecules, because within every one of them exists a rudimentary internal nature that guides them toward that end. Electrons assemble around nuclei to form atoms because they possess an attribute of internal nature which directs them toward that purpose. According to modern science, all particles that constitute atoms are made up of energy. For energy to form particles, it, too, must possess an internal nature which directs it to assume specific forms.

Probing deeper still, we search for the Ultimate Cause which brought this energy, with its elements of internal nature and external form, into existence. This being would be the First Cause of all the myriad things in the universe. As the First Cause, it must also possess the dual characteristics of internal nature and external form, which stand in the position of subject partner to the internal natures and external forms of all beings. We call this First Cause of the universe God, and we call God's internal nature and external form the *original internal nature* and *original external form*. As St. Paul indicated, by investigating characteristics that are universally present in the diverse things of creation, we can come to know the nature of God: God is the First Cause of the entire universe and its subject partner, having the harmonious dual characteristics of original internal nature and original external form.

We have already mentioned that entities require for their existence the reciprocal relationship between the dual characteristics of yang and yin. It is only natural to surmise that God, the First Cause of all things, also exists based on the reciprocal relationship between the dual characteristics of yang and yin. The verse "So God created man in his own image, in the image of God he created him; male and female he created them"[3] supports

---

3. Gen. 1:27

the idea that God is the subject partner, with dual characteristics of yang and yin in perfect harmony.

What is the relationship between the dual characteristics of internal nature and external form and the dual characteristics of yang and yin? God's original internal nature and original external form each contain the mutual relationship of original yang and original yin. Therefore, original yang and original yin are attributes of original internal nature and original external form. The relationship between yang and yin is similar to that which exists between internal nature and external form. Yang and yin thus have the following mutual relationships: internal and external, cause and result, subject partner and object partner, vertical and horizontal. For this reason, it is written in Genesis that God took a rib from the man, Adam, and created a woman, Eve, to be his helper.[4] In this case, the yang and yin of God were manifested in masculinity and femininity.

A human being attains perfection when he centers his life on his mind; likewise, the creation becomes complete only when God stands as its center. Hence, the universe is a perfect organic body that moves only according to God's purpose of creation. As one organic body, the universe exists in a relationship of internal nature and external form, with God as the internal nature and the created universe as the external form. For this reason it is written in the Bible that human beings, who are the center of the universe, are created in the image of God.[5] Before the creation, God existed alone as the internal and masculine subject partner. He therefore created the universe as His external and feminine object partner. This is supported by the Bible verse which states, "man . . . is the image and glory of God."[6] In recognition of God's position as the internal and masculine subject partner, we call Him "Our Father."

In summary, God is the Subject in whom the dual characteristics of original internal nature and original external form are in harmony. At the same time, God is the harmonious union of masculinity and femininity, which manifest the qualities of original internal nature and original external form, respectively. In relation to the universe, God is the subject partner having the qualities of internal nature and masculinity.

1.2 THE RELATIONSHIP BETWEEN GOD AND THE UNIVERSE

We have learned that every creation is God's substantial object part-

---

4. Gen. 2:22
5. Gen. 1:27
6. I Cor. 11:7

ner, formed in His likeness as a discrete projection of His dual characteristics. God exists as the incorporeal subject partner to all beings. Human beings are object partners embodied at the level of *image*, and the rest of creation are object partners embodied at the level of *symbol*. These object partners are called *individual embodiments of truth*, in image and symbol.

Individual embodiments of truth are discrete manifestations of the dual characteristics of God. Therefore, they can be distinguished broadly into two classes: those of yang qualities which resemble the original internal nature and masculinity of God, and those of yin qualities which resemble the original external form and femininity of God. Although individual embodiments of truth belong to either of these two classes, since they are all substantial object partners to God—resembling His original internal nature and original external form—they each possess within themselves both internal nature and external form, and likewise both yang and yin.

In light of our understanding of the dual characteristics, the relationship between God and the universe can be summarized thus: The universe as a whole is a substantial object partner to God. It is composed of individual embodiments of truth, each a unique manifestation of the dual characteristics of God at either the level of image or of symbol, as governed by the Principle of Creation. The myriad qualities of God, in their duality, are apportioned into diverse human beings, each an incarnate object partner at the level of image. These qualities are also apportioned into all the diverse things of creation, each an embodied object partner at the level of symbol. The relationship between God and the universe is similar to that between internal nature and external form. It is a mutual relationship like that between dual characteristics: internal and external, cause and result, vertical and horizontal, subject partner and object partner, and so forth.

Finally, from the viewpoint of the Principle of Creation, let us investigate the metaphysical concept at the root of East Asian philosophy which is based on the *Book of Changes (I Ching)*. There, the origin of the universe is the Great Ultimate (Ultimate Void). From the Great Ultimate arose yang and yin, from yang and yin came forth the Five Elements—metal, wood, water, fire and earth—and from the Five Elements all things came into existence.[7] Yang and yin together are called the Way *(Tao)*, or as the *Book of Changes* states, "One yang and

---

7. This is a paraphrase of the opening lines of *An Explanation of the Diagram of the Great Ultimate (T'ai-chi-t'u shuo)* by Chou Tun-i.
8. *Book of Changes*, Appended Remarks 4.

one yin: this is the Way."[8] The Way is traditionally defined as the Word. To put all this together, from the Great Ultimate arose yang and yin, or the Word, and all things came into being based on the Word. Accordingly, the Great Ultimate is the First Cause of all existing beings, the integral nucleus and harmonious subject partner of yang and yin.

It is written in the Gospel of John that "the Word was with God, and the Word was God,"[9] and that all things were made through the Word. Comparing this to the metaphysics rooted in the *Book of Changes,* we can surmise that the Great Ultimate, as the harmonious source of yang and yin or the Word, is none other than God who, as we have seen, is the harmonious subject partner of dual characteristics. According to the Principle of Creation, the fact that everything created through the Word has dual characteristics shows that the Word itself consists of dual characteristics. Consequently, the claim made in the *Book of Changes* that yang and yin together are the Word is valid.

However, this East Asian metaphysics observes the universe exclusively from the viewpoint of yang and yin while failing to recognize that all things also possess internal nature and external form. Therefore, although it reveals that the Great Ultimate is the subject partner of harmonious yang and yin, it fails to show that the Great Ultimate is also the subject partner of harmonious original internal nature and original external form. Hence, it does not comprehend that the Great Ultimate is a God with personality.

We have learned that the root concept of East Asian philosophy as based on the *Book of Changes* can be fully elucidated only with the help of the Principle of Creation. In recent years, Oriental medicine has become recognized to an increasing degree throughout the world. Its success is due to the fact that its founding principles, which focus upon the concepts of yang and yin, are in accordance with the Principle of Creation.

SECTION 2

UNIVERSAL PRIME ENERGY, GIVE AND TAKE ACTION, AND THE FOUR POSITION FOUNDATION

2.1 UNIVERSAL PRIME ENERGY

God, the Creator of all things, is the absolute reality, eternal, self-existent and transcendent of time and space. The fundamental energy of God's being is also eternal, self-existent and absolute. It is the ori-

---

9. John 1:1-3

gin of all energies and forces that allow created beings to exist. We call this fundamental energy *universal prime energy*.

2.2 GIVE AND TAKE ACTION

Through the agency of universal prime energy, the subject and object elements of every entity form a *common base* and enter into interaction. This interaction, in turn, generates all the forces the entity needs for existence, multiplication and action. The interaction generating these forces through this process is called *give and take action*. Universal prime energy and the forces generated by give and take action are in a reciprocal relationship of cause and result, internal and external, and subject partner and object partner. Universal prime energy may be thought of as a vertical force, while the forces generated by give and take action as horizontal forces.

Let us examine in detail God and His creation in terms of universal prime energy and give and take action. God's universal prime energy directs His eternal dual characteristics to form a common base for their mutual relationship. They then engage in give and take action. Based on the forces generated by this give and take action, the dual characteristics construct a foundation for their eternal reciprocation. This is the foundation for God's existence, upon which God eternally exists and generates all forces needed to create and sustain the universe.

In the created universe, the dual characteristics that make up each being are empowered by universal prime energy to establish a common base. They then engage in give and take action. Based on the forces generated by this give and take action, the dual characteristics construct a foundation for their continued reciprocation. This becomes the foundation for the existence of each individual being, upon which the being becomes an object partner to God and is able to generate all forces necessary for its continued existence.

For example, atoms come into existence when electrons assemble about a nucleus and engage in electromagnetic interaction, which is a type of give and take action. When positive ions and negative ions perform give and take action, they form molecules and produce chemical reactions. The give and take action between positive and negative electrical charges underlies all electrical phenomena.

The circulation of nutrients between xylem and phloem is one of the give and take actions in plants that sustain their life functions and promote their growth. The give and take action between stamen and pistil is the dominant means for the reproduction of plant life. Animals multiply and maintain their species through the give and take action between male and female. Animal and plant life co-exist through such give and take actions as the exchange of oxygen and carbon dioxide and the cooperation between bees and flowers.

With respect to the heavenly bodies, the solar system exists based on the give and take action between the sun and the planets. Their various movements give structure to the universe. The earth and the moon also maintain their rotations and their revolution in a set orbit through their give and take action.

The human body maintains its life through the give and take actions between arteries and veins, inhalation and exhalation, sympathetic and parasympathetic nerves, and so forth. The give and take action between mind and body enables an individual to carry out activities which further the purpose of life. The give and take between husband and wife in a family, among people in a society, between the government and citizens in a nation, and among the nations of the world are essential for them to live together in harmony and peace.

However evil a person may be, the force of his conscience, which impels him toward a virtuous life, is always active within his inner self. This is true for all people of all ages and places. No one can quell the force of conscience, which is powerfully at work even without one's conscious awareness. The minute a person commits an evil act, he immediately feels pangs of conscience. If the function of the conscience were absent in fallen people, God's providence of restoration would be impossible. How is this force of conscience generated? Since all forces are produced by give and take action, the conscience cannot generate the force needed for its operation all by itself. That is to say, the conscience can operate only when it forms a common base with some subject partner and engages in give and take action with it. The ultimate subject partner of our conscience is God.

The human Fall, in essence, severed our relationship with God. Rather than attaining oneness with God, our ancestors joined in a reciprocal relationship with Satan, thereby becoming one with him. Jesus was the only begotten Son of God; he attained oneness with God through perfect give and take action. When we unite with Jesus in a perfect reciprocal relationship, we can recover our original God-given nature. We can cultivate a give and take relationship with God and become one with Him. This is how Jesus serves as the mediator for fallen people;

---

10. John 3:16

he is our way, truth and life. Jesus came with love and sacrifice to give all that he had to humankind, even offering his life. If we turn to him in faith, we will "not perish but have eternal life."[10]

Christianity is a religion of love. It strives through love and sacrifice to open the path to restore the horizontal relationships of give and take between people in the love of Christ. On this horizontal foundation of love, the way is opened to restore our vertical relationship of give and take with God. In truth, this was the main purpose of all the teachings and deeds of Jesus. For example, Jesus said:

> Judge not, that you be not judged. For with the judgment you pronounce you will be judged, and the measure you give will be the measure you get. —*Matt. 7:1-2*

> So whatever you wish that men would do to you, do so to them; for this is the law and the prophets. —*Matt. 7:12*

> So everyone who acknowledges me before men, I will also acknowledge before my Father who is in heaven. —*Matt. 10:32*

> He who receives a prophet because he is a prophet shall receive a prophet's reward, and he who receives a righteous man because he is a righteous man shall receive a righteous man's reward. —*Matt. 10:41*

> And whoever gives to one of these little ones even a cup of cold water because he is a disciple, truly, I say to you, he shall not lose his reward. —*Matt. 10:42*

2.3 THE FOUR POSITION FOUNDATION WHICH REALIZES THE THREE OBJECT PURPOSE THROUGH ORIGIN-DIVISION-UNION ACTION

2.3.1 ORIGIN-DIVISION-UNION ACTION

The process of God's creation begins when the dual characteristics within God form a common base through the prompting of His universal prime energy. As they engage in give and take action, they generate a force which engenders multiplication. This force projects the dual characteristics into discrete substantial object partners, each relating to God as its center. These object partners to God then assume the position of subject partner and object partner to each other as they are prompted by the universal prime energy to form a common base and engage in give and take action. They then join together in one harmonious union to form a new object partner to God. This whole process—in which out of God, the Origin, two entities are separately manifested and reunited in oneness—is called *origin-division-union action*.

2.3.2 THE THREE OBJECT PURPOSE

As a result of origin-division-union action, four positions are formed: the origin at the center, the subject partner and the object partner (distinct substantial object partners to the origin in the pattern of its dual characteristics), and their union. Any one of the four positions may assume the position of subject partner and engage the other three as its object partners, forming a communion of three object partners. When each of the four then acts as the subject partner and enters into give and take with the other three revolving around it, they fulfill the *three object purpose*.

2.3.3 THE FOUR POSITION FOUNDATION

When through origin-division-union action, the origin, the subject partner and object partner projected from the origin, and their union all fulfill the three object purpose, the *four position foundation* is established.

The original significance of the number four derives from the four-position foundation. The original significance of the number three also derives from it, because it is the fulfillment of the three-object purpose. The four position foundation is realized by God, husband and wife, and children; they complete the three stages of origin-division-union action. Hence, the four position foundation is the root of the principle of three stages. Furthermore, each of the four positions in the four position foundation takes on three object partners in fulfilling the three object purpose. In total there are twelve object partners; hence, from it derives the original significance of the number twelve. The four position foundation is the fundamental foundation of goodness. It is the realization of God's purpose of creation. It is the fundamental foundation for the life of all beings, providing all the forces necessary for their existence and enabling God to abide in them. Therefore, the four position foundation is God's eternal purpose of creation.

2.3.4 THE MODE OF EXISTENCE OF THE FOUR POSITION FOUNDATION

All beings which have completed the four position foundation by fulfilling the three object purpose through origin-division-union action move in circular (elliptical) or spherical paths. As a result, they exist in three dimensions. Let us now investigate the reason for this.

Through origin-division-union action, the dual characteristics of God are projected to form two distinct and substantial object partners, which interact with each other as subject partner and object partner. The object partner responds to the subject partner to form a common base and begins give and take action around the subject partner. As they are held in balance by the force of giving (centrifugal) and the force of receiving (centripetal), the object partner revolves around the subject partner in a circular motion, and thus they become harmonious and unified. In the same manner, the subject partner becomes an object partner to God, revolving around God and thus attaining oneness with Him. When the object partner becomes completely one with its subject partner, their union can stand before God as a new object partner resembling His dual characteristics. Moreover, the way for any object partner to stand as an object partner before God is by making oneness with its subject partner.

In this union of subject partner and object partner, the subject partner and object partner are themselves composed of dual characteristics; these, by the same principle of give and take action, carry on their own circular motions. Thus, we see circular motions of give and take action within both the subject partner and object partner, which are simultaneously engaged in the greater circular motion within their union. Although there are moments when the two levels of circular motion among subject partners and object partners may happen to have orbits on the same plane, in general, because the angle of revolution around the subject partner is constantly changing, this circular movement becomes a spherical movement. In short, all beings which have completed the four position foundation carry on circular and spherical movement, and hence their mode of existence always becomes three-dimensional.

Let us take the solar system as an example. The planets, standing as object partners to the sun, each form a common base and engage in give and take action with the sun through centripetal and centrifugal forces. Revolving around the sun in elliptical orbits, the planets attain harmony and oneness with the sun to form the solar system. At the same time the planet Earth, as a composite body of dual characteristics, rotates on its own axis. This is also true of the sun and the rest of the planets; they are in continuous rotation on their own axes, because they too are composite bodies of dual characteristics. The orbits caused by give and take action in the solar system do not occupy exactly the same plane. Rather, due to the varied angles of their orbits and rotations, the solar system exhibits spherical motion in three dimensions. Likewise, all heavenly bodies exist in three dimensions by virtue of their circular and spherical movements. When the countless heavenly bodies carry on give and take action with each other, they form one body and thereby give structure to the universe. The universe exists in three dimensions as, governed by the same principle, its elements engage in spherical movements.

When an electron forms a common base with a proton and engages in give and take action, it moves about the proton in a spherical or otherwise three-dimensional pattern. Thus, they unite and form an atom (Hydrogen). The electron and the proton are themselves composed of dual characteristics that cause them to spin in continuous rotation. Therefore, the circular motion arising from the give and take action between the proton and electron is not limited to an orbit on one plane but, by continuously altering its angle of revolution, creates a spherical movement. Through spherical movement the atom thus exists in three dimensions. By the same token, the magnetic force between positive and negative poles causes electrically charged particles to precess in spherical movement.

Let us consider the example of human beings. As the object partner to the mind, the body establishes a common base with the mind and engages in give and take action with it. Figuratively speaking, the body then revolves about the mind and attains complete oneness with it. If and when the mind stands as an object partner before God and revolves around Him, resonating in oneness with Him, and when the body becomes one with this mind, the individual will resemble God's dual characteristics and thus stand as God's embodied object partner. Thereupon, the person fulfills the purpose of creation. The mind and body are also each composed of dual characteristics, so they carry on continuous movement within themselves. Thus, the circular movement produced through the give and take dynamic between mind and body ceaselessly alters the angle of revolution around God and becomes spherical. People who have realized the purpose of creation exist as three-dimensional beings who always lead their lives in spherical relationships centered on God. This is how they can attain mastery even over the incorporeal world.[11]

When the circular movement of the subject partner and the object partner on a single plane becomes a spherical movement in a three-dimensional orbit, the dynamism and creativity of the universe

---

11. cf. Creation 6.2

unfolds. Variations in each orbit's distance, shape, state, direction, angle, force and velocity are manifest as the beauty of creation in its infinite variety.

Just as all beings have internal nature and external form, there is a type of spherical motion that corresponds to internal nature and a type that corresponds to external form. Likewise, there is a center of motion that corresponds to internal nature and a center that corresponds to external form. These two centers have the same relationship as that between internal nature and external form.

What is the ultimate center of all these spherical movements? Human beings are the center of all created things, which are embodied object partners to God's dual characteristics in symbol. God is the center of human beings, who are created as His embodied object partners in image. Consequently, the ultimate center of all spherical movements in the universe is God.

Let us consider this further. Every object partner to God contains a subject partner and an object partner within itself. The center of their relationship is the subject partner, so the center of the union between subject partner and object partner is also the subject partner. Since God is the center of the subject partner, He is also the ultimate center of the union. As discussed above, the three substantial object partners to God (subject partner, object partner, union) also form common bases with each other. As each of the three takes the central position, and becomes one with the others through give and take action with God as their ultimate center, they fulfill the three object purpose and establish the four position foundation. Accordingly, the ultimate center of the four position foundation is God.

All things that have established four position foundations in this manner are individual embodiments of truth. As mentioned before, individual embodiments of truth are divided broadly into individual embodiments of truth in image (human beings) and individual embodiments of truth in symbol (the rest of the creation). The universe is composed of countless individual embodiments of truth, mutually related to each other in good order from those of the lowest level to those of the highest level. Among them all, human beings occupy the highest level.

Individual embodiments of truth revolve spherically around each other, with those of a lower level acting as object partners to those of a higher level. Thus, the center of any spherical movement is an individual embodiment of truth of a higher level which acts as the subject partner. The centers of the countless symbolic individual embodiments of truth are interconnected from the lowest to the highest. The highest centers are human beings, who are individual embodiments of truth in image.

Let us examine the centrality of human beings. Science holds that elementary particles are the most basic building blocks of matter and explains that they are composed of energy. Considering the purpose of existence of the individual embodiments of truth that make up the material universe at different levels, we can surmise: energy exists in order to form particles, particles exist to form atoms, atoms to form molecules, molecules to form matter, and matter exists for the creation of all the individual entities in the universe. Likewise, the activity of energy is for the purpose of forming particles, the activity of particles is for atoms, the activity of atoms is for molecules, the activity of molecules is for matter, and the activity of matter is for the purpose of constructing the universe.

What is the purpose of the universe? What is its center? The answer to both questions is none other than human beings. This is why God, after creating human beings, commanded them to have dominion over the universe.[12] If there were no people to appreciate the universe, then it could be likened to a museum without any visitors. The articles on display in a museum attain their true value and are cherished as historical relics only when there are people who appreciate, love and take delight in them. Their relationship with human beings gives value to their existence. If there were no one to appreciate them, then what meaning would their existence have? The same holds true for the universe, whose lords are human beings.

The diverse things in creation enter into mutual relationships with a common purpose when human beings discover the source and nature of matter, and when they identify and classify plants and animals of the water, land and air, and all the stars in the sky. Their common purpose is realized when they are assimilated into the human body as elements essential for people to maintain their physiological functions, and when they participate in the construction of a comfortable living environment for people. In these and other ways, human beings stand as the center of the created universe in terms of its external form.

In addition, people relate to the universe from their position as the internal center. While the relationships discussed above are physical relationships, here we consider mental or spiritual relationships. The human body, though consisting of matter, fully responds physiologically to the emotion, intellect and will of the human mind. This demonstrates

---

12. Gen. 1:28

that matter has within itself elements which resonate with emotion, intellect and will—elements which constitute the internal nature of matter. This is the reason all things in the universe respond to human emotion, intellect and will, albeit to different degrees. We become intoxicated with the beauty of the natural world and experience the rapture of mystical union. We experience this because we are the center of the internal natures of all things in the natural world. Human beings are thus created as the center of the universe, and the place where God and human beings become completely one is the center of the cosmos.

Let us discuss from another viewpoint how human beings are the center of the cosmos, which is composed of both the spirit world and the physical world. Every human being embodies all the elements in the cosmos. Yet, as we discussed earlier, everything in the cosmos can be divided broadly into subject partners and object partners. Had Adam, the first human ancestor, reached perfection, he would have embodied all the subject elements in the things of creation. Had Eve attained perfection, she would have embodied all the object elements in the things of creation. God created Adam and Eve to have dominion over the natural world. Growing together toward perfection, Adam was to become the king of all the subject elements in creation and Eve was to become the queen of all the object elements. If they had then become one as husband and wife, they would have become the center that could rule the entire universe consisting of subject partners and object partners.

Human beings are created to be the center of harmony of the whole cosmos. If Adam and Eve had attained perfection and united as husband and wife, it would have meant the joining into oneness of the two centers of the dual characteristics of all beings. Had Adam and Eve moved together in harmony and attained oneness, the whole cosmos with its dual characteristics would have danced in harmony. The place where Adam and Eve become perfectly one in heart and body as husband and wife is also the place where God, the subject partner giving love, and human beings, the object partners returning beauty, become united. This is the center of goodness where the purpose of creation is fulfilled. Here God, our Parent, draws near and abides within His perfected children and rests peacefully for eternity. This center of goodness is the object partner to God's eternal love, where God can be stimulated with joy for eternity. This is the place where the Word of God is incarnated and brought to fulfillment. It is the center of truth and the center of the original mind which guides us to pursue the purpose of creation.

Consequently, the entire universe will perform a spherical movement with a unified purpose when it is founded on the four position foundation established by a perfected man and woman who join as husband and wife centered on God. Tragically, the universe lost its center when human beings fell. This is why St. Paul wrote that the creation has been groaning in travail while longing for the children of God.[13] Creation awaits the people who have restored their original nature to appear and become its center.

2.4 The Omnipresence of God

We have learned that the four position foundation, built upon the three object purpose through the origin-division-union action, proceeds in spherical movement around God and becomes one with God. This is the fundamental foundation for all beings to receive God's governance and be provided with all the powers necessary for life. In a world where God's purpose of creation has been fulfilled, all individual beings embody God's original internal nature and original external form and initiate spherical movements to build the foundation for God's governance. God is thus omnipresent.

2.5 The Multiplication of Life

For living things to propagate their kind they must reproduce, and this multiplication takes place through origin-division-union action which is built upon good interactions. For example, in plants, seeds develop into flowers with stamens and pistils; through pollination they produce their seed and propagate their kind. Male and female animals mature, engage in courtship, mate and bear offspring. All cells in animals and plants divide through give and take action.

When the body acts according to the will of the mind, and the mind and body thus engage in give and take action, the individual will live a purposeful life. This individual will then attract like-minded people. As these companions work together productively, their group will grow. It may be said that the universe is formed by the multiplication of myriad substantial manifestations of God's original internal nature and original external form through their give and take action in the pursuit of the purpose of creation.

---

13. Rom. 8:19-22

2.6 THE REASON ALL BEINGS ARE COMPOSED OF DUAL CHARACTERISTICS

For any being to exist, energy is required, and energy can be produced only through give and take action. However, nothing can reciprocate without a partner. To generate the forces necessary for existence, a being must contain dual characteristics, a subject partner and an object partner, which can engage in give and take action.

A movement in a straight line cannot be sustained forever. For anything to have an eternal nature it must move in a circle; give and take action between a subject partner and an object partner is necessary for any circular motion. This is true even for God; having dual characteristics allows Him to live eternally. In order for God's creation to resemble His eternal nature and be His eternal object partner, it likewise must be composed of dual characteristics. Similarly, time maintains its perpetuity through its periodic cycles.

SECTION 3

THE PURPOSE OF CREATION

3.1 THE PURPOSE OF THE CREATION OF THE UNIVERSE

It is recorded in the Bible that after God completed each day of creation, He saw that it was good.[14] This suggests that God wanted His creations to be object partners embodying goodness that He might take delight in them. How can the creation give God the greatest joy?

God created human beings as the final step in creating the universe. He created them in His image, in the likeness of His internal nature and external form, and gave them sensibility to all feelings and emotions because it was His intention to share joy with them. After their creation, God blessed Adam and Eve:

> Be fruitful and multiply, and fill the earth and subdue it; and have dominion over the fish of the sea and over the birds of the air and over every living thing that moves upon the earth. —*Gen. 1:28*

These are the *three great blessings:* to be fruitful (mature and ready to bear fruit), multiply and have dominion over the creation. Had Adam and Eve obeyed this divine mandate and built the Kingdom of Heaven, there is no doubt that God would have felt the greatest joy as His sons

---
14. Gen. 1:4-31

and daughters rejoiced in the world of His ideal.

How can God's three great blessings be fulfilled? They can be realized only when the four position foundation, which is the fundamental foundation of creation, has been established. The three great blessings are fulfilled when the whole creation, including human beings, completes the four position foundation with God as the center. This is the Kingdom of Heaven, where ultimate goodness is realized and God feels the greatest joy. This is, in fact, the very purpose for which God created the universe.

The ultimate purpose of the universe, with human beings at its center, is to return joy to God. All entities have dual purposes. As was explained earlier, every entity has dual centers of movement, one of internal nature and another of external form. These centers pursue corresponding purposes—for the sake of the whole and for the sake of the individual—whose relationship is the same as that between internal nature and external form. These dual purposes relate to each other as cause and result, internal and external, subject partner and object partner. In God's ideal, there cannot be any individual purpose which does not support the whole purpose, nor can there be any whole purpose that does not guarantee the interests of the individual. The infinite variety of beings in the universe form one vast organic body interwoven by these dual purposes.

3.2 GOOD OBJECT PARTNERS FOR THE JOY OF GOD

To understand more precisely the issues concerning God's purpose of creation, let us first examine how joy is produced. Joy is not produced by an individual alone. Joy arises when we have an object partner in which our internal nature and external form are reflected and developed. Our object partner helps us to feel our own internal nature and external form through the stimulation it gives. This object partner may be intangible or it may be substantial. For example, an artist's object partner may be an idea in his mind, or the finished painting or sculpture which substantiates that idea. When he visualizes his idea or beholds his work, he is stimulated to feel his own internal nature and external form reflected in it and feels joy and satisfaction. When his idea alone is the object partner, it is not as stimulating, nor is the joy that it brings as profound as that from a finished work. This nature of human beings originates in God's nature. In like manner, God feels the fullness of joy when He is stimulated by His substantial object partners to feel His original internal nature and original external form through them.

It was explained earlier that when the Kingdom of Heaven is realized—through the fulfillment of the three great blessings and the establishment of the four position foundation—it becomes the good object partner that gives joy to God. Let us investigate how the Kingdom becomes God's good object partner.

The key to God's first blessing is the perfection of individual character. An individual's mind and body are discrete projections and object partners of God's dual characteristics. In order for an individual to perfect his character, he must form a four position foundation within himself whereby his mind and body become one through give and take action with God as their center. Such individuals become the temples of God,[15] achieve complete oneness with Him,[16] and acquire a divine nature. They experience the Heart of God as if it were their own. Hence, they understand His Will and live fully attuned to it. When a person abides in the state of individual perfection, he lives as the substantial object partner to his mind. Because the center of his mind is God, he also lives as the substantial object partner to God. Both the mind and God rejoice as they experience their internal nature and external form through the stimulation which their object partners give them. Accordingly, when people realize God's first blessing, they become God's beloved who inspire Him with joy. Sharing all the feelings of God as their own, they would never commit any sinful acts that would cause God grief. This means they would never fall.

God's second blessing was to be fulfilled by Adam and Eve after they had achieved individual perfection as object partners to God, each manifesting an aspect of God's dual characteristics. In order to construct the four position foundation in their family, Adam and Eve should have joined in loving oneness as husband and wife and raised children. This would have been the fulfillment of the second blessing. A family or society that has formed the four position foundation in line with God's ideal is patterned after the image of a perfect individual. It thus becomes the substantial object partner to the individual who lives in oneness with God, and consequently, it also becomes the substantial object partner to God. The individual feels joy, and likewise God feels joy, when each perceives in this family or community the manifestation of his own internal nature and external form. When God's second blessing is fulfilled, this family or community also becomes a good object partner giving joy to God.

Before we examine how a person upon attaining the third blessing establishes a good object partner giving joy to God, we must first inves-

---

15. I Cor. 3:16
16. John 14:20

tigate the relationship between human beings and the creation from the viewpoint of internal nature and external form.

Prior to creating human beings, God created the natural world by expressing partial reflections of the internal nature and external form He had conceived for human beings. Consequently, a human being contains within himself the sum total of the essences of all things. This is the reason he is called the microcosm of the cosmos.

When God created living things, He began with creatures of a lower order. Over the course of time, He created animals of a higher order with more complex biological functions, culminating with human beings at the highest level. Therefore, human beings contain all the elements, structures and qualities found in animals. For example, human vocal cords are so versatile that they can imitate virtually any animal sound. Because the human body contains all the beautiful curves and lines of the creation, an artist hones his skills by drawing nude models.

Although human beings and plants have different structures and functions, they are similar in that they both are composed of cells. All the elements, structures and characteristics of plants can be found in human beings. For example, a plant's leaf corresponds to the human lung in appearance and function. As leaves absorb carbon dioxide from the atmosphere, the human lung absorbs oxygen. Branches and stems of plants correspond to the human circulatory system, which distributes nourishment to the entire body; the xylem and phloem correspond to human arteries and veins. The roots of a plant correspond to the human stomach and intestines, which absorb nutrients.

Human beings were fashioned from clay, water and air; consequently they contain elements of the mineral kingdom. Moreover, the earth displays a similarity to the structure of the human body: the earth's crust is covered with plants, its underground waterways exist inside the substrata, and beneath it all lies a molten core surrounded by a rocky mantle. This resembles the structure of the human body, which has skin covered with hair, blood vessels running inside the musculature, and marrow lying deeper still within the bones.

The meaning of God's third blessing is the perfection of a human being's dominion over the natural world. To fulfill this blessing, the four position foundation of dominion must be established centered on God. Human beings and the natural world, which are the substantial object partners of God at the level of image and symbol respectively, must share love and beauty to become completely one.[17]

---

17. cf. Creation 5.2.3

The natural world is an object partner which exhibits human internal nature and external form in diverse ways. Hence, ideal human beings receive stimulation from the world of nature. Sensing their own internal nature and external form displayed throughout the creation, they feel immense joy. God also delights when He experiences the stimulation of His original internal nature and original external form from the universe; this is possible when it becomes His third object partner through the harmonious union of human beings and the natural world. Therefore, when human beings realize God's third blessing, the entire universe becomes yet another good object partner giving joy to God. Had God's purpose of creation been realized in this way, an ideal world without even a trace of sin would have been established on the earth. We call this world the Kingdom of Heaven on earth. When life in the Kingdom of Heaven on earth comes to a close, people are to enter the spirit world and naturally enjoy eternal life in the Kingdom of Heaven there.

Based on the discussion thus far, we can understand that the Kingdom of Heaven resembles a person who has achieved individual perfection, taking after God's original internal nature and external form. In an individual, the mind's command is transmitted to the whole body through the central nervous system, causing the body to act with one purpose. Likewise, in the Kingdom of Heaven, God's direction will be conveyed to all His children through the True Parents of humankind, guiding everyone to live as one.

Section 4

Original Value

4.1 The Process and Standard for the Determination of Original Value

How is a being's original created value determined? The value of an entity may be determined by the relationship between its purpose of existence and the desire that a human being has for it. To be more precise, the value of an entity intended at its creation is not fixed as an inherent attribute. Rather, it is established through the mutual relationship between the purpose of the entity according to God's ideal of creation, and people's original desire to treasure it and bring out its true worth. It finds its true value when it participates as an object partner in a God-centered four position foundation by relating with a person through give and take action and by their union becoming the third object partner to God.

What sets the standard by which the original value of an entity is determined? Since its original value is determined when it participates in a four position foundation, and since the center of this four position foundation is God, it is God who sets the standard for its value. Since God is absolute, the original value of an object partner determined in relation to this standard set by God must also be absolute.

Consider a rose; how is its original beauty determined? It is determined when the purpose for which God created the flower and the divinely given human desire to appreciate and bring out its beauty are fulfilled together. To put it another way, an ideal person feels the fullness of joy when his desire to pursue beauty is satisfied by the emotional stimulation that the flower gives him. At that moment, the flower manifests its original beauty. The flower's beauty becomes absolute when it achieves its inherent purpose, which is to give complete joy to its subject partner. The human desire to appreciate the beauty of the flower is an instance of the desire to feel aspects of one's own internal nature and external form through an object partner. The moment the flower's purpose for which it was created and the human desire to bring out its value are fulfilled, the subject partner and the object partner enter a state of harmonious oneness.

An entity attains its true value when it and a human being, its subject partner, enter a state of harmonious oneness and form the third object partner to God in the four position foundation. Through this process, the true values of all things are determined absolutely, based on their relationship with the absolute standard of value set by God. Until now, no object partner's value could become absolute; it has remained relative because its relationship with fallen people was not based on God's ideal of creation but was based on satanic purpose and desire.

4.2 Original Emotion, Intellect and Will; and Original Beauty, Truth and Goodness

The human mind has three faculties: emotion, intellect and will. The human body acts in response to the commands of the mind. When the body responds to the mind's emotion, intellect and will, its actions pursue the values of beauty, truth and goodness respectively. God is the subject partner to the human mind; hence, He is also the subject partner to human emotion, intellect and will. Desiring to realize his original value, a person responds to the perfect emotion, perfect intellect and perfect will of God through his mind, and acts accordingly through his body. Thus, he manifests the values of original beauty, original truth and original goodness.

4.3 LOVE AND BEAUTY, GOOD AND EVIL, RIGHTEOUSNESS AND UNRIGHTEOUSNESS

4.3.1 LOVE AND BEAUTY

When two entities, discrete manifestations of God's dual characteristics, form a common base and seek to unite as the third object partner to God and establish a four position foundation, they will engage in give and take action. In accomplishing this, the emotional force that the subject partner gives to the object partner is called *love*, and the emotional force that the object partner returns to the subject partner is called *beauty*. The force of love is active, and the stimulation of beauty is passive.

In the relationship between God and human beings, God gives love as the subject partner and human beings return beauty as object partners. In the relationship between a man and a woman, the man is the subject partner, giving love, while the woman is the object partner, returning beauty. In the universe, people are the subject partners who give love to the natural world, and the natural world returns beauty as an object partner. However, when the subject partner and object partner become completely one in harmony, love is found within beauty and beauty is found within love. This is because when a subject partner and object partner become one in a circular movement, the subject partner sometimes acts as an object partner, and the object partner sometimes acts as a subject partner.

In interpersonal relationships, the beauty that a subordinate returns in response to the love of a superior is called *loyalty*, and the beauty that children return in response to the love of their parents is called *filial piety*. The beauty that a wife returns in response to the love of her husband is called *fidelity*. The purpose of love and beauty is to enable two wholesome beings, springing forth from God, to establish the four position foundation and realize the purpose of creation. By sharing love and beauty with each other, they join in harmonious oneness, becoming the third object partner to God.

Next, let us investigate the nature of God's love. Had Adam and Eve attained perfection, each becoming a substantial object partner to God resembling one of His dual characteristics, they would have joined as husband and wife and raised children in a godly family. In so doing, they would have deeply experienced three kinds of original love with their three object partners: parental love, conjugal love and children's love. (The love of the first object partner, the love of the second object partner, and the love of the third object partner.) Only then would they complete the three object purpose and form the four position foundation. This would be the fulfillment of their purpose of creation.

God's love is the subject to the various kinds of love flowing through the four position foundation. Therefore, God's love is manifested through the various loves of the three object partners. God's love is the underlying force which breathes life into the four position foundation. Accordingly, the four position foundation is the vessel of perfect beauty through which we can receive and enjoy the fullness of God's love. It is also the home of perfect joy and the wellspring of goodness. Upon this ground, the purpose of creation is complete.

4.3.2 GOOD AND EVIL

An act or the result of an act is considered *good* when it fulfills God's purpose of creation. This takes place when a subject partner and object partner unite through the harmonious and spirited give and take of love and beauty, become the third object partner to God, and form the four position foundation. On the other hand, an act or its result is called *evil* when it violates God's purpose of creation by forming a four position foundation under the dominion of Satan.

For example, when an individual realizes God's first blessing and fulfills his true purpose, the actions to this end are good and the individual is good. These actions involve the free-flowing give and take of love and beauty between the mind and the body so that they unite in the way of God and form the individual four position foundation. When Adam and Eve achieve the second blessing by building a family that realizes God's purpose, their actions to this end are good and the family they form is good. These actions include joining as a couple in the way of God through the harmonious and passionate sharing of love and beauty, bearing and raising children, and thus establishing the family four position foundation. Moreover, when a perfect individual achieves the third blessing, the actions to this end are good and all things that he nurtures are good. By relating with the natural world as his second self and by becoming completely one with it, a union is formed which becomes the third object partner to God, thus constructing the four position foundation of dominion. Conversely, when a person forms a four position foundation under the bondage of Satan and realizes a purpose contrary to God's three blessings, this act or its result is called evil.

4.3.3 Righteousness and Unrighteousness

Righteousness refers to a way of life dedicated to the pursuit of goodness, practiced to further the goal of goodness. Unrighteousness refers to a way of life that runs to do evil, to further its satanic purpose. A righteous life is absolutely required for the attainment of goodness.

Section 5

The Process of the Creation of the Universe and Its Growing Period

5.1 The Process of the Creation of the Universe

According to the Genesis account of the creation of the universe, amidst the primordial state of chaos, void and darkness, God created light. God next separated the waters under the firmament from the waters above the firmament. He then divided the land from the ocean, created plants, fish, birds and mammals, and finally made humankind. All of this took a period of six "days." From this account, we can surmise that the process of creating the universe took some period of time represented by six days.

The process of creation recorded in the Bible bears some resemblance to the theory of the origin and formation of the universe as described by modern science. According to modern science, the universe began as expanding plasma. Out of the chaos and void of space, the heavenly bodies formed and gave light. As the molten earth cooled, volcanic eruptions filled the sky with a firmament of water. The land rose and the water fell as rain, creating the continents and oceans. Next, the lower plants and animals came into being. Then came fish, birds, mammals, and finally humankind, in that order. The age of the earth is calculated to be several billion years. Considering that the account of the creation of the universe recorded in the Bible thousands of years ago nearly coincides with the findings of modern scientific research, we are reassured that this biblical record must be a revelation from God.

The universe did not suddenly spring forth complete, without regard to the flow of time. In fact, its origin and development took an enormous length of time. Therefore, the biblical period of six days for the completion of the universe is not to be reckoned by the number of literal sunrises and sunsets. It symbolizes six ordered periods of time in the creation process.

5.2 THE GROWING PERIOD FOR THE CREATION

The fact that it took six days, that is, six time periods, to complete the creation of the universe implies that some period of time was also necessary to complete the creation of each of the individual entities that make up the universe. Furthermore, the way the Genesis account reckons each day reveals something about the passage of time required for the creation of an entity. The account has an unusual way of numbering each day of creation. When the first day of creation was completed, it states, "There was evening and there was morning, one day."[18] One would think that the arrival of the morning after the passage of an evening and a night would be reckoned as the second day, yet it is referred to as the first day. The Bible states "one day" to show that a created being must pass through a growing period, symbolized by the night, before it reaches perfection in the morning. Then, as it greets this new morning, it can step forward and realize its ideal of creation.

All phenomena occurring in the universe bear fruit only after the lapse of a certain interval of time. All things are designed to reach completion only after passing through a set *growing period*.

5.2.1 THE THREE ORDERED STAGES OF THE GROWING PERIOD

The universe unfolds and manifests God's original internal nature and original external form based on mathematical principles. Hence, we can infer that one aspect of God's nature is mathematical. God is the one absolute reality in whom the dual characteristics interact in harmony; therefore, He is a Being of the number three. All created beings, Having been conceived in the likeness of God, all created beings exist, move and grow through a course of three stages.

The four position foundation, which is God's purpose of creation, was to be completed through a three-stage process: the origin in God, the marriage of Adam and Eve, and the multiplication of children. In order to establish the four position foundation and carry on circular movement, a being must first perform the three-stage origin-division-union action and fulfill the three object purpose, with each position engaged in interaction with the other three. It is like what is needed for something to stand firm: it must be supported by at least three points. Accordingly, everything reaches perfection by passing through three ordered stages of growth: the *formation stage*, the *growth stage* and the *completion stage*.

---

18. Gen. 1:5

In the natural world, many things appear in threes. There are three kingdoms: mineral, plant and animal. Matter exists in three states: gas, liquid and solid. Most plants are composed of three parts: roots, branches or stems, and leaves. Animals consist of head, body and limbs.

There are also many examples of the number three in the Bible. Human beings could not fulfill the purpose of their existence because they fell without completing the three stages of the growing period. Hence, in their renewed efforts to realize their purpose, human beings must pass through these three stages. In the providence of restoration, God has worked to reclaim the number three, which explains why there are many records in the Bible of the number three and dispensations based on the number three: the Trinity (Father, Son and Holy Spirit); the three levels of Paradise; the three archangels; the three levels of Noah's ark; the three flights of the dove from the ark after the flood; the three offerings of Abraham; and the three-day journey before the sacrifice of Isaac. At the time of Moses there were: the three-day plague of darkness, the three days of purification at the start of the Exodus, the three forty-year periods for the journey to Canaan, and the three days of purification under Joshua's leadership just prior to crossing the Jordan River. In the life of Jesus we see: three decades of private life followed by three years of public ministry, the three wise men from the East who brought three gifts, the three disciples, the three temptations, the three prayers in the garden of Gethsemane, Peter's three denials, the three hours of darkness at the crucifixion, and Jesus' resurrection after three days in the tomb.

When did the first human ancestors fall? They fell during their growing period, when they were still immature. If human beings had fallen after they had attained perfection, then there would be no basis for belief in the omnipotence of God. If human beings had fallen after they had become perfect embodiments of goodness, then goodness itself would be imperfect. Accordingly, we would be forced to conclude that God, as the source of goodness, is also imperfect.

It is written in the Book of Genesis that God warned Adam and Eve, "Of the tree of the knowledge of good and evil you shall not eat, for in the day that you eat of it you shall die."[19] They had a choice to either ignore God's warning and lose their lives or to heed the warning and live. The fact that they had the potential either to fall or to become perfect demonstrates that they were still in a state of immaturity. The universe was designed to reach perfection after a certain growing period,

---

19. Gen. 2:17

described in the Bible as six days. As one of God's creations, human beings are also bound to this principle.

At what stage of the growing period did the first humans fall? They fell at the top of the growth stage. This can be demonstrated by examining the circumstances surrounding the fall of the first human ancestors and the history of the providence of restoration. These will be further clarified through a thorough study of this volume.

5.2.2 THE REALM OF INDIRECT DOMINION

During the growing period, all beings in the creation grow by virtue of the autonomy and governance given by God's Principle. God, the Author of the Principle, has regard only for the fruits of their growth which are based on the Principle. In this way, He governs all things indirectly. We call this growing period the realm of God's *indirect dominion* or the realm of dominion based on accomplishments through the Principle.

All things reach perfection after passing through the growing period (the realm of indirect dominion) by virtue of the autonomy and governance given by God's Principle. Human beings, however, are created in such a way that their growth requires the fulfillment of their own portion of responsibility, in addition to the guidance provided by the Principle. They must exercise this responsibility in order to pass successfully through the growing period and reach perfection. We can deduce from God's commandment to Adam and Eve[20] that the first human ancestors were responsible to believe in the Word of God and not eat of the fruit. Whether or not they disobeyed God and fell depended not on God, but on themselves. Hence, whether or not human beings attain perfection does not depend only on God's power of creation; it also requires the fulfillment of human responsibility. In His capacity as the Creator, God created human beings in such a manner that they can pass through the growing period (the realm of indirect dominion) and attain perfection only when they have completed their own portion of responsibility. Because God Himself created human beings in this way, He does not interfere with human responsibility.

God endowed human beings with a portion of responsibility for the following reason. By fulfilling their given portion of responsibility, with which even God does not interfere, human beings are meant to inherit the creative nature of God and participate in God's great work of creation. God intends human beings to earn ownership and become

---

20. Gen. 2:17

worthy to rule the creation as creators in their own right,[21] just as God governs them as their Creator. This is the principal difference between human beings and the rest of creation.

Once we fulfill our responsibility, we inherit God's creatorship and attain dominion over all things, including the angels. God provides us with a course through the realm of indirect dominion that we may attain this perfection. We fallen people, who have not yet attained the qualification to rule, must fulfill our responsibility according to the Principle of Restoration. By so doing, we can progress through the realm of indirect dominion and thereby restore our right to rule over all things, including Satan. This is the only way we can accomplish the purpose of creation. God's providence of salvation has been prolonged for so long because the central figures in charge of the providence of restoration repeatedly made mistakes while attempting to fulfill their portions of responsibility, with which even God could not interfere.

No matter how great the saving grace of the cross of Christ, the salvation knocking at our door will be for naught unless we fortify our faith, which is our portion of responsibility. It was God's responsibility to grant the benefit of resurrection through the crucifixion of Jesus, but to believe or not to believe is strictly one's own portion of responsibility.[22]

5.2.3 THE REALM OF DIRECT DOMINION

What is the realm of God's *direct dominion* and what is its purpose? Human beings abide in the realm of direct dominion when, as subject partner and object partner, they unite in the love of God to form a four position foundation and become one in heart with God. In this realm they freely and fully share love and beauty according to the will of the subject partner, thus realizing the purpose of goodness. The realm of direct dominion is the realm of perfection. Entering this realm is essential for the fulfillment of the purpose of creation.

What is the meaning of God's direct dominion over human beings? Once Adam and Eve had perfected themselves as individuals centered on God, they were to live together as one, forming the four position foundation in their family. With God-centered Adam leading his family to share the fullness of love and beauty, they were to live a life of goodness and become one in heart with God. In the realm of God's direct dominion, people will intensely experience God's Heart within themselves. Hence, they will know His Will and carry it out in their

---

21. Gen. 1:28
22. John 3:16; Eph. 2:8; Rom. 5:1

actions. Just as every part of the body spontaneously moves in response to the subtle directions of the mind, people will spontaneously carry out the Will of God in accord with the deeply felt intentions of His Heart. In this state of perfect resonance, the purpose of creation is realized.

What will the world be like when the natural world abides under the direct dominion of human beings? When a fully mature person relates with the diverse things in nature as his object partners, they come together to form a four position foundation. People who are in total resonance with God's Heart will lead the natural world in the free-flowing sharing of love and beauty, and the entire universe will realize goodness. In such a manner, human beings will exercise direct dominion over all things.

SECTION 6

THE INCORPOREAL WORLD AND THE CORPOREAL WORLD WHOSE CENTER IS HUMAN BEINGS

6.1 THE INCORPOREAL WORLD AND THE CORPOREAL WORLD AS SUBSTANTIAL REALITIES

The universe was created after the pattern of a human being, who is in the image of God's dual characteristics. Therefore, the structure of the universe and every entity in it resembles that of a human being, which consists most fundamentally of mind and body.[23] Corresponding to the human mind and body, the universe consists of the *incorporeal world* and the *corporeal world,* both of which are real and substantial. The incorporeal world is so called because we cannot perceive it through our five physical senses. Yet we can perceive it through our five spiritual senses. Those who have had spiritual experiences testify that the incorporeal world appears as real as the world in which we live. The incorporeal and corporeal worlds together form the *cosmos.*

The body cannot act apart from its relationship with the mind; a person cannot perform true actions apart from a relationship with God. Likewise, the corporeal world cannot manifest its true value apart from a relationship with the incorporeal world. Furthermore, just as we cannot discern a person's character without fathoming his mind, and we cannot understand the fundamental meaning of human life without understanding God, so we cannot completely understand the nature

---

23. cf. Creation 1.2

and structure of the corporeal world without understanding the nature and structure of the incorporeal world. The incorporeal world, or spirit world, is in the position of subject partner, and the corporeal world, or physical world, is in the position of object partner. The latter is like a shadow of the former.[24] When we shed our physical bodies after our life in the physical world, we enter the spirit world as spirits and live there for eternity.

6.2 The Position of Human Beings in the Cosmos

The position of human beings in the cosmos has three aspects. First, God created human beings to be the rulers of the universe.[25] The universe does not of itself have internal sensibility toward God. Hence, God does not govern the universe directly. Rather, God endowed human beings with sensibilities to all things in the universe and gave them the mandate to rule over the universe directly. God created the human body with elements from the physical world—such as water, clay and air—to allow us to perceive and govern it. To make it possible for us to perceive and govern the spirit world, God created our spirits with the same spiritual elements that compose the spirit world. On the Mount of Transfiguration, Moses and Elijah, who had died hundreds of years earlier, appeared before Jesus and ministered to him.[26] These were actually the spirits of Moses and Elijah, yet Jesus was able to converse with them and was glorified before them. Human beings, composed of flesh which can dominate the physical world and spirit which can dominate the spiritual world, likewise have the potential to rule both worlds.

Second, God created human beings to be the mediator and the center of harmony of the cosmos. When a person's flesh and spirit unite through give and take action and become God's substantial object partner, the physical and spiritual worlds can also begin give and take action with that person as their center. They thus achieve harmonious integration to construct a cosmos that is responsive to God. Like the air that enables two tuning forks to resonate with each other, a true person acts as the mediator and center of harmony between the two worlds. The ability to communicate between the two worlds also may be likened to a radio or television which transforms invisible waves into perceptible images and sounds. Thus, a person can accurately convey the realities of the spirit world to the physical world.

---

24. Heb. 8:5
25. Gen. 1:28
26. Matt. 17:3

Third, God created human beings to encapsulate in a substantial form the essences of everything in the cosmos. God created the universe by projecting and developing the pre-existent prototype of the human internal nature and external form into countless substantial forms. The human spirit encapsulates all of the elements found in the spirit world, since God created the spirit world as the unfolding of the spirit's internal nature and external form. The human body encapsulates all the elements of the physical world, since God created the material realm as the unfolding of the body's internal nature and external form. Accordingly, since human beings contain within themselves the essences of all things in the cosmos, each person is a microcosm.

However, due to the human Fall, the universe has lost its master. St. Paul wrote, "the creation waits with eager longing for the revealing of the sons of God"[27]—that is, people who have been restored to the original state. Tragically, with the Fall of human beings, who should have served as the center of universal harmony, the give and take between the physical and spiritual worlds was severed. The two worlds were rendered utterly unable to achieve integration and harmony. Since they remain divided, Paul continued, "the whole creation has been groaning in travail."[28]

Jesus came as the new Adam, perfect in flesh and spirit. He was the microcosm of the cosmos. This is why it is written, "God has put all things in subjection under his feet."[29] Jesus is our Savior. He came into the world to open the way for fallen people to become perfect as he was perfect, by moving our hearts to believe in him and become one with him.

6.3 THE RECIPROCAL RELATIONSHIP BETWEEN THE PHYSICAL SELF AND THE SPIRIT SELF

6.3.1 THE STRUCTURE AND FUNCTIONS OF THE PHYSICAL SELF

The *physical self* consists of the dual characteristics of the *physical mind* (subject partner) and the *physical body* (object partner). The physical mind directs the physical body to maintain the functions necessary for its survival, protection and reproduction. Instinct, for example, is an aspect of an animal's physical mind. For the physical self to grow in good health, it must have proper nourishment. It must absorb air and sunlight, which are intangible, yang types of nourishment, and must eat and drink food and water, which are tangible, yin types of nourishment.

---

27. Rom. 8:19
28. Rom. 8:22
29. I Cor. 15:27

The body has give and take with this nourishment through its digestive and circulatory systems.

Good or evil in the conduct of the physical self is the main determinant of whether the spirit self becomes good or evil. This is because the physical self provides a certain element, which we call the *vitality element*, to the spirit self. In our everyday experience, our mind rejoices when our physical self performs good deeds but feels anxiety after evil conduct. This is because vitality elements, which can be good or evil according to the deeds of the physical self, are infused into our spirit self.

6.3.2 The Structure and Functions of the Spirit Self

Our *spirit self*, or spirit, is a substantial yet incorporeal reality which can be apprehended only through the spiritual senses. It is the subject partner to our physical self. Our spirit can communicate directly with God and is meant to govern the incorporeal world, including the angels. In appearance our spirit self matches our physical self. After we shed the physical self, we enter the spirit world and live there for eternity. The reason we desire an eternal life is because our innermost self is the spirit self which has an eternal nature. Our spirit self consists of the dual characteristics of *spirit mind* (subject partner) and *spirit body* (object partner). The spirit mind is the center of the spirit self, and it is where God dwells.

The spirit grows through give and take action between two types of nourishment: *life elements* of a yang type that come from God, and vitality elements of a yin type that come from the physical self. The spirit self not only receives vitality elements from the physical self; it also returns an element to the physical self which we call the *living spirit element*. When people receive grace from a heavenly spirit, they undergo many positive changes in their physical self; they feel infinite joy and new strength welling up in them which can even drive away illness. Such phenomena occur because the physical self receives living spirit elements from the spirit self.

The spirit can grow only while it abides in the flesh. Thus, the relationship between the physical self and the spirit self is similar to that between a tree and its fruit. When the physical mind obeys the spirit mind and the physical self acts according to the good purpose of the spirit mind, the physical self receives living spirit elements from the spirit self and becomes wholesome. In return, the physical self provides good vitality elements to the spirit self, which enable the spirit self to grow properly in the direction of goodness.

Truth illuminates the innermost desires of the spirit mind. A person must first comprehend his spirit mind's deepest desire through the truth and then put this knowledge into action to fulfill his responsibility. Only then do the living spirit elements and vitality elements reciprocate within him, enabling him to progress toward goodness. The living spirit element and the vitality element have the relationship of internal nature and external form. Because all people have living spirit elements ever active within themselves, even an evil person's original mind inclines toward goodness. However, unless he actually leads a life of goodness, the living spirit elements cannot engage in proper give and take with the vitality elements, nor can they be infused into his physical self to make it wholesome.

It can be inferred from the above that the spirit self can attain perfection only during a person's earthly life. The spirit mind guides the spirit self as it grows in the soil of the physical self. The growth of the spirit self toward perfection progresses through the three orderly stages ordained by the Principle of Creation. A spirit in the formation stage of life is called a *form spirit;* in the growth stage, a *life spirit;* and in the completion stage, a *divine spirit.*

A spirit fully matures as a divine spirit when the person's spirit self and physical self unite through perfect give and take action centered on God and form the four position foundation. A divine spirit can accurately feel and perceive every reality in the spirit world. As these spiritual realities resonate through the body and manifest themselves as physiological phenomena, they can be recognized through the five physical senses. People of divine spirit, who thus resonate with the spirit world, build the Kingdom of Heaven on earth. When they shed their physical bodies, they will make a smooth transition into the Kingdom of Heaven in the spirit world. For this reason, the Kingdom of Heaven in heaven will be realized only after the Kingdom of Heaven on earth has been established.

All the sensibilities of a spirit are cultivated through the reciprocal relationship with the physical self during earthly life. Therefore, only when a person reaches perfection and is totally immersed in the love of God while on earth can he fully delight in the love of God as a spirit after his death. All the qualities of the spirit self are developed while it abides in the physical self: Sinful conduct during earthly life aggravates evil and ugliness in the spirit of a fallen person, while the redemption of sins granted during earthly life opens the way for his spirit to become good. This was the reason Jesus had to come to the earth in the flesh to save sinful humanity. We must lead a good life while we are on the earth. Jesus gave the keys to the Kingdom of Heaven to Peter, who remained on the earth,[30] and said, "whatever you bind on earth shall be bound in heaven, and whatever you loose on earth shall be loosed in heaven,"[31] because the primary objective of the providence of restoration must be carried out on the earth.

It is not God who decides whether a person's spirit enters heaven or hell upon his death; it is decided by the spirit himself. Humans are created so that once they reach perfection they will fully breathe the love of God. Those who committed sinful deeds while on earth become crippled spirits who are incapable of fully breathing in the love of God. They find it agonizing to stand before God, the center of true love. Of their own will, they choose to dwell in hell, far removed from the love of God.

Since the human spirit can grow only in the soil of the physical self, the multiplication of human spirits takes place at the same time that the multiplication of physical selves occurs: during earthly life.

6.3.3 The Spirit Mind, the Physical Mind and Their Relationship in the Human Mind

The human *mind* consists of the spirit mind and physical mind. The relationship between these two minds is like that between internal nature and external form. When they become one through give and take action with God as their center, they form a united functioning entity which guides the spirit self and physical self to become harmonious and progress toward the purpose of creation. This united entity is the mind of a human being.

The *conscience* is that faculty of the human mind which, by virtue of its inborn nature, always directs us toward what we think is good. However, due to the Fall, human beings have become ignorant of God and thus ignorant of the absolute standard of goodness. For this reason, we are unable to set the proper standard of judgment for our conscience. As the standard of goodness varies, the standard of our conscience also fluctuates; this causes frequent contention even among those who advocate a conscientious life.

The *original mind* is that faculty of the human mind which pursues absolute goodness. It relates to the conscience as internal nature to external form. A person's conscience directs him to pursue goodness according to the standard which he has set up in ignorance, even

---

30. Matt. 16:19
31. Matt. 18:18

though it may differ from the original standard. However, the original mind, being sensitive to the proper direction, repels this faulty standard and works to correct the conscience.

As long as our spirit mind and physical mind are under the bondage of Satan, the functioning entity they form through their give and take action is called the *evil mind*. The evil mind continually drives people to do evil. Our original mind and conscience direct us to repel the evil mind. They guide us in desperate efforts to reject evil desires and cling to goodness by breaking our ties with Satan and turning to face God.

Chapter 2

The Human Fall

All people have an original mind which inclines them to reject evil and pursue goodness. Yet, even without our being aware of it, we are driven by evil forces to abandon the goodness which our original mind desires and to perform evil deeds which, in our innermost heart, we do not want to do. As long as these evil forces assail us, the sinful history of humanity will continue unabated. In Christianity, the master of these evil forces is known as Satan. We have been utterly unable to liquidate the forces of Satan because we have not understood Satan's identity or how he came to exist. To extirpate evil by its root, and thereby end sinful history and usher in an era of goodness, we must first expose the motivation and origin of Satan and recognize the destruction he has wrought in human life. This explanation of the human Fall will clarify these issues.

Section 1

The Root of Sin

No one has known the root of sin, which lies deep within and ceaselessly drives people toward the way of evil. On the basis of the Bible, Christians have held to a vague belief that Adam and Eve's eating the fruit of the tree of the knowledge of good and evil was the root of sin. Some Christians believe that the fruit of the tree of the knowledge of good and evil was the fruit of an actual tree, while others believe that the fruit is a symbol, as much of the Bible is written in symbolic language. Let us consider the Bible's account of the human Fall and its differing interpretations in order to arrive at a complete explanation.

1.1 THE TREE OF LIFE AND THE TREE OF THE KNOWLEDGE OF GOOD AND EVIL

Adam and Eve fell when they ate the fruit of the tree of the knowledge of good and evil. Many Christians to this day have thought that this was the fruit of an actual tree. But would God, the loving Parent of humanity, make a fruit which could cause the Fall to look so attractive?[1] Would He place it where His children could reach it so easily? Furthermore, Jesus said, "Not what goes into the mouth defiles a man, but what comes out of the mouth, this defiles a man."[2] How, then, can a food which one eats cause one to fall?

Humankind is beset by the *original sin,* which has been inherited from our first ancestors. Yet how can something one eats cause a sin which can be transmitted to one's descendants? The only way something can be inherited is by being passed down through the lineage. The temporary ill effects of eating something cannot be perpetuated through the long descent of lineage.

There are those who believe that God made the fruit of the tree of the knowledge of good and evil and commanded Adam and Eve not to eat it in order to test their obedience to Him. We may ask: would the God of love test humans so mercilessly by a means that could cause their death? Adam and Eve knew they would die the moment they ate the fruit, for God had told them so. Yet still they ate it. Adam and Eve did not lack for food. They would not have risked their lives and disobeyed God only to obtain some delicacy. Therefore, we can surmise that the fruit of the tree of the knowledge of good and evil could not have been an ordinary fruit. Rather, it must have been something so extraordinarily stimulating that even the fear of death did not deter them from grasping it.

If the fruit of the tree of the knowledge of good and evil was not a material fruit, then it must be a symbol which represents something else. Why should we stubbornly adhere to a literal interpretation of the fruit when so much of the Bible makes use of symbolism and metaphor? We would do well to abandon such a narrow and old-fashioned attitude of faith.

To learn what the fruit of the tree of the knowledge of good and evil represents, let us first investigate the *tree of life,* which stood next

---

1. Gen. 3:6
2. Matt. 15:11

to the tree of the knowledge of good and evil in the Garden of Eden.[3] When we grasp the meaning of the tree of life, then we can also understand the meaning of the tree of the knowledge of good and evil.

1.1.1 THE TREE OF LIFE

According to the Bible, the hope of fallen people is to approach or attain the tree of life: "Hope deferred makes the heart sick, but a desire fulfilled is a tree of life."[4] Thus, the Israelites of the Old Testament Age looked to the tree of life as their hope. Likewise, the hope of all Christians from the time of Jesus until today has been to approach and partake of the tree of life: "Blessed are those who wash their robes, that they may have the right to the tree of life and that they may enter the city by the gates."[5] Since the ultimate hope of humankind is the tree of life, we can infer that the hope of Adam was also the tree of life.

It is written that when Adam fell, God blocked his path to the tree of life by stationing the cherubim with a flaming sword to guard it.[6] From this we can also deduce that Adam's hope before the Fall was the tree of life. Adam was cast out of the Garden of Eden without having attained his hope, the tree of life. For fallen people ever since, the tree of life has remained a hope unfulfilled.

What was the hope of Adam during the time he was immature and growing toward perfection? He must have hoped to become a man who would realize God's ideal of creation by growing to perfection without falling. The tree of life in fact symbolizes a man who has fully realized the ideal of creation. Perfected Adam was to be this ideal man. The tree of life thus symbolizes perfected Adam.

Had Adam not fallen but attained the tree of life, all his descendants could also have attained the tree of life. They would have built the Kingdom of Heaven on earth. But Adam fell, and God blocked his path to the tree with a flaming sword. Ever since, despite the best efforts of fallen people to restore the ideal of creation, the tree of life has remained an unattainable dream. Burdened by the original sin, fallen people cannot complete the ideal of creation and become trees of life by their own efforts alone. For this ideal to be achieved, a man who has completed the ideal of creation must come to the earth as a tree of life. All of humanity must then be engrafted with him[7] and become one

---

3. Gen. 2:9
4. Prov. 13:12
5. Rev. 22:14
6. Gen. 3:24
7. Rom. 11:17. As the Bible compares the relationship between Jesus and the believers to a vine and its branches (John 15:4-5) and portrays Jesus as the tree of life, the esoteric meaning of the olive tree in Rom. 11:17 is Jesus.—Ed.

with him. Jesus was the man who came as this tree of life. The tree of life for which the faithful people of the Old Testament Age longed[8] was none other than Jesus.

Ever since God blocked Adam's path to the tree of life by guarding it with the flaming sword, the tree could not be approached without first clearing the path. On the day of Pentecost, tongues of fire descended upon the saints, and they were filled with the Holy Spirit.[9] This event marked the clearing of the path and the moving aside of the flaming sword, which appeared as the tongues of fire preceding the rush of the Holy Spirit. It opened the way for all humanity to approach Jesus, the tree of life, and be engrafted with him.

Nonetheless, Christians have been engrafted with Jesus only spiritually. This is why the children of even the most devout Christian parents still inherit sin, which must be redeemed. Even the most faithful saints have not been free of the original sin, and thus cannot help but transmit it to their children.[10] For this reason, Christ must come again on earth as the tree of life. By engrafting all humankind with himself once more, he is to redeem their original sin. Christians thus impatiently await the tree of life, which in the Book of Revelation symbolizes Christ at his Second Coming.[11]

The purpose of God's providence of salvation is to restore the failure to attain the tree of life in the Garden of Eden by realizing the tree of life mentioned in the Book of Revelation. Due to the Fall, Adam could not fulfill the ideal of the first tree of life.[12] In order to complete the salvation of fallen humanity, Jesus, the "last Adam,"[13] must come again as the tree of life in the Last Days.

1.1.2 The Tree of the Knowledge of Good and Evil

God did not create Adam to be alone; He also created Eve to be Adam's spouse. Just as there was a tree in the Garden of Eden which symbolized a perfected man, there also should have been a tree which represented a woman who has fully realized the ideal of creation. The tree of the knowledge of good and evil, standing beside the tree of life,[14] was this tree which, by fulfilling its good purpose, represents the ideal woman, perfected Eve.

---

8. Prov. 13:12
9. Acts 2:3-4
10. cf. Messiah 1
11. Rev. 22:14
12. Gen. 2:9
13. I Cor. 15:45
14. Gen. 2:9

The Bible refers to Jesus using the metaphors of a vine[15] and a branch.[16] Likewise, to give us a hint about the secret of the human Fall, God provided the symbolism of two trees to represent perfected Adam and Eve.

1.2 The Identity of the Serpent

In the Bible we read that a serpent tempted Eve to commit sin.[17] What does the serpent symbolize? Let us investigate the true identity of the serpent, based on the Genesis account.

The serpent described in the Bible was able to converse with people. It caused the Fall of humans, who are spiritual beings. Furthermore, the serpent knew the Will of God, which strictly forbade human beings to eat the fruit of the tree of the knowledge of good and evil. This is compelling evidence that the being which the serpent symbolizes was a spiritual being.

It is written:

> The great dragon was thrown down, that ancient serpent, who is called the Devil and Satan, the deceiver of the whole world—he was thrown down to the earth. —*Rev. 12:9*

This ancient serpent is the very serpent which tempted Eve in the Garden of Eden. Having lived in heaven before it was thrown down, this Devil or Satan must be a spiritual being. In fact, ever since the time of the human Fall, Satan has been continually turning the hearts of people toward evil. Since Satan is a spiritual being, the serpent which symbolizes him must also represent a spiritual being. These strands of biblical evidence confirm that the serpent who tempted Eve was not an animal but a symbol for a spiritual being.

The question arises whether the spiritual being symbolized by the serpent existed before the creation of the universe or was created as a part of the universe. If this being existed before the creation of the universe and had a purpose contrary to that of God, then the conflict between good and evil in the universe would be unavoidable and perpetual. God's providence of restoration, then, would be in vain. Moreover, monotheism, which holds that everything in the universe was created by one God, would be unfounded. We are left with the conclusion that the spiritual being represented by the serpent was originally created with a good purpose, but later fell and became Satan.

---

15. John 15:5
16. Isa. 11:1; Jer. 23:5
17. Gen. 3:4-5

What kind of spiritual being in God's creation could have conversed with people, understood the Will of God, and lived in heaven? What kind of being, even after it had fallen and become degraded to an evil being, could transcend time and space to dominate the human soul? There are no beings endowed with such characteristics other than angels. The verse "God did not spare the angels when they sinned, but cast them into hell and committed them to pits of nether gloom"[18] supports the conclusion that the serpent, which tempted human beings and sinned, is an angel.

A serpent has a forked tongue. It depicts someone who utters contradictory things with one tongue and lives a two-faced life with one heart. A serpent twists its body around its prey before devouring it, a metaphor for someone who ensnares others for his own benefit. For these reasons, the Bible likened the angel who tempted human beings to a serpent.

1.3 The Fall of the Angel and the Fall of Human Beings

It is clear that the serpent who tempted the human beings to fall was an angel, and that this angel became Satan when he sinned and fell. Let us now investigate what kind of sin the angel and the human beings committed.

1.3.1 The Crime of the Angel

> And the angels that did not keep their own position but left their proper dwelling have been kept by him in eternal chains in the nether gloom until the judgment of the great day; just as Sodom and Gomorrah and the surrounding cities, which likewise acted immorally and indulged in unnatural lust, serve as an example by undergoing a punishment of eternal fire.
> —*Jude 6-7*

From this passage we can infer that the angel fell as a result of an illicit sexual relationship.

Fornication is a crime which cannot be committed alone. With whom did the angel commit the illicit sexual act in the Garden of Eden? In order to unveil this mystery, let us examine what kind of sin the human beings committed.

---

18. II Pet. 2:4

1.3.2 The Crime of the Human Beings

We read that before they fell, Adam and Eve were both naked, and were not ashamed.[19] After the Fall, however, they felt ashamed of their nakedness and sewed fig leaves together into aprons to cover their lower parts.[20] If they had committed a crime by eating some actual fruit from a tree called the tree of the knowledge of good and evil, then they certainly would have covered their hands or mouths instead. It is human nature to conceal one's faults. Thus, the act of covering their lower parts shows that these parts, and not their mouths, were the source of their shame. In Job 31:33 it is written, "If I have concealed my transgressions like Adam, by hiding my iniquity in my bosom."[21] Adam concealed his lower parts after the Fall; this indicates that his blemish was in his lower parts. Adam and Eve's sexual parts were the source of their shame because they were the instruments of their sinful deed.

In the world before the human Fall, what act would one be willing to carry out even at the clear risk of one's life? It could be nothing else but the act of love. God's purpose of creation, described in the blessings "be fruitful and multiply,"[22] can be achieved only through love. Accordingly, from the viewpoint of God's purpose of creation, love should be the most precious and sacred act. But because the sexual act was the very cause of the Fall, people often regard it with shame and even contempt. In conclusion, human beings fell through an act of illicit sexual intercourse.

1.3.3 The Illicit Sexual Act between the Angel and the Human Beings

Thus far, we have explained that an angel seduced human beings to fall, and that both the angel and the human beings fell due to illicit sexual love. Human beings and angels are the only spiritual beings in the universe who are capable of having love relationships. We can deduce that the illicit sexual relationship must have involved the angel and human beings.

Jesus said, "You are of your father the devil, and your will is to do your father's desires."[23] Since the Devil is identified as Satan,[24] we can assert that human beings are descendants of Satan, the "ancient serpent" who tempted human beings. Through what circumstances did

---

19. Gen. 2:25
20. Gen. 3:7
21. KJV
22. Gen. 1:28
23. John 8:44
24. Rev. 12:9

humankind become the descendants of the fallen angel, Satan? There was an illicit sexual relationship between the angel and the first ancestors. As the fruit of that relationship, all humanity is of the lineage of Satan. When St. Paul wrote, "we ourselves, who have the first fruits of the Spirit, groan inwardly as we wait for adoption as sons, the redemption of our bodies,"[25] he was acknowledging that we fallen people stem from the lineage of Satan, not the lineage of God. John the Baptist reproached the people, calling them "a brood of vipers,"[26] that is, children of Satan. Jesus said to the scribes and Pharisees, "You serpents, you brood of vipers, how are you to escape being sentenced to hell?"[27] These verses affirm that we are the offspring of an illicit sexual relationship involving the angel and our first ancestors. This, in fact, lies at the heart of the human Fall.

1.4 THE FRUIT OF THE TREE OF THE KNOWLEDGE OF GOOD AND EVIL

The tree of the knowledge of good and evil was shown earlier to symbolize Eve. What does the fruit of this tree represent? It signifies the love of Eve. As a tree multiplies by its fruit, Eve should have borne good children through her godly love. Instead, she bore evil children through her satanic love. Eve was created in an immature state; she was to reach full maturity only after going through a period of growth. Thus, it was possible for her to bear either good fruit or evil fruit through her love. This is why Eve's love is symbolized by the fruit of the tree of the knowledge of good and evil, and why Eve is symbolized by the tree.

What did eating the fruit of the tree of the knowledge of good and evil signify? When we eat something, we make it a part of ourselves. Eve was to have eaten the fruit of goodness by consummating her God-centered love. Then she would have received the essence of God's divinity and multiplied a good lineage. However, she ate of the fruit of evil by consummating her evil love centered on Satan. Hence, she received the essence of his evil nature and multiplied an evil lineage from which our sinful society descended. Accordingly, Eve's eating of the fruit of the tree of the knowledge of good and evil denotes that she consummated a satanic love relationship with the angel which bound her in blood ties to him.

God cursed the fallen angel, saying, "upon your belly you shall go, and dust you shall eat all the days of your life."[28] "Upon your belly you

---

25. Rom. 8:23
26. Matt. 3:7
27. Matt. 23:33
28. Gen. 3:14

shall go" means that the angel would become a miserable being, unable to function properly or to perform its original service. To "eat dust" means that ever since the angel was thrown down from heaven,[29] he has been deprived of life elements from God. Instead, he has had to subsist on evil elements gleaned from the sinful world.

1.5 THE ROOT OF SIN

We have learned from the above elucidation of the Bible that the root of sin was not that the first human ancestors ate a fruit, but rather that they had an illicit sexual relationship with an angel (symbolized by a serpent). Consequently, they could not multiply God's good lineage but instead multiplied Satan's evil lineage.

There is ample evidence which helps us recognize that the root of human sin stems from sexual immorality. We know that the original sin has been perpetuated through lineal descent from one generation to the next. This is because the root of sin was solidified by a sexual relationship that binds one in ties of blood. Furthermore, those religions which emphasize the need to purge sin regard fornication as a cardinal sin, and they have taught the virtues of chastity and restraint in order to curb it. This is an indication that the root of sin is found in lustful desires. The Israelites performed the rite of circumcision as a condition for sanctification. They qualified themselves as God's chosen people by draining blood, because the root of sin lies in having taken in through an unchaste act the evil blood which permeates our being.

Sexual promiscuity is a principal cause of the downfall of numerous heroes, patriots and nations. Even in the most outstanding people, the root of sin—illicit sexual desire—is constantly active in their souls, sometimes without their conscious awareness. We may be able to eradicate all other evils by establishing moral codes through religion, by thoroughly implementing various educational programs, and by reforming the socio-economic systems that foster crime. But no one can prevent the plague of sexual promiscuity, which has become increasingly prevalent as the progress of civilization makes lifestyles more comfortable and indolent. Therefore, the hope of an ideal world is an empty dream as long as this root of all evils has not been eradicated at its source. Christ at his Second Advent must be able to solve this problem once and for all.

---

29. Isa. 14:12; Rev. 12:9

SECTION 2

THE MOTIVATION AND PROCESS OF THE FALL

The initial cause of the human Fall lay within the angel, who, as we have seen, is symbolized by the serpent who tempted Eve. Therefore, before we can know the motivation and the process of the Fall, we must first learn about the angel.

2.1   ANGELS, THEIR MISSIONS AND THEIR RELATIONSHIP TO HUMAN BEINGS

Like all beings, angels were created by God. God created them prior to any other creation. In the biblical account of the creation of heaven and earth, we find that God spoke in the plural: "Let us make man in our image, after our likeness."[30] This is not because God was referring to Himself as the Holy Trinity, as many theologians have interpreted the passage. Rather, He was speaking to the angels, whom He had created before human beings.

God created angels to be His retainers, who would assist Him in creating and sustaining the universe. In the Bible we find many instances of angels working for the Will of God. Angels conveyed to Abraham important words of God's blessing;[31] an angel heralded the conception of Christ;[32] an angel unchained Peter and led him out of prison and into the city.[33] The angel who escorts John in the Book of Revelation calls himself "a servant,"[34] and in Hebrews angels are referred to as "ministering spirits."[35] The Bible often portrays angels honoring and praising God.[36]

Let us investigate the relationship between human beings and angels from the perspective of the Principle of Creation. Because God created us as His children and gave us dominion over all creation,[37] we are meant to rule over the angels as well. It is written in the Bible that we have the authority to judge the angels.[38] Many who communicate with the spirit world have witnessed hosts of angels escorting the saints in Paradise. These observations illustrate the fact that angels have the mission to minister to human beings.

---

30. Gen. 1:26
31. Gen. 18:10
32. Matt. 1:20, Luke 1:31
33. Acts 12:7-10
34. Rev. 22:9
35. Heb. 1:14
36. Rev. 5:11-12, 7:11-12
37. Gen. 1:28
38. I Cor. 6:3

2.2 THE SPIRITUAL FALL AND THE PHYSICAL FALL

God created human beings with two components: the spirit self and the physical self. The human Fall likewise took place in two dimensions: the spiritual and the physical. The fall which took place through the sexual relationship between the angel and Eve was the *spiritual fall*, while the fall which occurred through the sexual relationship between Eve and Adam was the *physical fall*.

How can an act of passionate love be consummated between an angel and a human being? All the emotions and sensations felt between a person and a spirit are exactly the same as those felt during contact between two earthly people. Undoubtedly, a sexual union between an angel and a person is possible.

We can understand this more clearly from the following evidence. There are reported cases of earthly people leading a married life with a spirit. In the Bible we have the account of an angel who wrestled with Jacob and put his thigh out of joint.[39] Three angels visited Abraham's family and ate a meal of veal, milk and curds.[40] Moreover, two angels visited the house of Lot and ate the unleavened bread he served them. When the townspeople saw the angels, they were excited with lecherous desires for them and surrounded Lot's house, shouting, "Where are the men who came to you tonight? Bring them out to us, that we may know them."[41]

2.2.1 THE SPIRITUAL FALL

God created the angelic world and assigned Lucifer[42] to the position of archangel. Lucifer was the channel of God's love to the angelic world, just as Abraham was the channel of God's blessing to the Israelites. In this position he virtually monopolized the love of God. However, after God created human beings as His children, He loved them many times more than He had ever loved Lucifer, whom He had created as His servant. In truth, God's love towards Lucifer did not change; it was the same before and after the creation of human beings. Yet when Lucifer saw that God loved Adam and Eve more than him, he felt as if there had been a decrease in the love he received from God. This situation is similar to that in the biblical parable of the laborers in the vineyard.[43] Although the laborers who had worked since morning

---

39. Gen. 32:25
40. Gen. 18:8
41. Gen. 19:5
42. Isa. 14:12 (KJV)—In the Revised Standard Version, the Archangel is called "Day Star, son of Dawn."
43. Matt. 20:1-15

received a fair wage, when they saw that those who came later and worked less received just as much, they felt underpaid. Lucifer, feeling as though he were receiving less love than he deserved, wanted to grasp the same central position in human society as he enjoyed as the channel of God's love in the angelic world. This was why he seduced Eve, and this was the motivation of the spiritual fall.

Everything in the universe is created to be governed by God through love. Thus, love is the source of life, the key to happiness, and the essence of the ideal to which all beings aspire. The more one receives love, the more beautiful one appears to others. When the angel, created as God's servant, beheld Eve, the daughter of God, it was only natural that she looked beautiful in his eyes. Moreover, when Lucifer saw that Eve was responding to his temptation, the angel felt the stimulation of her love to be deliciously enticing. At this point, Lucifer was seducing Eve with the mind to have her regardless of the consequences. Lucifer, who left his proper position due to his excessive desire, and Eve, who wanted to open her eyes and become like God[44] before the time was ripe, formed a common base and began give and take action. The power of the unprincipled love generated by their give and take led them to consummate an illicit sexual relationship on the spiritual plane.

All beings are created based on the principle that when they become one in love, they exchange elements with each other. Accordingly, when Eve became one with Lucifer through love, she received certain elements from him. First, she received feelings of dread arising from the pangs of a guilty conscience, stemming from her violation of the purpose of creation. Second, she received from Lucifer the wisdom which enabled her to discern that her originally intended spouse was to be Adam, not the angel. Eve was in the position to receive wisdom from the Archangel because she was immature and her wisdom was not as seasoned as that of the Archangel, who was already in a state of angelic maturity.

2.2.2 The Physical Fall

Perfect Adam and Eve were supposed to have become an eternal husband and wife in God's love. But Eve, who in her immaturity had engaged in the illicit relationship with the Archangel, joined with Adam as husband and wife. Thus, Adam fell when he, too, was still immature. This untimely conjugal relationship in satanic love between Adam and Eve constituted the physical fall.

---

44. Gen. 3:5-6

As mentioned above, through the spiritual fall with the Archangel, Eve received feelings of dread arising from the pangs of a guilty conscience and a new wisdom that her originally intended spouse was not the Archangel but Adam. Eve then seduced Adam with the hope that by uniting with him, her intended spouse, she could rid herself of the dread and once again stand before God. This was Eve's motivation which led to the physical fall.

Once Eve had united with the Archangel through their illicit sexual relationship, she stood in the position of the Archangel with respect to Adam. Thus, Adam, who was still receiving God's love, appeared very attractive to her. Seeing Adam as her only hope of returning to God, Eve turned to Adam and tempted him, playing the same role as the Archangel had played when he had tempted her. Adam responded and formed a common base with Eve, and they began give and take action with each other. The power of the unprincipled love generated in their relationship induced Adam to abandon his original position and brought them together in an illicit physical relationship of sexual love.

When Adam united in oneness with Eve, he inherited all the elements Eve had received from Lucifer. These elements in turn have been passed down to all subsequent generations without interruption. What if Adam had reached perfection without having yielded to fallen Eve's temptation? The providence to restore Eve alone would have been relatively easy because, although she had fallen, Adam still would have remained intact as her perfect subject partner. Unfortunately, Adam also fell, and humanity has multiplied in sin to the present day, perpetuating the lineage of Satan.

SECTION 3

THE POWER OF LOVE, THE POWER OF THE PRINCIPLE AND GOD'S COMMANDMENT

3.1 THE POWER OF LOVE AND THE POWER OF THE PRINCIPLE IN THE HUMAN FALL

Human beings are created through the Principle, and they are meant to live according to the way of the Principle. Therefore, it cannot be that the force inherent in the Principle would induce a person to deviate from the way of the Principle and cause him to fall. This may be compared to a train which cannot run off the track unless, aside from a breakdown in the track or locomotive, some outside force stronger than the train's forward momentum collides with it and pushes it in a different direction. Similarly, for human beings the force inherent in the Principle guides their growth in the proper direction. But if some stronger force from a different direction and with an unprincipled purpose collides with them, they will surely fall. The force which is stronger than the force of the Principle is none other than the power of love. While human beings are in the state of immaturity, it is possible that the power of unprincipled love can induce them to fall.

Why is the power of love stronger than the power of the Principle? Why did God create it stronger, when this leaves open the possibility that the power of deviant love might collide with a person in the state of immaturity and cause him to fall?

According to the Principle of Creation, God's love is the subject of all loves flowing within the four position foundation, which is established when its members have completed the three object purpose through their dynamic love for each other. Without God's love, there is no way to establish the true four position foundation; without God's love, there is no way for us to fulfill the purpose for which we were created. Love is truly the source and wellspring of our life and happiness.

Although God created human beings based on the Principle, He governs us through love. Accordingly, in order for love to fulfill its proper role, its power must be stronger than the power of the Principle. If the power of love were weaker than the power of the Principle, God could not govern human beings through love; rather, we would pursue the Principle more than the love of God. For this reason, Jesus tried to raise his disciples with the truth, but it was his love that saved them.

3.2 Why God Set Up the Commandment as an Object of Faith

Why did God nurture the faith of Adam and Eve by giving them the commandment, "Do not eat of the fruit"? In their immature state, Adam and Eve could not be directly governed by God through love. Because the power of love is stronger than the power of the Principle, God foresaw that if they ever formed a common base with the Archangel, there was a possibility that they could succumb to the power of deviant, unprincipled love and fall. To prevent this, God gave Adam and Eve the commandment that forbade them from relating with the Archangel in this way. No matter how powerful the unprincipled love of the Archangel might be, had Adam and Eve adhered to God's commandment, forming a common base with God and engaging in give and take with Him and no other, the power of the Archangel's unprincipled love would not have affected them and they would never have fallen. Tragically, Adam and Eve did not obey the commandment, but formed a common base with the Archangel and had give and take with him. Hence, the power of illicit love pushed them off the track.

It was not only to prevent their fall that God gave immature human beings the commandment. God also wanted them to enjoy dominion over the natural world—including the angels—by inheriting His creative nature. In order to inherit this creatorship, human beings should perfect themselves through their faith in the Word as their own portion of responsibility.[45]

God gave the commandment not to the Archangel but only to the human beings. God wished to exalt the dignity of human beings as bestowed by the Principle of Creation, which entitled them to stand as God's children and govern even the angels.

3.3 THE PERIOD DURING WHICH THE COMMANDMENT WAS NECESSARY

Was God's commandment not to eat of the fruit binding forever? God's second blessing was to be fulfilled when Adam and Eve entered God's direct dominion of love, by joining as true husband and wife and bearing and raising children in God's love.[46] Indeed, the Principle mandates that human beings eat of the fruit once they reach full maturity of character.

The power of love is stronger than the power of the Principle. Had Adam and Eve reached perfection, become a godly husband and wife, and experienced God's direct governance by the absolute power of His love, their conjugal love would have become absolute. No person, no power in the universe could ever break that bond of love. At this point, Adam and Eve would never fall. There would have been no way that the love of the Archangel, who is inferior to human beings, could ever have severed the conjugal love of Adam and Eve once it was grounded firmly in God. Accordingly, God's commandment, "Do not eat of the fruit," was binding upon Adam and Eve only while they were immature.

---

45. cf. Creation 5.2.2
46. Gen. 1:28

Section 4

The Consequences of the Human Fall

What were the consequences of the spiritual and physical fall of Adam and Eve for the entire universe, including humankind and the angels? Let us discuss some of the most serious consequences.

4.1 Satan and Fallen Humanity

Satan is the name given to the Archangel Lucifer after he fell. When the first human ancestors fell, they bound themselves in blood ties with Lucifer. They formed a four position foundation yoked to Satan, and thus all humanity became the children of Satan. This is why Jesus said to the people, "you are of your father the devil," and called them a "brood of vipers."[47] St. Paul wrote, "not only the creation, but we ourselves, who have the first fruits of the Spirit, groan inwardly as we wait for adoption as sons,"[48] indicating that no one belongs to the lineage of God. Instead, due to the Fall of the first human ancestors, human beings are of the lineage of Satan.

Had Adam and Eve reached full maturity and built a four position foundation centering on God, the world of God's sovereignty would have been established at that time. While still immature, however, they fell and formed a four position foundation centering on Satan. Consequently, this world has come under Satan's sovereignty. Hence, the Bible calls Satan "the ruler of this world" and "the god of this world."[49]

Once Satan came to dominate human beings, who were intended to be the lords of creation, he also achieved domination over everything in the universe. Accordingly, it is written, "the creation waits with eager longing for the revealing of the sons of God. . . . We know that the whole creation has been groaning in travail together until now."[50] These verses describe the agony of the creation under the domination of Satan as it longs for the appearance of unfallen people who have perfected their original nature; it yearns for the day when they will vanquish Satan and rule it in love.

4.2 Satan's Activities in Human Society

Satan is constantly accusing all people before God, as he did Job, in

---

47. John 8:44; Matt. 12:34, 23:33; cf. Matt. 3:7
48. Rom. 8:23
49. John 12:31; II Cor. 4:4
50. Rom. 8:19-22

order to drag them into hell.[51] However, even Satan cannot perpetrate his evil activity unless he first finds an object partner with whom he can form a common base and engage in give and take action. Satan's object partners are evil spirits in the spirit world. The object partners to these evil spirits are the spirit selves of evil people on the earth, and the vehicles through which these evil spirit selves act are their physical selves. Accordingly, the power of Satan is conveyed through evil spirits and is manifested in the activities of earthly people. For example, Satan entered into Judas Iscariot,[52] and Jesus once called Peter "Satan."[53] In the Bible, the spirits of evil earthly men are called "angels" of the devil.[54]

The Kingdom of Heaven on earth[55] is a restored world in which Satan can no longer instigate any activity. To realize this world, it is necessary for all humanity to eliminate their common base with Satan, restore their common base with God, and engage in give and take action with Him. The prophecy that in the Last Days God will confine Satan in a bottomless pit[56] signifies that Satan will be utterly incapable of any activity, since there will no longer be any counterpart with whom Satan can relate. In order to eliminate our common base with Satan and be capable of judging him,[57] we must understand the identity and crime of Satan and accuse him before God.

However, God endowed human beings and angels with freedom; therefore, He cannot restore them by force. Of their own free will, human beings are to bring Satan to voluntary submission by upholding the Word of God through fulfilling their responsibility. Only in this way can we be restored to the original ideal purposed by God at the creation. Because God works His providence based on this principle, the history of the providence of restoration has been repeatedly prolonged.[58]

4.3 Good and Evil Seen from the Viewpoint of Purpose

Having already defined good and evil,[59] let us further examine the nature of good and evil from the viewpoint of purpose. Had Adam and Eve loved each other as God intended and formed a four position foundation centered on God, they would have established a good world. But when they loved each other with a purpose contrary to God's intentions and established a four position foundation centered on Satan, they

---

51. Job 1:9-11
52. Luke 22:3
53. Matt. 16:33
54. Matt. 25:41
55. cf. Eschatology 2
56. Rev. 20:1-3
57. I Cor. 6:3
58. cf. Predestination 2
59. cf. Creation 4.3.2

ended up forming an evil world. This demonstrates that although good and evil elements or actions may take the same form, their true nature may be discerned through their fruits. They yield their fruits in accordance with the divergent purposes they pursue.

We find many cases where an aspect of human nature conventionally considered evil is, in fact, good if its purpose is directed toward the Will of God. Let us take the example of desire. Desire, which people often consider sinful, is actually God-given. Joy is the purpose of creation, and joy can only be attained when desire is fulfilled. If we had no desire, we could never experience joy. If we had no desire, we would not have any aspiration to receive God's love, to live, to perform good deeds, or to improve ourselves. Without desire, therefore, neither God's purpose of creation nor the providence of restoration could be fulfilled. An orderly, harmonious and flourishing human society would be impossible.

Desires, being part of our God-given nature, are good when they bear fruit for the purpose of God's Will, or are evil when they bear fruit for the purpose of Satan's will. On this basis, we can deduce that even this evil world will be restored to goodness and become the Kingdom of Heaven on earth if it changes its direction and purpose according to the guidance of Christ.[60] The providence of restoration may thus be interpreted as the process of changing the direction of this fallen world from its current satanic purpose to the purpose of building the Kingdom of Heaven, God's ideal of creation.

Any standard of goodness set during the course of the providence of restoration is not absolute but relative. In any particular period of history, obedient compliance with the doctrines expounded by the prevailing authorities is considered good, while actions in opposition to them are considered evil. But the change of an era ushers in new authorities and doctrines, with new goals and new standards of good and evil. For the adherents of any religious tradition or school of thought, complying with the precepts of its doctrine or philosophy is good, while opposing them is evil. But whenever a doctrine or philosophy undergoes a change, its standards of good and evil will also change according to its new goals. Similarly, if an adherent converts to a different religion or school of thought, then naturally his goals and standards of good and evil will change accordingly.

Conflicts and revolutions constantly plague human society, mainly because of the continual changes in standards of good and evil as

---

60. cf. Eschatology 2.2

people seek to fulfill divergent purposes. Yet throughout the endless cycles of conflict and revolution in human history, people have been seeking the absolute goodness which their original mind desires. Conflicts and revolutions in fallen human society will inevitably continue as people pursue this absolute goal, until the final achievement of the world of goodness. The standard of goodness will remain relative only as long as the course of restoration continues.

Once the sovereignty of Satan is expelled from the earth, then God, the eternal and absolute Being transcendent of time and space, will establish His sovereignty and His truth. In that day, God's truth will be absolute, and hence the purpose which it serves and the standard of goodness which it sets will both be absolute. This cosmic, all-encompassing truth will be firmly established by Christ at his Second Advent.

4.4 The Works of Good Spirits and Evil Spirits

We use "good spirits" as a general term for God, spirits on the side of God, and good angels. The general term for Satan and spirits on his side is "evil spirits." The works of good spirits and evil spirits, as in the case of good and evil acts generally, have a similar appearance at the outset but pursue contrary purposes.

Over time, the works of a good spirit will increase a person's sense of peace and righteousness and even improve his health. The works of evil spirits, on the contrary, will gradually lead to an increase of anxiety, fear and selfishness and cause his health to deteriorate. It may be difficult for someone who does not know the Principle to discern the works of spirits, but eventually, often belatedly, he will recognize the nature of the spirits by the fruits they bear. Since a fallen person stands in the midway position between God and Satan and relates with both of them, the works of a good spirit may be accompanied by the subtle influences of an evil spirit. In other cases, phenomena which begin as the works of evil spirits may, as time passes, merge with the works of good spirits. Discerning the spirits is thus very difficult for those who do not understand the Principle. It is a pity that many religious authorities, in their ignorance, condemn the works of good spirits by lumping them together with the works of evil spirits. This may place them in inadvertent opposition to the Will of God. In the present era, spiritual phenomena are becoming ever more prevalent. Unless religious leaders can correctly distinguish the works of good spirits from the works of evil spirits, they cannot properly instruct and guide those who experience spiritual phenomena.

4.5 SIN

Sin is a violation of heavenly law which is committed when a person forms a common base with Satan, thus setting a condition for give and take action with him. Sin can be classified into four kinds. The first is the original sin. This sin originated with the spiritual and physical fall of our first human ancestors. It is ingrained in our lineage and is the root of all sins. The second is hereditary sin. This is sin which one inherits from one's ancestors on account of their connection through lineage. It is written in the Ten Commandments that the sins of parents will be visited upon their descendants.[61]

The third is collective sin. This is sin for which a person is responsible as a member of a group, even though he neither committed the sin himself nor inherited it from his ancestors. An example of this kind of sin is the crucifixion of Jesus. Although only the chief priests and certain scribes committed the deed when they sent Jesus to be crucified, the Jewish people and humanity as a whole have together shouldered the responsibility for this sin. As a consequence, the Jewish people were cast into the position to undergo grievous suffering, and humanity as a whole has had to walk a path of tribulation, until the Second Coming of Christ. The fourth is individual sin, which an individual himself commits.

The original sin may be thought of as the root of all sins, hereditary sin as the trunk, collective sin as the branches, and individual sin as the leaves. All sins sprout from the original sin, which is their root. Without extirpating the original sin, there is no way to completely eradicate other sins. However, no man is able to unearth this root of sin, buried deep in the recesses of time. Only Christ, who comes as the root and True Parent of humanity, can grasp it and uproot it.

4.6 THE PRIMARY CHARACTERISTICS OF THE FALLEN NATURE

Eve inherited from the Archangel all the proclivities incidental to his transgression against God when he bound her in blood ties through their sexual relationship. Adam in turn acquired the same inclinations when Eve, assuming the role of the Archangel, bound him in blood ties through their sexual relationship. These proclivities have become the root cause of the fallen inclinations in all people. They are the primary characteristics of our *fallen nature*.

The fundamental motivation which engendered these primary characteristics of the fallen nature lay in the envy the Archangel felt toward

---

61. Exod. 20:5

Adam, the beloved of God. How can there be anything such as envy and jealousy in an archangel, whom God created for a good purpose? The Archangel was endowed with desire and intellect as a part of his original nature. Because the Archangel possessed an intellect, he could compare and discern that God's love for human beings was greater than the love God gave to him. Because he also possessed desires, he had a natural yearning for God to love him more. This desire of the heart was naturally conducive to envy and jealousy. Envy is an inevitable byproduct of the original nature, like the shadow cast by an object in the light.

After human beings reach perfection, however, they will never be induced to fall because of incidental envy. They will know deep inside that the temporary gratification they might feel by attaining the object of their desire is not worth the agony of self-destruction that would ensue. Hence, they would never commit such crimes.

A world that has fulfilled the purpose of creation is a society built upon organic inter-relationships much like the structure of the human body. Recognizing that the downfall of an individual would cause the whole to perish, society will keep its individual members from such self-destruction. In this ideal world, the envious desires that arise incidentally from the original nature will be channeled into spurring the progress of humanity. They will never cause people to fall.

The primary characteristics of the fallen nature can be divided broadly into four types. The first is failing to take God's standpoint. A principal cause of the Archangel's fall was his failure to love Adam with the same heart and perspective as God; instead he felt jealous of Adam. This led him to tempt Eve. An example of this characteristic of the fallen nature is when a courtier feels jealous of the king's favorite instead of sincerely respecting him as one whom the king loves.

The second is leaving one's proper position. Seeking more of God's love, Lucifer desired to enjoy the same position of love in the human world as he had in the angelic world. This unrighteous desire caused him to leave his position and fall. People are induced by unrighteous desires to step beyond the bounds of what is right and overreach themselves because of this primary characteristic of the fallen nature.

The third is reversing dominion. The angel, who was supposed to come under the dominion of human beings, instead dominated Eve. Then Eve, who was supposed to come under the dominion of Adam, dominated him instead. This disruption of the proper order has borne bitter fruit. Human society is thrown out of order by people who leave their proper position and then reverse the order of dominion. These repeated occurrences are rooted in this primary characteristic of the fallen nature.

The fourth is multiplying the criminal act. After her fall, had Eve not repeated her sin by seducing Adam, Adam would have remained whole. The restoration of Eve alone would have been relatively easy. However, Eve spread her sin to others by inducing Adam to fall. The proclivity of evil people to entangle others in an expanding web of crime stems from this primary characteristic of the fallen nature.

SECTION 5

FREEDOM AND THE HUMAN FALL

5.1 THE MEANING OF FREEDOM FROM THE VIEWPOINT OF THE PRINCIPLE

What is the meaning of true freedom? In light of the Principle, three characteristics of freedom stand out. First, there is no freedom outside the Principle. Freedom requires both free will and the free actions pursuant to that will. The former and the latter have the relationship of internal nature and external form, and perfect freedom is achieved when they are in harmony. Therefore, there cannot be any free action without free will, nor can free will be complete without free actions to accompany it. Free actions are generated by free will, and free will is an expression of the mind. Since the mind of an original, sinless person cannot operate outside of God's Word, that is, the Principle, it will never express free will or generate free action apart from the Principle. Undoubtedly, the freedom of a true person never deviates from the Principle.

Second, there is no freedom without responsibility. Human beings, created according to the Principle, can reach perfection only by fulfilling their responsibility based on their free will.[62] Accordingly, a person pursuing the purpose of creation as prompted by his free will ceaselessly strives to carry out his portion of responsibility.

Third, there is no freedom without accomplishment. When human beings exercise freedom and carry out their responsibility, they strive to accomplish results which complete the purpose of creation and bring joy to God. Free will ceaselessly pursues concrete results through free actions.

5.2 FREEDOM AND THE HUMAN FALL

To summarize, freedom cannot exist outside the Principle. Freedom is accompanied by the responsibility laid out in the Principle, and freedom pursues accomplishments that bring joy to God. Free actions gener-

---

62. cf. Creation 5.2.2

ated by free will bring about only good results. Therefore, it cannot be that freedom caused the human Fall. It is written, "where the Spirit of the Lord is, there is freedom."[63] This freedom is the freedom of the original mind.

As long as Adam and Eve were bound by God's warning not to eat of the fruit of the tree of the knowledge of good and evil, they should have kept this commandment by their free will and without God's intervention. Certainly, the freedom of their original mind, which is inherently responsible and seeks the good, was prompting them to obey it. When Eve was about to deviate from the Principle, the freedom of her original mind aroused fear and foreboding in her in an attempt to prevent her from deviating. Ever since the Fall, this freedom of the original mind has been working to bring people back to God. Working in this way, freedom could not possibly have caused human beings to fall. Rather, the human Fall was caused by the stronger power of unprincipled love, which overwhelmed the freedom of the original mind.

In truth, human beings lost their freedom as a result of the Fall. Yet even fallen people possess intact a seed of their original nature which seeks freedom, and this makes it possible for God to carry on the providence to restore it. With the progress of history, people have been ever more zealously aspiring for freedom, even at the cost of their lives. This is evidence that we are in the process of restoring our freedom, long lost due to Satan. The purpose of our search for freedom is to facilitate the accomplishment of our God-given responsibility, which is essential for fulfilling our purpose of creation.

5.3 Freedom, the Fall and Restoration

It is true that human beings were free to relate with angels, who were created to minister to them. However, since Eve's heart and intellect were still immature when she was tempted by the angel, she became confused emotionally and intellectually. Although the freedom of her original mind induced in her a sense of foreboding, because the power of the love between her and the angel was stronger, she crossed the boundary and fell. No matter how freely Eve was relating with the angel, if she had maintained unwavering faith in God's commandment and not responded to the angel's temptation, then the power of unprincipled love would not have been generated and she would not have fallen. Therefore, despite the fact that freedom permitted Eve to relate with the angel and brought her to the brink of the Fall, what pushed her over

---

63. II Cor. 3:17

the brink was not freedom but the power of unprincipled love.

Since Eve was created to interact in freedom with angels, she naturally related with Lucifer. Yet when Eve and Lucifer formed a common base and engaged in give and take action, the power of the unprincipled love which was generated caused them to fall. Conversely, since fallen people can also relate with God in freedom, if they follow the words of truth, form a common base and engage in give and take with Him, then the power of principled love can revive their original nature. Indeed, the freedom of the original mind yearns to cultivate fully the original nature. Hence, people in every age have been desperately crying out for freedom.

Due to the Fall, human beings became ignorant of God and His Heart. This ignorance has rendered the human will incapable of striving toward goals which are pleasing to God. As God has given "spirit and truth"[64] (meaning internal knowledge and external knowledge) to fallen people according to the merit of the age in the providence of restoration, their heart, which yearns for the freedom of the original mind, has gradually been revived. In step with this progress, their heart toward God has also been restored, strengthening their zeal to live according to His Will.

Moreover, as aspirations for freedom mount in intensity, people will demand a social environment conducive to its realization. When the social circumstances of an era cannot satisfy the desires of freedom-loving people, revolutions inevitably erupt. The French Revolution in the eighteenth century is one example. Revolutions will continue until true freedom has been fully restored.

Section 6

The Reasons God Did Not Intervene in the Fall of the First Human Ancestors

God, being omniscient and omnipotent, must have known about the deviant acts of the first human ancestors which were leading to their Fall and was surely capable of preventing them from carrying them out. Why, then, did God not intervene to prevent the Fall? This is one of the most important unsolved mysteries of the ages. We can put forward the following three reasons why God did not interfere with the human Fall.

---

64. John 4:23

6.1 To Maintain the Absoluteness and Perfection of the Principle of Creation

In accordance with the Principle of Creation, God created human beings in His image, with the character and powers of the Creator, intending that they govern over all things as He governs over humankind. However, for human beings to inherit the creative nature of God, they must grow to perfection by fulfilling their portion of responsibility. As explained above, the period of their growth is the realm of God's indirect dominion or the realm of dominion based on accomplishments through the Principle. While people are still in this realm, God does not directly govern them because He wishes to allow them to fulfill their own portion of responsibility. God will govern them directly only after they have reached full maturity.

If God were to interfere with human actions during their growing period, it would be tantamount to ignoring the human portion of responsibility. In that case, God would be disregarding His own Principle of Creation, according to which He intends to give human beings His creative nature and raise them to become the lords of creation. If the Principle were ignored, then its absoluteness and perfection would be undermined. Because God is the absolute and perfect Creator, His Principle of Creation must also be absolute and perfect. In summary, in order to preserve the absoluteness and perfection of the Principle of Creation, God did not intervene in the acts that led the human beings to fall.

6.2 That God Alone Be the Creator

God only governs over a principled existence which He has created and only sways the course of principled acts. God does not regulate any unprincipled existence which He did not create, such as hell; nor does He interfere with any unprincipled act, such as criminal acts. If God were to affect the course of such beings or acts, then they would necessarily be given the value of God's creations and be recognized as principled.

Consequently, if God were to have intervened in the Fall of the first human ancestors, He would have been attributing to those acts the value of His creations and recognizing them as principled. If God were to do this, He would in effect be creating a new principle that recognizes these criminal acts as lawful. Since it would actually be Satan who manipulated the situation to bring about this outcome, it would in fact be Satan who created another, new principle, and Satan would stand as the creator of all the fruits of the Fall. Therefore, in order that God remain the sole Creator, He did not intervene in the human Fall.

6.3 To Make Human Beings the Lords of Creation

God created human beings and blessed them with dominion over everything in the creation.[65] Human beings cannot rule other creatures if they stand on an equal footing with them. They must earn certain qualifications to exercise their God-given mandate to govern.

God is qualified to govern human beings because He is their Creator. Likewise, for human beings to gain the qualifications to rule all things, they must also possess the character and powers of the Creator. In order to give them creatorship and make them worthy to govern all things, God has human beings perfect themselves by accomplishing their own portion of responsibility until the end of their growing period. Only by perfecting themselves in accordance with the Principle can they earn the qualifications to rule the universe. If God were to rule directly and control the lives of human beings who are still in the state of immaturity, this would in effect grant the authority of a ruler to those who are unqualified to rule. That is, it would have the effect of granting this authority to those who have not yet fulfilled their responsibility or earned God's creatorship. It would contradict God's Principle because He would be treating an immature person as if he were mature. God, the Author of the Principle, would be disregarding His own Principle of Creation, which He established in order to enable human beings to inherit the nature of the Creator and govern the creation. Consequently, it was in order to bless human beings as the lords of creation that God had to restrain Himself from intervening in the acts of immature human beings, as He watched with trepidation their tragic fall.

---

65. Gen. 1:28

Chapter 3

Eschatology and Human History

We dwell in ignorance of history, uncertain about its origin, the direction in which it is heading, and its final destination. Concerning eschatology, or the doctrine of the *Last Days,* many Christians believe literally what is written in the Bible: "the heavens will be kindled and dissolved, and the elements will melt with fire";[1] "the sun will be darkened and the moon will not give its light and the stars will fall from heaven";[2] and "with the archangel's call, and with the sound of the trumpet . . . the dead in Christ will rise first; then we who are alive, who are left, shall be caught up together with them in the clouds to meet the Lord in the air."[3] One pertinent question for Christians is whether these events will take place literally or whether the verses are symbolic, as are many parts of the Bible. To address this issue, we should first understand such fundamental matters as the purpose of God's creation, the meaning of the human Fall, and the goal of the providence of restoration.

---

1. II Pet. 3:12
2. Matt. 24:29
3. I Thess. 4:16-17

Section 1

The Completion of God's Purpose of Creation and the Human Fall

1.1 The Completion of God's Purpose of Creation

We have discussed how God's purpose in creating human beings was to rejoice with them.[4] Thus, our purpose of existence is to bring joy to God. What must we do to bring joy to God and fully manifest our original value?

Created beings other than humans are endowed with the innate nature to grow to maturity naturally and become object partners which bring God joy. Human beings, on the other hand, can become true and authentic object partners who bring joy to God only through their free will and free actions.[5] They cannot become the object partners who inspire God with joy unless they understand His Will and make effort to live accordingly. Hence, human beings are endowed with emotional sensitivity to the Heart of God, intuition and reason to comprehend His Will, and the requisite abilities to practice it. A person who relates with God in this manner will attain perfection of his individual character. Adam and Eve prior to the Fall, as well as the prophets of every age, had some ability to converse with God because they had these innate faculties.

The relationship between God and a person who has attained individual perfection can be compared to that between the mind and the body. The body is the dwelling place of the mind and moves according to the mind's direction. Likewise, God abides within the mind of a fully mature person. Such a person becomes a temple of God and leads his life in harmony with His Will. A perfect individual is fully attuned to God, just as the body resonates with the mind. For this reason it is written, "Do you not know that you are God's temple and that God's Spirit dwells in you?"[6] and "In that day you will know that I am in my Father, and you in me, and I in you."[7] A person who has perfected his individual character becomes a temple of God, and the Holy Spirit abides within him. Living in oneness with God, he acquires a divine nature. Thus, it is impossible for him to commit sin or to fall.

A person who has perfected his individual character embodies total

---

4. cf. Creation 3
5. cf. Creation 5.2.2
6. I Cor. 3:16
7. John 14:20

goodness and fulfills the purpose of creation. If a person embodying total goodness could fall, this would lead to the illogical conclusion that goodness contains the seed of its own destruction. Moreover, if human beings, who were created by the omnipotent God, could fall even after becoming perfect, we would have reason to doubt the omnipotence of God. God is the absolute and eternal Subject. To give Him true joy, His object partner must necessarily also be eternal and absolute. For these reasons, a person who has perfected his individual character can never fall.

Had Adam and Eve reached perfection, being thereafter insusceptible to sin, they would have borne good children and founded a sinless family and society in complete concordance with God's blessings.[8] They would have founded the Kingdom of Heaven, which consists of one great family with the same parents. The Kingdom of Heaven has the form of an individual who has achieved perfection of character. Just as the members of the human body are coordinated in horizontal relationships with each other and move as one in response to the vertical commands of the brain, in this society people will form cooperative horizontal relationships with each other and live together in tune with the vertical directions emanating from God. No one will harm his neighbor, since if one person were to suffer pain, everyone in this society would experience the Heart of God who shares in that person's grief.

Regardless of the purity of the people of this society, if they were living in primitive circumstances like cavemen, this could not be considered the Kingdom of Heaven which both God and human beings desire. God gave us the mandate to have dominion over all things.[9] Hence, to realize the ideal of creation, people of perfected character should advance science, harness the natural world, and create an extremely pleasant social and living environment. This will be the Kingdom of Heaven on earth. Once people have attained full maturity and enjoyed life in God's earthly Kingdom, then when they shed their physical bodies and pass into the spirit world, they will form the Kingdom of Heaven in heaven. Accordingly, God's primary purpose of creation is to build the Kingdom of Heaven on earth.

1.2 Consequences of the Human Fall

Human beings fell while they were immature and still in their growing period. We have already clarified why the growing period was necessary and what the evidence is for the conclusion that the first human

---

8. Gen. 1:28
9. Ibid.

beings fell while immature.[10] Due to the Fall, human beings could not become temples of God; instead, they united with Satan and became his dwelling places. They failed to cultivate the divine nature; instead, they acquired an evil nature. People with evil nature have propagated evil through their children, constituting evil families, evil societies and an evil world. This is the hell on earth in which we have been living. In this hell, we cannot properly form cooperative horizontal relationships with one another because our vertical relationships with God have been severed. We perform deeds harmful to others because we cannot feel the pain and suffering of our neighbors as our own. Once people have accustomed themselves to living in hell on earth, when they end their physical life, they naturally enter hell in the spirit world. We have not built the Kingdom of God, but instead established the sovereignty of Satan. For this reason, Satan is called the "ruler of this world"[11] and the "god of this world."[12]

SECTION 2

GOD'S WORK OF SALVATION

2.1 GOD'S WORK OF SALVATION IS THE PROVIDENCE OF RESTORATION

The sinful world brings humankind sorrow and causes God to grieve.[13] Would God abandon this world in its present misery? God intended to create a world of goodness and experience from it the utmost joy; yet due to the human Fall, the world came to be filled with sin and sorrow. If this sinful world were to continue forever in its present state, then God would be an impotent and ineffectual God who failed in His creation. Therefore, God will save this sinful world, by all means.

To what extent should God save this world? He should save it completely. First, God must expel the evil power of Satan from this sinful world,[14] thereby bringing it back to its original state prior to the Fall of the human ancestors. Salvation must then continue until the good purpose of creation is fulfilled and God's direct dominion is established.[15] To save a sick person is to restore him to the condition of health he

---

10. cf. Creation 5.2.1
11. John 12:31
12. II Cor. 4:4
13. Gen. 6:6
14. Acts 26:18
15. Acts 3:21

had before the illness. To save a drowning person is to restore him to the state he was in before he fell in the water. Likewise, to save a person suffering under the yoke of sin means to restore him to his original, sinless state. In other words, God's work of salvation is the *providence of restoration*.[16]

The human Fall was undoubtedly the result of human mistakes. Nevertheless, God also assumes some responsibility for the outcome because it was He who created human beings. Therefore, God has felt compelled to conduct the providence to correct this tragic outcome and to restore human beings to their true, original state. Furthermore, God created us to live eternally. This is because God, the eternal subject partner, wanted to share eternal joy with human beings as His object partners. Having endowed human beings with an eternal nature, God could not, by the laws of the Principle, simply annihilate them just because they fell. If He were to do that, He would be violating His own Principle of Creation. The only choice left to God is to save fallen people and restore them to the original, pure state in which He initially created them.

When God created human beings, He promised to help us accomplish the three great blessings.[17] He declared through Isaiah, "I have spoken, and I will bring it to pass; I have purposed, and I will do it,"[18] meaning that despite the Fall, God has been working to fulfill His promise to us through the providence to restore these blessings. He sent Jesus to restore us to our original, ideal state, as we can discern from Jesus' words to his disciples, "You, therefore, must be perfect, as your heavenly Father is perfect."[19] An original, ideal person is one with God and has realized a divine nature; thus, with reference to the purpose of creation, he is perfect as God is perfect.

2.2 THE GOAL OF THE PROVIDENCE OF RESTORATION

What is the goal of the providence of restoration? It is the establishment of the Kingdom of Heaven, which in its totality is God's good object partner and the fulfillment of His purpose of creation. The center of God's Kingdom on earth is to be human beings. Although God created the first ancestors with that intention, they fell; hence, His Will for the earth was not realized. Since then, the primary goal of the providence of restoration has been nothing less than to rebuild the Kingdom

---

16. Acts 1:6; Matt. 17:11
17. Gen. 1:28
18. Isa. 46:11
19. Matt. 5:48

of Heaven on earth. Jesus, who came to complete this goal, told his disciples to pray, "Thy will be done on earth as it is in heaven."[20] He also said, "Repent, for the kingdom of heaven is at hand."[21] His words testify that the goal of the providence of restoration is the establishment of the Kingdom of Heaven on earth.

2.3 HUMAN HISTORY IS THE HISTORY OF THE PROVIDENCE OF RESTORATION

As clarified above, God's work of salvation is the providence of restoration. Human history can be seen as the history of the providence through which God has been trying to save fallen people and work through them to restore the original, good world. Let us examine this idea in various ways, beginning with the history of the development of cultural spheres.

All people, in all ages and places, including even the most evil, have an original mind which inclines them to repel evil and seek goodness. People's intellectual understanding of what goodness is and how goodness is achieved has differed according to time, place and individual viewpoint; this has been a source of the conflicts which have made history. Nevertheless, everyone cherishes the same fundamental goal of finding and establishing goodness. Why does the original mind irrepressibly induce people of every age and every place to do good? God, the Subject of goodness, created human beings as His good and worthy object partners in order to fulfill the purpose of the good. Despite Satan's crippling efforts, which have rendered fallen human beings incapable of leading a life of total goodness, the original mind remains intact within them and prompts them toward goodness. Hence, the ultimate desire of the ages is to attain a world of goodness.

However hard the original mind may struggle to attain goodness, we can hardly find any examples of true goodness in this world under the sovereignty of evil. Human beings have thus been compelled to seek the source of goodness in the world transcendent of time and space. This necessity has given birth to religion. Through religion, fallen people mired in ignorance have sought to meet God by ceaselessly striving toward the good. Even though the individuals, peoples and nations which championed a certain religion may have perished, religion itself has survived.

Religion has endured through history despite the rise and fall of many nations. In the history of China, the Chao dynasty and the Warring

---

20. Matt. 6:10
21. Matt. 4:17

States were followed by an era of unification in the Ch'in dynasty. This was followed by the Former Han, Hsin, Later Han, the Six Dynasties, and an era of unification in the Sui and T'ang periods. They were followed by the Five Dynasties, Northern Sung, Southern Sung, Yuan, Ming, Ch'ing, the Republic of China and the People's Republic of China. In its history, China has experienced many cycles of the rise and fall of dynasties and numerous transfers of political power, yet the religions of the Far East—Confucianism, Buddhism and Taoism—have continued to thrive. The history of India has witnessed the empire of Mauryas followed by the Guptas, Harsa, Calukyas, the Mughals, Maratha, the British Raj, and today's independent India. Despite the rise and fall of many kingdoms, the religion of Hinduism has survived and prospered. In the history of the Middle East, the Umayyad Caliphate was followed by the Abbasids, the Seljuk and Ottoman Turks, the colonial period, and today's Arab states. Despite these changes in political sovereignty, the religion of Islam has endured and continued to thrive. In the history of Western Europe, we find that the center of power changed many times, from Rome to the Carolingian court, to the cities of Renaissance Italy. Spain and Portugal then became the leading powers of Europe, followed briefly by France and the Netherlands, and then England. In the modern era, the leadership of the West has been divided between America and the Soviet Union. Despite these political changes, Christianity has continued to flourish. Even under the despotic regime of the Soviet Union, founded upon Marxist materialism, Christianity remains vital and inextinguishable.

If we were to examine the rise and fall of nations, we would find numerous instances in which those nations which persecuted religion have perished, while those which protected and fostered religion have flourished. Often, the position of leading nation was taken away from nations that persecuted religion and passed to those that most esteemed religion. History thus assures us that the day will surely come when the communist world, which is persecuting religion, will perish.

Many religions have left their mark on history. Among them, the religions with the greatest influence formed cultural spheres. The major cultural spheres which have existed at various times in world history numbered between twenty-one and twenty-six. With the flow of history, lesser cultural spheres were absorbed by, or merged into, the more advanced spheres. Through the evolution of cultural spheres, as they were buffeted by the rise and fall of nations, four great cultural spheres have survived to the present day: the East Asian sphere, the Hindu sphere, the Islamic sphere, and the Christian sphere. The current trend has these four spheres forming one global cultural sphere based on the Christian ethos. This historical development is evidence that Christianity has, as its final mission, the accomplishment of the goals of all religions which have sought the ideal of goodness. The history of the development of cultural spheres, each with its stages of expansion, decline and convergence, is ultimately aimed at constituting one global cultural sphere based on one religion. This demonstrates that the essence of human history has been the restoration of one united world.

Second, we can deduce that human history is the history of the providence of restoration by observing the progress of religion and science. It was discussed earlier[22] that the purposes of religion and science are to overcome the internal and external aspects of ignorance in fallen humankind. Although they have been working independently with little connection to each other, religion and science inevitably must converge. Today they are on the threshold of reaching this destination, where they will resolve all their problems together in one united undertaking. This trend shows that human history has been walking the providential course to restore the world to its original state.

Had it not been for the Fall, the development of the intellectual capacity of our early human ancestors would have enabled them to reach the highest level of spiritual knowledge, thus naturally stimulating their knowledge of the material world to develop to a corresponding degree. Science then would have advanced rapidly in an extremely short period of time, and today's level of science and technology would have been attained in those days. However, due to the Fall, human beings plunged into ignorance and could build only a primitive society, far beneath God's original ideal. Long ages passed before people could overcome this ignorance through the advancement of science. The modern world of highly developed technology has now brought us externally to the threshold of the ideal society.

Third, by examining trends in the history of conflict, we can understand that human history is the history of the providence of restoration. Battles over property, territory and people have continued without interruption, expanding their scope in step with the progress of human society. The scale of these struggles has broadened from the family level to the levels of tribe, society, nation and world until today, when the democratic world and the communist world confront each other in a final conflict. In these Last Days of human history, heavenly law has

---

22. cf. Introduction

descended upon the earth in the name of democracy, bringing an end to the long phase of history in which people sought to obtain happiness by seizing property, land and people. At the conclusion of World War I, the defeated nations gave up their colonies. At the end of World War II, the victors voluntarily liberated their colonies and provided them with material aid. In recent years, the great powers have invited weak and tiny nations, some smaller than one of their own cities, to become member states of the United Nations, giving them equal rights and status in the brotherhood of nations.

What form does this final war between democracy and communism take? It is primarily a war of ideologies. Indeed, this war will never truly cease unless a truth emerges which can completely overthrow the ideology of Marxism-Leninism that is threatening the modern world. Communist ideology negates religion and promotes the exclusive supremacy of science. Hence, the new truth which can reconcile religion and science will emerge and prevail over the communist ideology. It will bring about the unification of the communist and democratic worlds. The trend of the history of conflict thus confirms that human history is the providential history to restore the original, ideal world.

Fourth, let us investigate this issue from the words of the Bible. The purpose of human history lies in the restoration of the Garden of Eden with the tree of life standing at its center.[23] The Garden of Eden does not refer to a specific geographical location where Adam and Eve were created, but includes the entire earth. If the Garden of Eden were limited to the small region of the globe where they were created, how could humanity be confined to such a small place and still fulfill God's blessing to multiply and fill the earth?[24]

Because the first human ancestors fell, the Garden of Eden was claimed by Satan, and the way to the tree of life at its center was blocked.[25] It is written in the Book of Revelation:

> I am the Alpha and the Omega, the first and the last, the beginning and the end. Blessed are those who wash their robes, that they may have the right to the tree of life and that they may enter the city by the gates.
> —*Rev. 22:13-14*

Human history began with Alpha and will end with Omega. At the end of history, the hope of fallen people will be to wash their sin-stained robes, enter the restored Garden of Eden, and approach the long-lost tree of life.

---

23. Gen. 2:9; cf. Fall 1.1.1
24. Gen. 1:28
25. Gen. 3:24

Let us discuss further the significance of this verse. The tree of life represents the True Father of humanity who, as we have seen, was to have been Adam had he perfected his character. Due to the fall of the first parents, their descendants were corrupted with the original sin. To be restored to the state of true, original people, we, as Jesus said, must be reborn.[26] Therefore, history has been humankind's search for Christ, the True Father of humanity, the one who can give us rebirth. In this verse, the tree of life which the saints of the Last Days may approach is none other than Christ. Thus, the Bible teaches that the goal of history is the restoration of the Garden of Eden with Christ, who is to come as the tree of life, as its center.

When the Bible states that a new heaven and new earth will appear in the Last Days,[27] it means that the old heaven and old earth under the bondage of Satan will be restored as a new heaven and new earth under the God-centered dominion of Christ. The Bible also states that the whole creation, groaning in travail under satanic tyranny, awaits the revealing of the sons of God.[28] Created beings do not await the restoration of true children of God in order to be burned in fire and perish in the Last Days; rather, they wait to be made new.[29] They will be made new by being restored to their original position under their rightful masters, the true sons and daughters of God, who are able to govern them with love.

Having examined human history from various standpoints—the development of cultural spheres, the trend of religion and science, the trend of the history of conflict, and the evidence in the Bible—it has become clear that human history is the providential history to restore the original, ideal world.

Section 3

The Last Days

3.1 The Meaning of the Last Days

Due to the crime of the Fall, the three great blessings God had granted our first ancestors were not fulfilled based on God's love and Principle, but instead were actualized in an unprincipled way under the tutelage of Satan. Human history since then has been the history of God's providence of restoration. Despite its evil beginning, the world under the sov-

---

26. cf. Christology 4.1
27. Rev. 21:1
28. Rom. 8:19-22
29. Rev. 21:5

ereignty of Satan must one day be transformed into the world where goodness reigns, where the three great blessings are fulfilled centered on God. The Messiah comes at this time of transformation.

The Last Days is this time, when the evil world under satanic sovereignty is transformed into the ideal world under God's sovereignty. Hell on earth will be transformed into the Kingdom of Heaven on earth. Therefore, it will not be a day of fear when the world will be destroyed by global catastrophes, as many Christians have believed. In fact, it will be a day of joy, when the cherished hope of humankind, the desire of the ages, will be realized.

Since human beings fell, God has attempted more than once to consummate His providence to put an end to the sinful world and restore the original, good world.[30] Nevertheless, at each attempt, human beings failed to fulfill their portion of responsibility, thus thoroughly frustrating the Will of God. Consequently, dispensations of the Last Days have been repeated several times. This can be confirmed by a close study of the Bible.

3.1.1   Noah's Day Was the Last Days

God said to Noah, "I have determined to make an end of all flesh; for the earth is filled with violence through them; behold, I will destroy them with the earth."[31] This indicates that Noah's day was the Last Days. God wanted to destroy the corrupt, evil world which had been ruled by Satan since the time of the human Fall. He intended once and for all to purge sinful history, biblically reckoned as 1,600 years, by the Flood. In its aftermath, God intended to raise up Noah's family, who worshipped Him and no other, and resurrect the world of God's sovereignty upon the foundation of their faith. This is how the time of Noah can be considered the Last Days.[32] Nonetheless, when Ham, the second son of Noah, committed a sinful act which reaffirmed the Fall, Noah's family could not fulfill its portion of responsibility on behalf of humankind, and the Will of God was frustrated.[33]

3.1.2   Jesus' Day Was the Last Days

God has foreordained the fulfillment of His Will; hence, the goal of the providence of restoration is unchanging and shall be fulfilled

---

30. cf. Foundation 1
31. Gen. 6:13
32. cf. Foundation 2
33. Gen. 9:22

without fail.[34] Therefore, even though the providence of restoration was not accomplished through Noah, God called upon other prophets to prepare anew the basis of faith. Upon this foundation, God sent Jesus to vanquish the satanic sovereignty which has held this world in thrall and to establish the God-centered ideal world. Accordingly, Jesus' day was also the Last Days. This is why Jesus said that he came to bring judgment,[35] and why Malachi prophesied of Jesus' coming:

> Behold, the day comes, burning like an oven, when all the arrogant and all evildoers will be stubble; the day that comes shall burn them up . . . so that it will leave them neither root nor branch. —*Mal. 4:1*

Jesus came to restore the original, ideal world. However, when the people of Israel did not believe in him, the human portion of responsibility was left unaccomplished. This meant that the fulfillment of the Will of God had to be prolonged until Christ's Second Advent.

3.1.3 THE DAY OF CHRIST'S SECOND ADVENT IS THE LAST DAYS

When the disbelief of the chosen people led Jesus to go the way of the cross, he could accomplish only spiritual salvation. It remains for him to return and accomplish the goal of the providence of restoration both spiritually and physically and restore the Kingdom of Heaven on earth.[36] Hence, the day of the Christ's Second Advent is also the Last Days. For this reason Jesus said, "As it was in the days of Noah, so will it be in the days of the Son of man"[37] and prophesied that many natural calamities would break out at his return.[38]

3.2 BIBLE VERSES CONCERNING THE SIGNS OF THE LAST DAYS

Many Christians believe that in the Last Days natural calamities and radical changes beyond the imagination of modern men will take place, as is literally written in the Bible. However, if they understood that human history is the history of God's providence, which has been restoring the world to the original state intended by God at the Creation, then they would know that the signs of the Last Days prophesied in the Bible will not take place literally. Let us investigate what the prophecies concerning the Last Days actually symbolize.

---

34. cf. Predestination 1
35. John 5:22
36. cf. Messiah 1.4
37. Luke 17:26
38. Matt. 24:7, 29

3.2.1 Heaven and Earth Destroyed, and a New Heaven and New Earth Created

It is written that God determined to destroy the earth in Noah's time.[39] Noah's time was the Last Days, yet the world was not destroyed. The earth is eternal, as the following verses indicate: "A generation goes, and a generation comes, but the earth remains forever;"[40] "He built his sanctuary like the high heavens, like the earth, which he has founded forever."[41] The earth was created as the object partner of God. God, the subject partner, is eternal; likewise, earth, the object partner, should also be eternal. Almighty God would never be pleased with having created a world so fragile it could possibly perish because of Satan. What, then, is the meaning of the prophecies of the earth's destruction in the Last Days? For instance:

> The heavens will be kindled and dissolved, and the elements will melt with fire! But according to his promise we wait for new heavens and a new earth in which righteousness dwells. —*II Pet. 3:12-13*

> Then I saw a new heaven and a new earth, for the first heaven and the first earth had passed away. —*Rev. 21:1; cf. Isa. 66:22*

To destroy a nation is to overthrow its sovereignty, while to erect a new nation is to establish a new sovereignty. Likewise, the prophecies that heaven and earth will be destroyed mean that the tyranny of Satan will be overthrown. To create a new heaven and new earth means to restore heaven and earth to God's sovereignty founded on Christ.

3.2.2 Heaven and Earth Judged by Fire

What is the meaning of the prophecy that in the Last Days "the heavens will be kindled and dissolved and the elements will melt with fire"?[42] Malachi, prophesying of Jesus to come, spoke of a day burning with the fire of judgment.[43] Jesus came into the world to cast this judgment, as he said, "For judgment I came into this world."[44] Jesus also said, "I came to cast fire upon the earth."[45] "Fire" here represents the means of the judgment for which Jesus came into the world. Nevertheless, there is no record that in his time Jesus judged the world with literal fire. The verses referring to fire must be symbolic. It is written, "Is not my word like

---

39. Gen. 6:13
40. Eccl. 1:4
41. Ps. 78:69
42. II Pet. 3:12
43. Mal. 4:1
44. John 9:39; also John 5:22
45. Luke 12:49

fire, says the Lord?"[46] Therefore, judgment by fire represents judgment by the Word of God.

Let us look for some biblical examples concerning judgment by the Word: "He who rejects me and does not receive my sayings has a judge; the word that I have spoken will be his judge on the last day."[47] "The lawless one will be revealed, and the Lord Jesus will slay him with the breath of his mouth,"[48] that is, by his word. Moreover, "He shall smite the earth with the rod of his mouth, and with the breath of his lips he shall slay the wicked."[49] "He who hears my word and believes him who sent me, has eternal life; he does not come into judgment, but has passed from death to life."[50] It follows that the judgment by fire which Jesus came to bring was the judgment by the Word.

What is the reason that Jesus judges by the Word? Human beings are created through the Word.[51] God's ideal of creation was that the first human ancestors fulfill the purpose of the Word by incarnating the Word. Yet they did not keep the Word of God and fell; thus, they failed to fulfill the purpose of the Word. Since then, God has tried to fulfill the purpose of the Word by recreating fallen human beings through the Word. This is the providence of restoration based on truth, the Word as revealed in the Scriptures. It is written, "The Word became flesh and dwelt among us, full of grace and truth; we have beheld his glory, glory as of the only Son from the Father."[52] Jesus completely realized the Word. He will come again as the standard of the judgment by the Word and judge the extent to which humanity has fulfilled the purpose of the Word. Judgment in this context contributes to the attainment of the goal of restoration, which is the realization of the purpose of the Word. Hence, in the course of the providence, the Word must be set up as the standard through which judgment can be carried out. Jesus lamented, "I came to cast fire upon the earth; and would that it were already kindled!"[53] As the incarnation of the Word,[54] he was grieved that the people of Israel did not receive the life-giving words which he proclaimed.

---

46. Jer. 23:29
47. John 12:48
48. II Thess. 2:8
49. Isa. 11:4
50. John 5:24
51. John 1:3
52. John 1:14
53. Luke 12:49
54. John 1:14

3.2.3 The Dead Rising from Their Tombs

It is written in the Bible that in the Last Days the dead will rise from their graves:

> With the archangel's call, and with the sound of the trumpet of God. . . the dead in Christ will rise first. —*I Thess. 4:16*

We can understand the meaning of this prophecy by examining a similar event, when the dead rose from their tombs at the time of Jesus' death:

> The tombs also were opened, and many bodies of the saints who had fallen asleep were raised, and coming out of the tombs after his resurrection they went into the holy city and appeared to many. —*Matt. 27:52-53*

This verse does not mean that the decomposed bodies of the saints literally rose up from their graves.[55] If the physical bodies of the saints of the Old Testament Age had actually risen from their tombs and appeared before many people in Jerusalem, they would certainly have testified to the people about Jesus, since they already knew that he was the Messiah. After hearing such testimony, who among the inhabitants of Jerusalem would not have believed in the crucified Jesus? Additionally, if the saints really had risen from their tombs in the flesh, then surely their deeds would have been recorded in the Bible. However, we find no such records.

What does the Scripture mean when it says that the bodies of the saints rose from their tombs? This record was made by people who could perceive the spirits of the past saints being resurrected spiritually and appearing on the earth.[56] This is much like Moses and Elijah who, as spirits, briefly appeared before Jesus on the Mount of Transfiguration.[57] What does "the tomb" symbolize? The realm of form spirits, the region of the spirit world where the spirits of the Old Testament saints were abiding, appears to be a dark place when viewed from Paradise, the realm of the spirit world opened up by Jesus. Hence, it is referred to as a tomb. The spirits of these saints had all lived in that lower region of the spirit world before they appeared to spiritually-attuned believers on the earth.

---

55. cf. Resurrection 2.3
56. Ibid.
57. Matt. 17:3

3.2.4 People on Earth Caught Up to Meet the Lord in the Air

> Then we who are alive, who are left, shall be caught up together with them in the clouds to meet the Lord in the air; and so we shall always be with the Lord. —*1 Thess. 4:17*

The "air" mentioned in this verse does not refer to the sky over our heads. In the Bible, "earth" is often a symbol for the fallen world under the sway of evil sovereignty, while "Heaven" is often a symbol for the sinless world of good sovereignty. The omnipresent God certainly dwells everywhere on the earth, yet we pray, "Our Father who art in heaven."[58] Even though Jesus was born on the earth, he is referred to as "he who descended from Heaven, the Son of man."[59] Meeting the Lord in the air means that the saints will receive the Lord in the world of good sovereignty when Christ comes again and restores the Kingdom of Heaven on earth by defeating the kingdom of Satan.

3.2.5 The Sun Darkened, the Moon Not Giving Light and the Stars Falling from Heaven

In the Last Days, Jesus said, "the sun will be darkened, and the moon will not give its light, and the stars will fall from heaven."[60] How are we to understand this verse?

It is written that Joseph, the eleventh of the twelve sons of Jacob, had a dream:

> Then he dreamed another dream, and told it to his brothers, and said, "Behold, I have dreamed another dream; and behold, the sun, the moon, and eleven stars were bowing down to me." But when he told it to his father and to his brothers, his father rebuked him, and said to him, "What is this dream that you have dreamed? Shall I and your mother and your brothers indeed come to bow ourselves to the ground before you?" —*Gen. 37:9-10*

When Joseph later became the prime minister of Egypt, his parents and brothers bowed down before him, as the dream had foretold. In his dream, the sun and moon symbolized the parents, while the stars symbolized their children. As will be explained, Jesus and the Holy Spirit are the True Parents who came to give rebirth to humanity in place of Adam and Eve.[61] Therefore, in this prophecy from Matthew, the sun and

---

58. Matt. 6:9
59. John 3:13
60. Matt. 24:29
61. cf. Christology 4

moon represent Jesus and the Holy Spirit, while the stars represent the faithful believers who are their children. Elsewhere, Jesus is likened to the true light because he came as the incarnation of the Word and shone forth the light of truth.[62] Here, the sunlight means the light of the words of Jesus, and the moonlight means the light of the Holy Spirit, who came as the Spirit of truth.[63]

For the sun to be darkened and the moon to lose its light means that the New Testament Word given by Jesus and the Holy Spirit will lose its luster. How can the Word as revealed in the New Testament possibly lose its light? The Old Testament Word was eclipsed when Jesus and the Holy Spirit came and gave us the New Testament Word, which fulfilled the Old Testament Word.[64] Likewise, when Christ returns and gives the new truth[65] in order to fulfill the New Testament Word and build a new heaven and new earth,[66] the Word which he gave at his first coming will lose its light. It is said that the Word will lose its light because, with the coming of a new era, the period of the mission of the old truth will have lapsed.

The prophecy that the stars will fall from heaven signifies that in the Last Days many faithful Christian believers will make a misstep and fall from God's grace. At the time of Jesus, the leaders of the Jewish people were all yearning for the coming of the Messiah, but they met their downfall when they did not recognize Jesus as the Messiah and opposed him. Likewise, Christians who have been anxiously awaiting the return of Jesus are likely to make the same misjudgment and fall when he actually returns.[67]

Jesus asked, "Nevertheless, when the Son of man comes, will he find faith on earth?"[68] On another occasion he said he would declare to devout believers, "I never knew you; depart from me, you evildoers."[69] Jesus gave these warnings to the Christians of the Last Days because he foresaw that they would be likely to disbelieve and trespass against him at his Second Advent.

---

62. John 1:9, 14
63. John 16:13
64. II Cor. 3:7-11
65. cf. Eschatology 5.1
66. Rev. 21:1
67. cf. Second Advent 2.2
68. Luke 18:8
69. Matt. 7:23

Section 4

The Last Days and the Present Days

When Jesus was speaking to Peter of his fate, Peter asked him about John's future. Jesus replied, "If it is my will that he remain until I come, what is that to you?"[70] Upon hearing this, the disciples thought Jesus would return during John's lifetime. Moreover, Jesus said to his disciples, "you will not have gone through all the towns of Israel, before the Son of man comes"[71] and "Truly, I say to you, there are some standing here who will not taste death before they see the Son of man coming in his kingdom."[72] Based on these sayings, the disciples and many Christians since have believed that Jesus would return during their lifetime. They have been constantly haunted by a sense of urgency that the Last Days are at hand. This is because they fail to grasp the fundamental meaning of the Last Days.

We can deduce that today is in fact the Last Days by examining the various circumstances of the present age. We can recognize in these circumstances the restoration of the three great blessings, which God has purposed in His providence of restoration. As Jesus said:

> From the fig tree learn its lesson: as soon as its branch becomes tender and puts forth its leaves, you know that summer is near. So also, when you see all these things, you know that he is near, at the very gates.
> —Matt. 24:32-33

4.1 Signs of the Restoration of the First Blessing

The first blessing God gave to Adam and Eve was perfection of individual character.[73] In the modern world, there are various phenomena which indicate that God's providence to restore fallen people to their original state as perfected individuals is near its zenith.

First, we can observe that the spirituality of fallen people is being restored. We have already explained that when a person reaches perfection, he becomes completely one with God in heart and is able to build true relationships with others. Adam and Eve, though not quite perfect, were able to converse with God. When they fell from this state, they caused their descendants also to sink into ignorance of and insensibility to God. Gradually, the spirituality of fallen people has been reha-

---

70. John 21:22
71. Matt. 10:23
72. Matt. 16:28
73. cf. Creation 3.2

bilitated as they enjoy the merit of the age in the providence of restoration. In the Last Days, therefore, many faithful believers will acquire the ability to communicate with God, as was prophesied in the Bible:

> In the last days . . . I will pour out my spirit upon all flesh, and your sons and your daughters shall prophesy, and your young men shall see visions, and your old men shall dream dreams. —*Acts 2:17*

As we witness a profusion of spiritual phenomena taking place all around us, we can discern that the present era is the Last Days. We are entering an era when we can reach individual perfection and restore the first blessing of God.

A second sign that the first blessing is being restored in the present era can be seen in the historical trend toward the recovery of the freedom of the original mind. Due to the Fall, our original mind was shackled under the yoke of Satan, and we lost the freedom to come before God. In the present era, as people struggle for freedom at the cost of their lives, the zeal to gain true freedom has reached its height. This is an indication that we are now entering a new era in which we can attain individual perfection, long denied by Satan, and freely go before God.

A third sign of the renewal of the first blessing is the restoration of true human value. From the horizontal perspective, every person possesses equal value, but that does not do justice to his true worth. From the vertical perspective of Heaven, each individual possesses the loftiest cosmic value.[74] Human beings lost their original value because of the Fall. In the present era, as democratic ideals have flourished, people have been promoting the emancipation of slaves, the freedom of oppressed racial minorities, and the independence of small and weak nations. They are advocating human rights and equality between the sexes and among all peoples. More than ever before, people are zealously uplifting the value of the individual toward its original value. This demonstrates that we have arrived at the threshold of the Last Days, when fallen people can restore the first blessing of God.

A fourth sign that the first blessing is being renewed in the present age is the restoration of original, true love in fallen people. The world which has realized the ideal of God will be in the image of a perfected individual. Every person in that world is united with God vertically, and this forms the basis upon which they can naturally live in harmony with each other horizontally. Solidarity and empathy are attained only when people join together in the love of God. Due to the Fall, the vertical bond

---

74. cf. Christology 1

of love between God and people was broken, and this in turn caused the horizontal love among them to be severed. As a result, human history became one of perpetual conflict. In the present era, however, the philosophy of universal love has become widespread, and people are increasingly seeking for true, original love. This is more evidence that the present time is the eve of the Last Days, when we can restore God's first blessing and reach perfection of individual character grounded in the love of God.

4.2 Signs of the Restoration of the Second Blessing

God's second blessing was for Adam and Eve to attain True Parenthood and bear and raise good children, forming a family, society and world where goodness reigns. However, Adam and Eve fell and became evil parents multiplying evil children; their descendants (all humanity) formed a world oppressed by evil. Ever since, God has been conducting a twofold providence, internal and external, to restore the sovereignty of goodness.

God has founded religions and worked through them to elevate people's spirituality by internally purifying people of satanic elements. At the same time, God has been cutting off Satan's influence externally through conflicts and wars. By separating Satan both internally and externally, the providence of restoration has been raising up good children who will one day be able to serve Christ when he comes as the True Parent. In this way, human history has been paving the way for the restoration of God's second blessing. Accordingly, we can deduce that the present era is the Last Days by examining the signs of the internal and external restoration of God's sovereignty. These are manifested as trends in the history of the development of cultural spheres and in the history of the rise and fall of nations, both of which are rooted in religion.

First, let us investigate how the history of the development of cultural spheres has progressed to the point when, in the present era, we have arrived at the threshold of the Last Days. God sends prophets and saints to fallen humanity to found religions. He works to develop them through the original minds of those who seek the good. In this way, God builds up cultural spheres based upon religions. Although many cultural spheres have emerged in the course of history, with the passage of time most of them either merged with or were absorbed by others. In the present age, we see a clear trend toward the formation of one global cultural sphere based on Christian ideals. As this trend progresses, all races and peoples are increasingly coming to stand side by side as brothers and sisters under the love and guidance of Jesus Christ, thereby restoring the second blessing of God.

The main distinction between Christianity and other religions is that its purpose is to receive and honor the True Parents of humanity, through whom all people can be reborn as good children. In this way, Christianity should renew the world as the one global family which God purposed from the time of creation. This makes Christianity the central religion with the mission to fulfill the goal of the providence of restoration. In the present era, the world has been coalescing into one cultural sphere based on Christian ideals. As the world has been greatly influenced by the teachings of Jesus and the Holy Spirit, who are the True Parents of humankind,[75] the way has been opened for all people to become godly children. This trend is evidence that God's second blessing is being restored. Thus, we can conclude with certainty that the present age is the Last Days.

Next, let us investigate how the history of the rise and fall of nations has been progressing toward the goal of restoring the sovereignty of good, thereby leading us into the Last Days. It is an error brought about by ignorance of the fundamental providence of God to regard the cause of struggles and wars as mere conflicts of interests and contests between ideologies. Humankind has suffered through a sinful history ever since the first human ancestors fell under the subjugation of Satan. However, as long as God's purpose of creation still stands, the purpose of this history must be to cut our ties with Satan and restore God's kingdom. If there were no wars or divisions in this fallen world, then the sovereignty of evil would continue forever and the world would never be restored. Therefore, God has worked His providence to restore the heavenly sovereignty by degrees. He sends prophets and saints to the fallen world to found religions and raise the level of morality. He establishes governments with higher standards of goodness which come to oppose and destroy regimes with lower standards of goodness. To fulfill the providence of restoration, therefore, conflicts and wars are unavoidable.

To summarize some of these issues, many of which will be treated more thoroughly in Part II, human history has progressed through the providential course of restoration through indemnity. Although there have been times when evil seemed to prevail, in the end the relatively evil social and political forces declined and were absorbed by the more godly forces. The wars which have shaped the rise and fall of nations are thus unavoidable during the course of the providence to re-establish the reign of good.

---

75. cf. Christology 4

For example, in the Bible God ordered the Israelites to destroy the seven tribes of Canaan. When Saul disobeyed Him, leaving some of the Amalekites alive with their cattle, God severely punished him.[76] While on that occasion God commanded the Israelites to destroy the Gentiles, at another time, when the Israelites of the northern kingdom turned to evil, God delivered them into the hands of the Assyrians.[77] We must understand that God's only intention by these events was to obliterate the sovereignty of evil and restore the sovereignty of good. Therefore, fights between individuals within the same good sovereignty on the side of God are evil, because they can weaken and even cause the disintegration of the good sovereignty itself. On the other hand, wars conducted by a good sovereignty to destroy an evil sovereignty are good in that they further the fulfillment of the providence of restoration.

The history of conflicts among nations has served the purpose of cutting off Satan's ties to humankind. History has progressed to the point where God's side can now reclaim territories and wealth all over the world. The providence to reclaim people began from lone individuals called by God. God's foundation progressively expanded to families, societies and nations, and today has reached the world level. The providence to separate Satan began with the clan society and continued through stages of political and social development: feudalism, monarchy and, today, democracy. At present, our world is divided into two: the democratic world, which seeks to create societies on God's side, and the communist world, which has been establishing regimes on Satan's side.

In other words, although fallen human history began under the sovereignty of Satan, God's providence has brought about a progressive transformation of the hearts of people and has nurtured their original nature, which seeks goodness through religion, philosophy and ethics. This inner nurturing has inspired groups which seek a just rule to separate from the prevailing evil. This process of separation has culminated in the establishment of two opposing powers on the global level. These two sovereignties, with contrary purposes, can by no means peacefully coexist. As human history nears its consummation, they will surely arrive at the point of intersection, colliding internally in the realm of ideology. This inner conflict may spur them to fight external wars with military forces. At the conclusion of this conflict, Satan's sovereignty will perish forever and Heaven's sovereignty will be re-established as the one, eternal sovereignty of God. Today we are at this very point of intersection, when these two worlds are confronting each other in the final

---

76. I Sam. 15:18-23
77. II Kings 17:23

battle. This is yet more evidence that the present era is the Last Days.

The flow of human history, in which good and evil are gradually separated, may be compared to muddy water. When muddy water is flowing slowly, the mud sinks to the bottom while the clear water rises to the top, until eventually the mud and water are completely separated. Human history is similar: with the passage of time, the evil sovereignty slowly sinks to destruction while the good sovereignty gradually ascends on the path of prosperity. After these two sovereignties intersect near the end of history, the good sovereignty will remain as God's eternal Kingdom, while the evil sovereignty will perish in eternal darkness.

The era when the paths of these good and evil sovereignties intersect is the Last Days. This is also the time when Adam and Eve's fall from the top of the growth stage will be restored through indemnity. All people in this era will suffer through great ideological confusion, much as the first human ancestors at the point of their temptation were utterly confused as to whom they should obey and what should guide their actions.

During the course of the providence of restoration, there were several occurrences of the Last Days, when the good and evil sovereignties came to the point of intersection. The times of Noah and Jesus, as mentioned earlier, were also the Last Days. Hence, they too were times when the two sovereignties intersected. Yet because people failed to accomplish their portion of responsibility, God's efforts to destroy the evil sovereignty were frustrated, and He had to begin once again the providence to separate good from evil. At the time of Jesus' return, the two sovereignties will intersect once more. The course of the providence progresses in a spiral path, moving forward in pursuit of the purpose of creation while events periodically repeat themselves in a circular fashion. Consequently, history has repeated itself, producing parallel periods.[78]

4.3   Signs of the Restoration of the Third Blessing

Once Adam and Eve had attained perfection, they were to fulfill God's third blessing by gaining dominion over the natural world. Dominion over the natural world has two aspects: internal and external. Both these aspects of dominion were lost to humankind at the Fall, but we witness their restoration in the present era. This also suggests that the present era is the Last Days.

Internal dominion denotes dominion of the heart. A person who reaches perfection and comes fully to resonate with God in heart will experience God's Heart as his own reality. Hence, he will be able to

---

78.   cf. Periods 1

love the creation with the same love as that which emanates from God's Heart and appreciate its beauty with the same delight as God. This is the meaning of dominion of the heart. However, when human beings fell and could no longer experience God's Heart as a reality, they also could no longer relate to the creation with the same love as that which flows from God's Heart. God's providence of restoration through religion, philosophy, ethics and so forth, has gradually elevated the spirituality of fallen people toward God. In the modern world, there is evidence that people are regaining the worthiness to govern the creation through heart.

External dominion denotes proper mastery of the creation through science and technology. Had our first ancestors reached perfection and attained internal dominion over the creation, able to love it with the same heart as God, then their sensibility to the spiritual dimension of creation would have developed to the highest degree. This would have stimulated the rapid advancement of science, giving them external dominion over everything in the natural world. Humankind would have reached the stars long ago and harnessed the full potential of the universe. Economic progress would have accompanied the development of science and technology, creating a comfortable and pleasant living environment.

However, due to the Fall, people's spirituality declined, and they lost internal dominion over the natural world. Their spiritual sensibility became as dull as those of animals, and they descended to the level of primitive man. Consequently, they also lost external dominion over the natural world. Through God's providence of restoration, people's spirituality is being elevated and their internal dominion over the creation is being restored. As a result, their external dominion is also being renewed, leading to today's highly advanced science. Modern people have built an extremely comfortable and pleasant living environment through the economic progress that has accompanied scientific development. Fallen people have thus been restoring their dominion over the universe, advancing toward the re-establishment of God's third blessing. Observing this, we are assured that the present era is the Last Days.

To summarize, the world's cultural spheres are converging toward one global cultural sphere based on one religion. Concurrently, nations are moving toward forming an apparatus for international governance, having progressed from the League of Nations to the United Nations. Today, people are envisioning plans for a world government. In the sphere of economics, the world is moving in the direction of establishing one international market. Highly developed transportation and communication technology have overcome the separation of time and space. People today can travel and communicate with each other almost as if they were all living in the same village. People of all races, from East and West, can meet with one another as easily as if they were members of a large family. People on all six continents are crossing the oceans seeking friendship and brotherly love. However, a family can be formed only when there is a father and a mother; only then can true brotherly love arise. Only when Christ comes again as the Parent of humanity will all people join together in one great family and live harmoniously in the global village.

As these events unfold, we may know that today is surely the Last Days. There is yet one final gift that history must present to humanity: it is the cosmic teaching which can bind together all the strangers of the global village into one family through the love and guidance of the same parents.

Section 5

The Last Days, the New Truth and Our Attitude

5.1 The Last Days and the New Truth

Fallen people have been overcoming their internal ignorance by enlightening their spirituality and intellect with "spirit and truth"[79] through religion. "Truth" may be divided into two types: internal truth as taught by religion, which helps people overcome internal ignorance, and external truth as obtained through science, which helps people overcome external ignorance. Accordingly, we can discern two aspects within the intellect: the internal intellect, awakened by internal truth, and the external intellect, awakened by external truth. Religions develop as the internal intellect pursues internal truth, while science advances as the external intellect pursues external truth.

"Spirit" in this context denotes the inspiration of Heaven. Cognition of a spiritual reality begins when it is perceived through the five senses of the spirit self. These perceptions resonate through the five physical senses and are felt physiologically. Cognition of truth, on the other hand, arises from the knowledge gleaned from the physical world as it is perceived directly through our physiological sense organs. Cognition thus takes place through both spiritual and physical processes.

---

79. John 4:23

Human beings become complete only when their spirit self and physical self are unified. Hence, the experience of divine inspiration gained through spiritual cognition and the knowledge of truth obtained through physical cognition should become fully harmonized and awaken the spirituality and intellect together. It is only when the spiritual and physical dimensions of cognition resonate together that we can thoroughly comprehend God and the universe.

God thus assists ignorant, fallen people to elevate their spirituality and enlighten their intellect through spirit and truth. By these means, God conducts His providence to restore people to the original state before the Fall. In the course of history, people's spiritual and intellectual levels have gradually been elevated due to the merit of the age in the providence of restoration. Hence, the quality of spiritual experience and the depth of religious and scientific knowledge have risen accordingly.

Spirit and truth are unique, eternal and unchanging. However, the degree and scope of their teaching and the means of their expression will vary from one age to another as they restore humankind from a state of utter ignorance. For example, in the age prior to the Old Testament, when people were still unenlightened and could not directly receive the Word of truth, God commanded them to make sacrificial offerings as a substitute for the Word.[80] In the course of time, the spirituality and intellect of human beings were elevated to the point when, in Moses' day, God granted them the Law, and at the time of Jesus He gave the Gospel. Jesus made it clear that his words were not the truth itself; rather, he declared that he himself was "the way, the truth, and the life."[81] Jesus was the incarnation of the truth. His words were just a means by which he expressed himself. Thus, the scope and depth of Jesus' words and the method of his teaching varied according to whom he was speaking.

In this sense, we must understand that the verses in the Bible are only one means of expressing the truth and are not the truth itself. The New Testament is but an interim textbook given to enlighten the people of two thousand years ago, whose spiritual and intellectual levels were far lower than today. The modern, scientific-minded thirst for the truth cannot be satisfied by expressions of truth which are limited in scope and couched in symbols and parables aimed specifically at instructing the people of an earlier age. For modern, intellectual people to be enlightened in the truth, there must appear another textbook of higher and richer content, with a more scientific method of expres-

---

80. cf. Restoration 1.2.1
81. John 14:6

sion. We call this the new truth. This truth, as discussed previously,[82] must be able to reconcile science and religion as one united undertaking in order to overcome the internal and external aspects of people's ignorance.

Let us examine some other reasons a new expression of truth must appear. The Bible, as was noted, is not the truth itself, but rather is a textbook teaching the truth. It renders important parts of the truth in symbols and in parables. Since these are open to various interpretations, there have arisen numerous disagreements among believers, causing them to divide into many denominations. The primary cause of denominational divisions lies in the character of the Bible, not in the people. The strife between denominations will only grow more intractable unless a new truth emerges which can elucidate the symbols and parables obscuring the essential truths of the Bible. Without this new truth, God's providence, which comes through the unification of Christianity, can never reach its goal. This is why Jesus promised that in the Last Days he will give us the new Word of truth:

> I have said this to you in figures; the hour is coming when I shall no longer speak to you in figures but tell you plainly of the Father.
> — *John 16:25*

Due to the disbelief of the people of his time, Jesus died on the cross without being able to teach all that was in his heart. As he said, "If I have told you earthly things and you do not believe, how can you believe if I tell you heavenly things?"[83] What is more, Jesus added, "I have yet many things to say to you, but you cannot bear them now,"[84] disclosing how sorrowful he was about the inability of even his closest disciples to receive all that he wanted to share.

Nevertheless, the words that Jesus left unspoken will not remain forever a secret, but one day will be divulged through the Holy Spirit as a new expression of truth. As Jesus said:

> When the Spirit of truth comes, he will guide you into all truth; for he will not speak on his own authority, but whatever he hears he will speak, and he will declare to you the things that are to come. — *John 16:13*

---

82. cf. Introduction
83. John 3:12
84. John 16:12

Moreover, it is written:

> I saw in the right hand of him who was seated on the throne a scroll written within and on the back, sealed with seven seals. —*Rev. 5:1*

The words that Jesus wanted to give us are written down and sealed in this very scroll. When John wept because he could not find anyone worthy to open the scroll and read it in heaven, on earth or under the earth, one of the elders said, "Weep not; lo, the Lion of the tribe of Judah, the Root of David, has conquered, so that he can open the scroll and its seven seals."[85] The Lion of the tribe of Judah, the Root of David, signifies Christ. The day must come when Christ will open the seven seals of the scroll, whose contents have long remained secret to humankind, and reveal to the faithful the words of the new truth. This is why it is written, "You must again prophesy about many peoples and nations and tongues and kings."[86] It is also prophesied that in the Last Days:

> I will pour out my Spirit upon all flesh, and your sons and your daughters shall prophesy, and your young men shall see visions, and your old men shall dream dreams. —*Acts 2:17*

For all these reasons, we can expect the appearance of a new expression of truth in the Last Days.

5.2 Our Attitude in the Last Days

When we examine the progress of history in the providence of restoration, we find that a new dispensation begins when the old dispensation is about to end. Accordingly, the beginning of the new overlaps the conclusion of the old; As darkness falls on the old history, the new history is already dawning. At such a time, the good and evil sovereignties, which had their origins at the same point yet pursued contrary purposes and have each borne their fruits on the world level, come to the point of intersection. Hence, those who live in this period suffer internally from anxiety, fear and confusion due to the absence of a guiding ideology or philosophy. They suffer externally from strife and battles fought with fearsome weapons. In the Last Days, disasters and devastation will abound, as Jesus said, "For nation will rise against nation, and kingdom against kingdom, and there will be famines and earthquakes in various places."[87]

---

85. Rev. 5:3-5
86. Rev. 10:11
87. Matt. 24:7

In the Last Days, it is inevitable that such devastation take place in order to vanquish the power of evil and erect the rule of good. In the midst of such wretchedness, God without fail will establish the center of the emerging good sovereignty in order to usher in a new age. Noah, Abraham, Moses and Jesus were among those whom God raised up as the central figures of their respective new eras. Today, at this historical transition period, we must find the person whom God has designated as the central figure of the new dispensation in order that we might participate in this new age and give honor to God's wishes.

The providence of the new age does not begin on the ashes of the old age. On the contrary, the new age sprouts and grows amidst the final phases of the old age and comes into conflict with that age. Accordingly, it is difficult for a person steeped in the old tradition to understand or accept the new providence. This is why the saints and sages leading the dispensation of a new age were often persecuted and martyred as victims of the old age. Jesus, for example, who inaugurated the New Testament Age, came at the close of the Old Testament Age in such a way as to bewilder the faithful adherents of the Mosaic Law. He was ostracized by the Jewish people and eventually crucified. This is why Jesus said, "New wine must be put into fresh wineskins."[88]

Jesus is to come again at the close of the New Testament Age. He will give us the new truth with which to found a new age, signified by the Bible's vision of a new heaven and new earth.[89] Just as Jesus at his first coming was derided by the Jews as one possessed by Beelzebul,[90] he will similarly be persecuted by the Christians when he comes again. Jesus therefore prophesied that at his Second Advent, "he must suffer many things and be rejected by this generation."[91] At this historical transition period, those who are comfortably entrenched in the ways of the old age will surely face judgment, along with the old age.

Fallen people's spiritual sensibility is extremely dull. Hence, they generally tend to adhere strictly to the letter of the truth in their efforts to follow God's providence. Such people cannot readily adjust themselves to the dispensation of the new age, even though the providence of restoration is moving toward it. They are generally too strongly attached to the outdated perspective provided by the doctrines of the old age. This is well illustrated by the case of the Jewish people of Jesus' day who were so attached to the Old Testament that they could not

---

88. Luke 5:38
89. Rev. 21:1-7
90. Matt. 12:24
91. Luke 17:25

respond to Jesus' call to open a new chapter of the providence. On the other hand, those believers who receive divine inspiration through prayer are able to grasp spiritually the providence of the new age. Even though this may put them at odds with the doctrines of the old age, they will still respond to the promptings of the spirit and follow the calling of the new providence. Among the disciples of Jesus, there was not one who was overly attached to the Old Testament Scriptures. Rather, they all responded to the spiritual experiences which they could sense through their inner minds. In the Last Days, people who lead an ardent life of prayer or who live by their conscience will feel intense anxiety in their hearts. This is because in their hearts they vaguely sense a spiritual calling and want to follow the providence of the new age, yet they have not come in contact with the new truth which can guide them to act accordingly. These are the chosen ones who, once they hear the new truth, will be awakened simultaneously in their spirits and intellects by spirit and truth. They will then fully understand God's providential needs concerning the new age and will volunteer with great enthusiasm and delight.

We who are alive today are living in the Last Days. We should cultivate a humble heart and make the utmost effort to receive divine inspiration through prayer. We should not be strongly attached to conventional concepts, but rather should direct ourselves to be receptive to the spirit, in order that we may find the new truth which can guide us to the providence of the new age. When we come across this truth, we should ascertain whether it leads us to become one with Heaven's guidance. We should examine ourselves as to whether or not genuine, heavenly bliss springs forth abundantly from the depths of our soul. Only in this way can we, the seekers in the Last Days, discover the path to true salvation.

Chart 1: The Unfolding Manifestation of God's Word in the Creation of the Universe and the Providence of Restoration

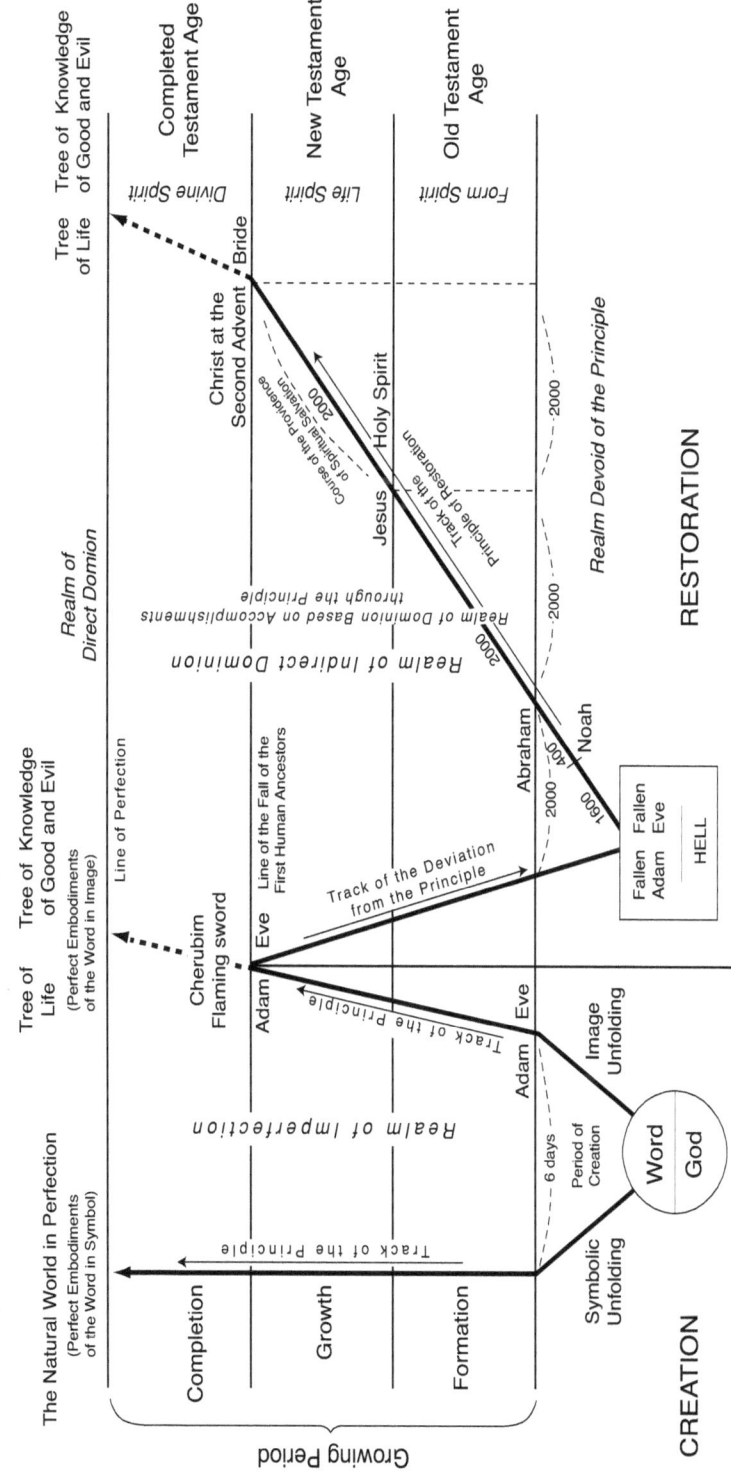

Chapter 4

The Messiah: His Advent and the Purpose of His Second Coming

The word "Messiah" in Hebrew means the "anointed one," signifying a king. The chosen people of Israel believed in the Word of God as revealed through the prophets, which promised that God would send them a king and savior. Such was their messianic expectation. God sent this Messiah in the person of Jesus Christ. "Christ" is the Greek word for Messiah.

The Messiah comes to fulfill the purpose of God's work of salvation. Human beings need salvation because of the Fall. Hence, before we can clarify the meaning of salvation, we must first understand the matter of the Fall. Furthermore, since the Fall implies the failure to accomplish God's purpose of creation, before we can clarify the significance of the Fall, we must first understand the purpose of creation.

God's purpose of creation was to be fulfilled with the establishment of the Kingdom of Heaven on earth. However, due to the human Fall, we have built hell on earth in place of God's Kingdom. Since the Fall, God has been repeatedly working His providence to restore the Kingdom. Being the history of the providence of restoration, human history's primary goal is to establish the Kingdom of Heaven on earth.[1]

---

1. cf. Eschatology 1-2

Section 1

Salvation through the Cross

1.1 The Purpose of Jesus' Coming as the Messiah

Jesus came as the Messiah for nothing less than the complete salvation of humanity; he was to fulfill the goal of the providence of restoration. Jesus was supposed to establish the Kingdom of Heaven, first on the earth. We can infer this from Jesus' own teaching to his disciples, "You, therefore, must be perfect as your heavenly Father is perfect."[2] According to the Principle of Creation, a person who has realized the purpose of creation does not commit sin, because he is in full harmony with God and possesses a divine nature. With respect to the purpose of creation, such a person is perfect as Heavenly Father is perfect. Jesus gave this teaching to his disciples with the hope that they could be restored as people who had realized the purpose of creation and become citizens of the Kingdom. Furthermore, Jesus taught people to pray that God's Will be done on earth as it is in heaven because he came to renew fallen humanity as citizens of God's Kingdom and build the Kingdom on earth. He also urged the people, "Repent, for the kingdom of heaven is at hand."[3] For the same reason, John the Baptist, who came to prepare the way of the Lord, also announced the imminence of the Kingdom.[4]

What will people be like once they have been restored as those who have realized the purpose of creation and become perfect as Heavenly Father is perfect? Such people are fully attuned to God and experience God's Heart within their innermost self. They possess a divine nature and live their life with God, inseparable from Him. Moreover, they do not have the original sin, and hence are not in need of redemption or a savior. They do not need to pray arduously or practice a faith, both of which are necessary for fallen people as they seek God. Furthermore, since they do not have the original sin, their children are naturally born good and sinless and likewise have no need of a savior for the redemption of their sins.

---

2. Matt. 5:48
3. Matt. 4:17
4. Matt. 3:2

1.2 Was Salvation Completed through the Cross?

Did Jesus' crucifixion, which brought us redemption from our sins, fulfill the purpose of the providence of restoration? If so, we would expect that faithful believers in Jesus would have restored their original nature and built the Kingdom of Heaven on earth. Yet in the entire history of Christianity, there has been no one, no matter how devout, who lived his life in inseparable oneness with God. Not one person has ever experienced God's Heart in its full intensity or possessed a divine nature. There has never been a believer who had no need of redemption or a life of ardent prayer and devotion. Even St. Paul, a great man of God, could not dispense with a life of faith and tearful prayer.[5] Moreover, no Christian parent, no matter how devout, has ever given birth to a child without the original sin, who could enter God's Kingdom without the grace of redemption by the Savior. Christian parents continue to transmit the original sin to their children.

What can be learned from this stark review of the Christian life? It teaches us that the grace of redemption by the cross has neither fully uprooted our original sin nor perfectly restored our original nature. Jesus, knowing that the redemption by the cross would not completely fulfill the purpose for which he came, promised he would come again. He understood that God's Will to restore the Kingdom of Heaven on earth is absolute and unchangeable. Thus, Jesus hoped to return and accomplish the Will of God completely.

Was Jesus' sacrifice on the cross for naught? Of course not.[6] If it were, Christianity would not have brought forth its illustrious history. Furthermore, our own personal experiences in faith make it plain how great is the grace of redemption by the cross. It is true that the cross has redeemed our sins; yet it is equally true that the cross has not entirely purged us of our original sin. It has not restored us to the unfallen state of perfected original nature in which we would never commit sin, and it has not enabled us to establish the Kingdom of Heaven on earth.

What is an accurate assessment of the extent of salvation through the cross? Unless this question is answered, it is difficult for people in the modern world to properly guide their faith. First, however, we must re-examine Jesus' death on the cross.

---

5. Rom. 7:18-25
6. John 3:16

1.3 Jesus' Death on the Cross

Was Jesus' death on the cross the most desired Will of God? Let us first examine the words and deeds of the disciples as recorded in the Bible. There was one unanimous feeling evident among the disciples concerning the death of Jesus: they were grief-stricken and indignant. Stephen, for example, burned with indignation over the ignorance and disbelief of the Jewish leaders, and he condemned their actions, calling them murderers and rebels.[7] Christians since then have commonly shared the same feelings as the disciples of Jesus' day. If Jesus' death had been the foreordained outcome for the fulfillment of God's Will, then it might have been natural for the disciples to grieve over his death, but they would not have been so bitterly resentful over it, nor so angry at those Jewish leaders who caused it. We can infer from their bitter reaction that Jesus' death was unjust and undue.

Next, let us examine from the viewpoint of God's providence whether the crucifixion of Jesus was inevitable as the predestined Will of God. God called the chosen people of Israel out of the descendants of Abraham. He protected them, nurtured them, and at times disciplined them with tribulations and trials. God sent prophets to comfort them with the unshakable promise that one day He would send them a Messiah. He prepared them to receive the Messiah by having them build the Tabernacle and the Temple. When Jesus was born, God proclaimed his advent. He sent the three wise men from the East as well as Simeon, Anna, John the Baptist and others to testify widely. Concerning John the Baptist in particular, many people knew that an angel had appeared and testified to his conception.[8] The miracles surrounding his birth stirred all of Judea in expectation.[9] Furthermore, John's ascetic life in the wilderness was so impressive that many people questioned in their hearts whether perhaps he was the Christ.[10] God's purpose behind sending such a great personality as John the Baptist to bear witness to Jesus as the Messiah was to encourage the Jewish people to believe in Jesus. Since God's Will was thus to have the Jewish people of that time believe that Jesus was their Messiah, the Jewish people, who were trained to live by God's Will, should have believed in him. Had they believed in him as God desired, would they have even entertained the thought of sending him to the cross? Would they have wanted any harm to come to the Messiah whom they had so

---

7. Acts 7:51-53
8. Luke 1:13
9. Luke 1:63-66
10. Luke 3:15

long and eagerly awaited? However, because they went against God's Will and did not believe that Jesus was the Messiah, he was delivered to be crucified. We must understand, therefore, that Jesus did not come to die on the cross.

Next, let us examine the words and deeds of Jesus himself to ascertain whether his crucifixion was in fact the way to completely accomplish his mission as the Messiah. Jesus' words and deeds were meant to engender belief on the part of the people that he was the Messiah. For example, when the people asked him what they must do to be doing the works of God, Jesus replied:

> This is the work of God, that you believe in him whom he has sent.
> —*John 6:29*

One day, when he was agonizing over the Pharisees' disbelief and having no one with whom to share his heart, Jesus looked down sadly over the city of Jerusalem. He wept as he lamented the fate of the Jewish people, whom God had so laboriously and lovingly guided for two thousand years. Jesus prophesied that the city would be so utterly laid waste that not one stone would be left upon another. He clearly pointed to the ignorance of the people, saying, "you did not know the time of your visitation."[11] On another occasion, Jesus lamented the stubbornness and disbelief of the people of Jerusalem, saying:

> O Jerusalem, Jerusalem, killing the prophets and stoning those who are sent to you! How often would I have gathered your children together as a hen gathers her brood under her wings, and you would not!
> —*Matt. 23:37*

Jesus reproached the people who refused to believe in him, even though they were familiar with the Scriptures which testified to him:

> You search the scriptures, because you think that in them you have eternal life; and it is they that bear witness to me; yet you refuse to come to me that you may have life. —*John 5:39-40*
>
> I have come in my Father's name, and you do not receive me . . . if you believed Moses, you would believe me, for he wrote of me.
> —*John 5:43-46*

How many miracles and signs did Jesus perform in his desperate efforts to lift the people from their disbelief! Yet, even as they were witnessing

---
11. Luke 19:44

the wondrous works of Jesus, the religious leaders mocked him as one possessed by Beelzebul.[12] In the midst of such a wretched situation, Jesus cried out:

> Even though you do not believe me, believe the works, that you may know and understand that the Father is in me and I am in the Father. —*John 10:38*

Then, confronting his opponents, he scathingly denounced their hypocrisy.[13] Through his words and deeds, Jesus tried to bring his people to believe in him, because it was God's Will that they do so. If they had followed God's Will and believed in Jesus as their Messiah, then who among them would have dared to send him to the cross?

From all the above evidence, we can deduce that Jesus' death on the cross was the unfortunate outcome of the ignorance and disbelief of the people of his day; it was not necessary for the complete fulfillment of his mission as the Messiah. This is well illustrated by Jesus' last words on the cross:

> Father, forgive them; for they know not what they do. —*Luke 23:34*

If God had originally predestined Jesus to die on the cross, Jesus would have expected to go that path as his due course. Why, then, did he pray three times, "My Father, if it be possible, let this cup pass from me; nevertheless, not as I will, but as thou wilt"?[14] In truth, Jesus offered those desperate prayers because he knew well that his death would shatter the hope of attaining the Kingdom of Heaven on earth. This would be a tragic disappointment to God, who had worked so laboriously to realize this hope through the long ages since the Fall. Furthermore, Jesus knew that humanity's afflictions would continue unrelieved until the time of his Second Coming.

Jesus said, "As Moses lifted up the serpent in the wilderness, so must the Son of man be lifted up."[15] When the Israelites lost faith in Moses on the way to Canaan, fiery serpents appeared and began to kill them. God commanded Moses to make a bronze serpent and set it on a pole, so that all who looked upon the serpent might live.[16] Similarly, Jesus foresaw that due to the chosen people's failure to believe in him, humankind

---

12. Matt. 12:24
13. Matt. 23:13-36
14. Matt. 26:39
15. John 3:14
16. Num. 21:4-9

would be consigned to hell. He foresaw that he would then be nailed to the cross like the bronze serpent in order to save all humankind, granting salvation to all who look to him. Foreseeing this eventuality, Jesus uttered this foreboding prophecy with a mournful heart.

Another indication that Jesus' death on the cross was not the Will of God, but rather due to the disbelief of the people, is that Israel declined after the crucifixion.[17] After all, it had been prophesied that Christ would come and sit on the throne of David and establish an everlasting kingdom:

> For to us a child is born, to us a son is given; and the government will be upon his shoulder, and his name will be called "Wonderful Counselor, Mighty God, Everlasting Father, Prince of Peace." Of the increase of his government and of peace there will be no end, upon the throne of David, and over his kingdom, to establish it, and to uphold it with justice and with righteousness from this time forth and for evermore. The zeal of the Lord of hosts will do this. —*Isa. 9:6-7*

An angel appeared to Mary prior to Jesus' conception and made a similar prediction:

> Behold, you will conceive in your womb and bear a son, and you shall call his name Jesus. He will be great, and will be called the Son of the Most High; and the Lord God will give to him the throne of his father David, and he will reign over the house of Jacob forever; and of his kingdom there will be no end. —*Luke 1:31-33*

God's clear intention for the chosen people of Israel, whom He had led through all manner of difficulty from the time of Abraham, was to send them a Messiah and build an eternal Kingdom on earth. Nevertheless, when the Jewish leadership persecuted Jesus and led him to the cross, Israel lost its qualification to be the founding nation of God's Kingdom. Within a few generations, the people of Israel would be scattered over the face of the earth. They have suffered oppression and persecution ever since. This can be viewed as the tragic consequence of the mistake their ancestors committed when they condemned to death the Messiah, whom they should have honored, thereby preventing the completion of the providence of restoration. Moreover, not only the Jews, but also many faithful Christians have shouldered the cross as their portion for the collective sin of having killed Jesus.

---

17. Luke 19:44

1.4 THE LIMIT OF SALVATION THROUGH REDEMPTION BY THE CROSS AND THE PURPOSE OF JESUS' SECOND ADVENT

What would have happened if Jesus had not been crucified? Jesus would have accomplished both the spiritual and physical aspects of salvation. He surely would have established the everlasting and indestructible Kingdom of Heaven on earth. This, after all, had been foretold by the prophet Isaiah, announced by the angel who appeared to Mary, and expressed by Jesus himself when he announced that the Kingdom of Heaven was at hand.[18]

When God created man, "the Lord God formed man of dust from the ground, and breathed into his nostrils the breath of life; and man became a living being."[19] Human beings were thus created in both spirit and flesh. Their Fall also happened both spiritually and physically. Since Jesus came to bring full salvation, he was responsible to complete it both spiritually and physically. To believe in Jesus means to become one with him. Hence, Jesus likened himself to a true vine and compared his disciples to its branches.[20] He also said, "In that day you will know that I am in my Father, and you in me, and I in you."[21] In order to save fallen people physically as well as spiritually, it was necessary that Jesus come in the flesh. Had the people believed in Jesus and so united with him in both spirit and flesh, they would have received salvation both spiritually and physically. Yet the people did not believe in Jesus; instead they led him to the cross. Jesus' body was exposed to Satan's assault, and he was killed. Therefore, even when faithful Christians are united with Jesus, their bodies remain exposed to Satan's attack, just as was Jesus' body.

Consequently, no matter how devout a believer may be, he cannot attain physical salvation through redemption by the cross of Jesus. His original sin, which has been passed down through the lineage from Adam, is not eliminated at its root. Even the most devout Christian still has the original sin and gives birth to children who also carry the original sin. In our personal faith, we may feel it necessary to mortify and deny our flesh in our efforts to prevent the intrusion of Satan, who continually tries to ensnare us through our bodies. We are taught to "pray constantly"[22] that we might remove the conditions by which Satan can attack us; these conditions stem from the original sin, which was not eradicated despite salvation through redemption by the cross.

---

18. Isa. 9:6-7; Luke 1:31-33; Matt. 4:17
19. Gen. 2:7
20. John 15:5
21. John 14:20
22. I Thess. 5:17

Jesus could not fulfill the goal of complete salvation, both spiritual and physical, because his body was struck down by Satan. However, Jesus laid the basis for spiritual salvation by securing the victorious foundation for his resurrection through the redemption by his blood on the cross. As a result, all believers since his resurrection have received the benefit of spiritual salvation, but not physical salvation. Salvation through redemption by the cross is spiritual salvation only. The original sin remains active in the flesh of even the most devout Christians and is transmitted through the lineage to their descendants. The more fervent a believer's faith, the more fiercely he must fight against the sin within. Even St. Paul, the most devout among the apostles, lamented over his inability to prevent sin from infiltrating his flesh:

> For I delight in the law of God, in my inmost self, but I see in my members another law at war with the law of my mind and making me captive to the law of sin which dwells in my members. Wretched man that I am! Who will deliver me from this body of death? Thanks be to God through Jesus Christ our Lord! So then I of myself serve the law of God with my mind, but with my flesh I serve the law of sin. —*Rom. 7:22-25*

This statement contrasts the bliss Paul felt upon receiving spiritual salvation with the agony he felt because he was unable to achieve physical salvation. John also confessed:

> If we say we have no sin, we deceive ourselves, and the truth is not in us. . . . If we say we have not sinned, we make him a liar, and his word is not in us. —*I John 1:8, 10*

We who receive salvation based on Jesus' crucifixion cannot unshackle ourselves from the chains of sin, due to the original sin still active deep within us. Therefore, to uproot the original sin, which he could not remove through the crucifixion, and to complete the work of physical salvation, Christ must come again on earth. Only then will the purpose of God's work of salvation be fulfilled both spiritually and physically.

1.5 Two Kinds of Prophecies Concerning the Cross

If Jesus' death on the cross were not predestined as necessary for the complete accomplishment of his purpose as the Messiah, why was it prophesied in Isaiah that he would suffer the ordeal of the cross?[23] We may think that the Bible contains only prophecies which foretold

---

23. Isa. 53

Jesus' suffering. However, when we read the Bible anew with knowledge of the Principle, we realize there are other prophecies to the contrary. As Isaiah prophesied[24] and as the angel announced to Mary,[25] it was foretold that Jesus would become the king of the Jews in his lifetime and establish an everlasting kingdom on the earth. Let us investigate why God gave two contrasting kinds of prophecies concerning Jesus.

God created human beings to reach perfection only by fulfilling their own portion of responsibility.[26] In reality, the first human ancestors did not fulfill their responsibility and fell. Thus, human beings have the potential to either accomplish their responsibility in accordance with God's Will or fail their responsibility contrary to God's Will.

To take some examples from the Bible, it was Adam's portion of responsibility not to eat of the fruit of the tree of the knowledge of good and evil. He either could obey the commandment of God and reach perfection or eat of the fruit and die. He chose the latter. In the Old Testament Age, God gave the Ten Commandments and the Mosaic Law, which the people were to obey as the condition for their salvation. It was their portion of responsibility to either uphold the Law and receive salvation or disobey it and come to ruin.[27] For the Israelites who left Egypt and journeyed toward Canaan, it was their responsibility to obey the instructions of Moses. They could either faithfully comply with Moses' directions and enter the land of Canaan or rebel against him and not enter the promised land. In fact, God had foretold that He would guide the Israelites into the land of Canaan[28] and commanded Moses to lead them there. Yet due to their lack of faith, the people perished in the wilderness, leaving only their descendants to reach the final destination.

Human beings thus have their own portion of responsibility; they can either fulfill it in accordance with God's Will or fail to fulfill it contrary to His Will. The nature of the fruits they bear depends upon whether or not they fulfill their portion of responsibility. For this reason, God gave two kinds of prophecies concerning the accomplishment of His Will.

To send the Messiah is God's portion of responsibility. However, belief in the Messiah is the human portion of responsibility. The Jewish people could either believe in the Messiah as God wished or not believe

---

24. Isa. 9, 11, 60
25. Luke 1:31-33
26. cf. Creation 5.2.2
27. Deut. 30:15-20
28. Exod. 3:8

in him in opposition to His desire. To cope with the contingency of human responsibility, God gave two kinds of prophecies concerning the accomplishment of His Will through Jesus. One kind foretold that Jesus would die due to the disbelief of the people.[29] Another kind foretold that the people would believe in and honor Jesus as the Messiah and help him to accomplish God's Will in glory.[30] When Jesus died on the cross due to the disbelief of the people, only the prophecies of the first kind were fulfilled. The prophecies of the second kind were left unfulfilled until the Second Coming of Christ.

1.6 Gospel Passages in Which Jesus Spoke of His Crucifixion as if It Were Necessary

There are several passages in the Gospels in which Jesus spoke of his suffering on the cross as if it were necessary for salvation. For example, when Peter heard Jesus' prediction of his imminent crucifixion and tried to dissuade him, Jesus rebuked him, saying, "Get behind me, Satan! You are a hindrance to me."[31] Why did Jesus chastise Peter so harshly? In truth, when Jesus spoke these words, the disbelief of the chosen people had already frustrated Jesus' efforts to complete the providence of salvation both physically and spiritually. By that time, Jesus had resolutely determined to accept the fate of the cross[32] as a condition of indemnity to open the way for at least the spiritual salvation of humankind. Peter's dissuasion could have hindered Jesus from paving the way for spiritual salvation through the cross. For this reason, Jesus rebuked him.

A second example is Jesus' last words on the cross, "It is finished."[33] Jesus did not utter these words to mean that through the crucifixion he had completely accomplished the providence of salvation. After he realized that the people's disbelief was unalterable, he chose the path of the cross in order to lay the foundation for spiritual salvation, leaving unfulfilled the task of achieving physical salvation until the time of the Second Advent. Hence, by the words, "It is finished," Jesus meant that he had finished laying the foundation for spiritual salvation. By this time, it had become the alternative goal of the providence.

In order for us to have proper faith, it is necessary first to have direct communion with God through spiritual experiences in prayer, and then

---

29. Isa. 53
30. Isa. 9, 11, 60; Luke 1:31
31. Matt. 16:23
32. Luke 9:31
33. John 19:30

to understand the truth through a correct reading of Scripture. This is the reason Jesus told us to worship in "spirit and truth."[34]

Since the time of Jesus, Christians have believed that Jesus came to this world to die on the cross. They have not known the fundamental purpose for which Jesus came as the Messiah and misunderstood the spiritual salvation which he brought us, thinking it to be all that his mission entailed. Jesus had wanted to live and fulfill his destiny, yet due to the people's disbelief in him, he died with a heart full of disappointment. Today, there must appear on earth faithful brides—pure-hearted believers—who can alleviate the bitter and grieving heart of Jesus. There must appear brides who can exalt the desires of Jesus' heart before Jesus can come again as the bridegroom. Yet Jesus lamented, "Nevertheless, when the Son of man comes, will he find faith on earth?"[35] for he foresaw that when he returned the people would likely be in darkness.

We have clarified from our study of the Bible that Jesus did not come to die on the cross. We can ascertain this fact even more clearly if we communicate with Jesus spiritually and ask him directly. If we cannot perceive spiritual realities, we should seek out the testimonies of those who are endowed with such gifts in order to properly understand his heart and deepen our faith. Only then will we be worthy to become the brides of Jesus who can receive him in the Last Days.

SECTION 2

THE SECOND COMING OF ELIJAH AND JOHN THE BAPTIST

The prophet Malachi foretold that Elijah would come again: "Behold, I will send you Elijah the prophet before the great and terrible day of the Lord comes."[36] Jesus testified that the prophesied coming of Elijah was realized in none other than John the Baptist:

> "I tell you that Elijah has already come, and they did not know him, but did to him whatever they pleased. . . ." Then the disciples understood that he was speaking to them of John the Baptist. —*Matt. 17:12-13*

---

34. John 4:24
35. Luke 18:8
36. Mal. 4:5

Nevertheless, John the Baptist did not recognize himself to be the second coming of Elijah,[37] and neither did the Jewish people. John's ignorance reinforced his doubts about Jesus.[38] Since many Jewish people esteemed John the Baptist, they respected John's point of view. This exacerbated their disbelief in Jesus. John's ignorance was a major factor in compelling Jesus to go the way of the cross.

2.1 THE JEWISH BELIEF IN THE RETURN OF ELIJAH

During the period of the united kingdom, God's ideal for His holy Temple was thwarted by Satan through the transgressions of King Solomon.[39] To restore the Temple and pave the way for the advent of the Messiah—who is the incarnation of the Temple—God sent four major and twelve minor prophets to Israel and worked through them to purify Israel of all satanic influences. Besides these, God sent the prophet Elijah to confront the prophets of Baal on Mt. Carmel; he defeated them with the power of God and cast down their altars to Baal. However, Elijah ascended to heaven in a whirlwind and a fiery chariot[40] before he could complete his divine mission. Satan's power revived and continued to plague God's providence. The way of the Messiah could not be made straight until Satan's influence was removed. Hence, before Jesus could realize the ideal of the incarnate Temple, another prophet should inherit and complete Elijah's unfinished mission of breaking people's ties with Satan. Due to this providential necessity, the prophet Malachi foretold that Elijah would come again.[41]

The Jewish people who believed in the prophecies of Scripture fervently hoped for the advent of the Messiah. Yet we should know that they longed just as eagerly for the return of Elijah. This was because God had clearly promised through the prophet Malachi that He would send the prophet Elijah prior to the advent of the Messiah to prepare the way of the Lord. Elijah had ascended to heaven about 850 years before the birth of Jesus; since then he has abided in the spirit world. We are familiar with the story of the Transfiguration, when Elijah and Moses spiritually appeared before the disciples of Jesus.[42] Many Jews believed that when Elijah came again he would descend from heaven in the same manner as he had ascended to heaven. Just as there are Christians today who are resolutely looking to the sky with the

---

37. John 1:21
38. Matt. 11:3
39. cf Parallels 3
40. II Kings 2:11
41. Mal. 4:5
42. Luke 9:28-36

expectation that Jesus will come in the clouds, Jews of Jesus' day were looking up at the sky, anxiously awaiting the coming of Elijah.

Nevertheless, before any news was heard about Elijah having come again to fulfill Malachi's prophecy, Jesus suddenly appeared and claimed to be the Messiah. It is no wonder that Jesus' appearance and proclamation stirred up all of Jerusalem in great confusion. Wherever Jesus' disciples went, they were bombarded with the question about Elijah, who was supposed to come first. Lacking an adequate answer themselves, the disciples turned to Jesus asking, "Then why do the scribes say that first Elijah must come?"[43] Jesus replied that John the Baptist was the very Elijah whom the people were awaiting.[44] Since the disciples already believed that Jesus was the Messiah, they willingly accepted his testimony that John the Baptist was Elijah. Yet how could others who did not know Jesus accept this controversial claim? Jesus himself expected that they would not readily believe it, and hence he said, "If you are willing to accept it, he is Elijah who is to come."[45] What made it even more difficult for the Jewish people to believe in Jesus' proclamation was the earlier denial by John the Baptist. John had insisted he was not Elijah: "And they asked him, 'What then? Are you Elijah?' He said, 'I am not.'"[46]

2.2 THE DIRECTION THE JEWISH PEOPLE WOULD CHOOSE

Jesus made it plain that John the Baptist was the very Elijah whom the people were so anxiously awaiting, while on the contrary, John the Baptist himself flatly negated this claim. Whose words were the Jewish people to believe? This matter obviously depended on which of the two, Jesus or John, appeared more credible and respectable in the eyes of the people of that time.

Let us examine how Jesus must have appeared to the Jewish people. Jesus was an uneducated young man who grew up in the poor and lowly home of a carpenter. This unknown young man suddenly appeared and called himself the "Lord of the Sabbath" while apparently defiling the Sabbath, which pious Jews kept with utmost reverence.[47] Jesus thus gained the reputation of one who wanted to abolish the Law, which for the Jews was the basis of salvation.[48] Therefore, the lead-

---

43. Matt. 17:10
44. Matt. 17:12-13
45. Matt. 11:14
46. John 1:21
47. Matt. 12:1-8
48. Matt. 5:17

ers of the Jewish community persecuted Jesus. Jesus was compelled to gather disciples from among simple fishermen and to befriend tax collectors, prostitutes and sinners, with whom he would eat and drink.[49] Even worse from the standpoint of the Jewish leaders, Jesus asserted that the tax collectors and prostitutes would enter the Kingdom of Heaven ahead of them.[50]

On one occasion, a prostitute came to Jesus, weeping, and began to wet his feet with her tears, wipe them with her hair, kiss them, and anoint them with a flask of precious ointment.[51] To accept such ministrations from a prostitute would be unseemly even in modern society; it was surely scandalous in Jewish society, with its austere ethical code wherein an adulterous woman would have been stoned to death. Yet Jesus not only approved of her lavish attendance; he even praised her and chastised his disciples when they rebuked the woman.[52]

Moreover, Jesus seemed to place himself on an equal footing with God[53] and asserted that no one could enter God's Kingdom except through him.[54] He insisted that people should love him more than they love their own parents, brothers and sisters, spouses or children.[55] Thus, to many, Jesus' words and deeds appeared blasphemous. Hence, it is not surprising that the Jewish leadership rebuked and mocked him, accusing him of being one possessed by Beelzebul, the prince of demons.[56] From all this, we can gather that Jesus was far from credible in the eyes of the Jewish people of his time.

How did John the Baptist appear to the Jewish people of that time? John the Baptist was born to a prominent family; he was the son of Zechariah, a priest. The miracles and signs surrounding John's conception and birth surprised all the hill country of Judea. One day, when Zechariah was burning incense in the Temple, an angel appeared before him and announced that his wife, who was old and barren, would soon conceive a son. When he did not believe the angel's words, he was struck dumb, and his tongue was loosed only upon the birth of the child.[57] Furthermore, John led an exemplary life of faith and discipline in the wilderness, surviving on locusts and wild honey. For these reasons, many Jewish people wondered whether perhaps he was the Christ, and a delegation of priests and Levites came to him and asked him this directly.[58] The Jewish people respected John to this extent.

---

49. Matt. 11:19
50. Matt. 21:31
51. Luke 7:37-38
52. Luke 7:44-50
53. John 14:9
54. John 14:6
55. Matt. 10:37, Luke 14:26
56. Matt. 12:24
57. Luke 1:9-66
58. Luke 3:15, John 1:20

Considering these circumstances, when the Jewish people of Jesus' day compared Jesus and John the Baptist, who appeared more credible to them? Without a doubt, John's words had more credibility. Therefore, they naturally believed John the Baptist when he denied being Elijah more than they believed Jesus' testimony that John was Elijah. Since the people believed John, they considered Jesus' words to be a fabrication concocted to support his dubious claim to be the Messiah. Consequently, Jesus was condemned as an impostor.

Once Jesus was condemned as an impostor, the people's disbelief in him intensified daily. They found his deeds and words more and more offensive. Since they believed John's words over Jesus' words, they could only think that Elijah had not yet come. Accordingly, they could not even imagine that the Messiah had already come.

As long as the Jewish people kept their faith in the prophecy of Malachi, they had to reject Jesus, who claimed to be the Messiah, because from their viewpoint Elijah had not yet come. On the other hand, to believe in Jesus they would have had to deny the biblical prophecy which asserted that the Messiah would come only after the return of Elijah. Since pious Jews would not even consider denying the prophecies of Scripture, they were left with no other choice but to disbelieve in Jesus.

2.3 THE FAITHLESSNESS OF JOHN THE BAPTIST

Many among the Jewish leadership and people of Jesus' day had the highest respect for John the Baptist; some even thought of him as the Messiah. Had John the Baptist announced that he was Elijah, as Jesus had testified, those who were eagerly waiting for the Messiah would have readily believed John's testimony and flocked to Jesus. Instead, John's ignorance of God's providence, which led him to insist that he was not Elijah, became the principal reason why the Jewish people did not come to Jesus.

John the Baptist testified to Jesus at the Jordan River:

I baptize you with water for repentance, but he who is coming after me is mightier than I, whose sandals I am not worthy to carry; he will baptize you with the Holy Spirit and with fire. —*Matt. 3:11*

I myself did not know him; but he who sent me to baptize with water said to me, "He on whom you see the Spirit descend and remain, this is he who baptizes with the Holy Spirit." And I have seen and have borne witness that this is the Son of God. —*John 1:33-34*

God had directly revealed to John that Jesus was the Messiah, and John bore witness to this revelation. Moreover, he said, "I am the voice of one crying in the wilderness, 'Make straight the way of the Lord,'"[59] and declared that he was the one who had been sent before the Christ.[60] Therefore, John should have realized through his own wisdom that he was the returning Elijah. Even if John did not realize this fact, since God had revealed to him that Jesus was the Messiah, he should have accepted the testimony of Jesus and, in obedience, proclaimed himself to be Elijah. However, John was ignorant of God's Will. He negated Jesus' testimony concerning him; moreover, he separated from Jesus and went his own way. We can imagine how sorrowful Jesus must have been as these events unfolded. How sorrowful must God have felt as He looked upon His Son in such a difficult situation.

In truth, John the Baptist's mission as a witness ended when he baptized Jesus and testified to him. What should his mission have been after that point? At the time of John's birth, his father Zechariah, filled with the Holy Spirit, had prophesied concerning the mission of his son to serve the Messiah, saying: "grant us that we . . . might serve him without fear, in holiness and righteousness before him all the days of our life."[61] In this light, after John the Baptist bore witness to Jesus, he more than anyone, should have served Jesus with ardent devotion as a disciple for the rest of his life. However, John left Jesus and went about baptizing independently. It is no wonder that the Jewish people were confused to the point of even supposing that John was the Messiah.[62] Their leaders were confused, too.[63] What is more, in one incident, a Jew who followed Jesus and the disciples of John the Baptist quarreled with each other over whose teacher was giving more baptisms.[64]

We can also discern from John's statement, "He must increase, but I must decrease,"[65] that in his heart John did not regard himself as sharing the same destiny as Jesus. If John the Baptist and Jesus were walking side by side and sharing the same destiny, how then could John ever decrease as Jesus was increasing? Indeed, John the Baptist should have been Jesus' foremost apostle, zealously proclaiming the Gospel of Jesus. Yet, due to his blindness, he did not fulfill his mission. His precious life, which was meant to be offered for Jesus' sake, was eventually lost over a relatively insignificant affair.[66]

---

59. John 1:23
60. John 3:28
61. Luke 1:74-75
62. Luke 3:15
63. John 1:19-20
64. John 3:25-26
65. John 3:30
66. Mark 6:14-29

When the mind of John the Baptist was focused on God, he recognized Jesus as the Messiah and testified to him. Later, when the inspiration left him and he returned to a mundane state, his ignorance returned and exacerbated his faithlessness. Unable to acknowledge that he was the return of Elijah, John began to regard Jesus in the same disbelieving way as other Jews viewed him, particularly after he was imprisoned. Jesus' every word and deed seemed to him only strange and perplexing. At one point, John tried to resolve his doubts by sending his disciples to Jesus, asking, "Are you he who is to come, or shall we look for another?"[67]

When Jesus was confronted with this question from John, he answered indignantly, with an air of admonition:

> Go and tell John what you hear and see: the blind receive their sight and the lame walk, lepers are cleansed and the deaf hear, and the dead are raised up, and the poor have good news preached to them. And blessed is he who takes no offense at me. —*Matt. 11:4-6*

John the Baptist had been chosen while still inside the womb for the mission of attending Jesus. He led an arduous, ascetic life in the wilderness, building his ministry in order to prepare the way for the coming Messiah. When Jesus began his public ministry, God revealed the identity of Jesus to John before anyone else and inspired John to bear witness to him as the Son of God. Yet John did not properly receive the grace that Heaven had bestowed on him. Therefore, when confronted with John's doubting question, Jesus did not answer explicitly that he was the Messiah; he instead answered in this circuitous way. Certainly, John the Baptist must have known about Jesus' miracles and signs. Despite this, Jesus gave a veiled answer, reminding John of the works that he was doing, with the hope of awakening him to his true identity.

We should understand that when Jesus said, "the poor have good news preached to them," he was expressing his deep sorrow over the disbelief of John the Baptist and the Jewish leadership. The prepared Jews, and John the Baptist in particular, were the rich people who had been blessed with an abundant wealth of God's love. Yet because they all rejected Jesus, he had to roam the seacoast of Galilee and the region of Samaria to search among the "poor" for those who would listen to the Gospel. These poor ones were uneducated fishermen, tax collectors and prostitutes. The disciples whom Jesus would have preferred to find were not such as these. Since Jesus came to establish the Kingdom

---

67. Matt. 11:3

of Heaven on earth, he was more in need of one leader who could guide a thousand than a thousand who would follow a leader. Did he not first preach the Gospel to the priests and scribes in the Temple? He went there in search of prepared and capable people.

Nonetheless, as Jesus indicated in a parable, because the guests who were invited to the banquet did not come, he had to roam the streets and byways to gather the poor and maimed, the blind and lame.[68] Faced with the miserable situation of having to offer the riches of his banquet to the uninvited outcasts of society, Jesus expressed his sorrow in these words of judgment: "Blessed is he who takes no offense at me."[69] Though John was greatly admired in his day, Jesus judged John's life by saying obliquely that one who took offense at him would not be blessed, no matter how great he might be. John took offense and thus failed in his mission to attend Jesus devotedly for the whole of his life.

After the disciples of John the Baptist finished questioning Jesus and left, Jesus remarked that although John may have been the greatest of all prophets, he failed to complete the mission God had entrusted to him:

> Truly, I say to you, among those born of women there has risen no one greater than John the Baptist; yet he who is least in the kingdom of heaven is greater than he. —*Matt. 11:11*

Everyone in heaven was born of woman and lived an earthly life. One would expect that since John was the greatest among all those born of women, he should also have been the greatest in the kingdom of heaven. Why was John less than even the least in the kingdom? Numerous prophets in the past had borne testimony to the Messiah indirectly, across the expanse of time. John, on the other hand, had the mission of testifying to the Messiah directly. If testifying to the Messiah was the main mission of the prophets, then John the Baptist was surely the greatest of prophets. Nevertheless, in terms of attending the Messiah, he was the least of all. Everyone in the kingdom of heaven, no matter how lowly, knew that Jesus was the Messiah and served him with devotion. Yet John the Baptist, who had been called upon to serve the Messiah more closely than anyone else, separated from Jesus and walked his own way. In terms of his devotion to Jesus, therefore, he was less than even the least in the kingdom of heaven.

Jesus continued, "From the days of John the Baptist until now the kingdom of heaven has been forcefully advancing, and forceful men lay

---

68. Luke 14:16-24
69. Matt. 11:6

hold of it."⁷⁰ John the Baptist was chosen from before his birth and led an arduous ascetic life in the wilderness. Had he attended Jesus with a sincere heart, the position of Jesus' chief disciple was surely reserved for him. However, because he failed in his mission to serve Jesus, Peter, a "forceful man," laid hold of the position of chief disciple. We can deduce from the expression "from the days of John the Baptist until now" that Jesus spoke the verses that follow⁷¹ in reference not primarily to the people in general but specifically to John the Baptist. Jesus concluded, "Wisdom is justified by her deeds."⁷² Had John acted wisely, he would not have left Jesus, and his deeds would have been remembered forever as righteousness. Unfortunately, he was foolish. He blocked the Jewish people's path to Jesus, as well as his own path. Here we have come to understand that the main reason why Jesus had to die on the cross was the failure of John the Baptist.

2.4 The Sense in Which John the Baptist Was Elijah

We have stated previously that John the Baptist was to inherit and complete the mission which Elijah had left unfinished on earth. As recorded in the Bible, he was born with the mission to go before the Lord, "in the spirit and power of Elijah, to turn the hearts of the fathers to the children, and the disobedient to the wisdom of the just, to make ready for the Lord a people prepared."⁷³ Hence, in terms of his mission, John was the second coming of Elijah. Furthermore, as will be discussed in greater detail,⁷⁴ Elijah in fact returned in spirit and was trying to help John the Baptist accomplish the mission which he himself had failed to complete during his earthly life. John the Baptist concurrently served as Elijah's body, through whom Elijah worked to complete his mission. Therefore, in terms of their common mission, John may be seen as the same person as Elijah.

2.5 Our Attitude toward the Bible

We have learned that John the Baptist's ignorance and disbelief in Jesus brought about the Jewish people's disbelief, which eventually led to Jesus' crucifixion. Until today, no one has ever uncovered this heavenly secret, because we have been reading the Bible based on the unquestioned belief that John the Baptist was a great prophet. Our new

---

70. Matt. 11:12 (NIV)
71. Matt. 11:16-19
72. Matt. 11:19
73. Luke 1:17
74. cf. Resurrection 2.3.2

insight into John the Baptist teaches us that we should dispense with the conservative attitude of faith which makes us afraid to question conventional beliefs and traditional doctrines. Would it not be an error to regard John as having failed in his mission if he actually succeeded? Likewise, it is certainly wrong to believe that John fulfilled his mission when in fact he did not. We should constantly make effort to have the right faith by searching both in spirit and truth. Even though our discussion of John the Baptist has been based on an examination of the Bible, those who are able to communicate spiritually can see the condition of John the Baptist and confirm that the above revelation about John is entirely correct and true.

Chapter 5

Resurrection

If we are to believe literally the prophecies of Scripture, we should expect that when Jesus comes again, the saints will come back to life in the flesh. Their bodies, buried in the earth and completely decomposed, will be reconstituted to their original state.[1] On the one hand, these prophecies are the Word of God, and as people of faith we must accept them. On the other hand, given the modern state of our knowledge, they do not make rational sense. This brings great confusion to the Christian faith. Therefore, it is important that we elucidate the true meaning of resurrection.

Section 1
Resurrection

Resurrection means to come back to life. To come back to life implies that we have been dead. To fathom the meaning of resurrection, we must clarify the biblical concepts of life and death.

1.1 The Biblical Concepts of Life and Death

When a follower asked Jesus if he could go home to bury his deceased father, Jesus said, "Leave the dead to bury their own dead."[2] From these words of Jesus, it is clear that the Bible contains two different concepts

---
1. I Thess. 4:16, Matt. 27:52
2. Luke 9:60

of life and death. The first concept of life and death concerns physical life. Here, "death" means the end of physical life, as was the case of the disciple's deceased father who was to be buried. "Life" in that sense means the state in which the physical self maintains its physiological functions.

The second concept of life and death concerns those living people who had gathered to bury the deceased man, those whom Jesus called "the dead." Why did Jesus refer to people whose bodies were alive and active as the dead? He meant that since they had not accepted Jesus, they were far removed from the love of God and were dwelling in the realm of Satan's dominion. This second concept of death does not refer to the expiration of physical life. It means leaving the bosom of God's love and falling under the dominion of Satan. The corresponding concept of life refers to the state of living in accordance with God's Will, within the dominion of God's infinite love. Therefore, even if a person's physical self is alive, if he dwells apart from God's dominion and is in servitude to Satan, he is dead as judged by the original standard of value. A similar conclusion can be drawn from the Lord's words of judgment upon the faithless people of the church in Sardis: "You have the name of being alive, and you are dead."[3]

On the other hand, even though a person's physical life may have expired, he remains alive in the true sense if his spirit abides in the Kingdom of Heaven in heaven, a realm in the spirit world where God governs through love. When Jesus said, "he who believes in me, though he die, yet shall he live,"[4] he meant that those who believe in him and live within the realm of God's dominion have life. Even after their physical bodies have returned to the soil, their spirits enjoy life in God's dominion. Jesus also said, "whoever lives and believes in me shall never die."[5] In saying that believers will never die, Jesus did not mean that they would live forever on earth. Rather, he meant that those who believe in Jesus during their earthly life will obtain eternal life within the bosom of God's love. They will be alive, both in this life and the next. Jesus' words assure us that death, in the sense of the end of physical life, has no effect on our eternal life.

Jesus said, "Whoever seeks to gain his life will lose it, but whoever loses his life will preserve it."[6] Those who transgress the Will of God in order to preserve the well-being of their flesh, though their bodies are alive, are dead. On the other hand, those who sacrifice their bodies for the sake of God's Will are alive, even though their bodies are buried and decayed. They live forever as spirits in the love of God.

---

3. Rev. 3:1
4. John 11:25
5. John 11:26
6. Luke 17:33

1.2 THE DEATH CAUSED BY THE HUMAN FALL

We have learned that there are two different biblical concepts of death. Which of the two refers to the death brought about by the Fall of the first human ancestors?

God created human beings to grow old and return to dust; physical death was allotted to human beings regardless of whether or not they fell. Adam died at the biblical age of 930 years, and his flesh returned to dust; but this was not the death caused by the Fall. According to the Principle of Creation, the flesh is the clothing of the spirit. Just as one discards worn-out clothes, the flesh is to be discarded when it has grown old and weak. Only the unclothed spirit self then enters the spirit world and lives there eternally. Nothing material can live forever. Human beings are no exception; our bodies cannot live eternally. If human beings were to live on earth forever in the flesh, why did God create the spirit world as our final destination? The spirit world was not created after the Fall as a place for fallen spirits to abide. Rather, it is part of the original creation, created as the place where individuals who fulfill the purpose of creation will enjoy eternal life as spirits after their life on earth has come to an end.

Most people are attached to their earthly life. They regret its passing because, due to the Fall, they are ignorant of the fact that after they discard their clothes of flesh, they are meant to live forever in the beautiful and eternal spirit world. The transition from physical life to life in the spirit world may be compared to the metamorphosis of a caterpillar into a butterfly. If the caterpillar had self-awareness, it might feel the same attachment to its limited existence, climbing about the leaves of a plant, as people do to their earthly life. It, too, would probably be reluctant to end its existence as a caterpillar, unaware that it is destined to enter a new phase of life as a butterfly, when it will enjoy fragrant flowers and sweet nectar to its heart's content.

The relationship between earthly existence and the life of a spirit is akin to the relationship of caterpillar and butterfly. Moreover, if there had been no Fall, earthly people would be able to relate with spirits just as naturally as they relate among themselves. They would know that death is not the final departure from their loved ones on earth. If people knew what a beautiful and happy world they will enter after they attain perfection on earth and die a natural death, they would look forward eagerly to the day they enter that world.

Since the Fall did not cause death in the sense of the expiration of physical life, we can surmise that what it brought was the other type of death. Let us examine this further. God told Adam and Eve that on the day they ate of the fruit of the tree of the knowledge of good and evil they would surely die.[7] Since God so warned them, it must be that when Adam and Eve ate of the fruit, they did in fact die. Yet Adam and Eve after the Fall continued their earthly life and bore children, who multiplied to form today's corrupt human society. We can conclude that the death caused by the Fall does not mean the end of physical life, but rather the descent from the good dominion of God into the evil dominion of Satan.

Let us draw additional support from the Bible. It is written, "We know that we have passed out of death into life because we love the brethren. He who does not love remains in death."[8] Love here means the love of God. A person who does not love his neighbors with God's love is dead, even though he remains active and alive on earth. This is also the sense of the verses "The wages of sin is death, but the free gift of God is eternal life"[9] and "To set the mind on the flesh is death, but to set the mind on the spirit is life and peace."[10]

1.3 THE MEANING OF RESURRECTION

Many have hitherto believed that the death caused by the Fall was physical death. Consequently, they have interpreted the biblical concept of resurrection as revival from physical death, and believed that resurrection of the dead involves the biological regeneration of their decomposed bodies. However, the Fall of the first human ancestors did not cause this kind of death. According to the Principle of Creation, the human body was created to return to dust after it grows old. A decomposed body cannot be restored to its original state. Furthermore, it is not necessary for a spirit to take on another physical body when he is meant to enjoy eternal life in the vast spirit world.

Resurrection may be defined as the process of being restored from the death caused by the Fall to life, from the realm of Satan's dominion to the realm of God's direct dominion, through the providence of restoration. Accordingly, whenever we repent of our sins and rise to a higher state of goodness, we are resurrected to that degree.

The Bible illustrates the process of resurrection: "He who hears my word and believes him who sent me, has eternal life; he does not come

---

7. Gen. 2:17
8. I John 3:14
9. Rom. 6:23
10. Rom. 8:6

into judgment, but has passed from death to life."[11] Based on this verse, we can affirm that resurrection means to leave the bosom of Satan and return to the bosom of God. It is also written, "For as in Adam all die, so also in Christ shall all be made alive."[12] This verse means that because we inherited Satan's lineage as a result of Adam's fall, we are dead; when we return to the lineage of God through Christ, we shall be resurrected to life.

1.4 What Changes Does Resurrection Cause in Human Beings?

According to God's Word, Adam and Eve died when they ate of the fruit of the tree of the knowledge of good and evil. Nevertheless, no significant external change took place in them. At most there were momentary changes in their countenances due to the anxiety and fear they felt over having fallen. Likewise, no significant external changes should be expected to take place in fallen people when they are resurrected to the state prior to the Fall. One who has been reborn through the Holy Spirit surely has experienced resurrection. Compare such a faithful person to a robber: One has been resurrected to the level of being reborn into God's realm, while the other is a spiritually dead person destined for hell. Yet the two people cannot be distinguished by their external appearance. One who believes in God according to Jesus' teaching is indeed resurrected from death to life. However, one cannot discern any obvious change in his physical body before and after he received Jesus and gained life through resurrection.

Jesus was truly a man who fulfilled the purpose of creation.[13] Nevertheless, judged by his outward appearance, Jesus was not noticeably different from ordinary people. If he had unmistakably displayed divinity in his outward appearance, then everyone around him would surely have believed in and followed him.

The changes a person experiences when he is resurrected and enters the governance of God take place in his heart and spirit. Having been liberated from Satan's dominion, a resurrected person can unite with God in heart and acquire a divine nature. These internal changes also purify his body, transforming it from a haunt of Satan into a temple of God. In this sense, we may say that our physical body is also resurrected. We may compare it to a building which was previously used for evil purposes and is now used as a place of worship. Although there may be no change in its outward appearance, it is now sanctified as a sacred building.

---

11. John 5:24
12. I Cor. 15:22
13. cf. Christology 2.2

SECTION 2

THE PROVIDENCE OF RESURRECTION

2.1 How Does God Carry Out His Work of Resurrection?

Resurrection means the process through which a fallen person is restored to the original state as intended by God. The providence of resurrection thus means the providence of restoration. Since the providence of restoration is God's work of re-creation, resurrection is a work of re-creation. Thus, the providence of resurrection is carried out in accordance with the Principle of Creation, in the following manner.

First, in the history of the providence of resurrection, many of those who were entrusted with a mission exerted themselves with utmost sincerity and faith to realize the Will of Heaven. Even though they may not have fully carried out their responsibilities, based on their devotion, they broadened the foundation upon which subsequent generations can form a relationship of heart with God. We call this foundation the *merit of the age* in the providence of restoration. The merit of the age has increased in proportion to the foundation of heart laid by the prophets, sages and righteous people who came before us. Therefore, resurrection is carried out based on the merit of the age.

Second, according to the Principle of Creation, it was God's responsibility to create human beings and give them His Word, while it was the human portion of responsibility to reach perfection by believing in and living according to it. Similarly, in conducting the providence of resurrection, God's responsibility is to give us His Word and guidance, and our responsibility is to believe and practice it in order to fulfill the providence.

Third, according to the Principle of Creation, a person's spirit can grow to perfection only through the physical self. Likewise, in the providence of resurrection, the resurrection of a spirit can be achieved only through earthly life.

Fourth, according to the Principle of Creation, a person is meant to reach perfection through the three ordered stages of the growing period. Therefore, the providence of resurrection for fallen people is also to be completed through three ordered stages, manifested as three ages in the providence of restoration.

2.2 The Providence of Resurrection for People on Earth

2.2.1 The Providence to Lay the Foundation for Resurrection

God began His providence to resurrect fallen humankind in Adam's family. However, the providence was prolonged because those who were entrusted with accomplishing God's Will did not fulfill their responsibilities. Two thousand biblical years later, God chose Abraham to be the father of faith, and through him God's Will began to be accomplished. Consequently, the two thousand years from Adam to Abraham resulted in the establishment of the foundation upon which God could begin His providence of resurrection in the following age. For this reason, we may call this period the age of the providence to lay the foundation for resurrection.

2.2.2 The Providence of Formation-Stage Resurrection

During the two thousand years from Abraham to Jesus, God worked to raise people to the formation stage of resurrection. Hence, this era may be called the age of the providence of formation-stage resurrection. All people who lived on earth during this age could receive the merit of the age based on God's work of formation-stage resurrection. In this era, God gave the Law of the Old Testament. By believing in and practicing it, the people could fulfill their responsibility and be justified before God. Therefore, this era has been called the age of justification by works. The people of this era who practiced the Law in their daily life were resurrected in spirit to the formation stage and became form spirits. Upon their death, those who achieved the level of form spirits while on earth entered and abided in the form-spirit level of the spirit world.

2.2.3 The Providence of Growth-Stage Resurrection

Due to the crucifixion of Jesus, resurrection was left incomplete, and its completion has been delayed until the time of his return. The two thousand years since then have been a time of prolongation, during which God has worked the providence to resurrect people to the growth stage through spiritual salvation. Hence, this era may be called the age of the providence of growth-stage resurrection. All who have lived in this age can receive the merit of the age based on God's work of growth-stage resurrection. In this era, people are to believe in the New Testament Word, which God gave them that they might fulfill their responsibility for the providence and be justified before God. Therefore, this era has been called the age of justification by faith.

Those who have lived in this era could be resurrected in spirit by believing in the Gospel during their earthly life. By being resurrected to the growth stage, they could become life spirits. Upon their death, those who became life spirits while on earth enter and abide in *Paradise*, the life-spirit level of the spirit world.

2.2.4 The Providence of Completion-Stage Resurrection

The era when people are to be resurrected both spiritually and physically through the returning Christ and complete the providence of resurrection is called the age of the providence of completion-stage resurrection. All those who live during this era are to receive the merit of the age based on God's work of completion-stage resurrection. Christ at the Second Advent brings the new truth with which to fulfill the promises of the Old and New Testaments; it may be called the Completed Testament.[14] Believing in this truth, people are to serve and attend the Lord on the earth, that they may fulfill their responsibility for the providence and be justified before God. Therefore, this era is called the age of justification by attendance. By believing in and serving the Lord and devoting themselves to his work, people of this era are to be fully resurrected both spiritually and physically, become divine spirits, and live in the Kingdom of Heaven on earth. When they shed their physical bodies, as spirits they will enter and abide in the Kingdom of Heaven in heaven, which is the divine-spirit level of the spirit world.

2.2.5 The Kingdom of Heaven and Paradise

Some Christians have been unclear in their concepts of the Kingdom of Heaven and Paradise because they lack a full understanding of the Principle. Had Jesus completed his mission as the Messiah on earth, the Kingdom of Heaven on earth would have been established in his day. The Kingdom of Heaven in heaven would also have been realized at that time, once people of perfect character living in the Kingdom of Heaven on earth had passed into the spirit world as divine spirits. However, because Jesus died on the cross, the Kingdom of Heaven on earth was not realized. The earth never saw the appearance of people who had reached the level of a divine spirit. No one has ever become a citizen of the Kingdom of Heaven in the spirit world, which was created as the

---

14. cf. Eschatology 5.1

home of divine spirits. Therefore, the Kingdom of Heaven in heaven remains empty and incomplete.

Why then did Jesus indicate that whoever believed in him would enter the Kingdom of Heaven? The original purpose for which he came on earth was to establish the Kingdom of Heaven. However, due to the people's disbelief in him, Jesus died on the cross before he could establish the Kingdom. Jesus promised the thief who was crucified at his right side that he would enter Paradise together with him.[15] The thief was the only person who believed in Jesus at the end, when everyone else had abandoned him. While Jesus had the hope of accomplishing his mission as the Messiah, he preached that people could enter the Kingdom of Heaven. But when he was at the point of dying on the cross without fulfilling this purpose, he told the thief that he would enter only Paradise. Paradise refers to the realm in the spirit world for those spirits who have attained the level of life spirits by believing in Jesus during their earthly life. There they remain in waiting until the day when the gate to the Kingdom of Heaven is opened.

2.2.6 Spiritual Phenomena in the Last Days

Adam and Eve fell at the top of the growth stage. Human beings are now being restored to the top of the growth stage through the providence of restoration, having passed through the Old Testament Age and the New Testament Age. The Last Days is the time when people return to the spiritual level reached by the first human ancestors just prior to the Fall. Today, being the Last Days, is the time when people throughout the world are reaching this level. Just as Adam and Eve prior to the Fall were able to converse directly with God, today many people on earth can communicate with the spirit world. The prophecy that in the Last Days, "I will pour out my Spirit upon all flesh, and your sons and daughters shall prophesy, and your young men shall see visions, and your old men shall dream dreams,"[16] may be explained based on this insight from the Principle.

In the Last Days, many people will receive the revelation, "You are the Lord." Often these people will be misled into believing that they are the Second Coming of Christ. Why do they stray from the right path?

Upon creating human beings, God gave them the mandate to rule over the universe.[17] Yet due to the Fall, they have been unable to fulfill this blessing. When fallen people are spiritually restored through the

---

15. Luke 23:43
16. Acts 2:17
17. Gen. 1:28

providence of restoration to the top of the growth stage, they will reach the level of heart comparable to that of Adam and Eve just before their Fall. God gives certain people who are at this stage the revelation that they are the Lord, in recognition that they have reached the level of maturity at which He had once blessed human beings with dominion over the universe.

Believers in the Last Days whose devout faith entitles them to receive the revelation that they are "the Lord" stand in a position similar to that of John the Baptist. John the Baptist came with the mission to make straight the way of Jesus.[18] In the same way, these people of faith are given the mission to prepare, in their particular areas of responsibility, the way for Christ at the Second Advent. Since they are to act as the Lord's representatives in their respective fields, God gives them the revelation that they are the Lord.

When someone who is gifted with spiritual communication receives the revelation that he is the Lord, he should understand this phenomenon through the teachings of the Principle. He should not act wrongly, mistaking himself for Christ at the Second Advent. Otherwise, he may end up playing the role of an antichrist. For this reason, the Bible contains prophecies that in the Last Days there will appear many antichrists.[19]

Spiritual mediums are often confused and fall into conflict among themselves, because the levels of the spirit world with which they are in communication and the content of the revelations they receive differ.[20] Although spiritually perceptive people are in contact with the same spirit world, because their circumstances and positions vary and their character, intellect and spirituality are at different levels, they will perceive the spirit world in different ways. These differences give rise to conflicts among them.

People who contribute to the providence of restoration usually are responsible for only a part of the providence. Focusing only on their vertical relationship with God, they are often not sensitive to their proper horizontal relationship with other spiritually attuned people. Strife can break out among them, as each thinks that the Will of God which he serves is different from that which the others are serving. Their conflicts are aggravated when each of them receives the revelation that he is the best. Yet God offers such encouragement to spur each on to do his very best in carrying out his particular mission within the greater

---

18. John 1:23
19. I John 2:18
20. I Cor. 15:41

providence. God also gives such revelations because each is, in truth, the one best suited for his respective area of mission.

In addition, when people of devout faith become spiritually open and reach the level of heart comparable to Adam and Eve just prior to their fall, they will face a test similar to that which Adam and Eve failed to overcome. If they are not careful, they may commit the mistake of the Fall. It is extremely difficult to overcome this temptation without understanding the Principle. Regrettably, many religious people have failed to overcome this test, nullifying in an instant accomplishments gained through years of devotion and exertion.

How can spiritually gifted people cope with these troubles? To accomplish the providence of restoration in a short period of time, God apportions different missions to numerous individuals and relates to each of them independently. It is thus virtually inevitable that conflicts break out among spiritually sensitive people. However, at the end of history, God will provide them with the new truth. The new truth will help them understand that the unique missions with which each has been entrusted are all for the sake of the same ultimate purpose of God. It will guide them to cooperate with each other and work in harmony to accomplish the greater purpose of the providence of restoration. In this era, all spiritually gifted people should cease their stubborn insistence that they alone have been serving the Will of God. They should search out the higher and more comprehensive words of truth which can help them correctly understand their positions and the true nature of their providential missions. Only then will they be able to overcome the confusion stemming from past horizontal conflicts. Only then can each arrive at the fulfillment of his individual path of faith and bring forth its beautiful fruits.

2.2.7 The First Resurrection

The "first resurrection" spoken of in the Bible describes the fulfillment of restoration for the first time in providential history. This will be accomplished through Christ at the Second Advent. He will cleanse people of the original sin and restore them to their true, original selves, enabling each to fulfill the purpose of creation.

The hope of all Christians is to participate in the first resurrection. But who in fact shall participate? It will be those who are the first to believe in, serve and follow Christ at the Second Advent. They will assist him in fulfilling all the indemnity conditions worldwide and in accomplishing the providence of restoration. In the process, they will be the first to have their original sin removed, become divine spirits, and fulfill the purpose of creation.

Next, let us investigate the meaning of the 144,000 mentioned in the Bible.[21] In order for Christ at the Second Advent to complete the providence of restoration, he must find a certain number of people who can restore through indemnity the missions of all the past saints who, despite their best efforts to do God's Will, fell prey to Satan when they failed in their responsibilities. He must find these people during his lifetime and lay the foundation of victory over Satan's world. The total number of saints whom Christ at the Second Advent must find to accomplish this task is 144,000.

In the course of God's providence of restoration, Jacob had twelve children with whom he set out on his mission to restore a family. Moses led twelve tribes in fulfilling the mission to restore a nation. If these twelve tribes were to multiply once more after the pattern of twelve tribes, they would total 144. Jesus, who came with the mission to restore the world, found twelve disciples in order to restore through indemnity, both spiritually and physically, the number 144. Yet due to his crucifixion, Jesus was able to restore it only spiritually. Jacob had twelve sons in order to restore through indemnity in his lifetime the vertical course of twelve generations from Noah, which had been claimed by Satan.[22] In the same way, Christ at the Second Advent must restore through indemnity in his lifetime, both spiritually and physically, the long providential course since the First Coming of Christ, who has set up the spiritual pattern of 144 tribes. To accomplish this, he must find a required number of believers, corresponding to the number 144.

2.3 The Providence of Resurrection for Spirits

2.3.1 The Purpose and the Way of Returning Resurrection

According to the Principle of Creation, the growth of the human spirit requires two kinds of nourishment: life elements received from God and vitality elements received through give and take action with the physical self. Spirits can neither grow nor be resurrected apart from a physical self. Consequently, the spirits of people who died before they could reach perfection during their earthly life can be resurrected only by returning to earth and completing their unaccomplished responsibility through cooperation with earthly people. By assisting people of

---

21. Rev. 14:1-4, 7:4
22. cf. Periods 2.2

faith living on the earth to fulfill their missions, the spirits may complete their missions at the same time. Herein lies the meaning behind the verse which foretold that in the Last Days the Lord will come "with his holy myriads."[23] We call this process *returning resurrection*.

How do spirits help people on earth fulfill the Will of God? When people become receptive to spirits through prayer or other spiritual activities, the spirits descend to them to form a common base with their spirit selves and work with them. Spirits perform various works. For example, they pour spiritual fire on earthly people and give them the power to heal diseases. They help people enter states of trance and perceive the realities of the spirit world. They give people revelations and the gift of prophecy. They can also give deep inspiration to the soul. In these various works, spirits act on behalf of the Holy Spirit, guiding people on the earth to accomplish the Will of God.

2.3.2 The Returning Resurrection of the Spirits of Israelites and Christians

2.3.2.1 Growth-Stage Returning Resurrection

Spirits of those who kept the Mosaic Law and worshipped God sincerely while living on earth during the Old Testament Age came to abide at the form-spirit level of the spirit world. After the advent of Jesus, these spirits all returned to earth and assisted faithful people on earth to accomplish the Will of God. By thus helping the people to attain the level of life spirit, they too received the same benefit: namely, they became life spirits and entered Paradise. We call this dispensation growth-stage returning resurrection.

Let us draw some examples from the Bible. Since Elijah appeared as a spirit before Jesus and his disciples,[24] it is clear enough that Elijah still lived in the spirit world. Yet Jesus referred to John the Baptist, who lived on the earth, as Elijah.[25] Jesus called him Elijah because in terms of their common mission, John's body concurrently served as Elijah's body. The spirit of Elijah descended to John the Baptist to help John fulfill the mission Elijah had left unfinished during his earthly life. This was Elijah's returning resurrection.

It is recorded in the Bible that when Jesus died on the cross, many bodies of the saints rose from their tombs.[26] This verse does not mean

---

23. Jude 14
24. Matt. 17:3
25. Matt. 17:12-13
26. Matt. 27:52

that these saints' decayed bodies were regenerated, enabling them to rise up in the flesh. Rather, it describes the spiritual phenomenon of returning resurrection. The spirits of the faithful Jews descended to the earth from the form-spirit level of the spirit world where they had been living. They returned to help the believers on earth, who had the opportunity to benefit from the redemption by the cross, to believe in Jesus and become life spirits. In doing so, the returning spirits also became life spirits. If the saints had risen bodily from their tombs, as is literally written in the Bible, they certainly would have testified to the fact that Jesus was the Messiah. Would anyone then have dared to persist in disbelieving in Jesus? Moreover, their deeds and works would have been recorded in the Bible, yet we have nothing other than the vague report that the saints rose from their tombs. This was a fleeting spiritual phenomenon perceptible only to those believers whose spiritual senses were open.

Compared to Paradise, which people could enter by virtue of the redemption by Jesus' crucifixion, the region of the spirit world where the spirits of the Old Testament saints were staying was relatively dark and miserable; thus it was called a "tomb."

2.3.2.2 Completion-Stage Returning Resurrection

The spirits of people who believed in Jesus while they lived on earth during the New Testament Age became life spirits and entered Paradise after death. After the Second Advent, these spirits will all return to the earth to help faithful people believe in and attend the returning Christ. By thus helping people on earth to attain the level of divine spirit, they too will receive the same benefit and become divine spirits. When the earthly saints pass over to the next world and enter the Kingdom of Heaven in heaven, the returning spirits will also enter the Kingdom. This dispensation is called completion-stage returning resurrection. In this dispensation, the spirits not only help earthly people; earthly people also assist in the resurrection of the spirits.

Let us elucidate the following verse:

> All these [saints of the Old Testament Age], though well attested by their faith, did not receive what was promised [permission to enter the Kingdom of Heaven], since God had foreseen something better [the Kingdom of Heaven] for us [earthly people], that apart from us they [spirits] should not be made perfect [citizens of the Kingdom of Heaven]. —*Heb. 11:39-40*

With this explanation, we can understand that this verse accurately depicts returning resurrection. It illustrates that spirits living in the spirit world cannot attain perfection apart from the cooperation of earthly people. Furthermore, it is written, "Whatever you bind on earth shall be bound in heaven, and whatever you loose on earth shall be loosed in heaven."[27] This verse teaches that unless the believers on earth first loose what is bound, the spirits also cannot loose what is bound in them. Since spirits can be resurrected only by cooperating with believers on earth to whom they descend, Jesus gave the keys of the Kingdom of Heaven to Peter, representing earthly believers, in order that he might unlock the gates to the Kingdom of Heaven here on earth.[28]

2.3.3 The Returning Resurrection of Spirits Who Abide Outside Paradise

There are several classes of spirits who abide outside Paradise; each has a way to achieve returning resurrection. First, let us examine the returning resurrection of spirits who believed in religions other than Christianity during their lifetime. Just as any two people must first form a common base with each other before they can work toward a common goal, earthly people and spirits can work to achieve a common providential goal only when they first form a common base. Therefore, a spirit who returns to the earth for his resurrection seeks a counterpart among the earthly people of the religion in which he believed during his earthly life. A spirit descends to the person of his choice and guides him. When he helps that person fulfill the purpose of the providence of restoration, they both receive the same benefit.

Second, let us examine the returning resurrection of spirits who lived a conscientious life even though they did not believe in a religion. No one among fallen humanity embodies perfect goodness because no one has resolved the original sin within himself. Hence, a good spirit is only relatively better than an evil spirit. These good spirits descend to good people on earth and cooperate with them in order to help them fulfill the purpose of God's providence of restoration. In the process, the spirits receive the same benefits as the people they have helped.

Third, let us examine the returning resurrection of evil spirits. In the Bible we read about the "cursed," who are liable to "the eternal fire prepared for the devil and his angels."[29] "His angels" here refers to evil spirits who live and work under the control of the Devil. The spiritual

---
27. Matt. 18:18
28. Matt. 16:19
29. Matt. 25:41

creatures commonly known as ghosts, whose features and identity are often unclear, are none other than evil spirits. Even evil spirits are able to receive the merit of the age by returning to the earth. However, the works of evil spirits do not always bear fruit and result in their receiving the benefit of returning resurrection. To receive such benefit, their works must have the effect of punishing earthly people, thereby enlisting their help in making indemnity conditions in accordance with God's plan to cleanse evil spirits through punishment. How, then, can the works of evil spirits result in casting judgment on behalf of Heaven?

Let us take an example. Suppose there is a person living on earth who, based on the merit of the age, is about to graduate from his current sphere of benefit to a higher sphere of benefit. He cannot graduate to the new sphere of benefit unless he first makes some condition of indemnity to remove the sins of the past. In the case of graduating from the family sphere to the clan sphere, a person must pay the debt of sin both for himself and for the ancestors of his clan. Heaven allows evil spirits to torment him as punishment for this sin. If he willingly endures the suffering given by the evil spirits and overcomes it, he will have successfully paid the indemnity through this condition and thus be entitled to enter the higher sphere of benefit at the clan level. The evil spirits who have tormented him receive a corresponding benefit. This is the way that, based on the merit of the age, the providence of restoration expands its sphere of benefit from the family level to the clan level, the national level, and the world level. Whenever humanity is to graduate to a higher level, the person leading the providence must make a condition of indemnity to resolve the sins which he or his forefathers have committed.

The works of evil spirits may help an earthly person fulfill indemnity conditions to purge his sin in two different ways. First, the spirit may trouble the earthly person directly. Second, the evil spirit may descend to the spirit self of another person living on earth who is about to commit a sin comparable to the sin of the person to be punished, and work through the second person to attack him. In either case, if the earthly person gratefully and willingly suffers the work of the evil spirit, he will make the indemnity condition to purge his and his ancestors' sin. This sin will then be resolved, and he will enter the higher sphere of benefit which has become available in the new era. Thus, the works of the evil spirit will have cast judgment on the person for his sin on behalf of Heaven. Consequently, the spirit will receive the same benefit as the earthly person; he, too, will enter the higher sphere of benefit.

2.4 THE THEORY OF REINCARNATION EXAMINED IN LIGHT OF THE PRINCIPLE OF RETURNING RESURRECTION

In seeking to fulfill the whole purpose of the providence of restoration, God has called upon many individuals and has apportioned to each a suitable mission. These individuals have passed down their particular missions to other individuals of similar character and circumstances, gradually fulfilling each area of mission over the long flow of history.

The providence of restoration begins with an individual, expands to the family, nation and world, and ultimately will bring restoration to all of heaven and earth. Although the mission given to each individual may be only a part of the greater whole, it also unfolds according to this pattern. Each mission begins at the individual level and expands its scope to the family, nation and world level. To take an example from the Bible, the mission begun with Abraham at the individual and family levels was passed down to Moses at the national level and to Jesus at the worldwide level.

Spirits who could not complete their missions during their earthly life must return to people on earth who share the same type of mission as they had during their lifetime. When a spirit assists an earthly person to fulfill God's Will, the person will fulfill not only his own mission, but also the mission of the spirit who has helped him. Hence, from the standpoint of mission, the physical self of the person concurrently serves as the physical self of the spirit. In a sense, he is the second coming of the spirit; hence he may sometimes be called by the spirit's name and appear to be the reincarnation of that spirit. In the Bible, John the Baptist was to have fulfilled the mission which Elijah left unfinished during his earthly life, since he received Elijah's assistance in carrying out his activities. Jesus called John "Elijah" because John's physical self concurrently served as the body of Elijah.[30]

In the Last Days, certain people on earth are entrusted with missions on the worldwide level. They must inherit and complete the responsibilities of all the spirits of the past who were devoted to the same field. These spirits will descend to these people and assist them in order to complete the spirits' own unfinished work. Since the earthly people are, in a sense, the second coming of these guiding spirits, they may think that they are their reincarnation. Hence, in the Last Days there are people claiming to be the second coming of Jesus, the Maitreya Buddha, Confucius, the Olive Tree, or the Tree of Life. The Hindu and Buddhist

---

30. cf. Resurrection 2.3.2.1

doctrines of reincarnation interpret these outward phenomena but without the benefit of knowing the principle of returning resurrection.

Section 3

The Unification of Religions through Returning Resurrection

3.1 The Unification of Christianity through Returning Resurrection

At the time of the Second Advent, all life spirits who dwell in Paradise descend to the people on earth who, by believing in and attending the Lord, can attain the level of divine spirit. By cooperating with these people to fulfill God's Will for the providence of restoration, the spirits can share the same benefit and enter the Kingdom of Heaven.[31] Accordingly, all the spirits will descend from Paradise in that day and assist the believers on the earth.

Although the time of visitation may vary according to an individual's faith, inborn nature, and the accomplishments of his ancestors for the providence, sooner or later each believer will be guided by the spirits from Paradise to go before Christ at the Second Advent and devote their lives for the sake of God's Will. For this reason, Christianity is destined to be united.

3.2 The Unification of All Other Religions through Returning Resurrection

As explained above, all religions, which have sought the same ultimate purpose, are gradually coalescing into one cultural sphere based on Christian ideals.[32] Christianity does not exist for its own sake, but has as its final mission the fulfillment of the purposes of all the religions in human history. Christ at the Second Advent, who is to come as the center of Christianity, is the person of the Maitreya Buddha who is to return according to the teachings of Buddhism, the True Man who is awaited in the Chinese religious tradition, and the Chŏngdoryŏng for whom many Koreans yearn. He is the central figure whose advent is expected in other religions as well.

Consequently, at the Second Coming of Christ, all spirits who believed in religions other than Christianity during their lifetime will,

---

31. cf. Resurrection 2.3.2.2
32. cf. Eschatology 4.2

like the spirits in Paradise, also return to earth to be resurrected, even though the timing of their return will vary depending upon their spiritual position. These spirits must guide the earthly believers of their respective religions to Christ at the Second Advent and assist them to believe in him and attend him in his work to fulfill God's Will. We can find a parallel example of this at the First Advent: the three wise men from the East, who were Zoroastrians, came in search of Jesus and worshipped him at his birth.[33] Accordingly, all religions will eventually be united around a revived Christianity.

3.3 The Unification of Non-Religious People through Returning Resurrection

Spirits who, in their lifetime, led a conscientious life but did not believe in any religion will also return to earth at the granted time to receive the benefit of returning resurrection. They will guide conscientious earthly people to seek out Christ at the Second Advent, attend him, and assist him in fulfilling God's Will.

The ultimate purpose of God's providence of restoration is to save all of humanity. Therefore, God intends to abolish hell completely after the passage of time necessary for each individual to make restitution for his sin. If hell were to remain eternally in the world where God's purpose of goodness is fulfilled, it would contradict the perfection of God, His ideal, and His providence of restoration.

Even fallen parents cannot feel joyful when one of their children is unhappy. Is this not even more true for God, our Heavenly Parent? It is written, "The Lord . . . is forbearing toward you, not wishing that any should perish, but that all should reach repentance."[34] Accordingly, hell cannot remain forever. No trace of hell will remain in the ideal world, which is the fulfillment of God's deepest desire. In the Last Days, when the time is ripe, evil spirits will descend to evil people on earth of the same spiritual level and assist them to accomplish God's Will. Indeed, even the demons testified that Jesus was the Son of God.[35]

By participating in these various dispensations over a long course of time, all people will gradually converge toward the goal of God's ideal world.

---

33. Matt. 2:1-12
34. II Pet. 3:9
35. Matt. 8:29

Chapter 6

Predestination

Theological controversy over predestination has caused great confusion in the religious lives of many people. Let us begin by examining the source of this controversy.

In the Bible, we find many passages which are often interpreted to mean that everything in an individual's life—prosperity and decline, happiness and misery, salvation and damnation, as well as the rise and fall of nations—comes to pass exactly as predestined by God. For example, St. Paul wrote:

> Those whom He predestined He also called; and those whom He called He also justified; and those whom He justified He also glorified. —*Rom. 8:30*

> "I will have mercy on whom I have mercy, and I will have compassion on whom I have compassion." So it depends not upon man's will or exertion, but upon God's mercy. —*Rom. 9:15-16*

> Has the potter no right over the clay, to make out of the same lump one vessel for beauty and another for menial use? —*Rom. 9:21*

It is also written that, even while they were still in their mother's womb, God loved Jacob and hated Esau and announced their destiny, saying, "the elder will serve the younger."[1] Thus, there are ample biblical

---
1. Rom. 9:11-13

grounds to justify the doctrine of God's absolute and complete predestination.

Yet we can also find sufficient evidence in the Bible to refute the doctrine of absolute predestination. For example, God warned the first human ancestors not to eat of the fruit in order to prevent their Fall.[2] We can deduce from this that the human Fall was not the outcome of God's predestination, but rather the result of man's disobedience to God's commandment. Again we read, "the Lord was sorry that he had made man on the earth and it grieved him to his heart."[3] If the human Fall were predestined by God, there would be no reason for Him to grieve over fallen human beings, who were acting in accordance with His predestination. Moreover, it is written in the Gospel of John that whoever believes in Christ shall not perish, but have eternal life,[4] implying that no one is predestined to damnation.

The doctrine that the outcome of human undertakings is determined not by God's predestination, but instead by human effort, is supported by the well-known biblical verse, "Ask, and it will be given you; seek, and you will find; knock, and it will be opened to you."[5] If every human undertaking were to turn out as God had predestined, why did Jesus emphasize the need for human effort? The Bible instructs us to pray for our sick brothers,[6] suggesting that illness and health do not depend solely on God's predestination. If everything were determined by inevitable fate, as predested by God, our tearful supplications would be to no avail.

We would expect that since God is absolute, when He has predestined something, it is fixed absolutely and cannot be altered by human effort. Therefore, if we accept the traditional doctrine that all things are absolutely predestined by God, then we have to conclude that no human endeavor, including prayer, evangelism or charity, can add anything more to God's providence of restoration. Any extra effort beyond the natural course of events would be completely useless.

Since there are ample grounds in the Bible to justify either of these two contrasting doctrines, controversy over the issue of predestination has been inevitable. How can the Principle solve this problem? We will consider the question of predestination by analyzing it under several topics.

---

2. Gen. 2:17
3. Gen. 6:6
4. John 3:16
5. Matt. 7:7
6. James 5:14-15

Section 1

The Predestination of God's Will

Before discussing the predestination of God's Will, let us first examine what is being willed. Let us remember: God could not accomplish His purpose of creation due to the human Fall. Accordingly, God's Will in carrying out His providence for fallen humanity is still to accomplish the purpose of creation. In this sense, God's Will is that restoration be accomplished.

Next, we should know that God predetermines His Will before He works toward its fulfillment. God determined when He created human beings that they accomplish the purpose of creation. When God could not fulfill His Will due to the Fall, He determined to fulfill His Will once more through the providence of restoration and since then has worked to accomplish it.

God must predestine His Will and bring about its realization in the ways of goodness, and not in the ways of evil. God is the Author of goodness. Hence, His purpose of creation is good; likewise, the purpose of the providence of restoration and His Will to accomplish its purpose are good. For this reason, God does not intend anything that obstructs or opposes the fulfillment of the purpose of creation. In particular, He could not have predestined the human Fall or sins which make fallen human beings liable to judgment. Nor could He predestine such events as the destruction of the cosmos. If such evils were the inevitable result of God's predestination, then God could not be the Author of goodness. Moreover, if God Himself had predestined such evil outcomes, He would not have expressed regret over them as He did, for example, over the depravity of fallen human beings,[7] or over King Saul when he lapsed into faithlessness.[8] Such verses illustrate that evil is not the result of God's predestination, but rather is the result of human beings failing to fulfill their responsibility and instead joining hands with Satan.

To what extent does God predestine His Will—the ultimate accomplishment of the purpose of creation? God is the absolute Being, unique, eternal and unchanging; therefore, the purpose of His creation must also be absolute, unique, eternal and unchanging. Likewise, His Will for the providence of restoration, the goal of which is the accomplishment of the purpose of creation, must also be absolute, unique and unchanging. It follows that God's predestination of His Will—that the purpose of creation one day be fulfilled—must also be absolute, as it is written,

---
7. Gen. 6:6
8. I Sam. 15:11

"I have spoken, and I will bring it to pass; I have purposed, and I will do it."⁹ Since God predestines His Will absolutely, if the person who has been chosen to accomplish His Will fails, God must continue to carry on His providence until its fulfillment, even though it may require Him to choose another person to shoulder the mission.

For example, God willed that His purpose of creation be fulfilled through Adam. Although this did not come to pass, God's predestination of this providential Will has remained absolute. Hence, God sent Jesus as the second Adam and attempted to fulfill the Will through him. When Jesus also could not bring about the complete fulfillment of the Will due to the disbelief of the Jewish people,[10] he promised he would return and fulfill it without fail.[11] Likewise, God's Will was to establish the family foundation for the Messiah through the dispensation based on Cain and Abel. When Cain killed Abel and this Will was not fulfilled, God made another attempt to fulfill it through Noah's family. When Noah's family also failed to fulfill the Will, God chose Abraham as yet another replacement and worked through him. We also see this with respect to the missions of individuals: God tried to remedy the failure to fulfill His Will through Abel by choosing Seth as his replacement.[12] God tried to fulfill His Will left unaccomplished by Moses by choosing Joshua in his stead.[13] When God's Will for Judas Iscariot was nullified by his betrayal of Jesus, God made a second attempt to fulfill this Will by electing Matthias in his place.[14]

SECTION 2

THE PREDESTINATION OF THE WAY IN WHICH GOD'S WILL IS FULFILLED

According to the Principle of Creation, God's purpose of creation can be realized only when human beings complete their portion of responsibility.[15] Although God's Will to realize this purpose through the providence of restoration is absolute and beyond human influence, its fulfillment necessarily requires the accomplishment of the human portion of responsibility. Originally, God's purpose of creation was to be fulfilled through Adam and Eve only when they completed their given responsibility and refrained from eating the fruit of the tree of the

---

9. Isa. 46:11
10. cf. Messiah 1.2
11. Matt. 16:27
12. Gen. 4.25
13. Josh. 1:5
14. Acts 1:24-26
15. cf. Creation 5.2.2

knowledge of good and evil.[16] Similarly, in the providence of restoration, God's Will is accomplished only when the central figure responsible for a mission completes his portion of responsibility. For example, the Jewish people, as the central nation of the providence, should have believed in Jesus and followed him unconditionally in order for God to accomplish complete salvation at that time. Because they disbelieved and failed to fulfill their responsibility, the fulfillment of the Will had to be postponed until the time of the Second Advent.

To what extent does God predestine the unfolding of the events in the providence? Although God's Will to realize the purpose of the providence of restoration is absolute, God predestines the process of its accomplishment conditionally, contingent upon the five percent responsibility of the central figure, which must be completed in addition to the ninety-five percent responsibility of God. The proportion of five percent is used to indicate that the human portion of responsibility is extremely small when compared to God's portion of responsibility. Yet for human beings, this five percent is equivalent to one hundred percent of our effort.

To cite some examples: God predestined that His Will be fulfilled through Adam and Eve only when they refrained from eating the fruit and completed their responsibility. In the dispensation of restoration through Noah, God predestined that His Will be fulfilled only after Noah completed his responsibility by exerting himself with the utmost devotion in building the ark. In the providence of salvation through Jesus, God predestined that His Will be fulfilled only after fallen people completed their responsibility by believing in Jesus as the Messiah and rendering him devoted service.[17] However, time and again human beings could not cope with even their small portion of responsibility. Consequently, God's providence has been repeatedly prolonged.

It is written in the Bible, "The prayer of faith will save the sick man,"[18] "Your faith has made you well,"[19] and "For every one who asks receives, and he who seeks finds, and to him who knocks it will be opened."[20] These verses confirm that God predestines His Will to be fulfilled contingent upon human beings' completing their portion of responsibility. We should recognize from these examples how minuscule the human portion of responsibility is in comparison to God's toil and grace, which is His por-

---

16. Gen. 2:17
17. John 3:16
18. James 5:15
19. Mark 5:34
20. Matt. 7:8

tion of responsibility. On the other hand, when we consider the fact that over and over again central figures in the providence could not cope with their responsibility, we can appreciate how extremely difficult it was for them to fulfill even this comparatively small portion.

Section 3
The Predestination of Human Beings

Adam and Eve were to become the good ancestors of humanity, conditional upon fulfilling their responsibility to obey God's commandment not to eat of the fruit. Accordingly, God did not absolutely predestine that Adam and Eve would become our good ancestors. The same holds for all fallen people: they can become the ideal people God has foreordained them to be only when they complete their responsibility. Therefore, God does not predestine in absolute terms what kind of people they actually turn out to be.

To what extent does God determine the fate of an individual? The fulfillment of God's Will through an individual absolutely requires that he complete his responsibility. Hence, even though God predestines someone for a particular mission, God's ninety-five percent responsibility and the person's five percent responsibility must be accomplished together before the person can complete his given mission and fulfill God's Will. If the person does not complete his responsibility, he cannot become the person God has purposed him to be.

For example, when God chose Moses, He predestined conditionally that when Moses fulfilled his responsibility, he would lead the chosen people into the blessed land of Canaan.[21] However, when Moses transgressed God's Will by striking the rock twice at Kadesh-barnea, he failed. Consequently, Moses died before reaching his final destination, and God's intention for him to lead the people into Canaan was not realized.[22] When God chose Judas Iscariot, He conditionally predestined that Judas would remain a loyal disciple of Jesus by faithfully completing his responsibility. Yet when Judas turned faithless, God's expectation for him was not realized, and he ended up a traitor. When God raised up the Jewish people, God predestined that they would be glorified as the chosen nation when they fulfilled their responsibility to believe in and attend Jesus. However, when their leaders sent Jesus to the cross, this preordained destiny was not brought to pass, and the Jewish nation was scattered.

---

21. Exod. 3:10
22. Num. 20:2-13; 27:13-14

Let us next examine God's predestination of central figures in the providence of restoration. The purpose of God's providence of restoration is to restore completely the fallen world to the original world which God intended. Therefore, although the times of their salvation may differ, all fallen people are predestined to be saved.[23] Yet, as was the case with God's creation, His providence of salvation—a work of re-creation—cannot be completed in an instant. It begins from one point and gradually expands to cover the whole. Therefore, in the providence of salvation, God first predestines one person to be the *central figure* and then calls him to a mission.

What qualifications should the person possess to merit such a calling? First, the central figure must be born into the chosen people. Next, even among the chosen people, he must come from an ancestral line with many good accomplishments. Among the descendants of this outstanding lineage, he must be endowed with the requisite character. Among those with the requisite character, he must develop the necessary qualities during his early life. Finally, among those who have acquired these qualities, God selects first the individual who lives in a time and place most fitting to His need.

Section 4

Elucidation of Biblical Verses Which Support the Doctrine of Absolute Predestination

So far, we have analyzed the various issues concerning predestination. Next, we shall look again at those biblical verses which seem to suggest that the outcome of every undertaking is determined by God's absolute predestination and elucidate their meaning.

Let us begin with the following verse:

> For those whom He foreknew He also predestined . . . those whom He predestined He also called; and those whom He called He also justified; and those whom He justified He also glorified. —*Rom. 8:29-30*

God, being omniscient, foreknows who has the qualifications necessary to become a central figure in the providence of restoration. God predestines those whom He foreknows; then He calls upon them to fulfill the purpose of the providence. Calling a person is God's responsibility, but that alone does not entitle the person to be justified before God and

---

23. II Pet. 3:9

given glory. Only when the person completes his responsibility after being called by God is he justified and then glorified. God's predestination concerning an individual's glorification is thus contingent upon the completion of his portion of responsibility. Because the biblical verse does not mention the human portion of responsibility, people may misinterpret it to mean that all affairs are determined solely by God's absolute predestination.

It is written,

> "I will have mercy on whom I have mercy, and I will have compassion on whom I have compassion." So it depends not upon man's will or exertion, but upon God's mercy. —Rom. 9:15-16

As was explained above, only God foreknows and chooses who is most suitable to fulfill the purpose of the providence of restoration. It is God's right to choose a person and have mercy or compassion on him; this depends not at all upon human will or human effort. This verse was written to emphasize the power and grace of God.

Paul also wrote,

> Has the potter no right over the clay, to make out of the same lump one vessel for beauty and another for menial use? —Rom. 9:21

It has been explained that God gave human beings a portion of responsibility as the condition based on which He could love them more than any other being in creation. God's intention in giving this condition was to make them worthy to be the lords of creation by having them take after His creative nature. Yet human beings themselves violated this condition and fell. They have become like refuse, fit to be discarded. In such a state, fallen people have no cause to complain, no matter how God may treat them. This is what this verse teaches us.

It is written that God loved Jacob and hated Esau even when they were still inside their mother's womb and had not done anything good or evil. God favored one and disfavored the other and told Rebecca that "the elder will serve the younger."[24] What was the reason for this favoritism? God favored one over the other in order to set up a certain course in the providence of restoration. Although further details will be discussed below,[25] God gave Isaac twin sons, Esau and Jacob, with the intention of having them stand in the positions of Cain and Abel. They were to make the conditions of indemnity necessary for accomplishing

---
24. Rom. 9:10-13
25. cf. Foundation 3.2

His Will to recover the birthright of the elder brother, which was lost when Cain killed Abel in Adam's family. God intended to realize this Will by having Jacob (in the position of Abel) win over his elder brother Esau (in the position of Cain). Since Esau was in the position of Cain, he was "hated" by God. Since Jacob was in the position of Abel, he could receive God's love.

Nevertheless, whether God would in the end favor or disfavor them depended on whether or not they completed their given portions of responsibility. In fact, because Esau obediently submitted to Jacob, he was able to rise above his previous condition of being hated by God and receive the blessing of God's love equal to Jacob's. Conversely, even though Jacob was initially in the position to receive God's favor, he would have ceased to receive it had he failed in his responsibility.

People such as John Calvin have propounded the doctrine of absolute and complete predestination, which is widely believed even in our present day. They have held to such a doctrine because they wrongly believed that the accomplishment of God's Will depends solely on the power and work of God. They were ignorant of the true relationship between God's portion of responsibility and the human portion of responsibility in the fulfillment of the purpose of the providence of restoration.

Chapter 7

Christology

For fallen people who seek salvation, perhaps the most important questions among the many they must resolve concern Christology. Issues which fall within its scope include the Trinity, which deals with the relationship between God, Jesus and the Holy Spirit, as well as rebirth and the relationship between Jesus, the Holy Spirit and fallen people. Until today, the controversies surrounding these issues have never been clearly settled. Consequently, considerable confusion remains in Christian doctrine and ways of faith. The key in approaching these matters is to understand the original value of human beings. We shall discuss this issue first, as a foundation for answering the other questions of Christology.

SECTION 1

THE VALUE OF A PERSON WHO HAS REALIZED THE PURPOSE OF CREATION

Let us discuss the value of a person who has realized the purpose of creation; that is, the value of Adam or Eve in perfection. We can understand such a person's value from several perspectives.

First, the relationship between God and a fully mature person resembles the relationship between the dual characteristics. Human beings were created with mind and body in the likeness of the dual characteristics of

God.[1] Similarly, the relationship between God and a person who has attained perfection of individual character may be compared to that between the dual characteristics of a person, that is, between mind and body. Just as the body is created in the likeness of the intangible mind to be its substantial object partner, a human being is created in the likeness of the intangible God to be His substantial object partner. Just as there is inseparable oneness between the mind and body of a true person centered on God, there is inseparable oneness between God and a true person who together form a four position foundation. In that union, the person experiences the Heart of God as his own reality. Having a fully mature character, such a person is a temple of God, in whom God can dwell continually, and comes to possess a divine nature.[2] Jesus spoke of this state of perfection, saying "You, therefore, must be perfect, as your heavenly Father is perfect."[3] Thus, we see that a person who has realized the purpose of creation assumes a divine value, comparable to God.

Second, let us consider the value of a human being from the perspective of the purpose for which he was created. God created human beings for the purpose of sharing joy with them. Every human being possesses a unique individual character. No matter how many billions of people are born on the earth, no two will ever have exactly the same personality. Each person is God's substantial object partner who manifests a distinctive aspect of God's dual characteristics. Hence, that person is the only one in the entire universe who can stimulate that distinctive aspect of God's nature to bring Him joy.[4] Every person who has completed the purpose of creation is thus a unique existence in the cosmos. We can thus affirm the truth in the Buddha's saying, "In heaven and on earth, I alone am the honored one."[5]

Third, let us consider the value of a human being based on his relationship with the universe, as clarified by the Principle of Creation. A person who has completed the purpose of creation can govern the entire universe.[6] Possessing both spirit and flesh, he can rule the spirit world with his spirit self and the physical world with his physical self. With human beings acting as mediators, the two worlds enter into a reciprocal relationship and form a unified cosmos which is a complete object partner to God.

---

1. cf. Creation 1.1
2. I Cor. 3:16; cf. Creation 3.2
3. Matt. 5:48
4. cf. Creation 3.2
5. The first words attributed to the Buddha after his birth. *Ch'ang A-han ching*, *T* 1.1.4c1-2; *Mahāpadāna Suttanta*, *Dīgha-nikāya* ii.15.
6. Gen. 1:28

We have learned through the Principle of Creation that the universe is the substantial unfolding of the dual characteristics of a human being. A person's spirit encapsulates all elements of the spirit world while his flesh encapsulates all elements of the physical world. A person who has completed the purpose of creation thus encapsulates all the essences of everything in the cosmos. This is why a human being is called a microcosm of the universe. For these reasons, a human being has the value of the entire cosmos. We can thus understand the saying of Jesus in a new light, "For what will it profit a man, if he gains the whole world and forfeits his life?"[7]

Suppose there is a perfect machine, whose every part is the only one of its kind in the world, and there is no way to either procure or make a replacement for any of them. No matter how small or insignificant a single part may be, its value is then the same as that of the whole machine. Similarly, a fully mature person is unique in all the universe. No matter how insignificant he may seem, his value is equivalent to that of the entire cosmos.

Section 2

Jesus and the Person Who Has Realized the Purpose of Creation

2.1 Perfected Adam, Jesus and the Restoration of the Tree of Life

Human history is the history of the providence of restoration. Its goal is the realization of the Kingdom of Heaven on earth when, at the end of history, the tree of life which was lost in the Garden of Eden will be regained.[8] We can understand the relation between perfect Adam and Jesus by comparing the tree of life in the Garden of Eden with the tree of life to be restored in the Last Days.

As was discussed earlier,[9] had Adam fully realized the ideal of creation, he would have become the tree of life and likewise all his descendants would have become trees of life. However, Adam's fall frustrated God's Will, and ever since, fallen humankind has hoped to be restored as trees of life.[10] Since a fallen person can never fully restore himself as a tree of life by his own efforts, a man who has completed the ideal of creation must come as the tree of life and engraft all people with himself. Jesus is this tree of life portrayed in the Bible. Adam, had he realized the ideal of

---

7. Matt. 16:26
8. Rev. 22:14; Gen. 3:24
9. cf. Fall 1.1.1
10. Prov. 13:12; Rev. 22:14

perfection symbolized by the tree of life in the Garden of Eden, and Jesus, symbolized by the tree of life in the Book of Revelation, would be identical in the sense of having realized the goal of creation. As such, they would have equal value.

2.2 JESUS, HUMAN BEINGS AND THE FULFILLMENT OF THE PURPOSE OF CREATION

Let us compare the value of Jesus with that of a person of perfect individual character. With respect to the purpose of creation, a fully mature person is perfect as God is perfect.[11] Having the same divine nature as God, he is infinitely precious. Since God is an eternal being, a person created to become His incarnate object partner in perfection must have an eternal life. A fully mature person is unique in all the cosmos. Furthermore, since he is the lord of the entire natural world, which cannot realize its full value without him, he possesses the value of the cosmos.

There is no greater value than that of a person who has realized the ideal of creation. This is the value of Jesus, who surely attained the highest imaginable value. The conventional Christian belief in Jesus' divinity is well founded because, as a perfect human being, Jesus is totally one with God. To assert that Jesus is none other than a man who has completed the purpose of creation does not degrade the value of Jesus in the least. In fact, the Principle of Creation elevates the true value of all people who fulfill the purpose of creation to a level comparable to Jesus.

Let us now examine some biblical evidence supporting the position that Jesus is a man who has fulfilled the purpose of creation. It is written:

> For there is one God, and there is one mediator between God and men, the man Christ Jesus. —*I Tim. 2:5*

> For as by one man's [Adam's] disobedience many were made sinners, so by one man's [Jesus'] obedience many will be made righteous. —*Rom. 5:19*
>
> For as by a man [Adam] came death, by a man [Jesus] has come also the resurrection of the dead. —*I Cor. 15:21*
>
> He has fixed a day on which he will judge the world in righteousness by a man whom he has appointed. —*Acts 17:31*

Thus, the Bible demonstrates plainly that Jesus is a man. Above all, he had to come as a human being that he might become the True Parent who can give rebirth to human beings.

---

11. Matt. 5:48

2.3 Is Jesus God Himself?

When Philip asked Jesus to show him God, Jesus said, "He who has seen me has seen the Father; how can you say, 'Show us the Father?' Do you not believe that I am in the Father and the Father in me?"[12] It is written of Jesus, "He was in the world, and the world was made through him, yet the world knew him not."[13] Jesus also said, "Truly, truly, I say to you, before Abraham was, I am."[14] Based on these biblical verses, many Christians have believed that Jesus is God, the Creator.

Jesus may well be called God because, as a man who has realized the purpose of creation and who lives in oneness with God, he has a divine nature. Nevertheless, he is not God Himself. The relationship between God and Jesus may be thought of as analogous to the relationship between the mind and body. Because the body is the substantial object partner to the mind, resembles the mind and acts in oneness with the mind, it may be understood to be the mind's second self; but it is not the mind itself. By analogy, since Jesus is one with God and the incarnation of God, he may be understood to be God's second self; but he is not God. It is true that he who has seen Jesus may be said to have seen God,[15] but Jesus did not mean by saying this that he was God Himself.

The Bible refers to Jesus as the Word made flesh.[16] This verse means that Jesus is the incarnation of the Word; that is, a man in whom the Word comes alive. We read that all things were made through the Word, and further, that the world was made through Jesus.[17] Hence, Jesus may be said to be the creator. To understand what these verses mean, consider that the universe according to the Principle of Creation is the substantial unfolding of the internal nature and external form of a human being of perfected character. All the elements of the universe are encapsulated in a fully mature person and resonate in harmony around him. In this sense, it can be said that the universe is created through a perfect human being. Furthermore, God intended that human beings be the creators and lords of the natural world by endowing them with the character and powers of the Creator; these are to be realized once they reach perfection through the fulfillment of their responsibility. Seen from this perspective, these verses are in agreement with our understanding of Jesus as the man who has completed the purpose of creation; they do not signify that Jesus is the Creator Himself.

---

12. John 14:9-10
13. John 1:10
14. John 8:58
15. John 14:9-10
16. John 1:14
17. John 1:3, 10

Jesus also said, "Before Abraham was, I am."[18] Jesus was the descendant of Abraham. Yet with respect to the providence of restoration, Jesus is the ancestor of Abraham because, as the one to give rebirth to all humankind, he came in the position of their first ancestor. We should understand that Jesus did not mean by this saying that he is God Himself. While on earth, Jesus was a man no different from any of us except for the fact that he was without the original sin. Even in the spirit world, where he has abided since his resurrection, Jesus lives as a spirit, as do his disciples. The only difference between them is that Jesus abides as a divine spirit, emitting brilliant rays of light, while his disciples, as life spirits, reflect that light.

It is written that since his resurrection, Jesus has been interceding for us before God[19] as he did while he was on earth.[20] If Jesus were God, how could he intercede for us before Himself? Moreover, Jesus called God "Father," thus acknowledging that he was not God Himself.[21] If Jesus were God, how could He be tempted by Satan, as Jesus was? We can conclude with finality that Jesus was not God Himself from the words he uttered on the cross, "My God, my God, why hast thou forsaken me?"[22]

SECTION 3

JESUS AND FALLEN PEOPLE

A fallen person has nothing of the value of a true person who has completed the purpose of creation. Rather, he has fallen to such a lowly status that he looks up to the angels, who were created to be his subordinates. On the other hand, because Jesus came with the full value of a true person who has completed the purpose of creation, "All things are put in subjection under him."[23] A fallen person with original sin is stained with the condition through which Satan can attack him. On the other hand, Jesus, having no original sin, had no condition in himself for Satan to invade him. A fallen person cannot fathom the Will and Heart of God. At most, he can catch only a glimpse of them. In contrast, Jesus not only understood the Will and Heart of God thoroughly, he also experienced God's Heart as his own reality in his daily life.

---

18. John 8:58
19. Rom. 8:34
20. Luke 23:34
21. John 17:1
22. Matt. 27:46
23. I Cor. 15:27

A person has virtually none of his original value as long as he remains in the fallen state. If, however, he were to be reborn spiritually and physically through Jesus, the True Parent, and become his good child cleansed of the original sin, he would be restored as a true person who has perfected the purpose of creation, like Jesus Christ himself. His relationship with Jesus would then be like the human relationship of a child with his parent. Even though their relationship will always maintain the vertical order of parent and child, their original values do not differ in the least. Thus, Christ is the head of the church,[24] and we are his body and members.[25] Jesus is the main temple, and we are the branch temples. Jesus is the vine, and we are the branches.[26] We, the wild olive shoots, are to be engrafted with Jesus, the true olive tree,[27] before we can become true olive trees ourselves. Accordingly, Jesus called us "my friends,"[28] and it is written that "when he appears we shall be like him."[29] Jesus alone is the "first fruits," but at his return, we who belong to Christ will be the next.[30]

SECTION 4

REBIRTH AND TRINITY

The doctrine of the Trinity has remained one of the most mysterious topics in Christian theology. Moreover, the related doctrine of rebirth, though seemingly evident to all, also needs deeper elucidation. We will examine these doctrines in this section.

4.1 REBIRTH

4.1.1 JESUS AND THE HOLY SPIRIT AND THEIR MISSION TO GIVE REBIRTH

Jesus told Nicodemus, "Truly, truly, I say to you, unless one is born anew, he cannot see the kingdom of God."[31] *Rebirth* means to be born a second time. Why must fallen people be born anew?

Had Adam and Eve realized the ideal of creation and become the True Parents of humanity, they would have borne good children without original sin and formed the Kingdom of Heaven on earth. However, Adam and Eve fell and became evil parents, multiplying evil children who created this hell on earth. Hence, as Jesus told Nicodemus, fallen people

---

24. Eph. 1:22
25. I Cor. 12:27
26. John 15:5
27. Rom. 11:17
28. John 15:14
29. I John 3:2
30. I Cor. 15:23
31. John 3:3

cannot see the Kingdom of God unless they are first born anew—as children without original sin.

We cannot be born without parents. Who, then, are the good parents through whom we can be born again, cleansed of original sin and able to enter the Kingdom of God? Parents who have original sin cannot give birth to good children who do not have original sin. Certainly, it is impossible to find sinless parents among fallen humankind. These parents must descend from Heaven. Jesus was the Parent who came from Heaven. He came as the True Father in order to give rebirth to fallen people, transforming them into good children, thoroughly cleansed of original sin and fit to build the Kingdom of Heaven on earth. Thus, it is written in the Bible, "By his great mercy we have been born anew to a living hope through the resurrection of Jesus Christ from the dead."[32] Jesus came as the True Father whom Adam had failed to become. For this reason, the Bible speaks of him as "the last Adam" and the "Everlasting Father."[33]

However, a father alone cannot give birth to children. There must be a True Mother, as well as a True Father, for fallen children to be reborn as good children. The Holy Spirit came as the True Mother. This is why Jesus told Nicodemus that no one can enter the Kingdom of God unless he is born anew through the Holy Spirit.[34]

There are many who have received the revelation that the Holy Spirit is feminine. This is because the Holy Spirit comes as the True Mother or second Eve. Since the Holy Spirit is the feminine aspect of divinity, without first receiving her we cannot go before Jesus as his brides. Being feminine, the Holy Spirit consoles and moves the hearts of people.[35] She cleanses people's sin, thereby atoning for the sin which Eve committed. Jesus, the masculine Lord, works in heaven (yang), while the Holy Spirit, his feminine counterpart, works on the earth (yin).

4.1.2 JESUS AND THE HOLY SPIRIT AND THE DUAL CHARACTERISTICS OF THE LOGOS

Logos is Greek for "rational principle" or "the Word." The Bible indicates that the Logos is an object partner to God,[36] engaged in a reciprocal relationship with Him. Since God, the subject partner of the Logos, exists with dual characteristics, the Logos as His object partner should

---

32. I Pet. 1:3
33. I Cor. 15:45; Isa. 9:6
34. John 3:5
35. Rom. 5:5; John 14:26-27; Acts 9:31
36. John 1:1

also be composed of dual characteristics. If the Logos were without dual characteristics, all things made through it[37] would not be composed of dual characteristics. Adam and Eve, the embodied object partners of God in image, were created separately out of the dual characteristics of the Logos.[38]

Had Adam as a man realized the ideal of creation and become the tree of life, and had Eve as a woman realized the ideal of creation and fulfilled the tree of the knowledge of good and evil, they would have stood together as the *True Parents* of humankind. They would have fulfilled God's three great blessings and established the Kingdom of God on earth. Instead, because they fell, this world became an earthly hell. Therefore, to give rebirth to fallen people, Jesus came as the second Adam,[39] the True Father of humankind, with the mission symbolized by the tree of life.[40] This being the case, should not there also have come the True Mother of humankind,[41] the second Eve with the mission symbolized by the tree of the knowledge of good and evil? The one who has come as the True Mother to give rebirth to fallen people is the Holy Spirit.

4.1.3 SPIRITUAL REBIRTH THROUGH JESUS AND THE HOLY SPIRIT

A new life is born through the love of parents. When we believe in Jesus as the Savior through the inspiration of the Holy Spirit,[42] we receive the love of the spiritual True Parents, which is generated through the give and take between Jesus, the spiritual True Father, and the Holy Spirit, the spiritual True Mother. Through this love, new life is infused into us, and our spirits are reborn as new selves. This is spiritual rebirth. Nevertheless, since human beings fell both spiritually and physically, we must be cleansed of original sin by being born again both spiritually and physically. Christ must return to earth to grant physical salvation to humanity, which is to be realized through our physical rebirth.

4.2 THE TRINITY

According to the Principle of Creation, God's purpose of creation is completed based upon the four position foundation, which is established by fulfilling the three object purpose through origin-division-union action. To fulfill the purpose of creation, Jesus and the Holy

---

37. John 1:3
38. cf. Creation 1.1
39. I Cor. 15:45
40. Rev. 22:14
41. Rev. 22:17
42. I Cor. 12:3

Spirit stand before God as object partners who separately manifest the dual characteristics of God. They unite through give and take with each other with God as the center and form the four position foundation. God, Jesus and the Holy Spirit thus become one, and this oneness constitutes the Trinity.

Originally, God's purpose for creating Adam and Eve was to form a trinity by raising them to be the True Parents of humankind united in harmonious oneness as husband and wife centered on God in a four position foundation. If Adam and Eve had not fallen, but had formed this trinity with God and become the True Parents who could multiply good children, their descendants would have also become good husbands and wives with God as the center of their lives. Each couple would thus have formed a trinity with God. The Kingdom of Heaven on earth fulfilling God's three great blessings would have been realized at that time. Instead, when Adam and Eve fell, they formed a four position foundation with Satan as their center; in other words, they formed a fallen trinity with Satan. Their descendants likewise have continued to form trinities with Satan, and so built a corrupt and immoral society.

Since the Fall, God has worked for the day when He could give rebirth to people and join them in trinities with Himself. For this purpose, God intended to exalt Jesus and his Bride as the second Adam and Eve to become the True Parents of humanity. However, the resurrected Jesus and the Holy Spirit in oneness with God could form only a spiritual trinity. They could fulfill only the mission of spiritual True Parents. Thus, Jesus and the Holy Spirit have been giving spiritual rebirth to people of faith as their spiritual children, restoring them to spiritual trinities.

Christ must return in the flesh and find his Bride. They will form on the earth a perfect trinity with God and become True Parents both spiritually and physically. They will give fallen people rebirth both spiritually and physically, removing their original sin and enabling them to build trinities on earth with God as the center. When fallen people are restored to the point where they can establish true four position foundations centered on God, they will finally be able to build the Kingdom of Heaven on earth where God's three great blessings are fulfilled.

Part II

Introduction to Restoration

The *providence of restoration* refers to God's work to restore human beings to our original, unfallen state so that we may fulfill the purpose of creation. As discussed in Part I, human beings fell from the top of the growth stage and have been held under Satan's dominion ever since.[1] To restore human beings, God works to cut off Satan's influence. Yet, as was explained in Christology, we must have the original sin removed before we can sever Satan's bonds and be restored to the state before the Fall. This is possible only when we are born anew through the Messiah, the True Parent. To explain further: we first need to go through a course to separate Satan from ourselves. We do this in order to restore ourselves in form to the spiritual level which Adam and Eve had reached before the Fall—the top of the growth stage. On this foundation, we are to receive the Messiah and be reborn, and thereby be fully restored to the original state of human beings before the Fall. Finally, by following the Messiah, we should continue our growth to maturity where we can fulfill the purpose of creation.

Since the providence of restoration is God's work of re-creation, which has as its goal the fulfillment of the purpose of creation, God works this providence in accordance with His Principle. In the course of the providence of restoration, this principle is called the *Principle of Restoration*. Let us study how the providence of restoration is to be accomplished.

---

1. cf. Creation 5.2.1; Fall 4.1

Section 1

The Principle of Restoration through Indemnity

1.1 Restoration through Indemnity

Before discussing the Principle of Restoration through Indemnity, we must first understand in what position, due to the Fall, human beings came to stand in relation to both God and Satan. If the first human ancestors had not fallen but had reached perfection and become one in heart with God, then they would have lived relating only with God. However, due to their Fall, they joined in a kinship of blood with Satan, which compelled them to deal with him as well. Immediately after the Fall, when Adam and Eve had the original sin but had not yet committed any subsequent good or evil deeds, they found themselves in the *midway position*—a position between God and Satan where they were relating with both. As a consequence, all their descendants are also in the midway position. Take, for example, a person in the fallen world who does not believe in Jesus but leads a conscientious life. As long as he leads a virtuous life, Satan cannot drag him into hell; yet God cannot bring him to Paradise either as long as he does not believe in Jesus. He remains in the midway position. His spirit ends up abiding in an intermediate region of the spirit world which is neither Paradise nor hell.

How does God separate Satan from fallen people who stand in the midway position? Satan relates with them on the basis of his connection with them through lineage. Therefore, until people make a *condition* through which God can claim them as His own, there is no way God can restore them to the heavenly side. On the other hand, Satan acknowledges that God is the Creator of human beings. Unless Satan finds some condition through which he can attack a fallen person, he also cannot arbitrarily claim him for his side. Therefore, a fallen person will go to God's side if he makes good conditions and to Satan's side if he makes evil conditions.

For example, when Adam's family was in the midway position, God instructed the children, Cain and Abel, to offer sacrifices that they might come into a position where God could work His providence through them. Yet because Cain killed Abel, the condition was made which allowed Satan to claim them instead. God sent Jesus to fallen people that they might stand on God's side through the condition of believing in him. Unfortunately, when he came, many rejected him and remained on Satan's side. This is the reason Jesus is both the Savior and the Lord of judgment.

What, then, is the meaning of restoration through indemnity? When someone has lost his original position or state, he must make some condition to be restored to it. The making of such conditions of restitution is called *indemnity*. For example, to recover lost reputation, position or health, one must make the necessary effort or pay the due price. Suppose two people who once loved each other come to be on bad terms; they must make some condition of reconciliation before the love they previously enjoyed can be revived. In like manner, it is necessary for human beings who have fallen from God's grace into corruption to fulfill some condition before they can be restored to their true standing. We call this process of restoring the original position and state through making conditions *restoration through indemnity*, and we call the condition made a *condition of indemnity*. God's work to restore people to their true, unfallen state by having them fulfill indemnity conditions is called the *providence of restoration through indemnity*.

How does a condition of indemnity compare with the value of what was lost? We can answer by listing the following three types of indemnity conditions.

The first is to fulfill a condition of equal indemnity. In this case, restoration is achieved by making a condition of indemnity at a price equal to the value of what was lost when one departed from the original position or state. Acts of restitution or compensation are indemnity conditions of this type. The verse "life for life, eye for eye, tooth for tooth,"[2] refers to this type of indemnity condition.

The second is to make a condition of lesser indemnity. In this case, restoration is achieved by making a condition of indemnity at a price less than the value of what was lost. For instance, when someone owes a huge debt, if the creditor displays good will in forgiving a portion of the debt, then the debtor can pay back less than the total amount and still satisfy the entire debt. The outstanding example of this is redemption through the cross. Merely by fulfilling a small indemnity condition of faith in Jesus, we receive the much greater grace of salvation, which entitles us to participate with Jesus in the same resurrection. By making the indemnity condition of baptism by water, we can be spiritually born anew through Jesus and the Holy Spirit. Furthermore, by taking a piece of bread and a cup of wine at the sacrament of Holy Communion, we receive the precious grace of partaking in Jesus' body and blood. All these are examples of conditions of lesser indemnity.

The third is to make a condition of greater indemnity. When a person has failed to meet a condition of lesser indemnity, he must make

---

2. Exod. 21:23-24

another indemnity condition to return to the original state, this time at a price greater than the first. For example, because Abraham made a mistake when offering the sacrifice of a dove, ram and heifer, he had to meet a condition of greater indemnity to rectify his failure. God thus asked him to offer his only son Isaac as the sacrifice. In the days of Moses, when the Israelites failed to believe in God's promise during their forty days of spying in the land of Canaan, they had to fulfill a condition of greater indemnity by wandering in the wilderness for forty years, calculated as one year for each day of the failed spy mission.[3]

Why is a condition of greater indemnity necessary when an indemnity condition is set up for the second time? Whenever a central figure in God's providence makes a second attempt to fulfill an indemnity condition, he must fulfill not only his own unfulfilled condition; in addition, he must make restitution for the failures of the people who came before him.

Next, let us study the method of fulfilling indemnity conditions. For anyone to be restored to the original position or state from which he fell, he must make an indemnity condition by reversing the course of his mistake. For instance, because the chosen people reviled Jesus and sent him to the cross, to be saved and restored to the original position of God's elect, the chosen people must go the opposite way: love Jesus and willingly bear the cross for his sake.[4] This is the reason Christianity became a religion of martyrdom. Furthermore, human beings caused tremendous grief to God by violating His Will and falling. To restore this through indemnity, we must seek to regain our pure, original nature and comfort God's Heart by living in obedience to God's Will. Similarly, because the first Adam forsook God, his descendants ended up in the bosom of Satan. Accordingly, in order for Jesus, the second Adam, to take people out of the bosom of Satan and return them to God, he had to worship and honor God even after being forsaken by Him. This is the complicated reason behind God's abandonment of Jesus on the cross.[5] Finally, a nation's laws impose punishment on criminals for the purpose of setting the indemnity conditions necessary for maintaining order in society.

Who should make indemnity conditions? Earlier, we learned that human beings should have become perfect by fulfilling their responsibility; they then would have had the authority to govern even the angels. Yet the first human ancestors failed in their responsibility and

---

3. Num. 14:34
4. Luke 14:27
5. Matt. 27:46

thereby fell to the state where they were dominated by Satan. To escape from Satan's domination and be restored to the state where we rule over him, we ourselves must fulfill the necessary indemnity conditions as our portion of responsibility.

1.2 The Foundation for the Messiah

The Messiah comes as the True Parent of humanity because only he can remove the original sin by giving rebirth to humanity, born of fallen parents.[6] For fallen people to be restored to their original state, we must receive the Messiah. Before we can receive the Messiah, however, we must first establish the *foundation for the Messiah*.

What indemnity conditions are required for establishing the foundation for the Messiah? To answer this question, we must first understand how Adam was to have realized the purpose of creation and how he failed to do it, because the condition of indemnity is made by reversing the course of the deviation from the original path.

For Adam to realize the purpose of creation, he was supposed to fulfill two conditions. First, Adam should have established the *foundation of faith*. The person to lay this foundation was Adam himself. The condition to establish this foundation was to keep strictly to God's commandment not to eat of the fruit of the tree of the knowledge of good and evil. In fulfilling this condition, Adam would have passed through a set growing period, which was the time allotted for him to fulfill his portion of responsibility. This period represents some numbers of providential significance. Hence, the growing period may be thought of as a period to fulfill certain numbers.

The second condition which Adam was supposed to fulfill in order to realize the purpose of creation was to establish the *foundation of substance*. Upon an unshakable foundation of faith, Adam was then to become one with God, thereby establishing the foundation of substance. This means he would have become the perfect incarnation of the Word[7] with perfect character, fulfilling God's first blessing. In this way, had he not fallen, Adam would have completed the purpose of creation. For a fallen person to establish the foundation for the Messiah, he must pass through a similar course: establishing first the foundation of faith and then the foundation of substance.

---

6. cf. Christology 4.1.1
7. John 1:14

1.2.1 The Foundation of Faith

Because Adam disobeyed the Word of God and fell, he could not establish the foundation of faith. Hence, he could neither become the perfect incarnation of the Word nor complete the purpose of creation. To restore the basis upon which they can complete the purpose of creation, fallen people must first restore through indemnity the foundation of faith which the first human ancestors failed to establish. There are three aspects to the indemnity condition required for restoring the foundation of faith.

First, there must be a *central figure*. From the time Adam failed to establish the foundation of faith, God has been looking for central figures who could restore the lost foundation of faith. God had Cain and Abel offer sacrifices for this purpose. Likewise, God called men such as Noah, Abraham, Isaac, Jacob, Moses, the kings and John the Baptist for the purpose of raising them up as central figures.

Second, an *object for the condition* must be offered. When Adam lost faith in God, he lost the Word of God which had been given him for the fulfillment of the condition to establish the foundation of faith. As a result, fallen people could no longer directly receive the Word of God to restore the foundation of faith. It then became necessary to offer objects for the condition as substitutes for the Word. Human beings were degraded by the Fall to a status lower than the things of creation, as it is written, "the heart is deceitful above all things."[8] Hence, in the age prior to the giving of the Old Testament, people could establish the foundation of faith by offering a sacrifice or its equivalent, such as the ark, procured from the natural world. Thus, the foundation of faith also functioned as the foundation to restore all things, which had been defiled by Satan. In the Old Testament Age, either the Word as revealed in the Law of Moses or representatives of the Word—such as the Ark of the Covenant, the Temple and various central figures—served as objects for the condition, substituting for the original Word. In the New Testament Age, the Word as revealed in the Gospels and Jesus, the incarnation of the Word, were the objects for the condition. From the standpoint of human beings, these objects for the condition are offered for the purpose of restoring the foundation of faith. From God's perspective, the offering of objects for the condition is for the purpose of securing God's ownership.

Third, a *numerical period of indemnity* must be completed. Questions such as why the length of this indemnity period should be

---
8. Jer. 17:9

based on certain providential numbers and what lengths those numerical periods have, will be discussed later in detail.[9]

1.2.2 THE FOUNDATION OF SUBSTANCE

As earlier stated, for fallen people to complete the purpose of creation, we must become perfect incarnations of the Word, a state our first ancestors failed to attain. Becoming perfect incarnations requires that first we be cleansed of the original sin through the Messiah. Before we can receive the Messiah, however, we need to lay a foundation for him, which is accomplished when we establish the foundation of substance on the basis of the foundation of faith. After receiving the Messiah and being restored to the position of the first human ancestors before their Fall, a path still remains to be trod: we must become one with the Messiah centered on the Heart of God, then follow him along the uncharted path to the summit of the growing period, and thus finally become perfect incarnations.

Fallen people can establish the foundation of substance by making an indemnity condition, the *indemnity condition to remove the fallen nature*. When the first human ancestors fell and acquired the original sin, they could not realize their God-given original nature. Instead, they harbored the primary characteristics of the fallen nature.[10] By making the indemnity condition to remove this fallen nature, a fallen person can lay the foundation of substance by which he can receive the Messiah, be cleansed of the original sin, and ultimately restore his original nature. In later chapters, we will discuss how this condition may be fulfilled.[11]

SECTION 2

THE COURSE OF THE PROVIDENCE OF RESTORATION

2.1 THE AGES IN THE COURSE OF THE PROVIDENCE OF RESTORATION

Let us now present an overview of the entire course of history since the time of Adam, as reckoned in the Bible, and survey the providential ages which comprise it. God's providence to have fallen people establish the foundation upon which they could receive the Messiah, and thence complete the purpose of creation, began with Adam's family.

---

9. cf. Periods 2.4
10. cf. Fall 4.6
11. cf. Foundation 1.2

However, God's Will was frustrated when Cain murdered Abel. Ten generations later, the unfulfilled Will was passed down to Noah's family. God judged the evil world with the flood in order to set apart Noah's family and conduct the providence of restoration. God intended to complete the providence by establishing the foundation for the Messiah in Noah's family and sending the Messiah on that basis. Yet due to the fallen act of Noah's second son, Ham, the providence for Noah's family and the ark failed. As a consequence, the ten generations and the forty-day flood which God had set up to prepare for this providence were lost to Satan.

After four hundred years had passed in order to restore through indemnity what had been lost to Heaven's side, God's Will was entrusted to Abraham. If Abraham had established the foundation for the Messiah on the family level exactly as God had intended, the foundation would have expanded to the national level, and thereupon the Messiah would have come. However, because Abraham failed in the symbolic offering, God's Will was frustrated once more. Consequently, the biblical two thousand years from Adam to Abraham,[12] during which God had sought a father of faith who could receive the Messiah, was claimed by Satan. Yet Abraham's situation differed from that of Noah. Although Abraham failed in the symbolic offering, the family foundation for the Messiah was eventually fulfilled through the three generations of Abraham's family: Abraham, Isaac and Jacob. On that basis, God multiplied the chosen people in Egypt and expanded the foundation for the Messiah to the national level. For this reason, Abraham is called the father of faith.[13] If we judge the significance of the age strictly by its outcome, we can understand that the two-thousand-year period from Adam to Abraham was for the purpose of finding one father of faith who could lay the foundation to begin the providence of restoration. Thus, God's work of restoration can be said to have begun with Abraham.

However, due to Abraham's mistake in making the symbolic offering, the two thousand years from Adam to Abraham were lost to Satan. Hence, a period had to be set up in which those lost years could be restored through indemnity to God's side; this is the significance of the two-thousand-year period from Abraham to Jesus. If Abraham had not failed in making the symbolic offering, the Messiah would have come and stood upon the national foundation for the Messiah built by Abraham's immediate descendants, and the providence of restoration

---

12. The traditional biblical reckoning of the date for the first human ancestors as six thousand years ago, or two thousand years before Abraham, is a symbolic chronology representing a much longer period of time, the determination of which is a matter for science. —Ed.
13. Rom. 4:11-12, 16-17

would have been completed at that time. Likewise, had the Jewish people believed in and attended Jesus, they would have supported him to stand representing the nation as the living sacrifice before God. They then would have laid the national foundation for the Messiah. Jesus, standing as the Messiah on that foundation, could then have completed the providence of restoration.

However, just as Abraham failed in his symbolic offering, the Jewish people failed to make their offering on the national level when their leaders sent Jesus to the cross. Thus, a period of two thousand years—this time from Abraham to Jesus—was lost yet again to Satan. As a consequence, a parallel period had to be set up in which the earlier two-thousand-year period could be restored through indemnity to God's side. This is the significance of the two-thousand-year period from Jesus' time until today. During this age, founded upon the cross of Jesus, Christians must establish the worldwide foundation for the Messiah.

2.2 Categorization of the Ages in the Course of the Providence of Restoration

The ages in the course of the providence of restoration show the progressive development of God's providence. They may be categorized according to six criteria.

2.2.1 The Ages Categorized with Reference to God's Word

(i) During the two-thousand-year period from Adam to Abraham, people had not yet fulfilled sufficient indemnity conditions to receive God's Word directly. At most, fallen people made indemnity conditions through offering sacrifices; but in doing so, they laid the foundation for the next period when God could begin to work His providence of restoration based on the Word. Hence, this period is called the age of the providence to lay the foundation for the Word.

(ii) During the two-thousand-year period from Abraham to Jesus, humanity's spirituality and intellect developed to the formation stage based on the Word revealed in the Old Testament. Hence, this period is called the formation stage of the providence, or the Old Testament Age.

(iii) During the two-thousand-year period from Jesus until the Second Coming, humanity's spirituality and intellect developed to the growth stage based on the Word revealed in the New Testament. Hence, this period is called the growth stage of the providence, or the New Testament Age.

(iv) During the period when the providence of restoration is to be completed after the Second Coming of Christ, humanity's spirituality and intellect are to develop through the completion stage based on the Completed Testament Word, which will be given for the fulfillment of the providence of restoration. Hence, this period is called the completion stage of the providence, or the Completed Testament Age.

2.2.2 The Ages Categorized with Reference to God's Work of Resurrection

(i) During the two-thousand-year period from Adam to Abraham, people offered sacrifices to lay the foundation to commence the Old Testament Age, when God would begin His work of resurrection. Hence, this period is called the age of the providence to lay the foundation for resurrection.

(ii) During the two-thousand-year period from Abraham to Jesus, people could be resurrected to the form-spirit level based on the Old Testament Word and the merit of the age in the providence of restoration. Hence, this period is called the age of the providence of formation-stage resurrection.

(iii) During the two-thousand year period from Jesus to the Second Advent, people could be resurrected to the life-spirit level based on the New Testament Word and the merit of the age in the providence of restoration. Hence, this period is called the age of the providence of growth-stage resurrection.

(iv) During the period when the providence of restoration is to be completed after the Second Coming of Christ, people are to be fully resurrected to the divine-spirit level based on the Completed Testament Word and the merit of the age in the providence of restoration. Hence, this period is called the age of the providence of completion-stage resurrection.

2.2.3 The Ages Categorized with Reference to the Providence to Restore through Indemnity the Lost Periods of Faith

(i) During the two-thousand-year period from Adam to Abraham, God laid the foundation for the Old Testament Age. Although this period was lost to Satan, God, by raising up Abraham, could commence the Old Testament Age, in which He would restore this first period through indemnity. Hence, this period is called the Age of the Providence to Lay the Foundation for Restoration (through indemnity).

(ii) During the two-thousand-year period from Abraham to Jesus, God restored through indemnity the previous period of two thousand years—lost to Satan due to Abraham's mistake in the symbolic offering—by working predominantly through the people of Israel. Hence, this period is called the Age of the Providence of Restoration (through indemnity).

(iii) During the two-thousand-year period from Jesus to the Second Advent, God has been restoring through indemnity the Old Testament Age—lost to Satan due to Jesus' crucifixion—by working predominantly through Christianity. Hence, this period is called the Age of the Prolongation of the Providence of Restoration (through indemnity).

(iv) During the period when the providence of restoration is to be completed after the Second Coming of Christ, God will work to restore through indemnity the entire course of the providence of restoration, which has been lost to Satan. Hence, this period is called the Age for Completing the Providence of Restoration (through indemnity).

2.2.4 THE AGES CATEGORIZED WITH REFERENCE TO THE EXPANDING SCOPE OF THE FOUNDATION FOR THE MESSIAH

(i) During the two-thousand-year period from Adam to Abraham, God laid the family foundation for the Messiah by raising up Abraham's family on the condition of the sacrifices they offered. Hence, this period is called the age of the providence to lay the family foundation for the Messiah.

(ii) During the two-thousand-year period from Abraham to Jesus, God worked to lay the national foundation for the Messiah by raising up Israel based on the Old Testament Word. Hence, this period is called the age of the providence to lay the national foundation for the Messiah.

(iii) During the two-thousand-year period from Jesus to the Second Advent, God has been laying the worldwide foundation for the Messiah by raising up worldwide Christianity based on the New Testament Word. Hence, this period is called the age of the providence to lay the worldwide foundation for the Messiah.

(iv) During the period when the providence of restoration is to be completed after the Second Coming of Christ, God will complete the cosmic foundation for the Messiah by working throughout heaven and earth based on the Completed Testament Word. Hence, this period is called the age of the providence to complete the cosmic foundation for the Messiah.

2.2.5 THE AGES CATEGORIZED WITH REFERENCE TO RESPONSIBILITY

(i) During the two-thousand-year period from Adam to Abraham, God laid the foundation upon which to conduct His providence in the subsequent Old Testament Age, a providence which was to be fulfilled by God shouldering the responsibility. Hence, this period is called the age of the providence to lay the foundation for God's responsibility.

(ii) During the two-thousand-year period from Abraham to Jesus, God took responsibility as the Creator of human beings and carried out the providence of restoration at the formation stage. God worked with the prophets and personally shouldered the first responsibility to defeat Satan. Hence, this period is called the age of the providence based on God's responsibility.

(iii) During the two-thousand-year period from Jesus to the Second Advent, Jesus and the Holy Spirit, who assumed the missions of Adam and Eve, have conducted the providence of restoration at the growth stage. Jesus and the Holy Spirit have shouldered the second responsibility to defeat Satan as they work to restore fallen people. Hence, this period is called the age of the providence based on Jesus and the Holy Spirit's responsibility.

(iv) During the period when the providence of restoration is to be completed after the Second Coming of Christ, the people of faith on earth and in heaven are to bear the third responsibility to defeat Satan, the fallen archangel, and complete the providence of restoration. They are to achieve this in accordance with the Principle of Creation, which lays out the way for human beings to gain the qualification to rule the angels. Hence, this period is called the age of the providence based on the believers' responsibility.

2.2.6 THE AGES CATEGORIZED WITH REFERENCE TO THE PARALLELS IN THE PROVIDENCE

(i) During the two-thousand-year period from Adam to Abraham, the foundation for the Messiah was restored by fulfilling parallel indemnity conditions of a symbolic type. Hence, this period is called the age of symbolic parallels.

(ii) During the two-thousand-year period from Abraham to Jesus, the foundation for the Messiah was restored by fulfilling parallel indemnity conditions of an image type. Hence, this period is called the age of image parallels.

(iii) During the two-thousand-year period from Jesus to the Second Advent, the foundation for the Messiah has been restored by fulfilling parallel indemnity conditions of a substantial type. Hence, this period is called the age of substantial parallels.

Section 3

The History of the Providence of Restoration and I

As an individual, each one of us is a product of the history of the providence of restoration. Hence, the person who is to accomplish the purpose of history is none other than I, myself. I must take up the cross of history and accept responsibility to fulfill its calling. To this end, I must fulfill in my lifetime (horizontally), through my efforts, the indemnity conditions which have accumulated through the long course of the providence of restoration (vertically). Only by doing this can I stand proudly as the fruit of history, the one whom God has eagerly sought throughout His providence. In other words, I must restore through indemnity, during my own generation, all the unaccomplished missions of past prophets and saints who were called in their time to carry the cross of restoration. Otherwise, I cannot become the individual who completes the purpose of the providence of restoration. To become such an historical victor, I must understand clearly the Heart of God when He worked with past prophets and saints, the original purpose for which God called them, and the details of the providential missions which He entrusted to them.

Yet there is no one among fallen humanity who can become such an historical victor by his efforts alone. For this reason, we must understand all these things through Christ at the Second Advent, who comes to fulfill the providence of restoration. Moreover, when we believe in him, become one with him, and attend him in his work, we can stand in the position of having fulfilled horizontally with him the vertical indemnity conditions in the history of the providence of restoration.

The path which all past saints walked as they strove to fulfill God's providential Will is the very path we must walk again today. Beyond that, we must continue on to the end of the path, even walking trails they left untrodden. Therefore, fallen people can never find the path that leads to life without understanding the particulars of the providence of restoration. Herein lies the reason why we must study the Principle of Restoration in detail.

Chapter 1

The Providence to Lay the Foundation for Restoration

SECTION 1

THE PROVIDENCE OF RESTORATION IN ADAM'S FAMILY

Even though the Fall resulted from human failure, God has felt responsible to save fallen humanity.[1] Therefore, God immediately began His providence to restore fallen people by having Adam's family lay the foundation for the Messiah.

Due to Adam's kinship of blood with Satan, he was in the midway position, relating with both God and Satan.[2] For a fallen person standing in the midway position to be purified, come to God's side and establish the foundation for the Messiah, he must fulfill a condition of indemnity. Consequently, for the providence of restoration to be accomplished in Adam's family, the members of his family had to make certain conditions of indemnity to restore the foundation of faith and the foundation of substance. On these two foundations, the foundation for the Messiah was to have been established, and the Messiah could have come to Adam's family.

---

1. cf. Messiah 2.1
2. cf. Restoration 1.1

1.1 The Foundation of Faith

To restore through indemnity the foundation of faith, fallen people must set up an object for the condition. Due to his faithlessness, Adam lost the Word of God, which had been given him in order to fulfill the condition necessary to establish the foundation of faith. He fell to the position where he could no longer receive the Word of God directly. Consequently, in restoring the foundation of faith, Adam had to faithfully offer in a manner acceptable to God some object for the condition, substituting for God's Word. For Adam's family, this object was a sacrificial offering.

To restore the foundation of faith, there must also be a central figure. One would expect that the central figure in Adam's family be Adam himself. It would seem that Adam should have offered the sacrifice, and that whether or not he made the offering in an acceptable manner would have determined success or failure in laying the foundation of faith.

Yet nowhere in the biblical record do we find Adam offering a sacrifice. Instead, his sons Cain and Abel offered them. What was the reason for this? According to the Principle of Creation, human beings were created to serve only one master.[3] God cannot conduct His providence in accord with the Principle with someone who serves two masters. If God were to accept Adam and his offering, Satan would use his ties of kinship with Adam as a condition through which to make a counter-claim upon him and his offering. In that case, Adam would be placed in the unprincipled situation of having to serve two masters: God and Satan. Since God could not conduct such an unprincipled providence, He took the course of symbolically dividing Adam, who embodied both good and evil, into two entities, one representing good and the other representing evil—an arrangement in line with the Principle. For this reason, God gave Adam two sons, representing good and evil, and set them in positions where each dealt with only one master, God or Satan. After setting up this arrangement, God had the two sons offer sacrifices separately.

Cain and Abel were both sons of Adam. Which one of them was to represent goodness and relate with God, and which was to represent evil and interact with Satan? Both Cain and Abel were the fruits of Eve's fall; hence, their relative positions were determined according to its course. Eve's fall was consummated through two different illicit love relationships. The first was the spiritual fall through her love with the Archangel. The second was the physical fall through her love with

---

3. Matt. 6:24

Adam. Certainly, the two relationships were both fallen acts. Yet between the two, the second act of love was more in line with the Principle and more forgivable than the first. Eve's first fallen act was motivated by her excessive desire to enjoy what it was not yet time for her to enjoy and have her eyes opened, like God.[4] This desire led her to consummate a relationship of unprincipled sexual love with the Archangel. In comparison, Eve's second fallen act was motivated by her heartfelt longing to return to God's bosom after she realized that her first fallen relationship had been illicit. This desire led her to consummate a relationship with Adam, her intended spouse according to the Principle, even though God did not yet permit it.[5]

Cain and Abel were both fruits of Eve's illicit love. God discriminated between them based on Eve's two illicit acts of love and accordingly placed Cain and Abel in two opposing positions. In other words, since Cain was the first fruit of Eve's love, signifying Eve's first fallen act of love with the Archangel, he was chosen to represent evil. Therefore, he was in a position to relate with Satan. Since Abel was the second fruit of Eve's love, signifying Eve's second fallen act of love with Adam, he was chosen to represent goodness. Therefore, he was in a position to relate with God.

For his part, Satan had seized control of the creation, which God had created by the Principle, and established an unprincipled world having only the outward form of God's intended universe. In the original, principled world, God intended to raise up the eldest son and have him inherit the birthright. Therefore, Satan felt a stronger attachment to the elder son than he did to the younger. Since Satan had already claimed the universe, he vied with God for the elder son, Cain, who was more valuable to him. Because Satan had a strong attachment to Cain, God chose to deal with Abel.

The Bible attests to the discrimination between first- and second-born sons. For example, God said to Cain, "If you do not do well, sin is couching at the door."[6] From this we may understand that Cain had a base to relate with Satan. When the Israelites were about to flee Egypt, God struck the firstborn of the Egyptians, even the firstborn of their livestock,[7] because the Egyptians, as Satan's vassals, stood in the position of Cain. When the Israelites were returning to the land of Canaan, only the Levites, who were in the position of the younger son

---

4. Gen. 3:5
5. cf. Fall 2.2
6. Gen. 4:7
7. Exod. 12:29

Abel, were allowed to carry the Ark of the Covenant.[8] It is written that God loved the second son Jacob and hated the first son Esau even while they were still inside their mother's womb.[9] They were placed in the positions of Cain or Abel based solely upon the distinction of who was to be the firstborn son. When Jacob was blessing his two grandchildren, Ephraim and Manasseh, he crossed his hands and laid his right hand on the head of Ephraim, the second son in the position of Abel, to give him the first and greater blessing.[10] According to this principle, God placed Cain and Abel in a position where each could deal with only one master, and had them offer sacrifices.[11]

When Cain and Abel offered their sacrifices, "The Lord had regard for Abel and his offering, but for Cain and his offering he had no regard."[12] Why did God accept Abel's offering but reject Cain's? God received Abel's sacrifice because he stood in a proper relationship with God. Also, he made the offering in an acceptable manner—through faith[13] and in line with God's will.[13] In this way, Abel successfully laid the foundation of faith in Adam's family. He serves as an example that any fallen person can make an offering acceptable to God provided he satisfies the necessary conditions.

God did not reject Cain's sacrifice because He hated him. Rather, because Cain stood in a position to relate with Satan which gave Satan rights over the sacrifice, God could not accept Cain's sacrifice unless he first made some condition justifying its acceptance. The example of Cain shows that in order for a person who has a connection with Satan to return to God's side, he must make a requisite indemnity condition. What indemnity condition should Cain have made? It was the indemnity condition to remove the fallen nature.

1.2 THE FOUNDATION OF SUBSTANCE

Had Cain fulfilled the indemnity condition to remove the fallen nature, God would have gladly accepted his sacrifice. The foundation of substance would then have been laid in Adam's family. How should Cain have made the indemnity condition to remove the fallen nature? The first human ancestors fell by succumbing to the Archangel, from whom they inherited the fallen nature. To remove the fallen nature, a

---

8. Num. 1:50-53; Deut. 31:25
9. Rom. 9:11-13
10. Gen. 48:14
11. Gen. 4:3-5
12. Gen. 4:4
13. Heb. 11:4

person must make an indemnity condition in accordance with the Principle of Restoration through Indemnity, by taking a course which reverses the process through which human beings initially acquired the fallen nature.

The Archangel fell because he did not love Adam; rather, he envied Adam, who was receiving more love from God than he. This was the cause of the first primary characteristic of the fallen nature: failing to take God's standpoint. To remove this characteristic of the fallen nature, Cain, who stood in the Archangel's position, should have taken God's standpoint by loving Abel, who stood in Adam's position.

The Archangel fell because he did not respect Adam as God's mediator and did not receive God's love through him; rather, he attempted to seize Adam's position. This was the cause of the second primary characteristic of the fallen nature: leaving one's proper position. To remove this characteristic of the fallen nature, Cain, who stood in the Archangel's position, should have received God's love through Abel, who stood in Adam's position, respecting him as God's mediator. In this way, Cain should have maintained his proper position.

The Archangel fell when he claimed dominion over Eve and Adam, who were his rightful lords. This was the cause of the third primary characteristic of the fallen nature: reversing dominion. To remove this characteristic of the fallen nature, Cain, who stood in the Archangel's position, should have obediently submitted to Abel, who stood in Adam's position. By accepting Abel's dominion, Cain should have rectified the order of dominion.

God told Adam not to eat of the fruit of the tree of the knowledge of good and evil. Adam should have conveyed this Will to Eve, who in turn should have conveyed it to the Archangel, thus multiplying goodness. Instead, the Archangel conveyed to Eve his evil will that it was permissible to eat of the fruit. Eve in turn conveyed this evil will to Adam and led him to fall. This was the cause of the fourth primary characteristic of the fallen nature: multiplying evil. To remove this characteristic of the fallen nature, Cain, who stood in the Archangel's position, should have been receptive to the intentions of Abel, who stood closer to God, and learned God's Will from him. Thus, Cain should have made a foundation to multiply goodness.

There are many instances in human life which correspond to the situation of Cain and Abel. When we look within ourselves, we find that our innermost mind delights in the law of God.[14] It is in the position of

---

14. Rom. 7:22
15. Rom. 7:25

Abel, while our body, which serves the law of sin,[15] is in the position of Cain. We can become good only if our body obediently follows our mind, which directs us toward goodness. All too often, however, our body rebels against the mind's directions, repeating by analogy Cain's murder of Abel. This is how evil grows within us. For this reason, the religious way of life requires that we make our body submit to the commands of our higher mind, just as Cain should have submitted to Abel and followed him.

We can also see this in the practice of making offerings. Since we fell to the position of being "deceitful above all things,"[16] the things of creation stand in the position of Abel. Hence, through offering them we can go before God. To give another example, the universal tendency to seek out good leaders and righteous friends stems from our innermost desire to come before God through an Abel figure who is closer to God. By uniting with him, we can come closer to God ourselves. The Christian faith teaches us to be meek and humble. By this way of life, we may meet our Abel figure and thus secure the way to go before God.

In relationships at every level of society—from those between individuals to those at the level of families, communities, societies, nations and the world—we find that one party is in the role of Abel and the other is in the role of Cain. In order to restore society at each level to the state originally envisioned by God, those in the Cain position should respect and obey those in the Abel position. Jesus came to this world as the Abel figure to whom all of humanity should have submitted and followed. For this reason, he said, "no one comes to the Father, but by me."[17]

If Cain had yielded to Abel and thus fulfilled the indemnity condition to remove the fallen nature in Adam's family, they would have established the foundation of substance. Together with the foundation of faith already laid, Adam's family would have established the foundation for the Messiah. The Messiah would then have come to them and restored the original four position foundation. Instead, Cain killed Abel. In murdering Abel, Cain repeated the sin of the Archangel. That is, he re-enacted the very process which had given rise to the primary characteristics of the fallen nature. Adam's family thus failed to lay the foundation of substance. Consequently, God's providence of restoration through Adam's family could not be fulfilled.

---

16. Jer. 17:9
17. John 14:6

1.3 The Foundation for the Messiah in Adam's Family

The foundation for the Messiah is established by first restoring through indemnity the foundation of faith and then establishing the foundation of substance. With regard to their requisite sacrifices, the foundation of faith is restored by making an acceptable *symbolic offering*, and the foundation of substance is established by making an acceptable *substantial offering*. Let us examine the meaning and purpose of the symbolic offering and the substantial offering.

The three great blessings, which are God's purpose of creation, were to be realized when Adam and Eve, having perfected their individual character, became husband and wife. They were to give birth to good children, raise a good family, and master the natural world. However, due to the Fall, the three great blessings were lost. The way to restore them requires us to take the opposite course. First, we must establish the foundation of faith by making the symbolic offering, which fulfills a condition of indemnity for the restoration of all things and a condition of indemnity for the symbolic restoration of people. Next, we must establish the foundation of substance by making the substantial offering, which fulfills an indemnity condition for the restoration of first the children and then the parents. On this basis, we can establish the foundation for the Messiah.

We can consider the meaning and purpose of the symbolic offering in two ways. First, as discussed above,[18] Satan gained dominion over the natural world through his domination of human beings, its rightful rulers. For this reason it is written, "the whole creation has been groaning in travail."[19] Thus, one purpose for making the symbolic offering of all things is to enable all things to stand as God's actual object partners in symbol. It fulfills an indemnity condition for the restoration of the natural world to its original relationship with God. Second, since human beings fell to a position lower than the things of creation,[20] in order for them to come before God, they must go through all things. This follows from the Principle of Creation, which requires that one approach God through that which is closer to Him. The second purpose for making the symbolic offering is thus to fulfill an indemnity condition for the symbolic restoration of human beings.

The substantial offering, on the other hand, is an internal offering. Following the order of creation, in which God created all things first and human beings afterwards, this internal offering to restore human

---
18. cf. Fall 4.1
19. Rom. 8:22
20. Jer. 17:9

beings can only be made on the basis of an acceptable symbolic offering. After the symbolic offering fulfills an indemnity condition both for the restoration of all things and for the symbolic restoration of human beings, we must make the substantial offering, which fulfills an indemnity condition for the complete restoration of human beings. The substantial offering means fulfilling the indemnity condition to remove the fallen nature. This is essential for the actual restoration of human beings. The substantial offering is carried out when a person in Cain's position honors the person in Abel's position and sets him above himself as an offering. Through this, they fulfill the indemnity condition to be restored as good children. At the same time, it is also reckoned as the indemnity condition for the restoration of their parents. In this manner, the substantial offering can meet God's expectation.

How can we understand the indemnity condition for the restoration of the parents? To establish the foundation for the Messiah in Adam's family, Adam should have been the one to establish the foundation of faith by making the symbolic offering. However, as explained above, Adam could not make the offering, because if he had tried, his two masters, God and Satan, would have contended over it—an unprincipled situation. In addition, there is another reason from the aspect of feeling and heart. Fallen Adam was the very sinner who caused God the heartache and grief which was to last many thousands of years. He was not worthy to be the beloved of God's Heart, with whom God could work directly to further the providence of restoration.

Accordingly, God chose Adam's second son Abel in his stead and had Abel make the symbolic offering. Abel fulfilled the indemnity conditions for the restoration of all things and the symbolic restoration of human beings. If Cain and Abel had then fulfilled the indemnity condition for the restoration of the children by making an acceptable substantial offering, their father Adam would have shared in the victory of this foundation of substance. Thus, Adam's family would have established the foundation for the Messiah.

Before the substantial offering can be made, the central figure of the offering, the one who is to be offered, must be chosen. God had Abel make the symbolic offering for two reasons: first, to have him establish the foundation of faith in Adam's place; second, to qualify him to be the central figure of the substantial offering.

Cain was the one to fulfill the indemnity condition to remove the fallen nature, yet his accomplishment would have resulted in the entire family of Adam fulfilling the condition. How was this possible? It may be compared to the situation of the first human ancestors, who could have helped God accomplish His entire Will had they obeyed His Word. It may also be compared to the situation of the Jewish people of Jesus' day, who could have helped Jesus accomplish his will to bring complete salvation to humankind had they believed in him. If Cain had yielded to Abel and fulfilled the indemnity condition to remove the fallen nature, both children would have been regarded as having fulfilled the indemnity condition together. Cain and Abel were the offspring of Adam, the embodiment of both good and evil. Had they unshackled themselves from Satan's chains by fulfilling the indemnity condition to remove the fallen nature, then Adam, their father, also could have separated from Satan and stood upon the foundation of substance. Thus, the foundation for the Messiah would have been established by the family as a whole. In short, had Cain and Abel succeeded in making the symbolic and substantial offerings, the indemnity condition for the restoration of the parents would have been fulfilled.

When Abel made his sacrifice in a manner acceptable to God, he fulfilled the indemnity condition to restore Adam's foundation of faith and firmly secured his position as the central figure of the substantial offering. However, when Cain murdered Abel, they re-enacted the Fall, in which the Archangel murdered Eve spiritually. Needless to say, they did not fulfill the indemnity condition to remove the fallen nature and failed to make the substantial offering. Hence, neither the foundation of substance nor the foundation for the Messiah could be established. God's providence of restoration in Adam's family came to naught.

1.4 Some Lessons from Adam's Family

The failure of God's providence of restoration in Adam's family teaches us something about God's conditional predestination of the accomplishment of His Will and His absolute respect for the human portion of responsibility. From the time of creation, God predestined that His Will be accomplished based on the combined fulfillment of God's portion of responsibility and the human portion of responsibility. God could not instruct Cain and Abel on how to properly make their sacrifices because it was their portion of responsibility that Cain make his sacrifice with Abel's help.

Second, even after Cain killed Abel, God began a new chapter of His providence by raising Seth in Abel's place. This shows us that God has absolutely predestined that His Will shall one day be fulfilled, even though His predestination concerning individual human beings is conditional.

God foreordained that Abel succeed as the central figure of the substantial offering contingent upon fulfilling his own portion of responsibility. Therefore, when Abel could not complete his responsibility, God chose Seth in his place and carried on His efforts to accomplish the Will, which is predestined to be fulfilled without fail.

Third, through the offerings of Cain and Abel, God teaches us that fallen people must constantly seek for an Abel-type person. By honoring, obeying and following him, we can accomplish God's Will even without understanding every aspect of it.

The providence which God worked to accomplish through Adam's family has been repeated over and over again due to the faithlessness of human beings. Consequently, this course remains as the indemnity course which we ourselves must walk. The providence of restoration in Adam's family thus provides us with many valuable lessons for our own path of faith.

Section 2

The Providence of Restoration in Noah's Family

Cain killed Abel, thereby preventing the providence of restoration in Adam's family from being accomplished. Nevertheless, God had predestined absolutely the fulfillment of the purpose of creation, and His Will remained unchangeable. Hence, upon the foundation of the loyal heart which Abel demonstrated toward Heaven, God chose Seth in his place.[21] From among Seth's descendants, God chose Noah's family to substitute for Adam's family and commenced a new chapter in His providence.

It is written that God judged the world by the flood: "And God said to Noah, 'I have determined to make an end of all flesh; for the earth is filled with violence through them; behold, I will destroy them with the earth.'"[22] This shows us that Noah's time was the Last Days. God intended to accomplish the purpose of creation after the flood judgment by sending the Messiah upon the foundation laid by Noah's family. For this reason, Noah's family was responsible to fulfill the indemnity condition to restore the foundation of faith, and then the indemnity condition to restore the foundation of substance. They were to restore through indemnity the foundation for the Messiah, which Adam's family had failed to lay.

---

21. Gen. 4:25
22. Gen. 6:13

2.1 THE FOUNDATION OF FAITH

2.1.1 THE CENTRAL FIGURE FOR THE FOUNDATION OF FAITH

In the providence of restoration through Noah's family, Noah was the central figure to restore the foundation of faith. God called Noah ten generations or sixteen hundred biblical years after Adam for the purpose of fulfilling the Will which He had intended to realize through Adam. Accordingly, God bestowed His blessings upon Noah, "be fruitful and multiply,"[23] much as earlier He had bestowed the three great blessings upon Adam.[24] In this sense, Noah was the second ancestor of humanity.

Noah was called when "the earth was filled with violence."[25] Enduring all kinds of derision and mockery, he worked for 120 years on a mountain to build the ark in absolute obedience to God's instructions. Upon this condition of faith, God could bring on the flood judgment centered on Noah's family. In this sense, Noah was the first father of faith. Although we commonly regard Abraham as the father of faith, in fact, Noah was to have had that honor. As we shall see, it was due to his son Ham's sinful act that the mission of the father of faith was transferred from Noah to Abraham.

In the case of Adam, it was explained that although he should have been the central figure to restore the foundation of faith, he could not offer the sacrifice himself. Noah's situation was different. He was called by God upon the foundation of Abel's loyal and faithful heart in making an acceptable symbolic offering. In regard to his lineage, Noah was a descendant of Seth, who had been chosen to replace Abel. Furthermore, Noah was a righteous man in the sight of God.[26] For these reasons, he was qualified to make the symbolic offering to God by building the ark.

2.1.2 THE OBJECT FOR THE CONDITION IN RESTORING THE FOUNDATION OF FAITH

The object for the condition by which Noah was to restore the foundation of faith was the ark. The ark was full of symbolic significance. Before Noah could stand in place of Adam as the second human ancestor, he first had to make an indemnity condition for the restoration of the cosmos, which had been lost to Satan due to Adam's fall. Hence,

---

23. Gen. 9:7
24. Gen. 1:28
25. Gen. 6:11
26. Gen. 6:9

the object for this condition, which Noah had to offer in an acceptable manner, should symbolize the new cosmos. He offered the ark as this object.

The ark was built with three decks, symbolizing the cosmos which had been created through the three stages of the growing period. The eight members of Noah's family who entered the ark represented the eight members of Adam's family who, having been invaded by Satan, had to be restored through indemnity. Thus, the ark symbolized the cosmos; Noah, its master, symbolized God; the members of his family symbolized humanity; and the animals brought into the ark symbolized the entire natural world.

After the ark was completed, God judged the world with the flood for forty days. What was the purpose of the flood? According to the Principle of Creation, human beings were created to serve only one master. Since humankind was under bondage to Satan, full of corruption and debauchery, for God to relate with them He would have to assume the position of a second master. That would be unprincipled. Therefore, God brought about the flood judgment, eliminating sinful humanity in order to raise up a family who would relate only with Him.

Why did God choose a forty-day period for the flood? The significance of the forty-day period should be understood in terms of the meaning of the numbers four and ten. The number ten signifies unity.[27] It was ten generations after Adam when God called upon Noah to restore through indemnity the Will which He could not fulfill through Adam. By fulfilling a period of indemnity containing the number ten, God meant to bring the dispensation back into unity with His Will. Furthermore, since the goal of restoration is to complete the four position foundation, God worked to raise up each of these ten generations by setting up an indemnity period to restore the number four. In total, the period from Adam to Noah was an indemnity period to restore the number forty. Due to the lustfulness of the people of those days, however, this indemnity period of the number forty was defiled by Satan. The dispensation of Noah's ark was God's new attempt to complete the four position foundation. Therefore, God set the period of the flood judgment at forty days as the indemnity period to restore the number forty, which had been defiled when the earlier period was lost to Satan. By fulfilling this numerical period of indemnity, God intended to restore the foundation of faith.

---

27. cf. Periods 2.4

The number forty thus became characteristic of *dispensations for the separation of Satan*, which are necessary for restoring the foundation of faith. There are many examples of this: Noah's forty-day flood; the four hundred years from Noah to Abraham; the Israelites' four hundred years of slavery in Egypt; Moses' two forty-day fasts; the forty days of spying in Canaan; the Israelites' forty years of wandering in the wilderness; the forty-year reigns of King Saul, King David and King Solomon; Elijah's forty-day fast; Jonah's prophecy that Nineveh would be destroyed in forty days; Jesus' forty-day fast and prayer in the wilderness; and the forty-day period from Jesus' resurrection to his ascension.

In the Bible we read that at the end of forty days of rain, Noah sent forth from the ark a raven and a dove.[28] Let us examine what future providential situations this foreshadowed, as it is written, "Surely the Lord God does nothing, without revealing his secret to his servants the prophets."[29] By building the ark and passing through the forty-day flood judgment, Noah fulfilled an indemnity condition for the restoration of the cosmos. The flood corresponds to the period of chaos before the creation of the universe when "the Spirit of God was moving over the face of the waters."[30] Accordingly, the works which God performed around the ark at the end of the forty-day flood symbolized the entire course of history following God's creation of heaven and earth.

What was foreshadowed when Noah sent forth the raven, which circled about looking for a place to land until the waters subsided? It signified that Satan would be looking for a condition through which he could invade Noah's family, just as the Archangel vied for Eve's love soon after the creation of human beings, and just as Satan couched at the door looking for an opportunity to invade the offerings of Cain and Abel.[31]

What was foreshadowed when Noah sent forth the dove three times? Although it is written in the Bible that Noah sent out the dove to see if the water had subsided, that was not its only purpose. Certainly Noah could have looked out the opening from which he set forth the dove to examine the situation for himself. The sending forth of the dove had a deeper significance connected with the mysterious Will of God. Seven days after God proclaimed the flood judgment through Noah, the flood began.[32] Forty days later, the dove was first sent out. It flew about but then returned to the ark because it found no place to land, and Noah

---

28. Gen. 8:6-7
29. Amos 3:7
30. Gen. 1:2
31. Gen. 4:7
32. Gen. 7:10

took it back inside.³³ The dove, when it was sent out the first time, represented the first Adam. God created Adam with the hope that His ideal of creation, which He had cherished from before time, would be realized in Adam as the perfect incarnation of the divine ideal on earth. Due to Adam's fall, however, God could not realize the divine ideal on earth through him. God thus had to withdraw His ideal from the earth for a time and postpone its fulfillment to a later date.

Seven days later, Noah sent forth the dove a second time. Still the water had not yet dried, and again the dove returned. This time it carried in its mouth an olive leaf, indicating that there would be a place for it to land the next time.³⁴ The dove, when it was sent out the second time, symbolized Jesus, the second Adam, whose coming would be God's second attempt to realize the perfect incarnation of the divine ideal on the earth. These verses foreshadowed that if the chosen people were to disbelieve in Jesus at his coming, then he would have "nowhere to lay his head"³⁵ and thus would not be able to realize God's complete Will on the earth. In that situation, Jesus would have to go to the cross and return to God's bosom, leaving behind the promise of the Second Advent. The dove returned to the ark because the water had not yet dried up. By analogy, had more of the Jewish people faithfully attended Jesus, he would have found a secure place to stand among them. He would not have been crucified and would have gone on to build the Kingdom of Heaven on earth.

After another seven days had passed, Noah sent out the dove for the third time. This time the dove did not return to the ark, for the ground was dry.³⁶ The dove, when it was sent out the third time, symbolizes Christ at the Second Advent, who is to come as the third Adam. This foreshadowed that when Christ comes again, he will surely be able to realize God's ideal of creation, which will never again be withdrawn from the earth. When the dove did not return, Noah finally disembarked from the ark and walked upon the earth, which had been purged of sin and made new. This foreshadowed that when the ideal of creation is realized on the earth through the work of the third Adam, the new Jerusalem will descend from Heaven and the dwelling of God will be with men.³⁷

The foreshadowing in this story should be interpreted in light of the principle explained earlier: God's providence of restoration may be

---

33. Gen. 8:9
34. Gen. 8:10-11
35. Luke 9:58
36. Gen. 8:12
37. Rev. 21:1-3

prolonged if the person entrusted with the providence fails in his responsibility.[38] Due to Adam's faithlessness and failure to complete his responsibility, Jesus had to come as the second Adam. Furthermore, if the Jewish people were to disbelieve in Jesus and thus fail to complete their responsibility, Christ would certainly have to come again as the third Adam. Just as the creation of heaven and earth took a seven-day period, the seven-day intervals for sending forth the dove indicate to us that the restoration of heaven and earth requires certain providential periods of time.

2.2 THE FOUNDATION OF SUBSTANCE

Noah successfully restored through indemnity the foundation of faith by fulfilling the dispensation of the ark and thereby making a symbolic offering acceptable to God. In doing so, Noah fulfilled both the indemnity condition for the restoration of all things and the indemnity condition for the symbolic restoration of human beings. Upon this foundation, Noah's sons, Shem and Ham, were then to have stood in the position of Cain and Abel, respectively. Had they then succeeded in the substantial offering by fulfilling the indemnity condition to remove the fallen nature, they would have laid the foundation of substance.

For Noah's family to make an acceptable substantial offering, Ham, Noah's second son, was to restore the position of Abel, Adam's second son. He was supposed to become the central figure of the substantial offering, just as Abel was the central figure of his family's substantial offering. In Adam's family, Abel had successfully made the symbolic offering in Adam's place to restore through indemnity the foundation of faith and to be qualified as the central figure of the substantial offering. In the case of Noah's family, it was Noah, not Ham, who made the symbolic offering. Therefore, for Ham to stand in the position of Abel, as one who has succeeded in making the symbolic offering, he had to become inseparably one in heart with his father, Noah. Let us examine how God worked to help Ham become one in heart with Noah.

The Bible reports that when Ham saw his father lying naked in his tent, he felt ashamed of Noah and took offense. Ham stirred up the same feelings in his brothers, Shem and Japheth. Swayed by Ham to feel ashamed of their father's nakedness and turning their faces so as not to behold the sight, they walked backwards and covered their father's body with a garment. This act constituted a sin, so much so that Noah

---

38. cf. Predestination 2

rebuked Ham, cursing his son to be a slave to his brothers.[39]

Why did God conduct this dispensation? Why was it such a sin to feel ashamed of nakedness? To understand these matters, let us first recall what constitutes sin.[40] Satan cannot manifest his powers—including the power to exist and act—unless he first secures an object partner with whom he can make a common base and engage in a reciprocal relationship of give and take. Whenever a person makes a condition for Satan to invade, it means that he has allowed himself to become Satan's object partner, thereby empowering Satan to act. This constitutes sin.

Next, let us examine why God tested Ham by having him behold Noah's nakedness. We saw that the ark symbolized the cosmos, and that the events occurring immediately after the dispensation of the ark represented the events which took place immediately after the creation of the cosmos. Hence, Noah's position right after the flood was much like that of Adam after the creation of heaven and earth.

Adam and Eve before the Fall were close in heart and innocently open with each other and with God; as it is written, they were not ashamed of their nakedness.[41] Yet after they fell, they felt ashamed of their nakedness. They covered their lower parts with fig leaves and hid among the trees of the garden, fearing that God would see them.[42] This shame was an indication of their inner reality, for they had formed a bond of blood ties with Satan by committing sin with their sexual parts. By covering their lower parts and hiding, they expressed their guilty consciences, which made them feel ashamed to come before God.

Noah, who had severed his ties to Satan through the forty-day flood judgment, was supposed to secure the position of Adam right after the creation of the universe. God expected that the members of Noah's family would react to Noah's nakedness without any feelings of shame and without any thought to conceal his body. God wanted to recover the joyful heart which He had felt when looking at Adam and Eve in their innocence before the Fall by taking delight in the innocence of Noah's family. To fulfill such a profound wish, God had Noah lie naked. Had Ham been one in heart with Noah, regarding him with the same heart and from the same standpoint as God, he would have looked upon his father's nakedness without any sense of shame. He thus would have fulfilled the indemnity condition to restore in Noah's family the state of Adam and Eve's innocence before the Fall.

---

39. Gen. 9:20-25
40. cf. Fall 4.5
41. Gen. 2:25
42. Gen. 3:7-8

We can thus understand that when Noah's sons felt ashamed of their father's nakedness and covered his body, it was tantamount to acknowledging that they, like Adam's family after the Fall, had formed a shameful bond of kinship with Satan and were thus unworthy to come before God. Satan, like the raven hovering over the water, was looking for a condition to invade Noah's family. He attacked the family by taking Noah's sons as his object partners when they in effect acknowledged that they were of his lineage.

When Ham felt ashamed of his father's nakedness and acted to cover it up, he made a condition for Satan to enter; hence his feeling and act constituted a sin. Consequently, Ham could not restore through indemnity the position of Abel from which to make the substantial offering. Since he could not establish the foundation of substance, the providence of restoration in Noah's family ended in failure.

Is it always sinful to regard nakedness with a sense of shame? No. Noah's was a special case. In the position of Adam, Noah had the mission to remove all of Adam's conditions which had left him vulnerable to Satan's attack. By demonstrating that they neither felt ashamed of Noah's nakedness nor would attempt to cover it, Noah's family would have fulfilled the indemnity condition to restore the position of Adam's family in its original innocence before it had joined with Satan in a kinship of blood. Therefore, this was an indemnity condition which only Noah's family was required to fulfill.

2.3 Some Lessons from Noah's Family

It is difficult for anyone to understand how Noah persisted in building the ark on the mountain over 120 long years, all the while enduring harsh criticism and ridicule. Ham knew well that his family had been saved by his father's labors. Considering these things, Ham should have had such respect for his father that he would overcome his personal offense at Noah's nakedness and have some understanding of it. Yet instead of trusting Noah, who had been justified by Heaven, Ham criticized him from a self-centered perspective and showed his displeasure by his actions. His disrespect had the effect of frustrating God's long labors to work His providence through Noah's family. We, too, need humility, obedience and patience to walk the path toward Heaven.

Next, the providence in Noah's family teaches us about God's conditional predestination of the fulfillment of His Will and His respect for the human portion of responsibility. God found Noah's family after sixteen hundred years of preparation. He guided Noah for 120 years while he constructed the ark and raised up his family at the cost of sacrificing the rest of humanity in the flood. However, even though they had been His beloved in the providence of restoration, when Ham made his seemingly small mistake, allowing Satan to taint them, the entire Will centering on Noah's family came to naught.

Finally, the providence through Noah's family teaches us about God's conditional predestination of human beings. Despite the fact that God had striven arduously for a long time to find Noah and raise him up as the father of faith, when his family could not fulfill its responsibility, God, though regretful, did not hesitate to abandon him and choose Abraham in his place.

SECTION 3

THE PROVIDENCE OF RESTORATION IN ABRAHAM'S FAMILY

Due to Ham's fallen act, the providence of restoration in Noah's family was not fulfilled. Nevertheless, God had absolutely predestined that the purpose of creation would one day be realized. Therefore, upon the foundation of Noah's heart of loyalty toward Heaven, God called Abraham and commenced a new chapter in the providence of restoration with his family.

Abraham's family was to restore the foundation for the Messiah, which Noah's family had left incomplete, and receive the Messiah upon that foundation. Thus, as Noah before him, Abraham had to restore through indemnity the foundation of faith, and his sons had to restore through indemnity the foundation of substance.

3.1 THE FOUNDATION OF FAITH

3.1.1 THE CENTRAL FIGURE FOR THE FOUNDATION OF FAITH

In the providence of restoration in Abraham's family, the central figure to restore the foundation of faith was Abraham. God chose Abraham to inherit the mission of fulfilling the Will which He had tried to fulfill with Noah. However, Abraham could not inherit this mission unless he first restored through indemnity all the conditions which had been given to Noah to fulfill, but which were lost to Satan due to Ham's sin.

The first conditions which Noah's family lost to Satan were the ten generations from Adam to Noah and the forty-day period of judgment. Therefore, Abraham had to restore through indemnity another ten generations. Each of these ten generations was to restore the number forty, which represented the flood judgment. Once the forty-day flood ended in failure, the restoration of each generation had to span its entire length; this could not be accomplished in only forty days. The providence to restore the flood in each of those ten generations had to take a longer period of time: forty years. This is similar to the situation in Moses' time, when restoration of the failed forty-day spying mission required the people to wander in the wilderness for forty years.[43] Therefore, after an indemnity period of ten generations and four hundred years had passed since Noah,[44] God chose Abraham to inherit Noah's mission.

The next set of conditions which Noah's family lost to Satan was the position of the father of faith and the position of Ham, who was to take up the role of Abel. Therefore, Abraham could not stand in Noah's position without first restoring through indemnity the roles of the father of faith and of Ham. To assume the role of the father of faith in place of Noah, Abraham had to make a symbolic offering in faith with a loyal heart, just as Noah did when he built the ark. Next, how could Abraham restore the position of Ham? Ham was to have represented Abel, the most beloved of God; both were second sons and chosen to be the central figures of the substantial offering. Since Satan claimed Ham, according to the principle of restoration through indemnity, God needed to claim someone whom Satan loved most. This is the reason God called Abraham, who was the firstborn son of Terah, an idolator.[45]

Abraham was to inherit the mission of Noah and thus the mission of Adam. In this capacity, he represented restored Adam. As God had blessed Adam and Noah, God also blessed Abraham:

> I will make of you a great nation, and I will bless you, and make your name great, so that you will be a blessing. I will bless those who bless you, and him who curses you I will curse; and by you all the families of the earth shall bless themselves. —*Gen. 12:2-3*

After receiving this blessing, in obedience to God's command, Abraham left his father's house in Haran and entered Canaan with his wife Sarah, his nephew Lot, and all his belongings and servants.[46] In this sense, God

---

43. Num. 14:34
44. According to the Bible, God shortened the human life-span immediately after Noah's generation. Hence, the ten generations from Adam to Noah took sixteen hundred years, while the ten generations from Noah to Abraham took only four hundred years.
45. Josh. 24:2-3
46. Gen. 12:4-5

set Abraham's course as the model course for restoring Canaan, which Jacob and Moses would walk in their days. Jacob and Moses would take their family members and all their belongings out of Haran and Egypt, respectively, and bring them back to Canaan while suffering many hardships along the way. Abraham's course also foreshadowed the course which Jesus would one day walk: to take humanity and all things out of Satan's world and bring them back to God's world.[47]

3.1.2 The Objects for the Condition Offered for the Foundation of Faith

3.1.2.1 Abraham's Symbolic Offering

God commanded Abraham to offer a dove and a pigeon, a ram and a goat, and a heifer.[48] These were the objects for the condition which he offered to restore the foundation of faith. But before he could make the symbolic offering, Abraham had to demonstrate right faith, just as Noah before him was accounted righteous prior to building the ark as his symbolic offering. The Bible does not explain clearly how Noah demonstrated his faith. But from the verse, "Noah was a righteous man, blameless in his generation; Noah walked with God,"[49] we can deduce that Noah demonstrated faith before he was deemed worthy to receive God's commandment to build the ark. In truth, those who walk the providence of restoration must continually strengthen their faith.[50] Let us investigate how Abraham strengthened his faith in preparation for making the symbolic offering.

Since Noah was the second human ancestor, for Abraham to restore the position of Noah, he also had to assume Adam's position. For this reason, he was required to make a symbolic indemnity condition to restore the position of Adam's family before he could make the actual symbolic offering.

In this regard, the Bible gives an account of a trip Abraham made to Egypt because of a famine.[51] In Egypt, Abraham feared that the Pharoh would desire his beautiful wife Sarah and kill him if he knew he was her husband. While she posed as Abraham's sister, the Pharoh took Sarah for himself. Thereupon, God chastised the Pharaoh, Abraham took back his wife along with his nephew Lot and the abun-

---

47. cf. Moses and Jesus 1.2
48. Gen. 15:9
49. Gen. 6:9
50. Rom. 1:17
51. Gen. 12:10-20

dant wealth which the Pharaoh had given him, and they left Egypt.

Without knowing it, Abraham walked this providential course to make a symbolic indemnity condition to restore the position of Adam's family. When the Archangel took Eve—capturing under his dominion all of Eve's descendants and the natural world—Adam and Eve were still brother and sister. For Abraham to make the indemnity condition to restore this, he was deprived of Sarah, who was playing the role of his sister, by the Pharaoh, who represented Satan. He then had to take her back from the Pharaoh as his wife, together with Lot as the representative of all humanity, and wealth symbolizing the natural world. This course which Abraham walked was the model course for Jesus to walk in his day. Once he had fulfilled this indemnity condition, Abraham was deemed ready to make the symbolic offering.

What was the significance of Abraham's symbolic offering? For Abraham to become the father of faith, he had to restore through indemnity the position of Noah, whom God had intended to raise up as the father of faith, as well as Noah's family. Furthermore, he had to restore the position of Adam and his family. Abraham was thus required to offer in an acceptable manner objects for the condition to restore all that Cain and Abel were supposed to accomplish through their sacrifices, and all that Noah's family was trying to accomplish through the dispensation of the ark. Abraham's symbolic offering consisted of objects with such symbolic meanings.

Abraham offered three types of objects as the condition for his symbolic offering: first, a dove and a pigeon; second, a ram and a goat; and third, a heifer. These three sacrifices symbolized the cosmos, which was completed through the three stages of the growing period. The dove represented the formation stage. When Jesus was baptized by John the Baptist at the Jordan River, the Spirit of God descended and alighted upon him in the form of a dove.[52] This is because Jesus came to bring completion to the Old Testament Age, which, as the formation stage of the providence, was symbolized by the dove. Moreover, there was a second reason for the vision of the dove alighting on Jesus. Jesus was to restore Abraham's mistake in offering this dove, which, as we shall see, Satan snatched away.

The ram represented the growth stage. Once Jesus had brought fulfillment to the Old Testament Age, thus restoring everything represented by the dove, he commenced the New Testament Age at the growth stage of the providence, when everything represented by the ram was to be restored. After John the Baptist testified that he had seen

---

52. Matt. 3:16

the Spirit descend on Jesus as a dove—meaning that Jesus was the one to complete the formation stage of the providence—he testified that Jesus would begin the growth stage mission, saying, "Behold, the Lamb of God, who takes away the sins of the world!"[53]

The heifer represented the completion stage. It is written that once, when Samson put forth a riddle to the Philistines, they obtained the answer by having Samson's wife press him to reveal it. Samson said to them, "If you had not plowed with my heifer, you would not have found out my riddle,"[54] here metaphorically calling his wife a heifer. Jesus came as the bridegroom to all humanity. All devout believers should become his brides, awaiting the time of his return. After these brides celebrate the marriage of the Lamb with Jesus, their bridegroom, they are to live in the Kingdom of Heaven in spiritual oneness with him as his wives. Therefore, the Completed Testament Age following the Second Advent of Jesus is the age of the heifer, or the age of the wife. The reason why some spiritual mediums have received the revelation that the present era is the age of a cow or heifer is because we are entering the completion stage.

What were the three sacrifices to indemnify? Abraham was to restore by this offering all that God could not restore through the symbolic offerings made by the families of Adam and Noah—offerings that were made properly but then forfeited to Satan due to subsequent failures. Abraham's offering was also to make a symbolic indemnity condition as restitution for their failures in making the substantial offering. In other words, the purpose of Abraham's symbolic offering of the three types of objects for the condition was to restore in his generation (horizontally) all the indemnity conditions which had accumulated in the course of the providence (vertically) through the three generations of Adam, Noah and Abraham.

Why did Abraham place the three sacrifices—the dove and pigeon, the ram and goat, and the heifer, symbolizing the formation, growth and completion stages—on one altar? Before the Fall, Adam was responsible to grow through all three stages in his one lifetime. Similarly, Abraham, now in the position of Adam, was supposed to restore, all at once, the long providence which God had conducted through the three providential generations of Adam (formation), Noah (growth) and Abraham (completion). Through one offering, he could restore all the defiled conditions containing the number three. The symbolism of Abraham's sacrifice reveals God's Will to fulfill the entire providence of

---

53. John 1:29
54. Judg. 14:18

restoration once and for all.

> Now let us study how Abraham made the symbolic offering:
>
> He said to him, "Bring me a heifer three years old, a she-goat three years old, a ram three years old, a turtledove, and a young pigeon." And he brought him all these, cut them in two, and laid each half over against the other; but he did not cut the birds in two. And when the birds of prey came down upon the carcasses, Abram drove them away. As the sun was going down, a deep sleep fell on Abram; and lo, a dread and great darkness fell upon him. Then the Lord said to Abram, "Know of a surety that your descendants will be sojourners in a land that is not theirs, and will be slaves there, and they will be oppressed for four hundred years."
> —Gen. 15:9-13

Because Abraham did not cut the dove and pigeon in two as he should have, birds of prey came down and defiled the sacrifices. As a result of his mistake, the Israelites were destined to enter Egypt and suffer hardships for four hundred years. Why was it a sin not to cut the birds in half? This question can be understood only with the help of the Principle.

Let us first investigate the reason why Abraham was instructed to cut the sacrifices in half. God's work of salvation aims to restore the sovereignty of goodness by first dividing good from evil and then destroying evil and uplifting the good. This is the reason Adam had to be divided into Cain and Abel before the sacrifice could be made. This is the reason why in Noah's day, God struck down evil through the flood judgment and winnowed out Noah's family as the good. God had Abraham cut the sacrifices in two before offering them, with the intention of doing the symbolic work of dividing good from evil, which was left unaccomplished by Adam and Noah.

The sacrifices were to be divided, first, to restore the situation in Adam's family in which Abel and Cain were divided into a representative of good and a representative of evil. Second, it was to restore the situation of having divided good from evil during the forty days of Noah's flood. Third, it was to make the symbolic condition to separate a realm of good sovereignty out of the universe ruled by Satan. Fourth, it was to make the condition to sanctify the offering by draining out the blood of death, which had entered fallen humanity when they were bound in blood-ties to Satan.

Why was it a sin not to divide the offering? First, not dividing the offering has the significance of not dividing Abel from Cain. Without being divided, the offering could not be acceptable to God because it did not provide Him with an Abel-type object partner which He could take. Consequently, the mistakes Cain and Abel had made in their sacrifices were not restored. Second, not dividing the offering was tantamount to repeating the failure of the providence in Noah's time, when good and evil remained undivided despite the flood. Like the failure of Noah's family, Abraham's failure to divide the offering also deprived God of His good object partner. Thus, it repeated the mistake which made the dispensation of the flood a failure. Third, not dividing the offering meant there was no symbolic condition to separate a realm of God's good sovereignty out of the universe under Satan's dominion. Fourth, because the blood of death was not drained out of it, not dividing the offering meant it could not be a sanctified offering acceptable to God. In other words, when Abraham offered the birds without first dividing them, it meant that he offered what had not been wrested from Satan's possession. His mistake had the effect of acknowledging Satan's claim of possession over them.

The dove, symbolizing the formation stage, remained in Satan's possession. Consequently, Satan also claimed the ram, symbolizing the growth stage, and the heifer, symbolizing the completion stage, both of which were to be fulfilled based upon the formation stage. Since it had the effect of handing over the entire symbolic offering to Satan, not dividing the birds constituted a sin.

Next, let us examine what is meant by the verse that birds of prey descended upon the carcasses. Since the Fall of the first human ancestors, Satan has always been stalking those with whom God worked to fulfill His Will. When Cain and Abel were making their sacrifices, Satan was couching at the door.[55] In the story of Noah, the raven circling about signifies how Satan was looking for an opportunity to invade Noah's family right after the flood.[56] Similarly, when Abraham was making his symbolic offering, Satan was on the lookout for an opportunity to seize the sacrifice. He profaned it as soon as he saw that the birds were not divided. The Bible describes this by the image of birds of prey descending upon the sacrifice.

Abraham's mistake in making the symbolic offering caused the offering to be defiled. All the conditions God intended to restore through it were lost. As a consequence, Abraham's descendants had to suffer oppression and slavery for four hundred years in the land of Egypt. Let us investigate the reason for this.

God called upon Abraham and commanded him to make the symbolic offering at the completion of a four-hundred-year period for the

---

55. Gen. 4:7
56. Gen. 8:7

separation of Satan. This period had been set up to restore through indemnity the ten generations from Adam to Noah and the forty-day period of the flood judgment, lost to Satan due to Ham's sin. It was also the indemnity period necessary to establish Abraham as the father of faith when he completed the symbolic offering. When Abraham's mistake in the symbolic offering allowed Satan to claim the offering as his, that four-hundred-year period was also lost to Satan. To re-create on the national level the situation before Abraham's failure in the symbolic offering, which was itself parallel to when Noah was called upon to build the ark, God set up another four-hundred-year period for the separation of Satan. During this period, the Israelites were slaves in Egypt. By enduring through this period, the Israelites were to restore—this time on the national level—the situations of Noah and Abraham at the outset of their missions as the fathers of faith, thereupon also laying the foundation for Moses to begin his mission. Hence, this period of slavery was both the time when the Israelites were being punished for Abraham's mistake and the time when they were laying the foundation to cut off ties to Satan and commence God's new providence.

As explained earlier, God had hoped to fulfill, all at once, the dispensations in the formation, growth and completion stages by having Abraham successfully make the symbolic offering of three types of sacrifices on one altar. Contrary to this plan, Abraham failed, repeating the mistakes of the past. Consequently, the providence centered on him was prolonged through the three generations of Abraham, Isaac and Jacob.

3.1.2.2 Abraham's Offering of Isaac

After Abraham failed in the symbolic offering, God commanded him to sacrifice his only son Isaac as a burnt offering.[57] In this way, God began a new dispensation for the purpose of restoring through indemnity Abraham's failure. According to the principle of predestination, when someone whom God has foreordained to accomplish a certain portion of His Will fails to complete his responsibility, God does not use him a second time. Why, then, did God work with Abraham again when he had him offer Isaac?

We can advance three reasons. First, the number three represents completion.[58] God's Principle requires that when the providence to lay the foundation for the Messiah takes place for the third time, it must be brought to completion. Therefore, God's providence to lay the foundation

---

57. Gen. 22:2
58. cf. Periods 2.4

for the Messiah, which began in Adam's family as the first dispensation and continued in Noah's family as the second dispensation, had to conclude in Abraham's family, which was the third dispensation. For this reason, Abraham was given the opportunity to fulfill a condition of indemnity, albeit at a greater price, and thereby make symbolic restoration of all he had lost when he failed in the earlier symbolic offering. This greater indemnity condition was the offering of his son Isaac as a sacrifice.

Second, as was explained earlier, when Abraham was making his sacrifice, he was in the position of Adam. Satan had attacked both Adam and his son Cain, defiling the family over the course of two generations. Hence, according to the principle of restoration through indemnity, God could work to take back Abraham and his son Isaac over the course of two generations.

Third, we learned that Noah could make the symbolic offering of the ark himself, even though he was in the same position as Adam who could not make the sacrifice directly. This is because he stood upon the merit of Abel, who had demonstrated a faithful heart when he succeeded in the symbolic offering. When Abraham was called by God, he stood on the merit of both Abel, who succeeded in the symbolic offering at the formation stage, and Noah, who succeeded in the symbolic offering at the growth stage. Upon this double foundation, Abraham was to make the symbolic offering at the completion stage. Accordingly, even though Abraham failed, God could raise him up and give him another chance to make an offering based on the accumulated merit of Abel's and Noah's faithful hearts.

Before he could offer Isaac as a sacrifice, Abraham once again had to demonstrate right faith by repeating the symbolic indemnity condition for the restoration of Adam's family, as he had when he was about to make the symbolic offering. This is the reason Abraham once again put Sarah in the position of his sister and let her be taken by a king, this time Abimelech of Gerar. After she became the king's wife, Abraham took her back. This time Abraham also took back with him slaves, who symbolized humanity, and riches, which symbolized the natural world.[59]

How did Abraham offer Isaac?

> When they came to the place of which God had told him, Abraham built an altar there, and laid the wood in order, and bound Isaac his son, and laid him on the altar, upon the wood. Then Abraham put forth his hand,

---

59. Gen. 20:1-18

> and took the knife to slay his son. But the angel of the Lord called to him from heaven, and said, "Abraham, Abraham!" And he said, "Here am I." He said, "Do not lay your hand on the lad or do anything to him; for now I know that you fear God, seeing you have not withheld your son, your only son, from me." —Gen. 22:9-12

Abraham's faith was absolute. In obedience to God's command, he was about to kill Isaac, his only son, intending to offer him as a burnt offering. God intervened at that moment and told Abraham not to kill the boy.

Abraham's zeal to do God's Will and his resolute actions, carried out with absolute faith, obedience and loyalty, lifted him up to the position of already having killed Isaac. Therefore, he completely separated Satan from Isaac. God commanded Abraham not to kill Isaac because Isaac, now severed of all ties to Satan, stood on God's side. We must also understand that when God said, "now I know . . ." He revealed both His reproach to Abraham for his earlier failure in the symbolic offering and His joy over the successful offering of Isaac. Because Abraham succeeded in his offering of Isaac, the providence of restoration in Abraham's family could be carried on by Isaac.

Abraham took three days to reach the place on Mt. Moriah where he was to offer his son Isaac as a burnt offering. This three-day period for purifying Isaac was to begin a new course in the providence. Thenceforth, a three-day period has been required for the separation of Satan at the start of new dispensations. We find many instances of such periods in the history of the providence. When Jacob was setting out from Haran with his family to begin the family course to restore Canaan, there was a three-day period for the separation of Satan.[60] Moses, too, led the Israelites through a three-day period for the separation of Satan as they left Egypt to begin the national course to restore Canaan.[61] When Jesus began the worldwide spiritual course to restore Canaan, he spent three days in the tomb to accomplish the separation of Satan.

3.1.2.3 Isaac's Position and His Symbolic Offering in the Sight of God

It was explained earlier that although Abraham's symbolic offering ended in failure, there remained some grounds in the Principle for the foundation for the Messiah to be established centered on him. Yet since he had failed to fulfill his responsibility, Abraham was not qualified to repeat the symbolic offering himself.[62] Somehow, God had to find a way

---

60. Gen. 31:20-22
61. Exod. 8:27
62. cf. Predestination 3

to regard Abraham as though he had not failed in the symbolic offering or caused the prolongation of the providence. To achieve this, God commanded Abraham to offer Isaac as a burnt offering.

God had previously promised Abraham that He would raise up a chosen people from the lineage of Isaac:

> Behold, the word of the Lord came to him, ". . . your own son shall be your heir." And he brought him outside and said, "Look toward heaven, and number the stars, if you are able to number them." Then he said to him, "So shall your descendants be." —*Gen. 15:4-5*

When Abraham was prepared to slay his son, even the son of the promise, he demonstrated utmost loyalty to Heaven. This act of faith was tantamount to Abraham killing himself—a self which had been defiled by Satan due to his earlier failure in the symbolic offering. Accordingly, when God saved Isaac from death, Abraham was also resurrected to life, now loosed from all the ties with which Satan had bound him when his symbolic offering was defiled. Furthermore, Abraham and Isaac attained inseparable oneness in their fidelity to God's Will.

Though Isaac and Abraham were two different individuals, when God brought them back to life, they became as one person in the sight of God. Even though the dispensation through Abraham had failed and was prolonged through Isaac, as long as Isaac succeeded, Isaac's victory would become Abraham's own victory. Therefore, God would be able to regard Abraham as not having failed and the dispensation as not having been prolonged.

It is not clear how old Isaac was when Abraham offered the boy as a sacrifice. He was old enough to carry the wood for the sacrifice,[63] and when he saw there was no lamb to be offered, he inquired of his father about it.[64] Isaac was apparently old enough to understand his father's intentions. We can infer that he helped his father, even though he knew that his father was preparing to offer him as the sacrifice.

If Isaac had resisted his father's attempt to offer him as a sacrifice, God definitely would not have accepted the offering. In fact, Isaac demonstrated a faith as great as that of Abraham. Together, their faith made the offering successful, and there was no way for Satan to retain his hold on them. In making the offering, Isaac and Abraham underwent a process of death and resurrection. As a result, two things were

---

63. Gen. 22:6
64. Gen. 22:7

accomplished. First, Abraham succeeded in the separation of Satan, who had invaded him because of his mistake in the symbolic offering. He restored through indemnity the position he had occupied before he had made the mistake and transferred his providential mission to Isaac from this restored position. Second, by faithfully obeying God's Will, Isaac inherited the divine mission from Abraham and demonstrated the faith which qualified him to make the symbolic offering.

After the divine mission had passed from Abraham to Isaac, Abraham offered the ram provided by God as the substitute for Isaac:

> Abraham lifted up his eyes and looked, and behold, behind him was a ram, caught in a thicket by his horns; and Abraham went and took the ram, and offered it up as a burnt offering instead of his son. —*Gen. 22:13*

In fact, this was the symbolic offering by which Isaac restored the foundation of faith. Since Isaac had carried the wood for the sacrifice, we can infer that he participated in the offering of the ram. Thus, even though it is written that Abraham made the symbolic offering, Isaac, who had united with Abraham and inherited his mission, was given providential credit for the offering. In this way, Isaac, having inherited Abraham's mission, made the symbolic offering and restored through indemnity the foundation of faith.

3.2 The Foundation of Substance

Isaac thus became the central figure to restore the foundation of faith in place of Abraham. He established the foundation of faith by making the symbolic offering of the ram in a manner acceptable to God. To establish the foundation for the Messiah in Isaac's family, the foundation of substance had to be laid next. For this purpose, Isaac's sons, Esau and Jacob, had to be placed in the divided positions of Cain and Abel respectively. By making the substantial offering, they were responsible to fulfill the indemnity condition to remove the fallen nature and lay the foundation of substance.

If Abraham had not failed in the symbolic offering, Isaac and his half-brother Ishmael would have stood in the positions of Abel and Cain. They would have been responsible to fulfill the indemnity condition to remove the fallen nature which Cain and Abel did not accomplish. However, because Abraham failed in the offering, God set up Isaac in the position of Abraham, and Esau and Jacob in the positions originally intended for Ishmael and Isaac. It was then up to Esau and

Jacob to fulfill the indemnity condition to remove the fallen nature.

For the purpose of making the substantial offering, Esau and Jacob were in the same positions under their father Isaac as Cain and Abel in relation to Adam, and as Shem and Ham in relation to Noah. Isaac's eldest son Esau represented Abraham's first symbolic offering defiled by Satan, while the second son Jacob represented the offering of Isaac by which Satan was separated. Moreover, Esau assumed the role of Cain as the representative of evil, while Jacob stood in the position of Abel as the representative of goodness. Esau and Jacob began fighting inside their mother's womb[65] because they were in these opposing positions. Even then, God loved Jacob and hated Esau,[66] but this was for a providential reason: they were supposed to restore through indemnity the mistakes which Cain and Abel had made in their offering.

However, before Esau and Jacob could fulfill the indemnity condition to remove the fallen nature and make the substantial offering, Jacob first had to fulfill the indemnity condition to restore the position of Abel. In all, Jacob had the following missions: First, he should fulfill the indemnity condition to restore the position of Abel, the central figure of the substantial offering. Next, he should make the substantial offering. Finally, as will be discussed in the next section, Jacob would enter Egypt to commence the four-hundred-year course of indemnity required of his descendants because of Abraham's mistake in the symbolic offering.

Jacob made the indemnity condition to restore the position of Abel in the following manner. First, Jacob fulfilled the condition of victory in the fight to restore on the individual level the birthright of the eldest son. Because Satan took dominion over the universe created by God, Satan assumed the position of the eldest son. God was cast in the position of the second son, from which He had to work His way toward restoring the birthright. For this reason, God has favored second sons over firstborn sons, as in the case of Esau and Jacob: "I have loved Jacob but I have hated Esau."[67] Jacob, as the second son who had the responsibility to restore the birthright of the firstborn son, cleverly obtained it from Esau in exchange for some bread and a pottage of lentils.[68] Because Jacob highly valued the birthright and worked to reclaim it from his brother, God had Isaac bless him.[69] On the contrary, God did not bless Esau, because he thought so little of his birthright that he traded it for a bowl of lentil pottage.

---

65. Gen. 25:22-23
66. Rom. 9:11-13
67. Mal. 1:2
68. Gen. 25:29-34
69. Gen. 27:27-29

Second, Jacob went to Haran, which represented the satanic world. After suffering through twenty-one years of drudgery, he triumphed over Laban in the fight to restore the birthright by gaining family and wealth as his due inheritance. After winning this victory, Jacob returned to Canaan.

Third, on his way back to Canaan, the land of the promised blessing, Jacob triumphed in wrestling with an angel at the ford of Jabbok, thereby restoring dominion over the angel in a substantial struggle. Through these three victories, Jacob restored through indemnity the position of Abel. Thereupon, Jacob became the central figure of the substantial offering.

Esau and Jacob thus secured the positions in which Cain and Abel had stood at the moment when God accepted Abel's offering. Accordingly, for Jacob and Esau to fulfill the indemnity condition to remove the fallen nature, Esau needed to love Jacob, respect him as his mediator to God, obediently submit to Jacob's directions, and finally, multiply goodness by inheriting goodness from the bearer of God's blessing. Indeed, when Jacob returned to Canaan with his family and wealth after enduring twenty-one years of hardship in Haran, he moved Esau to overcome his former hostility:

> And Jacob lifted up his eyes and looked, and behold, Esau was coming, and four hundred men with him. So he divided the children among Leah and Rachel and the two maids. And he put the maids with their children in front, then Leah with her children, and Rachel and Joseph last of all. He himself went on before them, bowing himself to the ground seven times, until he came near to his brother. But Esau ran to meet him, and embraced him, and fell on his neck and kissed him, and they wept. —*Gen. 33:1-4*

When Esau opened his arms and affectionately welcomed Jacob, they fulfilled the indemnity condition to remove the fallen nature. For the first time, the foundation of substance was laid successfully.

When Jacob and Esau succeeded in making the substantial offering, they restored through indemnity the previous failures in making substantial offerings: the failures of Cain and Abel in Adam's family and of Ham and Shem in Noah's family. Their victory in the providence centered on Abraham also restored through indemnity, horizontally in one family, the long vertical course of history in which God had been working to restore the foundation of substance.

Esau had been in the position to be hated by God from the time he was inside his mother's womb[70] only because he had been given the role of Cain, who was on Satan's side, for the purpose of setting up an

---
70. Rom. 9:11-13

indemnity condition in the providence of restoration. Once he submitted to Jacob and completed his portion of responsibility, he stood in the position of restored Cain and was at last able to receive God's love.

3.3 THE FOUNDATION FOR THE MESSIAH

God's work to lay the foundation for the Messiah, which He first tried to establish in Adam's family, had to be conducted three times because the central figures of the providence of restoration could not fulfill their portion of responsibility. The third attempt was in Abraham's time, yet even this was prolonged when he failed in the symbolic offering. Isaac and his family inherited the Will and laid the foundation of faith and the foundation of substance. At last, the foundation for the Messiah was established. One would expect that the Messiah would have come on the earth at that time.

However, the foundation for the Messiah also requires a social environment conducive to his coming. The foundation must make it feasible for this satanic world to be restored into God's Kingdom ruled by the Messiah. In the providence in Adam's and Noah's families, there were no other families which could possibly attack or corrupt the central family. If either of these families had laid the foundation for the Messiah on the family level, the Messiah could have come without opposition. However, by Abraham's time, fallen people had already built up satanic nations which could have easily overpowered Abraham's family. Hence, even though the foundation for the Messiah was laid at that time, it was a limited foundation, on the family level. The Messiah could not have safely come on that foundation. A foundation of a sovereign state was needed to cope with the nations of the satanic world.

Such support would have been necessary even if Abraham had not failed in the symbolic offering, but had succeeded with his sons, Isaac and Ishmael, in making the substantial offering to lay the family foundation for the Messiah. It still would not have been safe for the Messiah to come until Abraham's descendants had multiplied in Canaan and established a national foundation for the Messiah. As it was, though the descendants of Isaac had established the family foundation for the Messiah, they would leave their homeland and suffer in a foreign land for four hundred years as the penalty for Abraham's mistake. Despite their suffering in Egypt, they would flourish and consolidate as a people. They would return to Canaan and build the national foundation for the Messiah as a sovereign nation prepared for the Messiah and his work.[71]

---

71. cf. Moses and Jesus 2.2.3.3

A course of indemnity had been placed upon the shoulders of Abraham's descendants due to his mistake in the symbolic offering. Jacob was to begin this course of indemnity, not Isaac. Indeed, the one who shoulders the major burden in walking the course of indemnity is the Abel-type person who serves as the central figure of the substantial offering. Abel in Adam's family, Ham in Noah's family, Isaac in Abraham's family, and Jacob in Isaac's family carried the major burdens in walking the indemnity courses set down for their families. Among them, Jacob was the only Abel figure who stood upon the foundation for the Messiah. Therefore, he would walk the model course for the separation of Satan, setting the pattern for the Messiah to follow at his coming.[72]

Jacob's family stood upon the foundation for the Messiah which had been completed in Isaac's family. Inheriting the position of Isaac's family, they set out to complete the dispensation entrusted to Abraham by taking responsibility for Abraham's sin and embarking upon the four-hundred-year course of indemnity. In Isaac's family it was Jacob, in the position of Abel, who walked the entire course of indemnity. In Jacob's family it was Joseph, the son of Rachel—Jacob's wife on God's side—who was to secure the position of Abel by entering Egypt and walking the course of indemnity. After being sold into slavery by his brothers and brought to Egypt, Joseph rose to the office of prime minister of Egypt by the age of thirty. He witnessed the realization of a prophecy which God had given him in his dreams while he was still a child.[73] First, Joseph's half brothers, born of Leah—Jacob's wife on Satan's side—entered Egypt and surrendered themselves to him. Later, all of Jacob's children entered Egypt, and finally they brought their father to Egypt. In this way, Jacob's family began the indemnity course to build a nation which would one day receive the Messiah.

Jacob, as the central figure who laid the foundation for the Messiah in Isaac's family, was responsible to shoulder Abraham's sin. He was also responsible to embark upon an indemnity course to realize on the national level the Will which had been entrusted to Isaac. Therefore, as was the case with Abraham and Isaac, God regarded Abraham, Isaac and Jacob as the same person with respect to His Will, even though they were three different individuals. Accordingly, Jacob's success meant Isaac's success, and Isaac's success meant Abraham's success. The providence of restoration centering on Abraham, though it was extended to Isaac and Jacob, came to be regarded in the sight of God as having been

---

72. cf. Moses and Jesus 1
73. Gen. 37:5-11

accomplished in Abraham's own generation without any prolongation. It is written, "I am the God of your father, the God of Abraham, the God of Isaac, and the God of Jacob."[74] This verse indicates that although they were three generations, God regarded as one generation these ancestors who collectively accomplished His Will.

God intended to fulfill the goal of His providence by establishing the national foundation for the Messiah and sending the Messiah to that prepared nation. To accomplish this, God had Jacob's family enter Egypt, the satanic world, where they would suffer as slaves for four hundred years. Then, as promised to Abraham, God would raise them up as the chosen people and bring them back to Canaan.

The foundation for the Messiah established in Isaac's family became the basis upon which to begin the course of indemnity to establish the national foundation for the Messiah. The period of two thousand years from Adam to Abraham was in effect the period to lay the basis for this national providence to begin in the next era.

In conclusion, Jacob was victorious in taking responsibility for the indemnity course to pay for Abraham's mistake. By using his wisdom for the sake of God's Will, Jacob triumphed as an individual in his struggle with Esau to win the birthright. He entered Haran and, as a family, triumphed in a twenty-one-year struggle with his uncle Laban to win the birthright. On his way back from Haran to Canaan, Jacob was victorious in the fight with the angel. He was the first fallen man to fulfill the indemnity condition to restore dominion over the angel. Thereupon, he received the name "Israel,"[75] signifying that he set the pattern and laid the groundwork upon which the chosen people would be established. After returning to Canaan with these victories, Jacob won Esau's heart, and together they fulfilled the indemnity condition to remove the fallen nature.

Jacob thus victoriously completed the model course to bring Satan to submission. Moses, Jesus, and even the people of Israel would walk this course after the pattern set by Jacob. The history of Israel can serve as a good historical source for understanding the course to bring Satan to submission on the national level. For this reason, it is central to the study of the providence of restoration.

3.4 Some Lessons from Abraham's Course

First, Abraham's course demonstrates that God's predestination concerning the manner in which His Will is fulfilled is conditional. The

---

74. Exod. 3:6
75. Gen. 32:28

providence of restoration cannot be fulfilled by God's power alone; it can only be fulfilled in conjunction with the human portion of responsibility. Hence, although God called upon Abraham for the purpose of fulfilling the providence of restoration, when he failed to complete his responsibility, God's Will was not fulfilled.

Second, Abraham's course demonstrates that God's predestination concerning human beings is conditional. Although God preordained Abraham to be the father of faith by succeeding in his offering, when he could not complete his responsibility, this mission extended to Isaac and Jacob.

Third, Abraham's course shows us that when human beings fail to complete their responsibility, the fulfillment of God's Will is always delayed, and its restoration requires fulfillment of a greater indemnity condition. In Abraham's case, God's Will was to be accomplished by merely sacrificing animals; upon his failure, however, it had to be accomplished by offering his beloved son, Isaac, as a sacrifice and had to be completed through Isaac and Jacob.

Fourth, Abraham's cutting the sacrifices in two provides a lesson that each of us must divide our own self as an offering to separate good from evil. A life of faith involves putting ourselves in the position of an offering. Only by dividing good from evil in ourselves can we become living offerings pleasing to God. We should constantly separate good from evil within ourselves, according to the standard of God's Will. If we neglect to do this, a condition is set up for Satan to invade.

Chapter 2

Moses and Jesus in the Providence of Restoration

The Bible contains many secrets concerning God's work of salvation. It is written, "Surely the Lord God does nothing, without revealing his secret to his servants the prophets."[1] However, without knowing the principle behind God's providence, people have been unable to discern the mysteries concealed in the Bible. The biblical account of a prophet's life is not merely a record of history. Rather, through the life course of a prophet, the Bible discloses the way for fallen people to walk. In particular, we shall examine how God set up the providential courses of Jacob and Moses as models for Jesus' course to save humankind.

SECTION 1

THE MODEL COURSES FOR BRINGING SATAN TO SUBMISSION

We learned that in the providence of restoration in Isaac's family, Jacob was the central figure who laid the foundation of substance. He secured the position of Abel and labored to bring Satan to submission and fulfill the indemnity condition to remove the fallen nature. Jacob's entire course became the model course for Moses and Jesus. Jesus came

---

1. Amos 3:7

to bring Satan to submission in substantial terms. Before Jesus, Moses walked a course for the subjugation of Satan that was the image of the course Jesus would walk. Still earlier, God had Jacob walk a course that was a symbolic representation of Jesus' course. Moreover, Jacob's course is the model for the course which the Israelites and all of humanity must walk to bring Satan to submission and attain the goal of the providence of restoration.

1.1 Why Jacob's Course and Moses' Course Were Set Up as the Models for Jesus' Course

The goal of the providence of restoration is attained when human beings bring Satan to voluntary submission and become his master. They must do this by fulfilling their given portion of responsibility. Jesus, as the Messiah and the true human ancestor, came to help all people of faith bring Satan to voluntary submission. By himself, he pioneered the course to bring Satan to complete submission and has since guided people of faith to follow his example.

Satan, who does not meekly surrender even before God, would by no means readily surrender to Jesus, much less to ordinary believers. Therefore, God, who takes responsibility for human beings, whom He created, called upon Jacob and worked through him to show us, in symbolic form, the course for bringing Satan to submission.

Moses was able to subjugate Satan by following the pattern of the model course which was revealed symbolically in Jacob's course. In his course, Moses developed this to the level of image. Similarly, by building on the pattern of Moses' course, Jesus came to substantially bring Satan to submission. By walking in Jesus' footsteps, people of faith can also bring Satan to submission and master him. When Moses said, "The Lord God will raise up for you a prophet from your brethren as he raised me up. You shall listen to him in whatever he tells you,"[2] he was referring to Jesus. Jesus would stand in a position comparable to Moses and follow Moses' course as the model in order to walk the worldwide providence to restore Canaan—the Kingdom of God. Jesus said, "The Son can do nothing of his own accord, but only what he sees the Father doing; for whatever he does, that the Son does likewise."[3] By this he meant that he was following the model course which God had revealed to him through Moses. Moses thus prefigured Jesus.

---

2. Acts 3:22
3. John 5:19

1.2 Jacob's Course as the Model for Moses' and Jesus' Courses

Jacob pioneered the course to bring Satan to submission. This course takes the path opposite to the way by which Satan corrupted humanity. Moses and Jesus went through courses after the pattern of Jacob's course. Let us study these courses together in this section.

(1) The first human beings should have been absolutely determined to keep God's commandment not to eat of the fruit, yet they fell at the risk of their lives when the Archangel tempted them. Accordingly, for Jacob to complete the restoration of Canaan at the family level—that is, return to Canaan with his family and wealth and there restore the foundation to receive the Messiah—he had to triumph in a fight at the risk of his life with an angel, representing Satan. Jacob was desperate to overcome this trial as he wrestled with the angel at the ford of Jabbok. He triumphed and received the name "Israel."[4] In this trial, it was God who tested Jacob by putting the angel in the position of Satan. God's purpose in doing this was not to make Jacob miserable, but to help him secure the position of Abel and complete the restoration of his family by winning the qualification to rule the angel. Furthermore, through the angel playing the leading role in the trial, the way was opened for the angelic world to be restored.

In the case of Moses, before he could guide the Israelites into Canaan and thus complete the national restoration of Canaan, he first had to overcome a life-threatening trial in which the Lord tried to kill him.[5] We must understand that God gives such tests to people because He loves them. If Satan rather than God gave such tests and people were to fail, they would become Satan's prey. Similarly, Jesus had to overcome a trial before he could embark upon the worldwide restoration of Canaan—that is, to guide humanity into the Kingdom of Heaven on earth. He battled with Satan at the risk of his life and triumphed over him when he fasted for forty days and was tempted in the wilderness.[6]

(2) Since our fallen nature was acquired when Satan defiled our flesh and spirit, Jacob had to fulfill a comparable condition to remove it. For this reason, to restore the position of Abel for the fulfillment of the indemnity condition to remove the fallen nature, Jacob purchased the birthright from Esau with bread and lentils,[7] which symbolized flesh and spirit. To repeat this course in Moses' day, God fed the people with manna and quail,[8] also symbolizing flesh and spirit, and thereby

---

4. Gen. 32:25-28
5. Exod. 4:24
6. Matt. 4:1-11
7. Gen. 25:34
8. Exod. 16:13

strengthened their gratitude toward Him and heightened their awareness of being the chosen people. Through this provision, God wanted the people to obey Moses and fulfill the indemnity condition to remove the fallen nature on the national level.

Jesus said: "Your fathers ate the manna in the wilderness, and they died. . . . I say to you, unless you eat the flesh of the Son of man and drink his blood, you have no life in you."[9] Besides confirming that he walked the model course set by Moses, Jesus meant by these verses that all fallen humanity should become one with him in flesh and spirit. By faithfully following and uniting with Jesus, who at that time stood in the position of John the Baptist,[10] they would have fulfilled the worldwide indemnity condition to remove the fallen nature. By then devotedly attending Jesus as the Messiah, they were to restore their original nature.

(3) Due to the Fall, Satan defiled even the human corpse. Jacob's body was sanctified with the blessing which he had received in life. In death, the disposition of his corpse also fulfilled a condition of purification; thus the embalming took forty days.[11] In the case of Moses, the archangel Michael contended with the Devil over the proper disposition of his body.[12] We know that Jesus' body disappeared, to the bewilderment of the authorities, leaving an empty tomb.[13]

(4) At the Fall, Satan corrupted the first human ancestors during their growing period. To restore through indemnity this defilement, God has been working to set up conditions based on certain numbers, such as the number three, which signify the growing period.[14] When Jacob began his journey from Haran to Canaan, there was a three-day period for the separation of Satan before Laban was notified of his absence.[15] When Moses guided his people out of Egypt into Canaan, there was an initial period of three days.[16] Joshua lodged at the Jordan River for three days before he crossed it.[17] When Jesus was about to begin the worldwide spiritual course to restore Canaan, he spent three days in the tomb.[18]

Jacob had twelve sons[19] in order to restore through indemnity in his generation (horizontally) the indemnity conditions accumulated (vertically) through the twelve generations from Noah to Jacob, which had been lost to Satan. In Moses' day, there were the twelve tribes[20] and Jesus had twelve disciples[21] for similar reasons. To fulfill an indemnity

---

9. John 6:49-53
10. cf. Moses and Jesus 3.2.1
11. Gen. 50:3
12. Jude 9
13. Matt. 27:62-28:15
14. cf. Periods 2.4
15. Gen. 31:22
16. Exod. 5:3
17. Josh. 3:2
18. Luke 18:33
19. Gen. 35:22
20. Exod. 24:4
21. Matt. 10:1

condition to separate Satan from the seven days of God's creation which he had defiled, there were seventy members of Jacob's family,[22] seventy elders in Moses' time,[23] and Jesus' seventy followers,[24] all of whom played central, providential roles in their respective eras.

(5) A staff, which smites evil, leads the way and provides support when one leans on it, is a symbol of the Messiah.[25] Jacob crossed the Jordan River and entered the land of Canaan while leaning on a staff.[26] This foreshadowed that one day fallen humanity will cross the waters of this sinful world and arrive on the shore of the ideal world by following the Messiah: smiting injustice, following his guidance and example, and depending on him. Moses guided the Israelites across the Red Sea with a staff.[27] Jesus at his Second Coming will guide humanity across the turbulent waters of this fallen world to reach the shore of God's ideal with the rod of iron, symbolizing himself.[28]

(6) Eve's sin implanted the root of sin in the lineage of humankind, which bore fruit when Cain killed Abel. Since it was a mother and son who allowed Satan to enter and bear the fruit of sin, according to the principle of restoration through indemnity, a mother and son must separate from Satan through their joint efforts. Jacob could not have received the blessing and separated from Satan without his mother's devoted support and wise advice.[29] Moses could not have escaped death and been in the position to serve God's Will if not for his mother's help.[30] Finally, Mary saved Jesus' life by fleeing with him to Egypt, escaping from King Herod who sought to kill him.[31]

(7) The central figure entrusted with God's Will in the providence must return from Satan's world to God's world. This is why Jacob journeyed from Haran, the satanic world, to Canaan,[32] and Moses journeyed from Egypt to the promised land of Canaan.[33] After Jesus had taken refuge in Egypt shortly after his birth,[34] he returned to Galilee.

(8) The ultimate purpose of the providence of restoration is to eradicate Satan. Signifying this, Jacob buried the idols under an oak tree.[35] Moses tore down the golden calf, burned it with fire, ground it to a powder, scattered the powder upon the water, and made the Israelites drink it.[36] Jesus came to destroy this evil world by bringing Satan to submission with his words and power.[37]

---

22. Gen. 46:27
23. Exod. 24:1
24. Luke 10:1
25. cf. Moses and Jesus 2.2.2.2
26. Gen. 32:10
27. Exod. 14:16
28. Rev. 2:27; 12:5
29. Gen. 27:5-17, 42-45
30. Exod. 2:2
31. Matt. 2:13
32. Gen. 31-33
33. Exod. 3:8
34. Matt. 2:14-15
35. Gen. 35:4
36. Exod. 32:20
37. cf. Eschatology 3.2.2

Section 2

The Providence of Restoration under the Leadership of Moses

2.1 Overview of the Providence Led by Moses

The providence of restoration led by Moses was built upon the foundation for the Messiah laid in Abraham's family. Nevertheless, the Principle still required Moses himself to lay the foundation for the Messiah by restoring through indemnity the foundation of faith and the foundation of substance. Whenever the central figure for the providence changes, the new central figure cannot inherit the providential Will without first completing a similar responsibility of his own. Furthermore, in this case, the foundation had to be laid anew because the scope of the providence had expanded from a family to a nation. As we shall see, in the providence of restoration led by Moses, the indemnity conditions required to lay these foundations were quite different than before.

2.1.1 The Foundation of Faith

2.1.1.1 The Central Figure to Restore the Foundation of Faith

Moses was the central figure to restore the foundation of faith. A foundation of faith had to be laid anew to begin the course to return to the promised land of Canaan upon the conclusion of the four hundred years of slavery incurred because of Abraham's mistake in his symbolic offering. Before we study how Moses established the foundation of faith, let us first examine the providential position of Moses in relation to Jesus, and then in the next section investigate how he was different from all the previous central figures who were called to lay the foundation of faith.

First, Moses was put in the position representing God, acting in His stead. God told Moses that he should be as God to Aaron.[38] He also said, "See, I make you as God to Pharaoh; and Aaron your brother shall be your prophet."[39]

Second, God set up Moses to prefigure Jesus. By having Moses stand in God's position before Aaron and the Pharaoh, God set him up to prefigure Jesus, the only incarnation of God. By prefiguring Jesus, Moses pioneered the path for Jesus to one day walk. Like John the

---

38. Exod. 4:16
39. Exod. 7:1

Baptist after him,⁴⁰ Moses was to make straight the way for Jesus.

As the descendant of Jacob, who had established the foundation for the Messiah, Moses could serve as a central figure in the Age of the Providence of Restoration. In his providential path, Moses built upon the tradition and deeds of his ancestor, Jacob. Their courses served as models for the path which Jesus would later walk.

Moses also stood on the foundation which Joseph had laid when he entered Egypt. Joseph's life, too, prefigured that of Jesus. As the son of Rachel (Jacob's wife representing God's side) and the younger brother of the sons of Leah (Jacob's wife representing Satan's side), Joseph stood in the position of Abel. He narrowly escaped his older brothers' scheme to kill him, and when he was sold off to merchants, he entered Egypt as a slave. Yet he rose to the rank of prime minister of Egypt by the age of thirty. His brothers and father came to Egypt and humbly bowed before him, fulfilling a prophetic dream he had as a child.⁴¹ Based upon this providential victory, the Israelites entered Egypt and commenced a period of hardships for the purpose of severing Satan's ties. Joseph's course foreshadowed the course which Jesus would later walk. After coming to the satanic world, Jesus would endure a path of hardships and emerge as the King of Kings at the age of thirty. He was to bring all of humanity, including his forefathers, into submission, cut all their ties to the satanic world, and restore them to God's realm.

Moses' infancy, childhood and death also prefigured the course of Jesus. At his birth, Moses was in danger of being killed at the hands of the Pharaoh. After his mother nursed him in concealment, Moses entered the Pharaoh's palace and was brought up safely among his foes. Likewise, Jesus was born into a situation where he was in danger of being killed by King Herod. Jesus' mother took him, fled to Egypt, and raised him in concealment there. Later, she brought him back to King Herod's realm where he grew up safely among his foes. After Moses' death, no one knew the whereabouts of his body;⁴² this foreshadowed what would happen to Jesus' body after his death.

In all these ways, Moses' course to restore Canaan on the national level was the model for Jesus' course to restore Canaan on the worldwide level. And, as we mentioned earlier, the Bible attests through the words of Moses⁴³ and Jesus⁴⁴ that God disclosed through Moses' life a model for Jesus, prefiguring the path Jesus would walk in the future.

---

40. John 1:23
41. Gen. 37:5-11
42. Deut. 34:6
43. Deut. 18:18-19
44. John 5:19

2.1.1.2 The Object for the Condition in Restoring the Foundation of Faith

Moses was in a position different from earlier central figures who were entrusted with laying the foundation of faith. Unlike Abel, Noah and Abraham, Moses did not need to make a symbolic offering. Rather, he could restore the foundation of faith merely by obedience to God's Word while fulfilling a *dispensation of forty for the separation of Satan*.[45] There are three reasons for this difference.

First, Moses stood on the foundation of the three successful symbolic offerings by Abel, Noah and Isaac. They had completed the providence based on making symbolic offerings.

Second, symbolic offerings were objects for the condition made necessary as substitutes for the Word, because after the first human ancestors lost God's Word at the Fall, people were not able to receive God's Word directly. Hence, during the Age of the Providence to Lay the Foundation for Restoration (the age from Adam to Abraham), sacrifices had been offered as objects for the condition in laying the foundation of faith. However, by Moses' time that age had come to a close. Humanity had entered a new era, the Age of the Providence of Restoration (Old Testament Age), when they could once again receive God's Word directly. Thus, there was no longer any need of a symbolic offering in laying the foundation of faith.

Third, as the providence which had commenced with Adam's family was prolonged again and again, certain conditions of indemnity were needed to restore the providential periods which had been defiled by Satan. When Noah was laying the foundation of faith, he had to pass through a dispensation of forty for the separation of Satan while living in the ark. Abraham could make the symbolic offering to lay the foundation of faith only after he restored the previous period of four hundred years and thus stood on the foundation of a dispensation of forty for the separation of Satan. The Israelites suffered four hundred years of slavery in Egypt to fulfill a dispensation of forty for the separation of Satan and thereby restore the foundation of faith claimed by Satan due to Abraham's mistake. Likewise, in the Age of the Providence of Restoration, a central figure could lay the foundation of faith as long as he stood firmly upon the completion of the dispensation of forty for the

---

45. Literally, this term may be read "forty-day foundation for the separation of Satan." For the sake of clarity, we render it "dispensation of forty for the separation of Satan" for the following reasons. First, the "forty days" refers to Noah's flood which first set up this condition (cf. Foundation 2.1.2) and not to the length of the period required to fulfill it, which may take forty years or even four hundred years. Second, although a foundation is laid as a result, the text uses this term to discuss a dispensation of a fixed length. —Ed.

separation of Satan by upholding God's Word, now that an object for the condition was no longer required to serve as its substitute.

2.1.2 THE FOUNDATION OF SUBSTANCE

In the Age of the Providence to Lay the Foundation for Restoration, God worked to lay the family foundation of substance. Upon entering the Age of the Providence of Restoration, God worked to lay the national foundation of substance. Since Moses stood as God to the people and represented Jesus, he stood in the position of parent to the Israelites when laying the national foundation of faith. Concurrently, as a prophet with the mission to prepare the way for Jesus, Moses stood in the position of a child. Therefore, with respect to the Israelites, Moses stood in the position of Abel as the central figure for the national foundation of substance.

We recall that Abel made the symbolic offering from the position of a parent in Adam's stead and was thereby entitled to make the substantial offering from the position of a child. Likewise, Moses stood in the dual positions of parent and child. When he restored through indemnity the foundation of faith, he stood in the position of a parent. He thereby secured the position of Abel for the substantial offering, for which he stood in the position of a child.

Once Moses had secured the position of Abel, the Israelites, standing in the position of Cain, were supposed to fulfill the national indemnity condition to remove the fallen nature through their obedience to Moses. By doing so, they would establish the national foundation of substance.

2.1.3 THE FOUNDATION FOR THE MESSIAH

Moses was to restore through indemnity the national foundation of faith, and the Israelites under Moses' leadership were to restore through indemnity the national foundation of substance. This would have constituted the national foundation for the Messiah and the basis for a sovereign nation to which the Messiah could come. The Israelites were then to receive the Messiah, be reborn through him, be cleansed of their original sin, and restore their original nature by uniting with God in heart. In this way, they were to attain the ultimate goal of becoming perfect incarnations.

2.2 THE NATIONAL COURSES TO RESTORE CANAAN UNDER THE LEADERSHIP OF MOSES

Moses brought the Israelites out of Egypt, the satanic world, with miracles and signs, led them across the Red Sea, and had them wander through the wilderness before entering the promised land of Canaan. This foreshadowed the course on which Jesus would one day lead Christians, the Second Israel. With miracles and signs, Jesus would bring Christians out of lives of sin and lead them safely across the troubled sea of evil. He would take them through a desert devoid of life-giving water before guiding them into the Garden of Eden of God's promise. Just as the national course to restore Canaan under the leadership of Moses was prolonged as three courses because of the Israelites' faithlessness, the worldwide course to restore Canaan under the leadership of Jesus had to be undertaken three times because of the disbelief of John the Baptist and the Jewish people of that day. To avoid redundancy, a close comparison between Moses' course and Jesus' course will not be made here. Still, the parallels will become plain when one compares this section with the next.

2.2.1 THE FIRST NATIONAL COURSE TO RESTORE CANAAN

2.2.1.1 THE FOUNDATION OF FAITH

After four hundred years of slavery in Egypt, the indemnity period required of the Israelites due to Abraham's mistake came to an end. In order for Moses to become the central figure to restore the foundation of faith and be qualified to lead the Israelites out of Egypt, he as an individual had to inherit the four-hundred-year national indemnity period and complete a dispensation of forty for the separation of Satan. In addition, Moses had to restore through indemnity the number forty, which unfallen Adam should have fulfilled to establish his foundation of faith.[46] To achieve these purposes, Moses was brought into the Pharaoh's palace, the center of the satanic world, and he spent forty years there.[47]

While in the palace, Moses was educated by his mother, who, unknown to anyone, was hired to be his nurse. She secretly imparted to him the consciousness and pride of belonging to the chosen people. Despite the comforts of palace life, Moses maintained unshakable loyalty and fidelity to the lineage of Israel. After forty years, he left the

---

46. cf. Periods 2.4
47. Acts 7:23

palace, "choosing rather to share ill-treatment with the people of God than to enjoy the fleeting pleasures of sin."[48] Hence, during the forty years of his life in the Pharaoh's palace, Moses fulfilled the dispensation of forty for the separation of Satan and thereby restored the foundation of faith.

2.2.1.2 THE FOUNDATION OF SUBSTANCE

Moses was in the dual position of parent and child. When he laid the foundation of faith, he also secured the position of Abel for the foundation of substance. The Israelites, who were in the position of Cain, were supposed to follow and obey Moses in faith. By inheriting God's Will from Moses and multiplying goodness, they would fulfill the national indemnity condition to remove the fallen nature and lay the national foundation of substance. The Israelites were to lay the foundation of substance by following Moses from the time they left Egypt until they entered the blessed land of Canaan.

God commenced the *dispensation to start* the course with Moses' act of killing an Egyptian. Seeing one of his brethren being mistreated by an Egyptian taskmaster, Moses was incited by his burning love for his people; he struck and killed the man.[49] In a way, this was an expression of God's heart of burning indignation as He looked down upon the affliction of His people.[50] At that moment, whether or not the Israelites united with Moses would determine if they could successfully begin the course to return to Canaan.

When Moses killed the Egyptian, God used this act to achieve the following: First, the Archangel induced the first human ancestors to fall and Cain to kill Abel; these were the conditions by which Satan has controlled the progression of sinful history from the position of the eldest son. Therefore, before God could begin the providence to restore Canaan, someone on God's side should fulfill the condition to restore this through indemnity by prevailing over someone on the side of Satan who stands in the position of the eldest son. Second, this act effectively cut off any lingering attachment Moses had to the Pharaoh's palace and placed him in a situation where he could never return. Finally, by this act, God desired to induce the Israelites to trust Moses by showing them he was a patriotic Israelite. As we shall see, these were comparable to the reasons why in the second national course to restore Canaan, God struck all the firstborn among the Egyptians and their livestock.

---

48. Heb. 11:25
49. Exod. 2:11-12
50. Exod. 3:7

The Israelites, upon witnessing Moses' act of killing the Egyptian, should have been deeply inspired by his love for Israel, as was God. Had they felt this way, they would have respected Moses, trusted him and followed him with ardor. Then, through Moses' leadership, God would have brought them directly into the land of Canaan where they would have established the foundation of substance. In fact, they would not have had to cross the Red Sea or wander through the Sinai wilderness, but would have taken the straight route to Canaan by way of the land of the Philistines. In a twenty-one-day course, they would have restored Jacob's twenty-one years in Haran.

Later, in the second national course, God had reason to distrust the Israelites because their previous failure to follow Moses had aborted the first national course. It is written: "When Pharaoh let the people go, God did not lead them by way of the land of the Philistines, although that was near; for God said, 'Lest the people repent when they see war, and return to Egypt.'"[51] During the second national course to restore Canaan, God led the people across the Red Sea and in a detour through the wilderness because He had reason to fear they might turn faithless and return to Egypt without completing their journey.

2.2.1.3 THE FAILURE OF THE FIRST NATIONAL COURSE TO RESTORE CANAAN

Had the Israelites (Cain) wholeheartedly obeyed Moses (Abel) and followed him to return to Canaan, they would have fulfilled the national indemnity condition to remove the fallen nature and laid the foundation of substance. On the contrary, however, when they saw Moses strike and kill the Egyptian, they misunderstood him and spoke ill of him:

> When he went out the next day, behold, two Hebrews were struggling together; and he said to the man that did the wrong, "Why did you strike your fellow?" He answered, "Who made you a prince and a judge over us? Do you mean to kill me as you killed the Egyptian?" Then Moses was afraid, and thought, "Surely the thing is known." When Pharaoh heard of it, he sought to kill Moses. —*Exod. 2:13-15*

Moses was left with no choice but to escape from the Pharaoh. Reluctantly forsaking the Israelites, he fled into the wilderness of Midian. The foundation of substance was shattered, and the Israelites' course to restore Canaan under the leadership of Moses would be repeated a second and eventually a third time.

---

51. Exod. 13:17

2.2.2 The Second National Course to Restore Canaan

2.2.2.1 The Foundation of Faith

When the first national course to restore Canaan ended in failure due to the disbelief of the Israelites, Satan claimed the forty years of Moses' life in Pharaoh's palace during which he had laid the foundation of faith. Hence, for Moses to begin the second national course to restore Canaan, he had to lay anew the foundation of faith by completing another period of forty years to restore through indemnity his lost forty years in the palace. This was the purpose of Moses' forty-year exile in the wilderness of Midian.[52] During this forty-year period, the Israelites' lives in Egypt became even more miserable as the penalty for their disbelief in Moses.

Moses went through a second dispensation of forty for the separation of Satan during the forty years he spent in the wilderness of Midian. There he restored the foundation of faith needed to embark upon the second national course to restore Canaan. God then appeared before Moses and said:

> I have seen the affliction of my people who are in Egypt, and have heard their cry because of their taskmasters; I know their sufferings, and I have come down to deliver them out of the hand of the Egyptians, and to bring them up out of that land to a good and broad land, a land flowing with milk and honey, to the place of the Canaanites . . . and now, behold, the cry of the people of Israel has come to me, and I have seen the oppression with which the Egyptians oppress them. Come, I will send you to Pharaoh that you may bring forth my people, the sons of Israel, out of Egypt. —*Exod. 3:7-10*

2.2.2.2 The Foundation of Substance

Once Moses restored the foundation of faith in the wilderness of Midian, he also secured the position of Abel. Accordingly, as in the first national course to restore Canaan, if the Israelite people in the position of Cain had believed in and followed Moses with unquestioning faith and obedience, they would have entered the promised land, the land of milk and honey. In so doing, they would have fulfilled the indemnity condition to remove the fallen nature and laid the foundation of substance.

God worked the dispensation to start the first national course to restore Canaan when Moses struck and killed an Egyptian. Similarly, to work the dispensation to start the second national course to restore

---

52. Acts 7:30

Canaan, God granted Moses three signs and ten plagues with which to prevail over the Egyptians. The reasons God had Moses strike the satanic side were, as already elucidated: first, to restore through indemnity the position of the eldest son which Satan had defiled; second, to cut off the Israelites' attachment to Egypt; third, to let the Israelites know that Moses was sent by God.[53] There was yet another reason why Moses could strike the Egyptians. Although the Israelites had already completed the due indemnity period of four hundred years as slaves in Egypt, they had suffered thirty additional years of affliction.[54] God heard their cries and groaning and answered them with compassion.[55]

The three signs which God provided for Moses and Aaron to perform foreshadowed the work of Jesus. The first sign was given when God commanded Moses to cast down his staff, and it became a serpent.[56] When Aaron later performed this sign before the Pharaoh at Moses' command, the Pharaoh summoned his magicians and had them cast down their staffs, which also became serpents; but Aaron's serpent devoured their serpents.[57] This sign symbolically foreshadowed that Jesus would come as the Savior and destroy the satanic world.

The staff symbolized Jesus. Just as the staff displayed miraculous power in front of Moses, who represented God, Jesus was to come with such power and perform miracles before God Himself. Moreover, a staff provides protection and support for people to lean on; it smites injustice and leads people on the right path. Symbolizing Jesus, Moses' staff disclosed the missions which Jesus was to accomplish at his coming.

The transformation of Moses' staff into a serpent also symbolized the work of Jesus. Jesus likened himself to a serpent, saying, "As Moses lifted up the serpent in the wilderness, so must the Son of man be lifted up."[58] He also said to his disciples, "Be wise as serpents."[59] Jesus meant by this saying that he came as the good serpent of wisdom who entices and leads fallen people on the path of goodness. He was thus to restore through indemnity the Fall caused by the evil serpent who cunningly tempted the first human ancestors. Therefore, his disciples were to learn Jesus' wisdom and guide the sinful people in the way of goodness. Moreover, when Moses' serpent devoured the magicians' serpents, it signified that Jesus would come as the heavenly serpent to swallow up and destroy Satan, the evil serpent.

---

53. Exod. 4:1
54. Exod. 12:41
55. Exod. 2:24-25
56. Exod. 4:3-9
57. Exod. 7:10-12
58. John 3:14
59. Matt. 10:16

The second sign was given when Moses, upon God's command, put his hand into his bosom and it became leprous. Then God commanded him to put his hand into his bosom a second time, and it was healed.[60] This miracle foreshadowed symbolically that Jesus would come as the second Adam and, together with his would-be Bride (the second Eve, later manifested in the Holy Spirit)[61] perform the work of redemption. The first time Moses put his hand into his bosom and it became leprous symbolized the Archangel embracing Eve to his bosom, an act which tainted humanity with incurable sin. The second time Moses put his hand into his bosom and it was healed foreshadowed that Jesus, the True Father, would come and restore his Bride, the True Mother, and that they would embrace humanity to give them rebirth "as a hen gathers her brood under her wings."[62] Restoration would then be complete.

To perform the third sign, God instructed Moses to pour water from the Nile on the ground and it would turn to blood.[63] The symbolism of this sign lies in water, an inorganic substance, being transformed into blood, the substance of life. Water is a biblical symbol for the fallen multitudes[64] who have no life in them. Thus, this sign foreshadowed that Jesus and the Holy Spirit would come and resurrect fallen humanity, deprived of life, to become the living children of God. God had Moses and Aaron perform these three signs in order to fulfill symbolic indemnity conditions upon which Jesus and the Holy Spirit would later come to Israel as the True Parents. They would restore the original four position foundation which had been lost to Satan and give rebirth to all humanity as their children.

When Moses, who was not eloquent, asked God for someone to speak on his behalf, God provided Moses' older brother Aaron,[65] and also Miriam the prophetess, Aaron's sister.[66] This symbolically foreshadowed that Jesus and his would-be Bride, the incarnations of the Word,[67] would come and restore human beings—who had lost the Word at the Fall—as the incarnations of the Word. In the course to restore Canaan, Aaron and Miriam were given the mission to uphold the will

---

60. Exod. 4:6-7
61. cf. Christology 4.1. When describing the foreshadowing of Jesus' course, the Korean text uses "Holy Spirit" to refer to Jesus' female counterpart. However, the Holy Spirit became the spiritual female counterpart to Jesus only after he was crucified without fulfilling God's original providence, which included taking a Bride on the earth. Together Jesus and his would-be Bride were to have fulfilled the marriage of the Lamb and become the True Parents. For clarity, we will use "would-be Bride" when the text is alluding to Jesus' intended Bride on earth. —Ed.
62. Matt. 23:37
63. Exod. 4:9
64. Rev. 17:15
65. Exod. 4:14
66. Exod. 15:20
67. John 1:14

of Moses, who was in the position of God, and to exercise leadership on his behalf. In the future, Jesus and the Holy Spirit would uphold the Will of God in the worldwide course to restore Canaan and take on the mission to redeem our sin.

At God's command, Moses went to meet the Pharaoh. On his way, the Lord appeared before him and tried to kill him. Moses' life was saved when his wife Zipporah circumcised their son.[68] She helped Moses overcome the trial and saved their family. This circumcision made it possible for the Israelites to be liberated from Egypt. It foreshadowed that even when Jesus came, God's work of salvation could not be accomplished unless the people underwent an internal circumcision.

Let us examine the deeper significance of circumcision. When the first human ancestors fell through a sexual relationship with Satan, they inherited the blood of death through the male sexual organ. In the course for fallen people to be restored as God's children, God established the rite of circumcision as a condition of indemnity: cutting the foreskin of the male sexual organ and letting blood flow from it. Circumcision signifies removing the blood of death. Circumcision is also a sign of the restoration of man's right of dominion and a sign of promise that God will restore people as His true children. There are three types of circumcision: circumcision of the heart,[69] circumcision of the foreskin,[70] and circumcision of all things.[71]

Through the ten plagues, God had Moses liberate the Israelites from Egypt.[72] This, too, foreshadowed that in the future Jesus would come with miracles and signs to save God's chosen people. When Jacob was suffering twenty-one years of hardship in Haran, Laban cheated Jacob ten times and did not give him his due wages.[73] Likewise, in Moses' course, which was patterned after Jacob's course, the Pharaoh not only continued to afflict the Israelites beyond the preordained time period, he also deceived them ten times with the false promise that he would release them. As recompense for this, God was entitled to strike the Pharaoh with the ten plagues. Among them, the ninth and tenth plagues had particular significance.

For the ninth plague, God blanketed Egypt in thick darkness for three days, while in the places where the Israelites dwelt there was light.[74] This foreshadowed that when Jesus came, darkness would blanket Satan's

---

68. Exod. 4:24-26
69. Deut. 10:16
70. Gen. 17:10
71. Lev. 19:22-23
72. Exod. 7:14-12:36
73. Gen. 31:7
74. Exod. 10:21-23

realm while light would shine upon God's people, and the two sides would be separated. For the tenth plague, God killed all the firstborn among the Egyptians and their cattle, while instructing the Israelites to paint lamb's blood on the lintel and door posts of their houses so that the angel of death would pass over them. The firstborn of the Egyptians, on the satanic side, were in the position of Cain. God struck them in order to restore the Israelites, in the position of the second son Abel, to the position of the eldest son. Satan had seized the position of the eldest son and thus took the lead in the course of history, leaving God in pursuit.[75] This plague foreshadowed that at Jesus' coming, the side of Satan would perish, while God's side, in the position of the second son, would be saved by the redemption of Jesus' blood. Moses brought abundant wealth out of Egypt.[76] This foreshadowed the restoration of all things, to take place at Jesus' coming.

After each plague, God hardened the Pharaoh's heart.[77] There were several reasons for this. First, by repeatedly manifesting His powers, God wanted to show the Israelites that He was God.[78] Second, God wanted the Pharaoh to make his best efforts in holding on to the Israelites before forcing him to give them up; then the Pharaoh would realize how powerless he was and abandon any lingering attachment to the Israelites after they left. Third, God wanted the Israelites to cut off their attachment to Egypt by provoking in them strong feelings of hostility against the Pharaoh.

God worked the dispensation to start the first national course to restore Canaan when Moses killed the Egyptian. However, this course was aborted when the people distrusted Moses. In the dispensation to start the second national course, God granted the Israelites the three signs and ten plagues. When the Israelites witnessed these miracles, they came to believe that Moses was truly sent by God as their leader. They believed and followed Moses, the Abel figure who had laid the national foundation of faith. Hence, the Israelites could embark upon the second national course to restore Canaan.

However, the indemnity condition to remove the fallen nature required more of the Israelites than a short-lived trust in and obedience to Moses while he was working these miracles. Due to their previous failure to fulfill this condition, Satan had claimed the entire providential course to restore Canaan. Now the Israelites had to restore that course by remaining faithful and obedient to Moses for the duration of

---

75. cf. Parallels 7
76. Exod. 12:35-36
77. Exod. 4:21; 10:27
78. Exod. 10:1-2

their journey. Only in this way would they fulfill the national indemnity condition to remove the fallen nature. Until they had traversed the wilderness with unwavering faith in Moses and entered the land of Canaan, the national foundation of substance would not be established.

The dispensation to start the second national course to restore Canaan was conducted with greater grace than that of the first course. Yet, since the prolongation had been due to their disbelief, the indemnity condition which the Israelites would have to fulfill was correspondingly heavier. In the first course, if the Israelites had followed Moses, they would have been led along the direct route by way of the land of the Philistines and would have entered Canaan in twenty-one days—a period corresponding to Jacob's twenty-one-year course in Haran. However, in the second course, God did not lead the people along the direct route. He was worried that when they encountered the warlike Philistines, they might again turn faithless and return to Egypt.[79] Instead, God led them across the Red Sea and through the wilderness in a long detour. God planned to bring them into Canaan after twenty-one months.

Thus, the Israelites began a twenty-one-month wilderness course under Moses' leadership. Let us study this course and examine how it served as the model course for Jesus to lead humanity on the worldwide course to restore Canaan.

When the Pharaoh grudgingly gave Moses permission for the Israelites to make sacrifices in Egypt, Moses demanded more, saying:

> It would not be right to do so; for we shall sacrifice to the Lord our God offerings abominable to the Egyptians. If we sacrifice offerings abominable to the Egyptians before their eyes, will they not stone us? We must go three days' journey into the wilderness and sacrifice to the Lord our God as he will command us. —*Exod. 8:26-27*

Moses asked for three days' leave with the intention to deceive the Pharaoh and lead the people out of Egypt altogether.

This three-day period had the same significance as Abraham's three-day journey to Mt. Moriah, which he needed in order to sever his ties to Satan before he could offer Isaac as a sacrifice. Since Abraham's time, this has been the indemnity period required for the separation of Satan at the outset of a providential course. When Jacob embarked upon the course to restore Canaan, there was a three-day period when he cut off ties to Satan by deceiving Laban and leaving Haran.[80]

---
79. Exod. 13:17
80. Gen. 31:19-22

Likewise, at the outset of this national course, Moses asked for a leave of three days with the intention of deceiving the Pharaoh and liberating his people from bondage. Jesus, too, would begin the spiritual course of restoration only after passing through three days for the separation of Satan before his victorious resurrection.

The Israelites, who numbered some 600,000 according to the Bible, departed from Rameses on the fifteenth day of the first month by the Hebrew calendar.[81] They upheld God's Will throughout the three-day journey to their first campsite at Succoth. From that time forth, God granted them the grace of a pillar of cloud by day and a pillar of fire by night to guide their way.[82] The pillar of cloud which led the Israelites by day (yang) symbolized Jesus, who would one day lead the people of Israel in the worldwide course to restore Canaan. The pillar of fire by night (yin) symbolized the Holy Spirit, who would guide them as the feminine Spirit.

At the shore of the Red Sea, upon God's command, Moses stretched out his staff and parted the waters; then he led the Israelites across on dry ground. The Egyptians chasing them in chariots were drowned when the waters closed up and engulfed them.[83] As was explained earlier, Moses represented God before the Pharaoh,[84] and Moses' staff symbolized Jesus, who would manifest God's power in the future. Hence, this miracle foreshadowed what was to happen when Jesus came. Satan would pursue the faithful ones who followed Jesus in walking the worldwide course to restore Canaan, but Jesus would raise the rod of iron[85] and strike the troubled sea[86] of this world. The waters would divide and reveal a smooth path upon which the believers would walk, while Satan in pursuit would perish.

The Israelites crossed the Red Sea and arrived at the wilderness of Sin on the fifteenth day of the second month. From then until the day they arrived at habitable land, God fed them with manna and quail.[87] The manna and quail signified the life-giving flesh and blood of Jesus, which God would provide during the worldwide course to restore Canaan. Thus, Jesus said:

> Your fathers ate the manna in the wilderness, and they died. . . . I am the living bread which came down from heaven; if anyone eats of this bread, he will live forever . . . unless you eat the flesh of the Son of man and drink his blood, you have no life in you. *—John 6:49-53*

---

81. Exod. 12:37; Num. 33:3
82. Exod. 13:21
83. Exod. 14:21-28
84. Exod. 7:1
85. Rev. 2:27; Ps. 2:9. The rod of iron signifies God's Word; cf. Eschatology 3.2.2.
86. The Bible uses water as a symbol for the sinful world. (Rev. 17:15) Hence, this world is sometimes referred to as a "troubled sea."
87. Exod. 16:13-35

When the Israelites left the wilderness of Sin and camped at Rephidim, there was no water for the people to drink. God commanded Moses to strike the rock at Horeb that water might spring forth from it. Moses did so and gave the people water which saved their lives.[88] St. Paul wrote, "The Rock was Christ."[89] Accordingly, the miracle of water from the rock foreshadowed that the Messiah would save all humanity with the water of life, of which Jesus said, "Whoever drinks of the water that I shall give him will never thirst."[90] The two tablets of stone Moses received on Mt. Sinai symbolized Jesus and his would-be Bride; the rock, which was the root of the tablets of stone, symbolized God. When Moses struck the rock and gave the people water, this laid the foundation upon which he could receive the tablets of stone and build the Ark of the Covenant and the Tabernacle.

Joshua fought with the Amalekites at Rephidim. Whenever Moses held up his hands, the Israelites prevailed; whenever Moses let his hands drop, they suffered a reverse. Aaron and Hur had Moses sit on a pile of stones and held his hands up on the left and the right, thus enabling Joshua to vanquish the king of the Amalekites and his troops.[91] This also foreshadowed what would happen when Jesus came. Joshua symbolized the believers, the Amalekites symbolized the satanic world, and Aaron and Hur symbolized Jesus and the Holy Spirit. Aaron and Hur holding up Moses' hands and enabling Joshua to vanquish the Amalekites foreshadowed that faithful people who worship the Trinity—God, Jesus and the Holy Spirit—will defeat every devil who confronts them.

2.2.2.3 The Providence of Restoration and the Tabernacle

The Israelites received the tablets of stone, the Tabernacle, and the Ark of the Covenant. Let us first examine how they received them. The Israelites arrived in the wilderness of Sinai at the beginning of the third month, after their victory over the Amalekites.[92] Moses then took seventy elders and climbed Mt. Sinai to meet God. Moses alone was called to the summit of Mt. Sinai, where God commanded him to fast for forty days to receive the Ten Commandments inscribed on the tablets of stone.[93] During his fast, Moses received God's instructions concerning the Ark of the Covenant and the Tabernacle.[94] When the forty-day fast

---

88. Exod. 17:6
89. I Cor. 10:4
90. John 4:14
91. Exod. 17:10-13
92. Exod. 19:1
93. Exod. 24:9-10, 18
94. Exod. 25-31

was over, Moses received two tablets of stone, inscribed by the finger of God with the Ten Commandments.[95]

When Moses came down from Mt. Sinai with the two tablets of stone and went before the Israelites, he found them worshipping a golden calf. During Moses' absence, they had instructed Aaron to make it, and when he had fashioned it, they proclaimed that this was the god who had led them out of Egypt. Moses' anger burned hot when he saw this. He threw down the tablets of stone and broke them at the foot of the mountain.[96] God appeared again to Moses and told him to carve another pair of stone tablets identical to the first pair, promising that He would again give them the Ten Commandments. Moses presented himself before God on the mountain and fasted for forty days a second time. God dictated the Ten Commandments to Moses, and Moses wrote them on the tablets.[97] Moses took these tablets and went before the Israelites again. This time they honored Moses. In obedience to his directions, they built the Ark of the Covenant and constructed the Tabernacle.[98]

2.2.2.3.1 The Significance and Purpose of the Tablets of Stone, the Tabernacle and the Ark of the Covenant

What did the tablets of stone signify? When Moses received the tablets of stone inscribed with God's Word, this signified the passing of the Age of the Providence to Lay the Foundation for Restoration, when fallen people could relate with God only through sacrifices, and the beginning of the Age of the Providence of Restoration, when they could relate with God through the revealed Word. It was previously explained that if Adam and Eve, who were created by the Word, had become perfect, they would have become the incarnations of the Word. Instead, they fell and lost the Word.[99] Moses received the two tablets inscribed with the Word at the end of a forty-day period for the separation of Satan. This signified the symbolic restoration of Adam and Eve as incarnations of the Word. Accordingly, the two tablets symbolized restored Adam and Eve, and also symbolized Jesus and his would-be Bride who were to come as the incarnations of the Word. Christ is symbolized in the Bible by a white stone,[100] and it is written, "the Rock was Christ."[101] As symbols of Jesus and his would-be Bride, the tablets of stone were also symbols of heaven and earth.

---

95. Exod. 31:18
96. Exod. 32:1-19
97. Exod. 34:1, 27-28
98. Exod. 35-40
99. cf. Restoration 1.2.1
100. Rev. 2:17
101. I Cor. 10:4

Next, what did the Tabernacle symbolize? Jesus likened his body to the Temple in Jerusalem.[102] We who believe in him are called God's temples.[103] The Temple was thus a representation of Jesus in image. If the Israelites had succeeded in the first course to restore Canaan under Moses' leadership, then as soon as they entered the land of Canaan they would have built the Temple and prepared to receive the Messiah. Yet due to their disbelief, the first course was aborted at the start. In the second course, God led them in a roundabout way across the Red Sea and through the wilderness. God could not have them build the Temple, but instead had to settle for the Tabernacle, which could be moved from place to place, as its substitute. Like the Temple, the Tabernacle was a representation of Jesus, but in symbol. When God commanded Moses to build the Tabernacle, He said, "And let them make me a sanctuary, that I may dwell in their midst."[104]

The Tabernacle was divided into two parts: the holy place (sanctuary) and the most holy place (holy of holies). Only the high priest could enter the most holy place, and only once a year when making the sacrifice of the Day of Atonement. The most holy place was where the Ark of the Covenant was kept. Here was the place where God made Himself present. It symbolized the spirit of Jesus. The holy place contained a lampstand, an incense altar and a table for the bread of the Presence, which were tended daily by the priests. It symbolized the body of Jesus. Furthermore, the most holy place symbolized the spiritual world, while the holy place symbolized the physical world. When Jesus was crucified, the curtain between the holy place and the most holy place was torn in two, from top to bottom.[105] This meant that Jesus' crucifixion laid the basis for spiritual salvation, when the gate was opened between spirit and flesh, or between heaven and earth.

What did the Ark of the Covenant symbolize? Enshrined in the most holy place, the Ark contained the testimonies to God's covenant. It contained the two tablets of stone, which symbolized Jesus and his would-be Bride and heaven and earth. It also contained manna, the main staple of the Israelites during the wilderness course, which symbolized the body of Jesus. The manna was placed inside a golden urn, which symbolized the glory of God. The Ark of the Covenant also contained Aaron's staff, which had demonstrated God's power by budding and putting forth sprouts.[106] The Ark thus represented the cosmos and, at the same time, was a smaller representation of the Tabernacle.

---

102. John 2:19-21
103. I Cor. 3:16
104. Exod. 25:8
105. Matt. 27:51
106. Heb. 9:4

The mercy seat was placed on top of the Ark of the Covenant. Two cherubim made of hammered gold were placed on either end of the mercy seat, overshadowing it with their wings. God promised that He would personally appear above the mercy seat, between the cherubim, and there He would give guidance to the Israelites.[107] This foreshadowed that when Jesus and his Bride, symbolized by the tablets of stone, come and cleanse the people's sins, God would appear over the mercy seat and open a path between the cherubim which had blocked the way to the tree of life in the Garden of Eden.[108] Everyone would then be able to come before Jesus, the tree of life, and receive the fullness of God's Word.

For what purpose did God give the tablets of stone, the Tabernacle, and the Ark of the Covenant? When the Israelites set out for the wilderness after completing the four-hundred-year indemnity period incurred due to Abraham's mistake in the offering, God struck the Egyptians with signs and plagues and drowned a host of Egyptian soldiers who tried to follow the Israelites across the Red Sea. The Israelites could not return to Egypt, not only because God's Will forbade it, but because they had become bitter enemies of the Egyptians. They had no choice but to complete the journey to Canaan; God had driven them to the point of no return. Nevertheless, the Israelites repeatedly fell into faithlessness during their journey. In the end, there was danger that even Moses might act faithlessly. To cope with this situation, God set up an object of faith, one which would remain unchanged even though the people might change. As long as even one person revered the object with absolute faith, God could continue the providential Will through him. That person would inherit the mission to attend the object of faith, as a baton is handed from one runner to the next in a relay race.

The Tabernacle, enshrining the Ark of the Covenant and the tablets of stone, was this object of faith. Since the Tabernacle represented the Messiah, when the Israelites built the Tabernacle, it signified that the Messiah had already come in a symbolic sense.

The Israelites were to revere and honor the Tabernacle as if it were the Messiah and to return to the blessed land of Canaan under Moses' leadership. Thus, they would establish the national foundation of substance. Even if all the Israelites were to fall into faithlessness along the way, as long as Moses continued to exalt the Tabernacle, the people would then be allowed to indemnify their faithlessness and be restored upon Moses' intact foundation. Furthermore, if even Moses were to become faithless, as long as any single Israelite exalted the Tabernacle in Moses' place, God could work through that person to restore all the people.

---

107. Exod. 25:17-22
108. Gen. 3:24

If the Israelites had trusted Moses and entered Canaan in the first national course, Moses' family would have served in the role of the Tabernacle, and Moses himself would have fulfilled the roles which were taken by the tablets of stone and the Ark of the Covenant. Moses' family would have become the bearer of the heavenly law. The Israelites could then have built the Temple in the land of Canaan without any need for the tablets, the Ark, or the Tabernacle. These were given as the means of salvation only after the people had become faithless. The Tabernacle, as the representation in symbol of Jesus and his would-be Bride, was needed only until the construction of the Temple. The Temple, as the representation in image of Jesus and his would-be Bride, was needed only until the Messiah's coming as the Temple incarnate.

2.2.2.3.2 The Foundation for the Tabernacle

Just as a foundation must be laid before we can receive the Messiah, a foundation had to be laid before the Israelites could build and exalt the Tabernacle, the symbolic representation of the Messiah. Needless to say, to establish the foundation for the Tabernacle, foundations of faith and substance for the Tabernacle had to be laid. Let us investigate how the Israelites were to lay these two foundations under the leadership of Moses.

Moses was to follow God's instructions and lay the foundation of faith for the Tabernacle by fasting and praying for forty days, a period for the separation of Satan. Upon this foundation of faith for the Tabernacle, the Israelites were to faithfully obey and support Moses as he worked to realize the ideal of the Tabernacle. They would thus fulfill the indemnity condition to remove the fallen nature and lay the foundation of substance for the Tabernacle. The Tabernacle in this discussion includes the tablets of stone and the Ark of the Covenant.

The First Foundation for the Tabernacle

Human beings were created on the sixth day to become the incarnations of the Word.[109] Hence, to give the Word of re-creation to fallen people for their restoration, God first had to restore the number six, representing the period of creation defiled by Satan. For this reason, God sanctified Mt. Sinai by covering it with clouds of glory for six days, and on the seventh day He appeared and called Moses from amidst the clouds. From that moment, Moses began his fast of forty days and

---

109. John 1:3

forty nights.[110] God directed Moses to set up a forty-day period for the separation of Satan in order to establish the foundation of faith for the Tabernacle, the symbolic Messiah. God saw that this was necessary because the Israelites had fallen into faithlessness after crossing the Red Sea.[111]

As mentioned above, the indemnity condition to remove the fallen nature during the Israelites' course to restore Canaan could not be fulfilled by their believing and following Moses only for the short time that he manifested God's power. Rather, its fulfillment required that the people maintain such faith and obedience until they entered Canaan, built the Temple, and received the Messiah. Likewise, to fulfill the indemnity condition to remove the fallen nature and lay the foundation of substance for the Tabernacle, the Israelites should have faithfully obeyed Moses from the moment he climbed the mountain to undertake the forty-day fast until they had finished constructing the Tabernacle. However, while Moses was fasting and praying on the mountain, the people all fell into faithlessness and worshipped the golden calf. Consequently, the foundation of substance for the Tabernacle was not established.

Since human beings themselves had lost the basis for the Word, it is their portion of responsibility to recover the basis upon which to receive it again. Hence, God does not intervene in people's actions when they are working to restore the Word. For this reason, although God had led the Israelites with signs and miracles, He did not intervene when they sinned.

When Moses saw the people worshipping the idol and dancing around it, he raged in anger. He threw down the tablets and shattered them.[112] As a result, Satan invaded the foundation of faith for the Tabernacle. As was explained above, the two tablets of stone symbolized Jesus and his would-be Bride, who were to come as the restored second Adam and Eve. This event foreshadowed that if Jesus came and found the Jewish people faithless, he might have to die on the cross without completing his original God-given mission with his would-be Bride.

The faithlessness of the Israelites at Mt. Sinai undermined God's providence to establish the foundation for the Tabernacle. It nullified God's arduous efforts to separate Satan from the people and cultivate their obedience to Moses. Due to their continued faithlessness, God's providence to establish the foundation for the Tabernacle had to be prolonged through a second and then a third attempt.

---

110. Exod. 24:16-18
111. Exod. 16:1-12; 17:2-4
112. Exod. 32:19

The Second Foundation for the Tabernacle

The Israelites proved faithless in the dispensation to receive the tablets of stone, and hence to build the Tabernacle, but because they stood on the foundation of having drunk the water from the rock at Rephidim—the symbolic root of the tablets—they were given a second chance. God appeared before Moses after he had broken the tablets and promised him another inscription of His Word. This time, God required that Moses himself carve the blank tablets upon which He would write the inscription. Furthermore, Moses could not restore the tablets of stone or build the Tabernacle around them without first restoring the foundation of faith for the Tabernacle by fulfilling once again a dispensation of forty for the separation of Satan. Therefore, Moses had to fast forty more days before he could obtain the second pair of tablets with the inscription of the Ten Commandments[113] and establish the Tabernacle as the object of faith. This time, the Israelites faithfully waited for Moses to return.

Moses' successful efforts to restore the broken tablets by forty days of fasting, and the Israelites' faith in him, foreshadowed that Jesus, though crucified, could return and make a new beginning in his work of salvation if the believers devotedly fulfilled the indemnity condition to receive him during the forty days of the Lord's resurrection—a dispensation of forty for the separation of Satan.

By remaining faithful while Moses was fasting on the mountain, and then obeying his instructions to build the Tabernacle, the Israelites fulfilled the indemnity condition to remove the fallen nature. This laid the foundation of substance for the Tabernacle, and hence the foundation for the Tabernacle. The Tabernacle was built by the first day of the first month of the second year.[114] However, as was mentioned earlier, the foundation of substance in the second national course to restore Canaan required much more than the mere construction of the Tabernacle. In fact, until they entered Canaan and built the Temple, the Israelites were supposed to honor the Tabernacle more than they valued their own lives; they were to keep the same faith until they received the Messiah.

On the twentieth day of the second month of the second year, the Israelites set out from the wilderness of Sinai, arrayed in formation around the Tabernacle and led by the pillar of cloud.[115] Yet before long, they began to complain about their hardships and murmur against Moses. Even after God destroyed their camp in His burning wrath, the

---

113. Exod. 34:28
114. Exod. 40:17
115. Num. 10:11-12

Israelites did not repent. They continued to complain, lamenting that they had nothing to eat but manna. They were resentful toward Moses and longed for the meat, fruit, vegetables and luxuries of Egypt.[116] Thus, the Israelites failed to maintain the second foundation for the Tabernacle, and it was invaded by Satan. The providence to restore this foundation was prolonged to a third attempt.

The Third Foundation for the Tabernacle

Although Satan defiled the second foundation for the Tabernacle, Moses' faith and devotion to the Tabernacle remained unchanging. Therefore, the Tabernacle stood firmly upon the foundation of faith which Moses had laid, while the Israelites still stood upon the foundation of having drunk the water from the rock at Rephidim.[117] The rock, we recall, was the root of the tablets of stone, which was at the center of the Tabernacle. Upon this foundation, the Israelites were allowed to attempt yet another dispensation of forty for the separation of Satan. By obeying Moses, who still honored the Tabernacle, they were to restore through indemnity the foundation for the Tabernacle in their third attempt. The forty-day mission to spy out the land of Canaan was given as the condition to achieve this.

God had Moses choose a leader from each of the twelve tribes of Israel and send them to spy out the land of Canaan for forty days.[118] When they returned, all the spies except Joshua and Caleb presented faithless reports:

> The people who dwell in the land are strong, and the cities are fortified and very large . . . [it] is a land that devours its inhabitants; and all the people that we saw in it are men of great stature . . . and we seemed to ourselves like grasshoppers, and so we seemed to them. —*Num. 13:28, 32-33*

They concluded that the Israelites could not capture Canaan's fortified cities or defeat its people. Upon hearing this report, the Israelites again murmured against Moses. They called for another leader who would take them back to Egypt. Only Joshua and Caleb called for the people not to be afraid but to attack the Canaanites in obedience to God's command:

> Do not rebel against the Lord; and do not fear the people of the land, for they are bread for us; their protection is removed from them, and the Lord is with us; do not fear them. —*Num. 14:9*

---

116. Num. 11:1-6
117. Exod. 17:6
118. Num. 13:1, 25

The Israelites did not accept this exhortation and attempted to stone Joshua and Caleb. At that moment, the glory of the Lord appeared to all the people, and God said to Moses:

> How long will this people despise me? And how long will they not believe in me, in spite of all the signs which I have wrought among them?
> —Num. 14:11

> But your little ones, who you said would become a prey, I will bring in, and they shall know the land which you have despised. But as for you, your dead bodies shall fall in this wilderness. And your children shall be shepherds in the wilderness forty years, and shall suffer for your faithlessness, until the last of your dead bodies lies in the wilderness. According to the number of the days in which you spied out the land, forty days, for every day a year, you shall bear your iniquity, forty years, and you shall know my displeasure. —Num. 14:31-34

As a result of their lack of faith, the third foundation for the Tabernacle ended in failure. Their twenty-one-month course in the wilderness was extended to forty years.

2.2.2.4 The Failure of the Second National Course to Restore Canaan

Due to the Israelites' faithlessness, the foundation for the Tabernacle was invaded by Satan three times. Therefore, the national indemnity condition to remove the fallen nature was not fulfilled, and the foundation of substance for the second national course to restore Canaan was not laid. Consequently, the entire second national course to restore Canaan ended in failure. God's providence was prolonged to a third national course.

2.2.3 The Third National Course to Restore Canaan

2.2.3.1 The Foundation of Faith

Because the Israelites turned faint-hearted upon hearing the report of the faithless spies, the second national course to restore Canaan ended in failure. The forty years Moses had spent in the wilderness of Midian to restore the foundation of faith were invaded by Satan. As a result of the failure of the mission to spy out the land, the people had to wander in the wilderness for forty years, one year for each day of the forty-day spy mission, until they returned to Kadesh-barnea. For Moses, this forty-year period was to separate Satan, who had invaded the previous foundation of faith, and to restore through indemnity the foundation of faith for the third course. Moses honored the Tabernacle with faith and loyalty throughout the entire forty years of wandering in the wilderness. By the time he returned to Kadesh-barnea, he had completed the foundation of faith for the third national course to restore Canaan. Accordingly, he also secured the position of Abel for the foundation of substance.

2.2.3.2 The Foundation of Substance

The foundation of substance for the second course ended in failure when, due to the people's persistent disbelief, Satan defiled the foundation for the Tabernacle. However, at least the foundation of faith for the Tabernacle remained, preserved by Moses' continued devotion. If, upon this foundation, the Israelites had faithfully followed Moses through the forty years of wandering in the wilderness, thus establishing the basis for the separation of Satan, they would have set up the foundation of substance for the Tabernacle and completed the foundation for the Tabernacle. If they had then honored and obeyed Moses and entered Canaan in faith, they would have completed the foundation of substance for the third national course to restore Canaan.

For Moses, the forty years of wandering in the wilderness was the period required to establish the foundation of faith for the third national course. For the Israelites, the goal for this period was to accomplish the dispensation to start the third course. They were to do this by establishing the foundation for the Tabernacle, thereby returning to the state of grace which they had enjoyed in the second course when they first constructed the Tabernacle under Moses' direction.

2.2.3.2.1 The Foundation of Substance Centered on Moses

The tablets, the Tabernacle, and the Ark of the Covenant became necessary in the second course only because the Israelites lost faith in the wilderness. Soon after they crossed the Red Sea, they forgot the three signs which God had granted when conducting the dispensation to start. To restore this through indemnity, God tested the people through a forty-day period while Moses was on the mountain. He then gave them three manifestations of divine grace: the tablets of stone, the Ark of the Covenant and the Tabernacle. Moreover, God had granted the ten plagues, which were to restore Laban's ten deceptions of Jacob in Haran. Yet when the Israelites lost faith even after witnessing these, God attempted to restore the ten plagues through indemnity by giving the Ten Commandments. If the Israelites had renewed their faith by honoring the three manifestations of divine grace and obeying the Ten Commandments, they would have returned to the state of grace they had enjoyed when they left Egypt under the power of these miracles.

Accordingly, in the third course the Israelites should have completed the forty-year indemnity period by following Moses in faith and obedience through the wilderness. After they returned to Kadesh-barnea, they should have stood with Moses upon the foundation for the Tabernacle and exalted the tablets, the Tabernacle and the Ark. Had they done so, they would have stood in the position they had enjoyed at the completion of the dispensation to start the second course, when God struck the Egyptians with the three signs and ten plagues. The tablets were a smaller representation of the Ark; the Ark was a smaller representation of the Tabernacle; hence, the tablets were a smaller representation of the Tabernacle. The Ark and the Tabernacle may thus be represented by the tablets or their root, the rock. Therefore, the third national course to restore Canaan was to begin at Kadesh-barnea upon completing a dispensation to start based on the rock. Henceforth, had the Israelites honored the Tabernacle with faith and devotion and followed Moses into Canaan, they would have fulfilled the indemnity condition to remove the fallen nature required for the foundation of substance in the third national course.

How did God intend to conduct the dispensation to start based on the rock? During the forty years of wandering in the wilderness, the Israelites again fell into complaint and faithlessness. To save them, God instructed Moses to strike the rock with his staff that it might yield water and give drink to the people.[119] Moses should have struck the rock only once. The awe-struck Israelites then should have united with him, thereby standing with him upon the foundation for the Tabernacle. In this way, they would have fulfilled the dispensation to start based on the rock.

However, when Moses heard the people murmuring against him and complaining that they had no water to drink, he raged in uncontrolled anger and struck the rock twice. Whereupon God said to him:

> Because you did not believe in me, to sanctify me in the eyes of the people of Israel, therefore you shall not bring this assembly into the land which I have given them. —*Num. 20:12*

By striking the rock twice when he should have struck it only once, Moses undermined the dispensation to start based on the rock. As a

---

119. Num. 20:4-5, 8

consequence, he was not permitted to enter the promised land. He could only gaze upon it from a distance at the end of his life.[120]

Let us investigate why Moses should have struck the rock just once, and why his striking it twice constituted a sin. The rock is a symbol for Jesus Christ.[121] Since Christ came as the tree of life,[122] the rock may also be seen as the tree of life. The tree of life is also a symbol for perfected Adam in the Garden of Eden; hence the rock symbolized Adam in perfection.

In the Garden of Eden, Adam should have matured to become the ideal represented by the rock. Yet when Satan struck him and caused him to fall, Adam could not become the tree of life or the rock which could give his descendants the water of eternal life. Therefore, the waterless rock, before Moses struck it the first time, symbolized fallen Adam. To indemnify Satan's act of striking Adam and preventing him from becoming the rock which could give the water of life, God had Moses strike the rock once. When he hit the rock once and it yielded water, Moses fulfilled an indemnity condition to restore Adam as the water-giving rock. The rock, struck once, symbolized Jesus who was to come and give fallen humanity the water of life. Therefore, Jesus said:

> Whoever drinks of the water that I shall give him will never thirst; the water that I shall give him will become in him a spring of water welling up to eternal life. —*John 4:14*

Thus, God intended that Moses strike the rock once as an indemnity condition for fallen Adam to be restored in the person of the second, perfected Adam—Jesus. However, when Moses struck the rock the second time, after it had already brought forth water, it represented the possibility that Jesus might be struck. In other words, Moses' act of striking the rock twice in anger at the faithlessness of the Israelites set up the condition that when Jesus came, if the Jewish people were to turn faithless, Satan would have grounds to confront Jesus, the fulfillment of the rock. This is why Moses' act constituted a sin.

Although Moses' act of breaking the tablets of stone could be restored, his mistake of striking the rock the second time could not be restored. Why is this so? In the context of the providence of restoration, the tablets of stone and the rock were related as external and internal. The tablets of stone, inscribed with the Ten Commandments, were the

---

120. Num. 27:12-14
121. I Cor. 10:4; Rev. 2:17
122. Rev. 22:14; cf. Fall 1.1.1

core of the Mosaic Law and the heart of the Old Testament. The Israelites could receive the salvation available in the Old Testament Age by upholding the ideals contained in the tablets. In this sense, the tablets of stone were an external representation of Jesus who was to come.

The rock, on the other hand, not only symbolized Christ; as the root of the tablets of stone, it also symbolized God, the origin of Christ. The tablets of stone were external; the rock was internal. If we liken the tablets to the body, the rock corresponds to the mind; if we liken the tablets to the holy place, the rock corresponds to the most holy place; if we liken the tablets to the earth, the rock corresponds to heaven. In short, as an internal representation of Christ, the rock had greater value than the tablets of stone.

As an external representation of Jesus, the tablets of stone also symbolized Aaron. Aaron was an external representative of Jesus as he stood before Moses, the representative of God.[123] When the Israelites pressured Aaron to make the golden calf,[124] Aaron himself lost faith, and this led to the breaking of the tablets. Nevertheless, Aaron could be revived because he repented while still standing upon the foundation of having drunk the water from the rock at Rephidim.[125] When he did so, the tablets of stone symbolizing Aaron could also be refashioned and restored based on the internal foundation of the water from the rock. However, since the rock—the root of the tablets of stone—symbolized not only Jesus but also God, his origin, striking the rock the second time could not be undone.

What were the consequences of striking the rock twice? Moses struck the rock the second time because he was overcome by uncontrolled rage at the people's faithlessness.[126] He acted under the influence of Satan, even on Satan's behalf. Consequently, the dispensation to start which God had intended to carry out based on the rock was defiled by Satan.

Although externally Moses' act of striking the rock a second time proved to be a satanic act, still in a deeper, internal sense he gave drink to the people with the water which flowed from it and saved their lives. This reaffirmed the prophecy God had given earlier[127] that the external Israelites, those who were adults when they left Egypt, could not enter Canaan as was promised, except for Joshua and Caleb. Moses,

---

123. Exod. 4:16; 7:1
124. Exod. 32:4
125. Exod. 17:6
126. Ps. 106:32-33
127. Num. 14:28-34

too, would die without fulfilling his long-cherished dream of entering the promised land.[128] On the other hand, the internal Israelites, those who were children at the time of the Exodus from Egypt or were born during the wilderness course when the people drank water from the rock and honored the Tabernacle, would enter Canaan under the leadership of Joshua,[129] who succeeded Moses.[130]

Since Moses' act of striking the rock twice allowed Satan to invade, we would not expect the rock to have yielded water. How, then, was it possible for water to flow from it? Moses had already brought forth water from the rock at Rephidim[131] in the second national course to restore Canaan, thus laying the foundation to bring forth water from the rock. The tablets of stone, the Tabernacle and the Ark of the Covenant erected upon this foundation were sustained into the third national course, despite the people's faithlessness, by Moses' unwavering devotion. He firmly maintained the foundation of faith for the Tabernacle, which he had laid during his forty-day fast. Although Moses' faith faltered in a moment of anger, his heart toward God remained unchanging. Furthermore, Joshua had laid the foundation for the Tabernacle through his absolute faith during the forty days of spying, and he continued to uphold the tablets, the Tabernacle and the Ark from that time forth. Thus, the foundation to bring forth water from the rock, which had been established at Rephidim, remained intact centered on Joshua. In sum, although the second dispensation based on the rock was invaded by Satan externally due to Moses' outward act of faithlessness, it remained sound internally. The rock brought forth water for the people due to Moses' and Joshua's internal attitude of unswerving faith and devotion.

When Moses struck the rock the second time, he in effect struck it from the position of Satan. Satan, therefore, took possession of the stone. Accordingly, when in Jesus' time the people disbelieved, Jesus, as the fulfillment of the stone, had to personally enter the wilderness and recover the stone. This is the reason behind his first temptation, when Satan challenged him to turn the stone into bread.

Due to the faithlessness of the Israelites, Moses became enraged and struck the rock twice. This gave Satan a lien on his body, which bound Moses to die outside the promised land. However, he was able to enter Canaan in spirit because he had brought forth water from the rock by virtue of his indomitable faith. This foreshadowed what could happen when Jesus came as the true manifestation of the rock. If the Jewish

---

128. Deut. 34:4-5
129. Num. 32:11-12
130. Num. 27:18-20
131. Exod. 17:6

people disbelieved, Jesus' body would also suffer attack by Satan, even to the extent of being hung on the cross. He would die before completing the restoration of Canaan worldwide. Nevertheless, he would still be able to accomplish the spiritual portion of restoration through his resurrection.

Shortly after this episode, the Israelites again complained along the way, and God sent fiery serpents which bit and killed many of them. When they repented, God had Moses make a bronze serpent and set it on a pole, that anyone might look at it and be saved.[132] The fiery serpents symbolized Satan, the ancient serpent[133] who had caused Eve to fall; the bronze serpent set on the pole symbolized Jesus, who was to come as the heavenly serpent. This foreshadowed what might happen in Jesus' time, as he said: "As Moses lifted up the serpent in the wilderness, so must the Son of man be lifted up."[134] Although God let the Israelites fall prey to the satanic serpent when they became faithless, He saved their lives with the bronze serpent when they repented and renewed their faith. Likewise, in Jesus' time, if the people were to disbelieve, God would have to leave them vulnerable to Satan's attack, and Jesus would have to be hung on the cross as the heavenly serpent to save humanity. Whoever then repented of his faithlessness and believed in the redemption by the cross would be saved. Indeed, the episode of the fiery serpents was a remote cause of Jesus' walking the path of the crucifixion to begin the course of spiritual salvation.

When the Israelites were faithless and Moses struck the rock twice, God declared that Moses would not be permitted to enter the land of Canaan.[135] Although Moses desperately prayed to God and begged God to allow him to enter Canaan,[136] he was denied entrance and died outside its borders. After his death, his body was buried in a valley in the land of Moab, but no one knew the place of its burial.[137] This also foreshadowed what might happen to Jesus: if the people were to reject him, he would be crucified. Even though he might pray desperately to avoid this fate and realize the Kingdom of Heaven—as he in fact did in the Garden of Gethsemane when he prayed, "let this cup pass from me"— he would die unable to accomplish this goal. Furthermore, after his death no one would know the whereabouts of his body.

---

132. Num. 21:6-9
133. Rev. 12:9
134. John 3:14
135. Num. 20:12
136. Deut. 3:25
137. Deut. 34:6

2.2.3.2.2 The Foundation of Substance Centered on Joshua

When at Kadesh-barnea Moses struck the rock twice, the dispensation to start the journey to Canaan, which was to have been based on the rock, was not brought to pass. Although Satan invaded externally, nevertheless the foundation which Moses had laid internally when he had brought forth water from the rock at Rephidim remained intact, and he could bring forth water from the rock at Kadesh-barnea for the people to drink. This set the pattern for what would follow. The external Israelites born in Egypt, who became faithless in the wilderness, all perished except for Joshua and Caleb, who had shown firm faith during the forty-day mission to spy out the land.[138] The internal Israelites, the younger generation who were born and raised in the wilderness when the people drank water from the rock and were upholding the Tabernacle, entered the land of Canaan under the leadership of Joshua.

God instructed Moses to commission Joshua in his stead:

Take Joshua the son of Nun, a man in whom is the spirit, and lay your hand upon him; cause him to stand before Eleazar the priest and all the congregation, and you shall commission him in their sight. You shall invest him with some of your authority, that all the congregation of the people of Israel may obey. —*Num. 27:18-20*

When the people were beset with fear upon hearing the reports of the spies, only Joshua and Caleb remained firm in their faith upon the foundation of faith Moses had laid through the Tabernacle. With absolute faith and loyalty, they thus established the foundation for the Tabernacle and would honor it to the end. Although Moses' faith faltered later on, the tablets of stone, the Ark and the Tabernacle all remained intact upon the foundation for the Tabernacle which Joshua laid.

Therefore, God worked the dispensation to start the course anew, this time based on the water from the rock, by elevating Joshua to Moses' place and having the internal Israelites obey him and stand with him upon the foundation for the Tabernacle. On this basis, they were to enter the land of Canaan, where they were to fulfill the national indemnity condition to remove the fallen nature. In this way, God intended to establish the foundation of substance centered on Joshua in the third national course.[139]

When Moses had satisfactorily accomplished the period of forty years in the wilderness of Midian, God appeared before him and commanded

---
138. Num. 32:11-12
139. Deut. 3:28

him to guide the Israelites to the land of Canaan, the land of milk and honey.[140] Likewise, when Joshua accomplished with faith and devotion the period of forty years of wandering in the wilderness, God personally called him to serve in the position of Moses, commanding:

> Moses my servant is dead; now therefore arise, go over this Jordan, you and all this people, into the land which I am giving to them, to the people of Israel. . . . As I was with Moses, so I will be with you; I will not fail you or forsake you. Be strong and of good courage; for you shall cause this people to inherit the land which I swore to their fathers to give them. —Josh. 1:2, 5-6

Upon receiving this direction from God, Joshua summoned the officers of the people and conveyed God's instructions to them.[141] They replied:

> All that you have commanded us we will do, and wherever you send us we will go. . . . Whoever rebels against your commandment and disobeys your words, whatever you command him, shall be put to death. Only be strong and of good courage. —Josh. 1:16-18

They pledged with their lives to follow Joshua. In succeeding Moses' mission to restore Canaan, Joshua prefigured Christ at the Second Advent, who will come to complete the mission which Jesus left unfinished. Just as Joshua's course was to restore through indemnity Moses' course, the course of Christ at the Second Advent must restore through indemnity, both physically and spiritually, Jesus' course of spiritual restoration.

In the second national course, Moses sent twelve spies to Canaan.[142] Upon the foundation of heart laid by the two spies who had faithfully completed their mission, Joshua sent two men to spy out the fortified city of Jericho.[143] When they returned from Jericho, the two spies made a faithful report: "Truly the Lord has given all the land into our hands; and moreover all the inhabitants of the land are fainthearted because of us."[144] The younger generation of Israelites raised in the wilderness all believed the spies' words, and this faith indemnified the sins of their parents, who had not properly completed the previous forty-day mission to spy out the land.

Having pledged with their lives to obey Joshua, who stood upon the foundation for the Tabernacle, the internal Israelites could stand with him

---

140. Exod. 3:8-10
141. Josh. 1:10
142. Num. 13:1-2
143. Josh. 2:1
144. Josh. 2:24

on that foundation. By restoring the dispensation to start based on the water from the rock, they assumed the same position as their parents had when, under Moses' leadership, they had participated in the dispensation to start at the Exodus from Egypt when God provided the three signs and ten plagues. Just as the Israelites under Moses' leadership had passed through a three-day course before they crossed the Red Sea, the Israelites under Joshua's leadership passed through a three-day course before they crossed the Jordan River.[145] In the second national course, after the three-day course was completed, the pillar of cloud and the pillar of fire led the Israelites to the Red Sea. Similarly, after the Israelites under Joshua's leadership completed the three-day course, the Ark of the Covenant led them to the Jordan River.[146] The tablets lying at the center of the Ark, and the pillars of cloud and fire both symbolized Jesus and his would-be Bride.

Moses used his staff to guide the way and split the Red Sea in two. Likewise, Joshua placed the Ark of the Covenant in front of the troops to guide their way. When the priests bearing the Ark of the Covenant entered the Jordan River, its waters parted, opening the way for the people following the Ark to walk on the riverbed.[147] Moses' staff symbolized Jesus; similarly, the Ark containing the tablets of stone, manna and Aaron's staff symbolized Jesus and his would-be Bride. Therefore, the parting of the Jordan River before the Ark, which allowed the Israelites to enter the land of Canaan safely, foreshadowed what would happen in the presence of Jesus and his Bride: sinful humanity, symbolized by water,[148] would be divided between the righteous and the wicked and face the judgment. All faithful believers would then complete the restoration of Canaan worldwide.

Upon reaching the Jordan River, God commanded Joshua, saying:

> Take twelve men from the people, from each tribe a man, and command them, "Take twelve stones from here out of the midst of the Jordan, from the very place where the priests' feet stood, and carry them over with you, and lay them down in the place where you lodge tonight." —*Josh. 4:2-3*

And thus the people did:

> The people came up out of the Jordan on the tenth day of the first month, and they encamped in Gilgal, on the east border of Jericho. And those twelve stones, which they took out of the Jordan, Joshua set up in Gilgal. —*Josh. 4:19-20*

---

145. Josh. 3:2
146. Josh. 3:3, 6
147. Josh. 3:16-17
148. Rev. 17:15

What did this foreshadow? As was discussed earlier, the stone symbolized Jesus. Accordingly, when the twelve leaders representing the twelve tribes each carried a stone from the middle of the Jordan River after its waters had been divided by the Ark, it foreshadowed what the twelve disciples of Jesus, representing the twelve tribes, should do at his coming: uphold him at the very place where his Word judges this sinful world and divides it into good and evil.

After they took the twelve stones and set them up in the camp at Gilgal in the land of Canaan, Joshua said, "So that all the peoples of the earth may know that the hand of the Lord is mighty; that you may fear the Lord your God for ever."[149] This foreshadowed that the twelve disciples of Jesus should become one in heart; only then could they complete the restoration of Canaan worldwide, that all the people of the world might praise the power of God eternally.

Just as Jacob built a stone altar wherever he went, the representatives of the twelve tribes, descendants of the twelve sons of Jacob, gathered together the twelve stones and built an altar in praise of God. They were eventually to construct the Temple. This foreshadowed that the twelve disciples of Jesus should join together and honor Jesus as the Temple. For this reason, when his disciples were not uniting, Jesus said, "Destroy this temple, and in three days I will raise it up."[150] The twelve disciples in fact failed to unite with each other, and one of them, Judas Iscariot, even sold Jesus to his foes. Only after Jesus suffered crucifixion and resurrected after three days was he able to bring together his scattered disciples. The disciples then honored the resurrected Jesus as the spiritual Temple. Only at his Second Coming will his followers be able to serve him as the incarnate Temple.

When the Israelites left Egypt and set out for the land of Canaan, they observed the feast of Passover on the fourteenth day of the first month.[151] Likewise, the Israelites under Joshua's leadership, who encamped at Gilgal, observed the feast of Passover on the fourteenth day of the first month of that year. Afterward, they set out for the city of Jericho. When they began to live on the produce of the land, God stopped giving the manna which He had been providing for forty years. From that time forth, they were to make a living with their own sweat. Furthermore, until they had overthrown every last satanic city, they had to strive to the utmost to fulfill their responsibility.

---

149. Josh. 4:24
150. John 2:19
151. Exod. 12:17-18

As they approached Jericho, in accordance with God's command, the Israelites put forty thousand soldiers at the forefront while seven priests blew seven trumpets as they marched behind the soldiers. Following behind them was the Ark of the Covenant carried by the Levitical priests, and the rest of the Israelite army marched at the rear. The Israelites marched around the fortified city in this formation once a day for six days, but this caused no change in the city. With patience and obedience, the people were restoring through indemnity the six-day period of creation which had been invaded by Satan. After they faithfully endured through six days, on the seventh day the seven priests circled the city walls seven times, blowing the seven trumpets, and Joshua said to the people: "Shout; for the Lord has given you the city."[152] The people raised a great shout and the city walls tumbled down. The conquest of Jericho[153] foreshadowed that by the power of Christ and the work of his followers, the satanic barrier between Heaven and earth will crumble. Once dismantled, this wall will never be erected again. Thus, Joshua proclaimed:

> Cursed before the Lord be the man that rises up and rebuilds this city, Jericho. At the cost of his firstborn shall he lay its foundation, and at the cost of his youngest son shall he set up its gates. —*Josh. 6:26*

Joshua then launched attacks on the enemy with insurmountable force. He defeated thirty-one kings altogether.[154] This foreshadowed that Christ will come as the King of Kings to build the unified Kingdom of Heaven on earth by bringing all gentile kings to complete surrender and winning the hearts of their people.

2.2.3.3 THE FOUNDATION FOR THE MESSIAH

We have learned that the Israelites failed in the second national course to restore Canaan when they could not fulfill the forty-day mission to spy out the land as a condition to separate Satan. To pay indemnity for this failure, during the third national course they wandered in the wilderness for forty years. During this period, Moses laid the foundation of faith for the third course, and the Israelites stood upon the foundation for the Tabernacle. Yet Satan defiled these two foundations due to the people's faithlessness and Moses' mistake of striking the rock twice. Consequently, the older generation of Israelites, except for

---

152. Josh. 6:16
153. Josh. 6
154. Josh. 12:9-24

Joshua and Caleb, perished in the wilderness. Joshua and Caleb had faithfully fulfilled the forty-day spy mission while standing upon the foundation of faith for the second course and the foundation of faith for the Tabernacle which Moses had laid. They thereby established the foundation for the Tabernacle. The younger generation of Israelites crossed the Jordan River while bearing the Ark of the Covenant with utmost faith under the leadership of Joshua, who succeeded Moses. Then, destroying the fortified city of Jericho, they entered Canaan, the promised land. Based on this victory, they laid the foundation of substance in the third national course and established the foundation for the Messiah for this course—albeit as a people without sovereignty.

The family foundation for the Messiah had been fulfilled in the days of Abraham. His descendants passed through a four-hundred-year course of indemnity as slaves in Egypt before they could enter Canaan and there complete the national foundation for the Messiah. This required more than merely entering and conquering Canaan. As was discussed earlier in detail,[155] fallen people had already founded powerful nations such as Egypt, led by satanic rulers who opposed God's providence of restoration. Therefore, even though the national foundation for the Messiah was established under Joshua's leadership, it would be necessary to build a sovereign kingdom from which the Messiah could confront the satanic nations of the world. However, once the younger generation of Israelites entered Canaan, they also became faithless. Hence, God's providence was prolonged again, and would suffer repeated setbacks until the time of Jesus.

2.3 SOME LESSONS FROM MOSES' COURSE

Throughout history, people of faith have read the biblical account of Moses and thought it was merely a record of Moses' life and Israel's history. No one truly understood that God intended to reveal by this account certain secrets of the providence of restoration. Jesus only intimated it, saying, "The Son can do nothing of his own accord, but only what he sees the Father doing; for whatever he does, that the Son does likewise."[156] He passed away without divulging the true significance of Moses' course.[157]

In these pages, we have revealed how Moses walked the model course or formula course for the providence of restoration. By making a comparison between this section and the next section, readers will understand more clearly how, through Moses' course, God foreshadowed the path

---

155. cf. Foundation 3.3
156. John 5:19
157. John 16:12

Jesus would walk. Yet even by studying the providence centered on Moses alone, we cannot but come to the conclusion that God exists and has been guiding human history toward the realization of one absolute purpose.

Moses' course also demonstrates that the actual outcome of a person's life depends upon whether or not the person fulfills his portion of responsibility, regardless of God's foreordained plan for him. God's predestined Will cannot be achieved through the person entrusted with its fulfillment if he does not complete his portion of responsibility. Specifically, God foretold that He would have Moses lead the Israelites into Canaan, the land of milk and honey, and commanded him to carry this out. Nevertheless, when Moses and his people did not fulfill their responsibility, only Joshua and Caleb among the first generation entered Canaan. The rest died in the wilderness.

Moreover, God does not intervene in the human portion of responsibility but acts only upon the actual result a person brings. Although God guided the people with amazing signs and miracles, He did not interfere in their actions when they worshipped the golden calf while Moses was away on the mountain. He did not intervene to restrain Moses when he struck the rock twice. When they did so, they were carrying out their portions of responsibility which were theirs alone to fulfill. However, once they had acted either to fulfill their responsibility or to fail in it, God regarded their result and acted accordingly.

Moses' course demonstrates the absoluteness of God's predestined Will. God predetermines absolutely that His Will be fulfilled and continually attempts to accomplish it until it is done. Thus, when Moses could not complete his responsibility, God found a successor, Joshua, and worked determinedly to accomplish His Will through him. In general, when someone in the Abel position whom God has chosen does not complete his given mission, someone in the Cain position who has demonstrated the utmost devotion will replace the Abel figure and inherit his mission. Jesus described a comparable situation when he said, "From the days of John the Baptist until now the kingdom of heaven has been forcefully advancing, and forceful men lay hold of it."[158]

Moses' course shows that the greater one's mission, the greater the test one will face. Because the first ancestors fell when they did not believe in God but turned away from Him, central figures restoring the foundation of faith must overcome a test in which God abandons them. Moses had to overcome a trial in which God tried to kill him[159] before he could rise as the leader of the Israelites.

---

158. Matt. 11:12 NIV; cf. Messiah 2.3
159. Exod. 4:24

With the Fall as a condition, Satan bound human beings in a relationship with him. Consequently, God does not grant grace to people without a necessary condition, for if He were to do so, Satan would make accusations. Therefore, when God is about to give grace, He puts the person through a test, either before or after the grace, to prevent Satan's accusation. Moses' course provides examples of this. God granted Moses the grace to begin the first course to depart from Egypt only after he had completed the test of living in the Pharaoh's palace for forty years. God granted him the grace to begin the second course to depart from Egypt only after he had completed the test of living in the wilderness of Midian for forty years.[160] Only after giving the test in which God tried to kill Moses[161] did He grant the three signs and ten plagues.[162] Only after giving the test of the three-day course[163] did God grant the pillars of cloud and fire.[164] Only after giving the test of crossing the Red Sea[165] did God give the grace of manna and quail.[166] After giving the test of the battle with the Amalekites,[167] God granted the grace of the tablets of stone, the Tabernacle, and the Ark of the Covenant.[168] The grace of the water from the rock[169] was given only after the test of wandering for forty years in the wilderness. When God sent the fiery serpents, the people's repentance was the condition for God to give the grace of the bronze serpent.[170]

These are lessons which Moses' course teaches us.

SECTION 3

THE PROVIDENCE OF RESTORATION UNDER THE LEADERSHIP OF JESUS

In the beginning, Adam should have governed the angels;[171] but due to his fall, human beings came under Satan's dominion and formed a hellish world. To restore this through indemnity, Jesus came as the second Adam to personally bring Satan to submission and establish the Kingdom of Heaven. However, Satan, who does not submit even to God, would by no means readily yield to Jesus and people of faith. Therefore, taking responsibility for having created human beings, God raised up Jacob and Moses and revealed through them the model course by which Jesus could subjugate Satan.[172]

---

160. Exod. 4:2-9
161. Exod. 4:25
162. Exod. 7:10
163. Exod. 10:22
164. Exod. 13:21
165. Exod. 14:21-22
166. Exod. 16:13
167. Exod. 17:10
168. Exod. 31:18
169. Num. 20:9
170. Num. 21:6-9
171. I Cor. 6:3
172. cf. Moses and Jesus 1.1

Jacob walked the symbolic course to bring Satan to submission, while Moses walked the image course. Their courses pioneered the way for Jesus to walk the actual course. In walking the worldwide course to restore Canaan, Jesus followed the model demonstrated in the national course to restore Canaan when Moses was working to subjugate Satan.

God told Moses, "I will raise up for them a prophet like you from among their brethren; and I will put my words in his mouth, and he shall speak to them all that I command him."[173] By "a prophet like you," God was referring to Jesus, who was to walk the same course Moses walked. When Jesus said, "the Son can do nothing of his own accord, but only what he sees the Father doing; for whatever he does, that the Son does likewise,"[174] he meant that God had revealed the model course through Moses and that he was following in Moses' footsteps. Let us examine the providence of restoration centered on Jesus, drawing relevant comparisons between the three national courses to restore Canaan under Moses' leadership and the three worldwide courses to restore Canaan under Jesus' leadership.

3.1 THE FIRST WORLDWIDE COURSE TO RESTORE CANAAN

3.1.1 THE FOUNDATION OF FAITH

In the first worldwide course to restore Canaan, the central figure entrusted with the mission to restore the foundation of faith was John the Baptist. From what position was John supposed to accomplish this mission? In the national course to restore Canaan under Moses' leadership, Moses broke the tablets of stone and struck the rock twice. This set up conditions for Satan to strike the body of Jesus—the fulfillment of the tablets and the rock—should the Jewish people of his day not believe in him.

For Jesus to be released from this condition, the chosen people entrusted with the mission to prepare for his coming should have united around the Temple, the image representation of the Messiah who was to come. However, over the years the Israelites repeatedly lapsed into faithlessness and thus multiplied conditions for Satan to attack Jesus. To erase these conditions, God sent the prophet Elijah. Elijah worked to separate Satan by defeating the prophets of Baal and Asherah, 850 altogether,[175] and then ascended to heaven.[176] Yet, because Elijah did not complete his

---
173. Deut. 18:18
174. John 5:19
175. I Kings 18:19
176. II Kings 2:11

entire mission he had to return.[177] John the Baptist was the prophet who came as Elijah[178] to complete this unfinished mission to separate Satan and make straight the way of the Lord.[179]

The Israelites had suffered hardships in Egypt for four hundred years without a prophet to guide them. They finally met Moses, the one man who could lead them into Canaan as a nation in preparation to receive the Messiah. In a similar fashion, the Jewish people suffered all kinds of tribulations under the oppression of the gentile nations of Persia, Greece, Egypt, Syria and Rome without a prophet to guide them during the four-hundred-year period of preparation for the advent of the Messiah, which began at the time of the prophet Malachi.[180] They finally met John the Baptist, the one man who could lead them to the Messiah, who was coming to restore Canaan worldwide.

Thus, John the Baptist, like Moses, was called on the foundation of a four-hundred-year period for the separation of Satan. Moses had learned to love his brethren and the traditions of his fathers while living in the Pharaoh's palace. Likewise, John the Baptist learned the way of faith and obedience to Heaven and made preparations for the Messiah while living on locusts and wild honey in the wilderness. His life was so exemplary that many people, including the priests and Levites, wondered whether he might be the Messiah.[181] In this way, John the Baptist successfully established the dispensation of forty for the separation of Satan and was able to lay the foundation of faith for the first worldwide course to restore Canaan.

3.1.2   The Foundation of Substance

Since John the Baptist stood in the same position as Moses, he likewise stood in the dual positions of parent and child. From the position of parent, he restored through indemnity the foundation of faith. From the position of child, he secured the position of Abel for the fulfillment of the indemnity condition to remove the fallen nature.[182] John the Baptist recovered a foundation on the world level comparable to that of Moses when he laid the foundation of faith for the first national course after forty years inside the Pharaoh's palace.

In Moses' day, God's desire at the first dispensation to start was that the Israelites develop trust in Moses when they witnessed him killing

---

177. Mal. 4:5
178. Matt. 11:14; 17:13
179. John 1:23
180. cf. Periods 3.6
181. John 1:19; Luke 3:15
182. cf. Moses and Jesus 2.1.2

an Egyptian taskmaster. The Israelites were then to leave the satanic world of Egypt and travel to the land of Canaan. In John the Baptist's time, however, the Jewish people were not to leave the Roman Empire and set out for another land. They were to remain within the empire, win over its people, and restore the empire to God's side. God conducted the dispensation to start by encouraging the Jewish people to believe in John through the miracles surrounding his life.

At John's conception, an angel gave a wondrous prophecy concerning the child. When his father Zechariah did not believe it, he was struck dumb, and his speech returned only after he circumcised and named the child. Through these and other miracles, the Israelites were convinced that John was a prophet sent by God:

> Fear came on all their neighbors. And all these things were talked about through all the hill country of Judea; and all who heard them laid them up in their hearts, saying, "What then will this child be?" For the hand of the Lord was with him. —*Luke 1:65-66*

Moreover, John led an illustrious life of prayer and asceticism in the wilderness, living on locusts and wild honey. The general public and even the priests admired him so highly that many thought he might be the Messiah.[183]

When Moses finished the forty-year indemnity period in the Pharaoh's palace and killed the Egyptian, the Israelites should have been deeply inspired by his love for his people and followed him with faith. They would have then gone straight into Canaan, without having to cross the Red Sea or wander in the wilderness, and without need of the tablets of stone, the Ark of the Covenant or the Tabernacle. Likewise, the Jewish people in Jesus' time were to believe in and follow John the Baptist, whom God had raised up through miracles and signs as the focus of their faith. Thus, they would fulfill the indemnity condition to remove the fallen nature and lay the foundation of substance, thereby immediately establishing the foundation for the Messiah.

3.1.3 THE FAILURE OF THE FIRST WORLDWIDE COURSE TO RESTORE CANAAN

The Jewish people stood upon the foundation of faith laid by John the Baptist and followed John as if they were following the Messiah.[184] Thereupon, they brought an end to the Old Testament Age and were ready to embark upon a new course to restore Canaan worldwide. Yet,

---

183. Luke 3:15; John 1:19
184. John 1:19; Luke 3:15

as was explained earlier,[185] John the Baptist harbored doubts toward Jesus, even though he had testified to him. He sent a delegation and asked Jesus, "Are you he who is to come, or shall we look for another?"[186] He denied that he was Elijah even though he in fact came to fulfill Elijah's mission.[187] This not only blocked the Jewish people's path to Jesus, it even led them to oppose him. In effect, John left the position of Abel, depriving the Jewish people of the central person with whom they could fulfill the indemnity condition to remove the fallen nature. This blocked their way to complete the foundation of substance or the foundation for the Messiah. Consequently, the first worldwide course to restore Canaan was aborted. As was the case in Moses' days, it was prolonged to a second and then a third course.

3.2 THE SECOND WORLDWIDE COURSE TO RESTORE CANAAN

3.2.1 THE FOUNDATION OF FAITH

3.2.1.1 JESUS TAKES ON THE MISSION OF JOHN THE BAPTIST

In relationship to Jesus, the perfect Adam, John the Baptist came in the role of the restored Adam. He was to establish the foundation for the Messiah, thus completing all the unfinished missions of the central figures of the past who had labored to restore the foundations of faith and substance. Upon this foundation, he was to present all the fruits of providential history to Jesus and guide the Jewish people, who trusted and followed him, to receive Jesus. Finally, he himself should have attended Jesus with faith and devotion.

Even though John the Baptist did not know it, the baptism which he gave to Jesus at the Jordan River[188] was in truth a ceremony of offering Jesus all of John's lifelong accomplishments for the sake of God's Will.

Nevertheless, because John the Baptist gradually came to doubt Jesus and finally even undermined his work, the Jewish people, who had the highest esteem for John, were compelled to disbelieve in Jesus.[189] Consequently, the foundation of faith which John had laid for the first worldwide course to restore Canaan was invaded by Satan. Jesus himself now had to take on John's mission and restore through indemnity the foundation of faith in order to set out on the second

---

185. cf. Messiah 2
186. Matt. 11:3
187. John 1:21
188. Matt. 3:16
189. cf. Messiah 2.2

worldwide course to restore Canaan. When Jesus fasted for forty days in the wilderness, it was to separate Satan for the very purpose of restoring the foundation of faith; however, for this he lowered himself to assume the position of John the Baptist.

Jesus, who came as God's only begotten Son and the Lord of Glory, was not meant to walk a path of suffering.[190] Rather, it was for John the Baptist, born with the mission to make straight the way of Jesus,[191] to go through tribulations. However, because John did not complete his responsibility, Jesus had to undergo suffering in John's place. Jesus enjoined Peter not to reveal to the Jewish people that he was the Messiah[192] because, although he was the Messiah, he had assumed John's role for the purpose of beginning this phase of the providence.

3.2.1.2 Jesus' Forty-Day Fast and Three Temptations in the Wilderness

Let us examine the remote and immediate causes behind Jesus' forty-day fast and his three temptations. In the national course to restore Canaan, when Moses stood before the rock, he turned faithless and struck the rock twice. As a result, the rock, symbolizing Jesus,[193] was defiled by Satan. This act affirmed the possibility that centuries later, when Jesus came to walk in the footsteps of Moses' course, John the Baptist might become faithless and Satan could then attack Jesus, the fulfillment of the rock. Moses' act also affirmed the possibility that Satan might invade the foundation of faith laid by John the Baptist. Hence, Moses' act of striking the rock twice was the remote cause which, should John lose faith, would compel Jesus to endure a forty-day fast and face three temptations in the wilderness for the purpose of restoring the foundation of faith.

John the Baptist actually did become faithless[194] and Satan invaded the foundation of faith which John had laid. This was the immediate cause of Jesus undertaking a dispensation of forty for the separation of Satan by fasting for forty days and overcoming the three temptations. By doing this from the position of John the Baptist, Jesus restored through indemnity the foundation of faith.

It is written that after forty days, Satan tested Jesus three times. First, he showed Jesus stones and tempted him to turn them into loaves of bread. Next, he took Jesus to the pinnacle of the Temple and challenged him to throw himself down. Finally, Satan took Jesus to a very

---

190. I Cor. 2:8
191. John 1:23; Luke 1:76
192. Matt. 16:20
193. I Cor. 10:4
194. cf. Messiah 2.3

high mountain and offered to give Jesus all the kingdoms of the world if he would fall down and worship him.[195]

What was Satan's purpose in giving Jesus the three temptations? In the beginning, God created human beings and gave them three great blessings—perfection of individual character, multiplication of children, and dominion over the natural world[196]—by which they might accomplish the purpose of creation. By inducing the first human ancestors to fall, Satan deprived humankind of the three great blessings and thus prevented the fulfillment of the purpose of creation. Jesus came into the world to accomplish the purpose of creation by restoring these blessings. Therefore, Satan tempted Jesus three times in an attempt to prevent him from restoring the three blessings and accomplishing the purpose of creation.

How, then, did Jesus confront and overcome the three temptations? First, let us examine how Satan came to be in a position to impose temptations on Jesus. Satan first took such a dominant position when, in the national course to restore Canaan, he claimed possession of the rock and the tablets of stone, which symbolized Jesus and his would-be Bride. This was possible because Moses broke the tablets of stone and struck the rock twice in anger at the faithlessness of the people. In the worldwide course, when John the Baptist failed his responsibility, the Jewish people became as disbelieving and disobedient as the Israelites were in Moses' time. Therefore, as God had already foreshadowed in Moses' course, Satan rose to a position of power from which he could impose temptations on Jesus.

After Jesus completed the forty-day fast in the wilderness, Satan appeared before him and tempted him, saying, "If you are the Son of God, command these stones to become loaves of bread."[197] Satan had possession of the stone. He had claimed the water-giving rock and the tablets of stone based on the condition first set by Moses' mistakes and then brought to fruition by John the Baptist's faithlessness. Moses had first obtained the stone after fulfilling dispensations of forty for the separation of Satan in the wilderness. To purify and recover the stone, Jesus fasted in the wilderness for forty days. Satan was well aware that Jesus went into the wilderness for this purpose, and his intention in giving the first temptation was to keep the stone in his possession. Jesus suffered from hunger in the wilderness, just as the Israelites had in Moses' day. When the Israelites could not overcome their hunger but

---

195. Matt. 4:1-10
196. Gen. 1:28
197. Matt. 4:3

fell into faithlessness, this eventually let Satan claim possession of the stone. Likewise, if Jesus were to lose faith and satisfy his hunger by turning the stone into bread, abandoning his effort to restore the stone, Satan would possess the stone forever.

Jesus' answer to this temptation was, "Man shall not live by bread alone, but by every word that proceeds from the mouth of God."[198] Originally, human beings were created to live on two kinds of nourishment. The body lives on the nourishment obtained from the physical world, while the spirit lives by receiving the love and truth of God. However, since fallen people cannot receive the Word directly from God, their spirits have life by the words of Jesus, who came as the incarnation of God's Word.[199] Jesus said, "I am the bread of life. . . . unless you eat the flesh of the Son of man and drink his blood, you have no life in you."[200] He meant that a person does not live a complete and wholesome life merely by eating bread to keep his body alive. His life is not full unless he lives by Jesus, who came as the life-giving nourishment for the spirit.

Indeed, the stone in Satan's hands—signifying the rock and the tablets of stone which Moses had lost—symbolized the very self of Jesus[201] who was being subjected to this temptation. In his reply, Jesus meant that although he was starving, he was less concerned about obtaining the bread which could keep his body alive than he was with becoming the incarnate Word of God who could nourish every spirit with life. With that heart, Jesus was determined to triumph over Satan. Furthermore, this test was conducted so that Jesus might re-establish the position of the Messiah, the one who has attained perfection of his individual character, by overcoming the temptation from the position of John the Baptist. Jesus defeated Satan because he spoke and acted in full accordance with the Principle. By his victory over this temptation, Jesus fulfilled the condition to restore the individual nature to perfection and thereby established the basis for the restoration of God's first blessing.

Next, Satan brought Jesus to the pinnacle of the Temple and challenged him, saying, "If you are the Son of God, throw yourself down."[202] Jesus referred to himself as the Temple,[203] and it is written that Christians are temples of God[204] and members of the body of Christ.[205] From this we can understand that Jesus is the main temple while the

---

198. Matt. 4:4
199. John 1:14
200. John 6:48-53
201. I Cor. 10:4; Rev. 2:17
202. Matt. 4:6
203. John 2:19
204. I Cor. 3:16
205. I Cor. 12:27

believers are like branch temples. Jesus came as the Lord of the Temple. Even Satan had to acknowledge his position; thus he put Jesus on the top of the Temple. When Satan dared Jesus to throw himself down, it meant that he wanted to usurp Jesus' position as the Lord of the Temple by enticing Jesus to fall from that position to the lowly state of a fallen person.

At that moment Jesus answered him, "You shall not tempt the Lord your God."[206] Originally, angels were created to be governed by people who have realized their God-given nature. Hence, even fallen angels should rightfully submit to Jesus, their Lord. Accordingly, it was an unprincipled act for an angel to attempt to usurp the position of the Lord of the Temple from Jesus. Jesus' response meant that Satan should not test God by tempting Jesus, the incarnation of God, who works His providence in strict accordance with the Principle. Moreover, by prevailing in the first temptation and restoring his individual character as the incarnate Temple, Jesus had already secured the position of the Lord of the Temple. Therefore, Satan had no condition to tempt Jesus again, but should have retreated at that point. By overcoming the second temptation, Jesus, the main temple, the bridegroom and the True Parent of humanity, opened the way for all people of faith to be restored to the positions of branch temples, brides and true children. Jesus thus established the basis upon which to restore God's second blessing.

Finally, Satan took Jesus to a very high mountain and showed him all things under heaven and all their glory, saying, " All these I will give you, if you will fall down and worship me."[207] Due to Adam's fall, human beings lost the qualification to be the lords of creation. They fell under the dominion of Satan, who usurped Adam's position as the creation's master. Coming in the capacity of a perfected Adam, Jesus was the Lord of creation, as it is written, "For God has put all things in subjection under his feet."[208] Because Satan knew this from his understanding of the Principle, he led Jesus to the top of the mountain in recognition of his position as the Lord of creation. Satan then tempted Jesus, hoping that Jesus, the second Adam, might also submit to him as Adam had submitted in the beginning.

Jesus replied, "Begone, Satan! for it is written, 'You shall worship the Lord your God and him only shall you serve.'"[209] Angels were created as ministering spirits[210] to revere and serve God, their Creator. By his answer, Jesus indicated that according to the Principle even a fallen

---

206. Matt. 4:7
207. Matt. 4:9
208. I Cor. 15:27
209. Matt. 4:10
210. Heb. 1:14

angel like Satan should worship God; by the same token, he should honor and attend Jesus, who came as the body of the Creator. Furthermore, by overcoming the two previous temptations, Jesus already had laid the basis upon which to restore God's first and second blessings. Upon this foundation, he would naturally restore God's third blessing and govern the creation. Jesus said, "Begone, Satan!" because there was no longer any basis for Satan to contend with Jesus over the natural world, which already stood on the firm foundation of his victory. By prevailing in the third temptation, Jesus set up the condition to restore dominion over the natural world—God's third blessing.

3.2.1.3 The Result of the Forty-Day Fast and the Three Temptations

According to the Principle of Creation, God's purpose of creation is to be realized only when human beings pass through the three stages of origin, division and union and establish the four position foundation. However, Satan blocked this ideal while the first human ancestors were still in the process of building the four position foundation. Therefore, in the course of the providence of restoration, with its prolongations through three stages, God has tried to restore through indemnity all that was lost by working to fulfill dispensations of forty for the separation of Satan. Jesus prevailed over the three temptations and fulfilled the forty-day fast as a dispensation of forty for the separation of Satan. Thereupon, Jesus restored through indemnity, all at once, the following conditions which God had been seeking to fulfill through all the dispensations of forty for the separation of Satan throughout history.

First, in the position of John the Baptist, Jesus restored through indemnity the foundation of faith for the second worldwide course to restore Canaan. In so doing, Jesus restored all that had been offered to God over the course of the providence for the purpose of laying the foundation of faith, including: the offerings of Cain and Abel, Noah's ark, Abraham's sacrifice, Moses' Tabernacle and King Solomon's Temple. Furthermore, Jesus restored through indemnity, all at once, all the dispensations of forty for the separation of Satan conducted during the four thousand years since Adam, lost despite the best efforts of central figures to lay the foundation of faith. These included: Noah's forty-day flood judgment, the three forty-year periods in the life of Moses and his two forty-day fasts, the forty-day mission to spy out the land, the Israelites' forty years of wandering in the wilderness, the four hundred years from Noah to Abraham, the four hundred years of slavery in Egypt, and all other periods characterized by the number forty which had been lost since the Exodus.

Second, by rising from John the Baptist's position to the position of the Messiah, Jesus paved the way for the fulfillment of God's three great blessings and the restoration of the four position foundation. Having successfully made his offering, Jesus stood as the fulfillment of the tablets of stone, the Ark of the Covenant, the Tabernacle, the rock and the Temple.

3.2.2 The Foundation of Substance

Jesus came as the True Parent of humanity, yet he restored through indemnity the dispensation of forty for the separation of Satan while standing in the position of John the Baptist. Therefore, after he restored the foundation of faith (and rose to the position of Messiah and True Parent) he stood in the position of a parent. At the same time, when he secured the position of Abel for fulfilling the indemnity condition to remove the fallen nature, he stood in the position of a child (still in the role of John the Baptist with respect to that condition). In that capacity, Jesus through his forty-day fast attained the same position on the world level that Moses had assumed just after he had laid the foundation of faith for the second national course to restore Canaan by enduring a forty-year exile in the wilderness of Midian.

God conducted the dispensation to start the second national course to restore Canaan by providing the three signs and ten plagues. God conducted the dispensation to start the third national course to restore Canaan by having the people uphold the three manifestations of divine grace—the tablets of stone, the Ark of the Covenant and the Tabernacle—and obey the Ten Commandments. These, as we recall, were given upon the foundation for the Tabernacle to restore the three signs and ten plagues lost due to the faithlessness of the Israelites. Jesus was the fulfillment of the three manifestations of grace and the Ten Commandments. Therefore, God conducted the dispensation to start the second worldwide course to restore Canaan based on Jesus' own words and miraculous deeds. If the Jewish people (Cain) had been moved to believe in and follow Jesus, who was in the position of John the Baptist (Abel), they would have fulfilled the indemnity condition to remove the fallen nature and restored the foundation of substance. The foundation for the Messiah would thus have been laid. Standing upon this foundation, Jesus would have risen from the position of John the Baptist to the position of the Messiah. Then, by engrafting all people with himself,[211] humankind would have been reborn, cleansed of the

---

211. Rom. 11:17

original sin, and would have become one with God in heart. They would have restored their original, God-given nature and built the Kingdom of Heaven on earth in Jesus' day.

3.2.3 THE FAILURE OF THE SECOND WORLDWIDE COURSE TO RESTORE CANAAN

When the first worldwide course to restore Canaan ended in failure due to John the Baptist's faithlessness, Jesus took John's mission upon himself and suffered hardships in the wilderness for forty days. Thus, Jesus restored through indemnity the foundation of faith for the second worldwide course to restore Canaan. It is written that Satan, who was defeated in the three temptations, left Jesus' side "until an opportune time,"[212] indicating that Satan had not left Jesus for good but might confront him at a future date. As a matter of fact, Satan did confront Jesus, working primarily through the Jewish leadership, the priests and scribes who disbelieved in Jesus. In particular, Satan confronted Jesus through Judas Iscariot, the disciple who betrayed him.

Due to the faithlessness of such people, Jesus could lay neither the foundation of substance nor the foundation for the Messiah for the second worldwide course to restore Canaan. The second worldwide course thus ended in tragic failure.

3.3 THE THIRD WORLDWIDE COURSE TO RESTORE CANAAN

3.3.1 THE SPIRITUAL COURSE TO RESTORE CANAAN UNDER JESUS' LEADERSHIP

In discussing the third worldwide course to restore Canaan, we should first understand in what respects this course was different from the third national course to restore Canaan. As was explained in detail, the focus of faith for the Israelites in the third national course was the Tabernacle, the symbol of the Messiah. Even when the Israelites fell into faithlessness, the Tabernacle remained intact, standing upon the foundation of faith for the Tabernacle which Moses had laid during his forty-day fast. When Moses also became faithless, the Tabernacle remained intact, preserved by Joshua's stewardship and the foundation for the Tabernacle which he had laid during the forty-day mission to spy out the land.

However, in the worldwide course to restore Canaan, the focus of faith for the Jewish people was Jesus himself, who came as the fulfillment of the Tabernacle. When even his disciples became faithless, Jesus had to walk the path of death and be crucified, as he had foretold, "As Moses lifted up the serpent in the wilderness, so must the Son of man

---

212. Luke 4:13

be lifted up."²¹³ As a consequence, the Jewish people lost the one who should have been the spiritual and physical focus of their faith. They no longer had a basis upon which to begin the third worldwide course to restore Canaan as a substantial course, as the Israelites had when they commenced the third national course. Rather, Christians, as the Second Israel, were to begin this course as a spiritual course by exalting the resurrected Jesus as their focus of faith. Foreseeing this, Jesus said, "Destroy this temple, and in three days I will raise it up."²¹⁴

Then, just as Joshua succeeded to Moses' mission and completed the third national course, Christ at the Second Advent will succeed the mission of Jesus. He will complete, both spiritually and physically, the third worldwide course to restore Canaan. Accordingly, unless the returning Christ comes in the flesh, as Jesus did, he cannot inherit Jesus' mission, much less fulfill the purpose of the providence of restoration.

3.3.1.1 The Spiritual Foundation of Faith

When the second worldwide course to restore Canaan ended in failure due to the Jewish people's rejection of Jesus, the foundation of faith which Jesus had laid during his forty-day fast from the position of John the Baptist was lost to Satan. After Jesus gave up his body on the cross, he resumed John the Baptist's mission spiritually. During the forty-day period from his resurrection to his ascension, Jesus triumphed over Satan and broke all his chains. By doing so, Jesus restored the foundation of faith for the spiritual course in the third worldwide course to restore Canaan. This is the heretofore undisclosed reason behind this forty-day period. How, then, did Jesus lay the spiritual foundation of faith?

God had personally been guiding His beloved chosen people until the time Jesus appeared as the Messiah. Yet from the moment they turned against His only begotten Son, God tearfully had to turn His back and allow Satan to lay claim to them. Nonetheless, God's purpose in sending the Messiah was to save the Jewish people and all humanity. God was determined to save humankind, even though it meant delivering Jesus into the hands of Satan. Satan, on the other hand, was fixed on killing one man, Jesus Christ, even though he might have to hand back all of humanity, including the Jewish people, to God. Satan knew that the primary goal of God's four-thousand-year providence of restoration was to send the Messiah. He thought that by killing the Messiah he could destroy the entire providence of God. In the end, God handed

---

213. John 3:14
214. John 2:19

over to Satan as the condition of indemnity to save all humankind, including the Jewish people who had turned against Jesus and fallen into Satan's realm.

Satan exercised his maximum power to crucify Jesus, thereby attaining the goal he had sought throughout the four-thousand-year course of history. On the other hand, by delivering Jesus to Satan, God set up as compensation the condition to save sinful humanity. How did God achieve this? Because Satan had already exercised his maximum power in killing Jesus, according to the principle of restoration through indemnity, God was entitled to exercise His maximum power. While Satan uses his power to kill, God uses His power to bring the dead to life. As compensation for Satan's exercise of his maximum power in killing Jesus, God exercised His maximum power and resurrected Jesus. God thus opened the way for all humanity to be engrafted with the resurrected Jesus and thereby receive salvation and rebirth.

It is clear from the biblical record that the resurrected Jesus was not the same as he had been when he had lived with his disciples before his crucifixion. The resurrected Jesus was no longer a man seen through physical eyes, because he transcended time and space. He appeared to his disciples inside a room with closed doors.[215] He accompanied two disciples traveling toward Emmaus for a long distance. Yet they did not recognize him until much later, when he made himself known, at which point he suddenly vanished out of sight.[216] By passing through the forty-day period of his resurrection and thereby separating Satan, Jesus laid the foundation of faith for the spiritual course. He thus opened the way to redeem humanity's sins.

3.3.1.2 The Spiritual Foundation of Substance

Through his resurrection appearances, Jesus fulfilled the dispensation of forty for the separation of Satan while standing in the position of John the Baptist in spirit. He thereby laid the foundation of faith for the spiritual course in the position of the spiritual True Parent. At the same time, from the position of a child, he secured the position of Abel for fulfilling the indemnity condition to remove the fallen nature. This spiritual foundation of faith which Jesus laid for the third worldwide course to restore Canaan was comparable to the foundation of faith which Moses laid for the third national course through forty years in the wilderness.

---

215. John 20:19
216. Luke 24:15-31

God had worked the dispensation to start in Moses' day by having him establish the foundation for the Tabernacle. However, the resurrected Jesus was himself the spiritual fulfillment of the tablets of stone, the Ark of the Covenant and the Tabernacle. He gathered his scattered disciples from all over Galilee and worked the dispensation to start by giving them the power to perform signs and miracles.[217]

The resurrected Jesus stood spiritually in the position of John the Baptist and the position of Abel. The faithful believers stood in the position of Cain. By believing in Jesus and following him devotedly, they fulfilled the indemnity condition to remove the fallen nature and restored the spiritual foundation of substance.

3.3.1.3 The Spiritual Foundation for the Messiah

Upon Jesus' crucifixion, his eleven remaining disciples were demoralized and scattered. After his resurrection, however, Jesus gathered them in one place and commenced a new phase of the providence: the restoration of spiritual Canaan. The disciples chose Matthias to replace Judas Iscariot and fill the vacancy among the twelve. By believing in Jesus and following him at the cost of their lives, they laid the spiritual foundation of substance and the spiritual foundation for the Messiah. Upon this foundation, Jesus ascended from the position of the spiritual mission-bearer for John the Baptist to the position of the spiritual Messiah and sent the Holy Spirit. Thereupon, Jesus and the Holy Spirit became the spiritual True Parents and began the work of giving rebirth. Ever since the descent of the Holy Spirit at the Pentecost,[218] the resurrected Jesus as the spiritual True Father and the Holy Spirit as the spiritual True Mother have worked in oneness to grant spiritual rebirth by spiritually engrafting believers with themselves. This is the work of spiritual salvation,[219] which established a realm of resurrection inviolable by Satan.

Even though we may by faith unite with Jesus in spirit, our bodies are still liable to Satan's attack, as was the case with Jesus himself. In other words, our physical salvation still remains unaccomplished. Still, if we believe in the resurrected Jesus, he will guide us to enter spiritually his realm of resurrection, which is invulnerable to satanic invasion. There we are released from the conditions which allow Satan to accuse us, and we are spiritually saved.

---

217. Matt. 28:16-20; Mark 16:15-18
218. Acts 2:1-4
219. cf. Messiah 1.4

3.3.1.4 THE RESTORATION OF SPIRITUAL CANAAN

By believing in and serving the resurrected Jesus, who stands upon the spiritual foundation for the Messiah, Christians can accomplish the restoration of spiritual Canaan and enter its realm of grace. On the other hand, the physical bodies of Christians stand in the same position as Jesus' body, which was assaulted by Satan through the crucifixion. Christians are still stained with the original sin[220] and are just as much in need of purifying themselves from satanic influences as were people who lived before the coming of Jesus. Hence, Christians still must walk the course for the separation of Satan to prepare for the Second Coming of Christ.[221]

The resurrected Jesus is the spiritual fulfillment of the Temple. He realized worldwide the ideal of the Tabernacle which Moses had upheld in the national course to restore Canaan. The most holy place and the holy place, representing the spirit and flesh of Jesus, were fulfilled as spiritual realities through Jesus and the Holy Spirit. The ideal of the mercy seat has been realized through the works of salvation given by Jesus and the Holy Spirit, enabling God to appear in their works and impart His Word. On the mercy seat, where God's Word is proclaimed, the cherubim that had blocked our path since the Fall were parted, opening our way to enter the Ark of the Covenant and receive Jesus, the Tree of Life. There we can partake of the manna provided by God and witness the greatness of God's power that once caused Aaron's staff to bud.[222]

As we have learned by studying Moses' course, the delays in God's providence were not predetermined, but were caused by people's faithlessness. Likewise, Jesus' crucifixion and the need for his return were not originally predestined by God.

3.3.2 THE COURSE TO RESTORE SUBSTANTIAL CANAAN UNDER THE LEADERSHIP OF CHRIST AT THE SECOND ADVENT

We have already explained why the third worldwide course to restore Canaan began as a spiritual course, not as a substantial course like the third national course to restore Canaan. This spiritual providence began when, upon the spiritual foundation for the Messiah, Jesus could stand as the spiritual Messiah and his followers believed and obeyed him. This providence has passed through a long two-thousand-year course of history, expanding to construct a worldwide spiritual dominion.

---
220. Rom. 7:25
221. cf. Messiah 1.4
222. Heb. 9:4-5

While Moses could enter Canaan only in spirit, Joshua walked the national course as a substantial course and actually conquered the promised land. Likewise, while Jesus has been restoring Canaan as a worldwide spiritual realm, Christ at the Second Advent is to complete this third worldwide course as a substantial course and build the actual Kingdom of Heaven on earth. Christ at the Second Advent must realize, on earth, God's ideal which was left unfulfilled at the First Coming. For this reason, he must be born on earth in the flesh.[223]

Since Christ at the Second Advent must restore through indemnity the course of the providence of restoration left unfinished at Jesus' coming, he may have to follow a similar course. Jesus encountered disbelief among the Jewish people and had to walk a course of bitter suffering. Likewise, if Christians, the Second Israel, reject Christ at the Second Advent, he will have to go through tribulations comparable to those Jesus suffered. He will have to repeat Jesus' painful course and restore it through indemnity, but this time during his earthly life. For this reason, Jesus said, "But first he must suffer many things and be rejected by this generation."[224]

At the First Coming, Jesus at the end had to forsake the First Israel, which had been called for his sake, and elect the Christians as the Second Israel to commence the new spiritual providence. Similarly, at Christ's Second Coming, if the Christians reject him in disbelief, he will have to abandon them, raise up a Third Israel, and work with them to bring the providence to its fulfillment on the earth. If the Lord's forerunners, who are entrusted with missions like that of John the Baptist, do not complete their responsibilities, then he will have to lower himself to assume the role of John the Baptist and establish the foundation of faith for the substantial course in the third worldwide course to restore Canaan. In such an eventuality, he will walk a path of suffering.

However arduous the path he may walk, Christ at the Second Advent will not die without fulfilling the providence of restoration. This is because God's providence to raise up the True Parents of humankind[225] and fulfill the purpose of creation through them will be successful on the third attempt. This providence began with Adam, was prolonged through Jesus, and will bear its fruit without fail at the Second Advent. Moreover, as will be discussed below,[226] God's spiritual providence of restoration during the two thousand years since Jesus' day has prepared a democratic social and legal environment which will protect Christ at

---

223. cf. Second Advent 2.2
224. Luke 17:25
225. cf. Christology 4.1.1
226. cf. Parallels 7.2.6

the Second Advent. Jesus was killed after being branded a heretic by the Jews and a rebel by the Roman Empire. In contrast, even if Christ at the Second Advent is persecuted as a heretic, in the democratic society to which he will come, such accusations will not be sufficient grounds for him to be condemned to death.

Therefore, no matter how bitter his tribulations may be, Christ at the Second Advent will be able to lay the foundation of faith on the earth. Standing upon it, he will gather disciples of indomitable faith. He will guide these followers to fulfill the indemnity condition to remove the fallen nature and establish the foundation of substance. The foundation for the Messiah for the substantial course in the third worldwide course will be established without fail.

When Moses was the central figure in the third national course to restore Canaan, God worked the dispensation to start based on the rock. When Joshua was the central figure, God conducted the dispensation to start based on the water from the rock, which is more internal than the rock. Similarly, at Jesus' coming, God conducted the dispensation to start through miracles and signs, but at Christ's Second Advent God will conduct the dispensation to start based on the Word, which is more internal than miracles and signs. As was explained earlier,[227] although human beings were created through the Word,[228] due to the Fall they could not fulfill its purpose. To accomplish the purpose of the Word, God has been working His providence of restoration by setting up external conditions of obedience to the Word. Finally, at the consummation of providential history, God will again send the Christ, the incarnation of the Word, and complete the providence of salvation based on the Word.

The deepest explanation of God's purpose of creation is revealed in terms of relationships of heart. As our invisible, internal Parent, God created human beings as His substantial children. Adam and Eve were created in the image of God, as the substantial object partners to God in the pattern of His dual characteristics. As God's first substantial object partners, they were meant to be the Parents of humankind. They were meant to become husband and wife, bear and raise children, and form a family intertwining the heart of parents, the heart of husband and wife, the heart of brothers and sisters, and the heart of children. Their family would have manifested the true love of parents, the true love of husband and wife, and the true love of children. This would have been the four position foundation which realizes the three object purpose.[229]

---

227. cf. Eschatology 3.2
228. John 1:3
229. cf. Creation 2.3.3

In this manner, God intended to build the Kingdom of Heaven on earth through His own children, born of His heavenly lineage.

The primary significance of the Fall was that the first human ancestors formed a bond of blood ties with the Archangel; therefore, all of humanity has been bound to Satan's lineage.[230] Every human being has been born as a child of the Devil.[231] The first human ancestors fell to the position where they no longer had any connection to God's lineage. Accordingly, the ultimate purpose of God's providence of restoration is to transform fallen people, who have no connection to God's lineage, into children born of God's direct lineage. Let us look further at the Bible for evidence of this hidden purpose behind God's providence.

Adam's family, whose members committed the Fall and the first murder, was bereft of any relationship with God. At Noah's time, a direct relationship with God could not be restored due to the mistake of his second son, Ham. Nevertheless, because Noah had demonstrated utmost devotion, his family could stand in an indirect relationship with God, as a servant of servants.[232] This was the nature of humankind's relationship with God attainable prior to the Old Testament Age.

Abraham, the father of faith, with his family established the family foundation for the Messiah. They and their descendants, God's chosen people, were elevated to the position of God's servants.[233] This was the nature of humankind's relationship with God attainable in the Old Testament Age.

In the days of Jesus, the disciples, who stood upon the foundation of faith Jesus had laid from the position of John the Baptist, were elevated from the position of servants to the position of adopted children. To rise further from this state and become the children of God's direct lineage, they should have first established the foundation of substance and the foundation for the Messiah by serving and obeying Jesus absolutely. Had Jesus stood as the Messiah upon that foundation, they could have been engrafted with him both spiritually and physically and attained complete oneness with him.

Jesus is the only Son of God, sinless and born of His direct lineage. He is the true olive tree who came to engraft all fallen people, the wild olive trees, with himself.[234] By thus joining them in oneness with himself, he was to cleanse them of the original sin and restore them as children born of God's lineage. This is the work of rebirth, which was to have been conducted by Jesus and his Bride.[235]

---

230. cf. Fall 1.3.3
231. Matt. 3:7; 23:33; John 8:44
232. Gen. 9:25
233. Lev. 25:55
234. Rom. 11:17
235. cf. Christology 4

Unfortunately, even Jesus' own disciples lost faith, and Jesus died on the cross without having ascended from the position of John the Baptist or commenced the duties proper to the Messiah. After his resurrection, Jesus began his spiritual course. He laid the spiritual foundation of faith through the forty days from his resurrection to his ascension—a period for the separation of Satan—while standing in the position of spiritual John the Baptist. His disciples repented and returned to serve him with faith; thus, Jesus and his disciples established the spiritual foundation of substance and the spiritual foundation for the Messiah. Upon this foundation, Jesus stands as the spiritual Messiah and has been engrafting his faithful followers with himself—though only spiritually. As a result, faithful Christians have been elevated to become God's spiritual children. This has been the nature of humankind's relationship with God attainable from the time of Jesus until today.

In this spiritual providence of restoration, the spirit world has been restored first, just as in the order of creation God made the spirit world first. Humanity has been elevated to stand as God's object partners, but only spiritually. However devout a Christian may be, since the original sin passed down through the flesh has not yet been removed, he is no different from a faithful person of the Old Testament Age in the sense that both are still bound to Satan's lineage.[236] Christians are, at best, God's adopted children, because they do not stem from His lineage. This explains why St. Paul lamented, "we ourselves, who have the first fruits of the spirit, groan inwardly as we wait for adoption as sons."[237]

Christ will return and restore all humanity to be God's true children. He will return in the flesh and be born on the earth, as at his First Coming. He will restore through indemnity the course of his First Coming by walking it again. As was explained above, the returning Christ will conduct the dispensation to start based on the Word and then complete the foundation for the Messiah both spiritually and physically. Upon that foundation, he will engraft all humanity with himself, cleansing them of the original sin and restoring them to be God's children, born of His lineage.

At the First Coming, Jesus laid a family foundation by choosing twelve disciples and appointing three of the twelve as his chief disciples. In this, he intended to restore through indemnity the position of Jacob, who had been the central figure for the family foundation for the Messiah. By raising up seventy followers, Jesus then expanded the scope of his foundation to the clan level. In the same manner, Christ at

---
236. cf. Messiah 1.4
237. Rom. 8:23

the Second Advent will begin by laying, both spiritually and physically, the family foundation for the Messiah. He will then expand its scope to the clan, society, nation, world and cosmos. When this foundation is secure, he will finally be able to build the Kingdom of Heaven.

God's purpose in raising up the people of the First Israel was to prepare the foundation for Jesus, that he might accomplish the goal of building the Kingdom of Heaven when he came. When they turned against him, God elected the Christians to be the Second Israel. Similarly, God's purpose in raising up Christianity was to prepare the foundation for Christ at the Second Advent to achieve the goal of building the Kingdom of Heaven. If the Christian world should likewise turn against him, God will be left with no alternative but to forsake them and elect a Third Israel. Therefore, although Christians in the Last Days may enjoy great blessings, in fact, like the Jewish people of Jesus' day, their situation is extremely precarious. They are liable to fall into disgrace and great misfortune.

3.4 Some Lessons from Jesus' Course

First, Jesus' course instructs us about God's predestination of His Will. God predestines absolutely that His Will be accomplished and then works unceasingly until it is fulfilled. When John the Baptist failed his mission, Jesus tried to accomplish God's Will at any cost, even to the extent of taking on John's responsibility. When disbelief on the part of the Jewish people frustrated his attempts to build the Kingdom of Heaven, Jesus still remained absolute in his determination and promised to fulfill the Will at his return.

Next, Jesus' course demonstrates that God's predestination concerning the manner in which His Will is to be accomplished through an individual or a nation is conditional, not absolute. That is to say, although God may have chosen a certain individual or nation to accomplish a purpose in the providence of restoration, if he fails to complete his responsibility, God will surely choose another person or nation to continue His work. Jesus chose John the Baptist to be his chief disciple, but when he failed to complete his responsibility, Jesus chose Peter to replace him. Jesus chose Judas Iscariot to be one of his twelve disciples, but when Judas failed, Matthias was chosen to take his place.[238] Similarly, God chose the Jewish people to accomplish the central responsibility in His providence of restoration, but when they failed, their mission passed to the Gentiles.[239] These instances illustrate that

---
238. Acts 1:25
239. Acts 13:46; Matt. 21:33-43

when God chooses a person or a nation to accomplish His Will, He never predestines in absolute terms whether that person or nation will, in fact, accomplish the Will.

Jesus' course also demonstrates that God does not interfere with a person's efforts to fulfill his portion of responsibility, but treats him according to the results of his actions. God must have known that John the Baptist and Judas Iscariot were losing their faith. He certainly had the power to stop them from sinning. Yet God did not interfere at all in their faith, but dealt with them only based on the results of their deeds.

Finally, Jesus' course shows that the greater a person's mission, the greater the test he will confront. Jesus came as the second Adam. To complete his mission, he had to restore through indemnity the position Adam had occupied prior to the Fall. Since Adam became faithless and forsook God, Jesus had to restore Adam's mistake by enduring when God forsook him, all the while showing unchanging faith. Therefore, Jesus was tempted by Satan in the wilderness and forsaken by God on the cross.[240]

---

240. Matt. 27:46

Chapter 3

The Periods in Providential History
and the Determination of Their Lengths

SECTION 1
PARALLEL PROVIDENTIAL PERIODS

Examining the course of human history, we often find cases where the various circumstances of a period in history are repeated in similar form during a later age. Some historians are impressed by these phenomena and point out that history progresses in a spiral movement. Yet they do not understand the underlying cause. When a period of history repeats the events of a previous period, albeit with differences in scope and degree, the two periods are called *parallel providential periods*. As will be explained below, the reason for using this terminology is because the principal cause behind these parallels lies in God's providence of restoration.

How do parallel providential periods come about? The course of history has been shaped by various events in the providence of restoration, which drives history toward a fixed goal. When a central figure in the providence fails his responsibility to restore the foundation for the Messiah, the providential period centering on that person comes to a close. Yet, since God has predestined the absolute and eventual fulfillment of His Will,[1] He chooses another person to carry on the mission and opens another historical period in the providence to restore through indemnity the foundation for the Messiah. Since this new period restores through indemnity the previous period, a course with similar events will be repeated. This is how the periods come to be parallel to one another.

However, parallel periods do not have exactly the same form and content, because the central figure in a particular period must restore in his time (horizontally) the unfulfilled indemnity conditions of the previous periods (vertically). The more the providence of restoration is prolonged and past indemnity conditions accumulate, the heavier will be the conditions of indemnity which the new central figure must fulfill. Consequently, the new parallel period will differ from the previous parallel period in content and scale.

The three stages of the growing period may be classified according to different degrees of manifestation: the formation stage is a manifestation in symbol, the growth stage in image, and the completion stage in substance. Likewise, in the development of history, the parallel periods in the providence of restoration have repeated similar events according to this pattern. Thus, the entire history of the providence of restoration may be divided according to the form of the parallels: the Age of the Providence to Lay the Foundation for Restoration is the age of symbolic parallels, the Age of the Providence of Restoration is the age of image parallels, and the Age of the Prolongation of the Providence of Restoration is the age of substantial parallels.

Next, let us examine the main factors which determine the formation of parallel providential periods. Parallel providential periods recur because of repeated dispensations to restore the foundation for the Messiah. Accordingly, the factors which determine the formation of parallel providential periods are: first, the three conditions necessary for the foundation of faith (the central figure, the object for the condition and the numerical period of indemnity) and second, the indemnity condition to remove the fallen nature, which is necessary to restore the foundation of substance.

Based on these factors, two characteristics of parallel providential periods stand out. First, the lengths of the parallel providential periods are determined based on a fixed number of generations or years of the

---

1. cf. Predestination 1

indemnity period necessary for restoring the foundation of faith. In the providence of restoration, when a central figure has failed to complete his responsibility and caused the prolongation of the Will, God repeats His work through other central figures until the final restoration of the lost foundation of faith is achieved. In each dispensation, the numerical period of indemnity for restoring this foundation must be repeated in some form. For this reason, the parallel periods in history have similar lengths, each representing the same fixed number of years or generations. The purpose of this chapter is to discuss this matter in detail.

Second, the parallels in history are shaped by the other three providential factors: the central figure and the object for the condition offered for the foundation of faith, and the indemnity condition to remove the fallen nature for the foundation of substance. The goal of the providence of restoration is ultimately to restore the foundation for the Messiah. Accordingly, when the providence is prolonged, the various dispensations involved in restoring this foundation are also repeated. Since the foundation for the Messiah can be established only by first laying the foundation of faith through the symbolic offering and then laying the foundation of substance through the substantial offering, providential history has been repeating dispensations to restore these two offerings. These dispensations have shaped the parallels between providential periods. We will elaborate on this matter in the next chapter.

SECTION 2

THE NUMBER OF GENERATIONS OR YEARS IN THE PERIODS OF THE AGE OF THE PROVIDENCE TO LAY THE FOUNDATION FOR RESTORATION

2.1 WHY AND HOW THE PROVIDENCE OF RESTORATION IS PROLONGED

God's providence for humankind to lay the foundation for the Messiah, receive the Messiah, and attain the ultimate goal of restoration was prolonged from Adam's day through the days of Noah, Abraham, Moses and finally to Jesus' day. When Jesus was killed without accomplishing his ultimate purpose due to the people's disbelief, the providence of restoration was prolonged again until the time of the Second Coming.

Why has the providence of restoration been prolonged? This question can only be answered with an understanding of the principle of predestination. According to this principle, since God absolutely predestines

His Will, He surely will realize it one day. However, whether God's Will is fulfilled through any particular individual is conditional upon the fulfillment of his portion of responsibility, which is in addition to God's portion of responsibility. Accordingly, when the Will is not fulfilled because the responsible person fails, God will choose another person in a different era to take his place. God will continue His work until its complete fulfillment, prolonging the providence in the process.

Let us next examine how the providence of restoration has been prolonged. According to the Principle of Creation, God is a being of the number three. All things created in His likeness manifest themselves through a three-stage process with respect to their mode of existence, movement and growth. For any entity to fulfill the purpose of creation by establishing the four position foundation with its spherical motion, it must go through the three stages of origin-division-union action and engage in interaction with three object partners to achieve the three object purpose. The providence to restore the purpose of creation is one of re-creation based on the Word. Therefore, whenever the providence of restoration is prolonged, it may extend to as many as three stages. On the basis of the Principle of Creation, up to three attempts are allowed.

For example, when in Adam's family Cain and Abel failed to make the substantial offering, the dispensation was repeated in the families of Noah and Abraham, and fulfilled on the third attempt. When Abraham made his mistake in the symbolic offering, the dispensation was prolonged through Isaac and fulfilled by Jacob. The courses to restore Canaan under the leadership of Moses and Jesus each were extended to three courses. When King Saul failed to build the Temple, this dispensation was prolonged through two more kings: David and Solomon. God's ideal of creation, which was not realized with Adam, has awaited a second and a third providence for its realization: through Jesus, the second Adam, and then through Christ at the Second Advent. Common proverbs, such as the Korean saying "If not accomplished at the first attempt, it surely will be done at the third," exemplify this aspect of the Principle expressed as everyday wisdom.

2.2 Vertical Indemnity Conditions and Horizontal Restoration through Indemnity

To inherit and complete the missions of his predecessors in providential history, a central figure responsible for the providence of restoration must fulfill, in a short time, all the indemnity conditions which his predecessors tried to fulfill. If this central figure also fails in his mission, all the indemnity conditions he tried to fulfill are passed down to the next person entrusted with the same responsibility. The conditions which accumulate in the course of providential history due to central figures' failures to complete their responsibility are called *vertical indemnity conditions*. The task of the central figure to fulfill all these conditions in a short time is called *horizontal restoration through indemnity*.

For example, Abraham had to restore horizontally through indemnity all the vertical indemnity conditions which Adam's family and Noah's family before him had tried to fulfill. In offering the three sacrifices at one time on the same altar, Abraham was to restore horizontally through indemnity the vertical indemnity conditions accumulated during the three dispensations of the prolonged providence. The three offerings represented all the conditions which Adam and Noah could not fulfill, as well as those which Abraham had to fulfill as the new central figure.

Jacob, in his course, had to fulfill in a short time a condition to horizontally restore through indemnity the vertical indemnity conditions accumulated through the twelve generations since Noah. For this purpose, he was given twelve sons from whom descended the twelve tribes of Israel.

Jesus employed this method to restore horizontally through indemnity all the accumulated vertical indemnity conditions left unfulfilled by the forefathers, prophets and kings who had led the providence during the four thousand years of biblical history until his time. For instance, Jesus chose twelve disciples and seventy followers in order to restore in a short time the vertical indemnity conditions which had accumulated from Jacob's course, in which God had worked with Jacob's twelve sons and seventy kinsmen, and from Moses' course, in which God had worked with the twelve tribes of Israel and seventy elders. Moreover, Jesus fasted for forty days to restore horizontally all the vertical indemnity conditions in the form of dispensations of forty for the separation of Satan, which were required for the foundation of faith. In this sense, we can understand that each central figure in the providence of restoration stands not only for himself as an individual, but represents all the forefathers, prophets and sages who had the same mission in the past. He bears within him the fruits of their labors in history.

2.3 Horizontal Restoration through Indemnity Carried Out Vertically

Sometimes horizontal restoration is achieved through a vertical dispensation which may span several generations. This was the case with the providence of restoration in Abraham's family. By making an acceptable symbolic offering, Abraham was supposed to restore horizontally through indemnity all the vertical indemnity conditions which had accumulated due to the mistakes of Adam's family and Noah's family. His mistake in the offering caused yet another failure and delay in the providence. As was explained above, since this was the third attempt in the providence to restore the family foundation for the Messiah, the Principle required that his family accomplish God's Will without fail. Therefore, in spite of his failure, God sought a way to regard Abraham as if he had not made the mistake, but had restored horizontally the vertical indemnity conditions without any prolongation. To this end, God set up a special dispensation: He had Abraham, Isaac and Jacob fulfill the necessary indemnity conditions while regarding these three individuals as one person with respect to His Will. Therefore, despite this vertical prolongation through three generations, Jacob's victory and Isaac's victory became Abraham's own victory, as if achieved in his generation without any delay.[2] The oneness of these three generations is signified by God's appellation of Himself as "the God of Abraham, the God of Isaac, and the God of Jacob."[3]

Thus, God could credit Abraham with having fulfilled, in his own generation, the horizontal indemnity conditions which he had failed to complete, by completing them vertically through the generations of Isaac and Jacob. This type of restoration is called *horizontal restoration through indemnity carried out vertically*.

2.4 Numerical Indemnity Periods for Restoring the Foundation of Faith

A central figure has to fulfill one or more numerical indemnity periods in order to restore the foundation of faith.[4] Let us examine the reasons for this. God exists upon His Principle, which has a numerical aspect. The universe, with human beings at its center, was created based on numerical principles to be the unfolding of the dual characteristics of the invisible God as His substantial object partner. This is the

---

2. cf. Foundation 3.1.2.3, Foundation 3.3
3. Exod. 3:6
4. cf. Restoration 1.2.1

reason science, which seeks to discover the external laws governing the universe, progresses through research conducted with the aid of mathematics. The first human ancestors were to become complete by passing through a growing period characterized by certain numbers, thus laying the foundation of faith. In their perfection, they were to embody the quality of these numbers. We must investigate these matters because restoration of the foundation of faith requires not only that we offer an object for the condition, symbolizing the universe in bondage to Satan, but also that we pass through a numerical period of indemnity to restore the numbers defiled by Satan.

Based upon what numbers were the first human ancestors, prior to the Fall, to lay the foundation of faith? What numbers were they to have embodied in their perfection? We learned in the Principle of Creation that no entity can exist or thrive without first forming a four position foundation. Accordingly, Adam and Eve in their immaturity had to each form a four position foundation for their existence. Each position in the four position foundation is to pass through the three stages of the growing period, making a total of twelve. Furthermore, each position in the four position foundation accomplishes the three object purpose by taking three object partners, making a total of twelve object partners and fulfilling the twelve object purpose. Hence, the growing period during which Adam was to establish the foundation of faith was a period for fulfilling the number twelve. While in their immaturity, the first human ancestors were to lay the foundation of faith based on the number twelve, and in perfection they were to attain the twelve object purpose and thus embody the quality of the number twelve. Due to their fall, Satan defiled this number. Therefore, a central figure in the providence of restoration must pass through a period of indemnity to restore the number twelve in laying the foundation of faith. Only on that basis can he lay the foundation of substance for the restoration of the perfect embodiment of the quality of the number twelve.

Some examples of the indemnity period to restore the number twelve are: the 120 years it took Noah to build the ark, the 120 years of the providence to restore Canaan under Moses' leadership, and the 120 years from when Abraham was called by God until Jacob purchased the birthright from Esau for some bread and lentils. As we will discuss below, this last period was to be restored by the 120-year period of the united kingdom in the Old Testament Age, and in the New Testament Age by the corresponding 120-year period of the Christian empire under Charlemagne and his sons.

The maturation process during which Adam and Eve were laying the foundation of faith also required a period to fulfill the number four. They were to pass through the three stages of the growing period and enter the realm of God's direct dominion, which is the fourth stage. At that point, they would have completed the four position foundation. By thus fulfilling the number four, the first human ancestors were to become its perfect embodiments. Due to the Fall, this number was defiled by Satan. Therefore, central figures in the providence must complete an indemnity period to restore the number four in laying the foundation of faith. Only on that basis can they lay the foundation of substance for the restoration of the perfect embodiment of the quality of the number four.

It was already explained that indemnity periods to restore the number four are necessary to restore the foundation of faith.[5] Examples include: Noah's forty-day flood judgment, Moses' forty-day fasts, the forty-day mission to spy out the land of Canaan, Jesus' forty-day fast, and the forty days of the ministry of the resurrected Jesus.

The growing period is also the period to fulfill the number twenty-one. The first human ancestors were to have become the perfect embodiments of the number twenty-one by laying the foundation of faith through a period based on the number twenty-one and then realizing the purpose of creation. However, due to the Fall, this number was defiled by Satan. Hence, central figures in history must complete an indemnity period to restore the number twenty-one in laying the foundation of faith. Only on that basis can they lay the foundation of substance for the restoration of the perfect embodiment of the quality of the number twenty-one.

To understand the significance of the number twenty-one, we should first understand the significance of the numbers three, four and seven in the Principle. God, whose dual characteristics exist in harmonious oneness, is a Being of the number three. The creation is perfected when it attains oneness with God in the four position foundation. Thus, for an individual to become perfect, he must form within himself a four position foundation in which God, the mind and body form a trinity, the center of which is God. For a man and a woman to become a perfect husband and wife, they must build a four position foundation in which they form a trinity with God as their center. For the universe to reach its perfection, it must form a four position foundation in which human beings and the natural world form a trinity with God as their center. Furthermore, for created beings to realize a four position foundation by becoming one centered on

---

5. cf. Foundation 2.1.2

God, they must first pass through the three stages of the growing period and complete the three object purpose. For these reasons, the number three is the number of Heaven, or the number of perfection.

When a subject partner and an object partner form a trinity by becoming one centering on God, the resulting union is an individual embodiment of truth which completes the four position foundation. Having thus secured the status of God's creation, it comes to have position and extension in the four directions: north, south, east and west. In this sense, the number four is the number of the earth.

When a created being passes through the three stages of the growing period and builds the four position foundation, it becomes perfectly established in the qualitative dimensions of time and space, respectively. Thus, every creation becomes the perfect embodiment of the number seven, which is the sum of the number of Heaven and the number of earth. This is the reason why the Bible recounts the creation of heaven and earth as having taken seven days. Just as the period of creation fulfills the number seven, any period for attaining completion may be regarded as a period to fulfill the number seven. Looking at the three stages of the growing period in this manner, the period to complete the formation stage, the period to complete the growth stage, and the period to complete the completion stage are each periods which fulfill the number seven. In total, the entire growing period may be regarded as a period to fulfill the number twenty-one.

Examples of indemnity periods of the number twenty-one include the following: After the flood, God had Noah send out a dove three times to foreshadow His providence, which was to be carried out in three stages. The dove was sent out in seven-day intervals; hence the entire period adds up to twenty-one days.[6] When Jacob walked the family course to restore Canaan, he labored in exile in Haran before returning home to Canaan, enduring three seven-year periods which add up to twenty-one years. In the Old Testament Age, there was the 210-year period of the Israelites' exile in Babylon and their return to Israel, which was to restore through indemnity this twenty-one-year course of Jacob. In the New Testament Age, there was the 210-year period from the papal captivity in Avignon to the eve of the Reformation, which was also to restore through indemnity the twenty-one-year course of Jacob.

The growing period is also the period to fulfill the number forty. The first human ancestors were to perfectly embody the quality of the number forty by laying the foundation of faith based on the number forty and then

---

6. Gen. 7:4; 8:10, 12

realizing the purpose of creation. Satan's attack at the Fall defiled this number. Hence, the central figures in the providence must fulfill an indemnity period to restore the number forty in laying the foundation of faith. Only on that basis can they lay the foundation of substance for the restoration of the perfect embodiment of the quality of the number forty.

To understand how the number forty is fulfilled in the growing period, we must first study the significance of the number ten. If we divide each of the three stages of the growing period into three sub-stages, we arrive at a total of nine levels. Herein lies the significance of the number nine in the Principle. As a numerical unfolding of the dual characteristics of the invisible God, each of God's creations passes through the nine levels of the growing period. Each then fulfills its purpose of creation when it becomes one with God in the realm of His direct dominion, which constitutes the tenth level. For this reason, we call the number ten the number of unity. God set up the ten generations after Adam to fulfill the indemnity period to restore the number ten before he called upon Noah. By this condition, God wanted to have Noah complete the Will which Adam had left unfinished, and then have him become one with God.

In the four position foundation which Adam and Eve should have established, each position was to pass through the ten levels in their course to maturity, fulfilling in total the number forty. Thus, the course of their maturation was a period to fulfill the number forty, and their four position foundation would have become the perfect embodiment of the number forty. Some examples of indemnity periods of the number forty set up to restore this foundation include: the forty days from the time Noah's ark came to rest on Mt. Ararat until he sent out the dove, the forty years of Moses' life in the Pharaoh's palace, his forty-year exile in the wilderness of Midian, and the forty years in the wilderness during the national course to restore Canaan.

We can deduce that there are two types of periods of the number forty in the providence of restoration. One type is an indemnity period to restore the number four; in restoration, it is multiplied by the number ten, the number of unity, to form forty. The second type is the indemnity period to restore the number forty itself, which Adam should have fulfilled before the Fall, as was just described. The forty years in the wilderness for the national course to restore Canaan was set up to restore both these types of periods of forty at the same time. It restored through indemnity the forty-day spy mission and Moses' forty-day fast, which were periods to restore the number four. It also restored through indemnity Moses' forty years in the Pharaoh's palace and forty years in the wilderness of Midian, which were periods to restore the number forty. Such a phenomenon occurs when the central figure for the foundation of faith is restoring through indemnity horizontally all the vertical indemnity conditions in the history of the providence.

When such a dispensation to horizontally restore periods of the number forty is again prolonged, it can be extended by a rule of multiplication by ten, because the required period of indemnity may have to be expanded through ten stages. Thus, a period of forty years may be expanded to four hundred or even four thousand years. Examples include: the four-hundred-year period from Noah to Abraham, the four hundred years of slavery in Egypt and the four thousand biblical years from Adam to Jesus.

Let us summarize the numerical periods of indemnity a central figure in the providence must fulfill to restore the foundation of faith. Had the first human ancestors not fallen, they would have laid the foundation of faith based on significant numbers, including twelve, four, twenty-one and forty. When they then accomplished the purpose of creation, they would have become the perfect embodiments of the quality of these numbers. Yet due to their fall, all these numbers were claimed by Satan. Therefore, the central figures in providential history must fulfill numerical periods of indemnity to restore the numbers twelve, four, twenty-one and forty before they can restore the foundation of faith. Only on that basis can they lay the foundation of substance for the restoration of the perfect embodiment of the quality of these numbers.

2.5 The Parallel Periods Determined by the Number of Generations

According to the Bible, God chose Noah to shoulder the providence ten generations and sixteen hundred years after Adam. Let us examine what significant numbers were restored by the sixteen hundred years and the ten generations.

The number ten is the number of unity with God. The course of growth to maturity requires a period to fulfill the number ten, through which Adam and Eve were to become the perfect embodiments of the number ten. When this number was defiled by Satan due to their Fall, God sought a central figure in order to restore this number and begin His work to unite the people with Himself by restoring them as perfect embodiments of the quality of the number ten. For this purpose, God would require the central figure to complete an indemnity period to restore the number ten. This is why God called Noah ten generations after Adam.

It was discussed earlier that the first human ancestors were to pass through a course to maturity which fulfilled the number forty and thereby become perfect embodiments of the number forty. For fallen people to become the central figures who will pave the way for the restoration of perfect embodiments of the number forty, they must establish the four position foundation necessary for restoration and then fulfill an indemnity period to restore the number forty. Each position of the four position foundation should fulfill the indemnity period to restore the number forty, yielding an indemnity period to restore the number 160. Moreover, since fallen people were to fulfill this number through ten generations—ten signifying unity with God—they had to complete an indemnity period of the number sixteen hundred. This is the reason the period from Adam to Noah was sixteen hundred years, by biblical reckoning.

After the failure of the providence of restoration in Noah's family, God waited four hundred years, until another ten generations had elapsed, before calling Abraham to carry the burden of the providence. Set according to the number of generations, the period from Noah to Abraham was parallel to the period from Adam to Noah, and was to restore that earlier period through indemnity.

It was discussed earlier why this period was made four hundred years.[7] God had Noah endure the forty-day flood judgment for the purpose of accomplishing the goal of the providence of restoration, which He had pursued by setting up the ten generations and sixteen hundred years. When this forty-day flood judgment was defiled by Satan due to Ham's mistake, God had to work through another central figure to restore it. From Adam to Noah, God worked to fulfill indemnity periods to restore the number 160 in each of ten generations. In the parallel period of ten generations from Noah to Abraham, God set each generation as the indemnity period to restore the number forty, which is derived from the flood judgment.

The failure of the forty-day flood judgment had to be restored through a period of the number forty. Since the restoration of each subsequent generation had to span its entire length, it could not be fulfilled in only forty days. Hence, God set the indemnity period to be fulfilled by each generation as forty years. A day of the flood was indemnified by a year, just as in Moses' time when the failure of the forty-day mission to spy out the land was restored through forty years of wandering in the wilderness.[8] Since the dispensation in which each generation was set as a forty-year indemnity period continued through ten generations, the entire span of the indemnity period came to be four hundred years.

---

7. cf. Foundation 3.1.1

2.6 Providential Periods of Horizontal Restoration through Indemnity Carried Out Vertically

As explained earlier, each central figure of the providence is called to restore horizontally all the vertical indemnity conditions accumulated up to his time. Hence, the longer providential history is prolonged, the heavier the indemnity conditions will be for the central figures of later generations to fulfill horizontally. In the providence of restoration in Adam's family, there were as yet no vertical indemnity conditions because the providence had just begun. Therefore, the foundation for the Messiah could have been laid quite simply by Cain and Abel properly making the symbolic offerings and the substantial offering. It would have merely required that once Abel had made his offering in a manner acceptable to God, Cain should have obeyed and followed Abel to fulfill the indemnity condition to remove the fallen nature. In regard to the numerical indemnity periods to restore the foundation of faith, these could have been completed in the short time necessary for making the symbolic and substantial offerings. However, when the providence of restoration was prolonged due to the failure of Adam's family, vertical indemnity conditions began to accumulate in the form of various numerical indemnity periods. Therefore, in restoring the foundation of faith, the central figures since Adam's day have had to complete numerical indemnity periods to restore such numbers as twelve, four, twenty-one and forty.

In the case of Noah, he was supposed to restore in his time all of these vertical indemnity conditions. To restore the foundation of faith, he had to go through several numerical indemnity periods: 120 years to build the ark, forty days of the flood judgment, twenty-one days during which he sent out the dove three times at seven-day intervals, and the forty-day period from the time the ark came to rest on Mt. Ararat until he sent out the dove.

Noah faithfully fulfilled these numerical indemnity periods, but due to Ham's mistake they were invaded by Satan. Consequently, they were again left behind as vertical indemnity conditions. Abraham had the opportunity to restore them all at once through his symbolic offering. However, because Abraham failed in his offering, the indemnity periods could not be restored horizontally. They then had to be restored vertically: by prolonging the fulfillment of His Will through Isaac and Jacob, God worked to fulfill in succession indemnity periods to restore the numbers twelve, four, twenty-one and forty.

---

8. Num. 14:34

In the providence in Abraham's family, the following indemnity periods, which should have been fulfilled horizontally, were instead carried out in vertical succession to restore the foundation of faith: 120 years from the time Abraham left Haran until Jacob purchased the birthright from Esau with bread and a pottage of lentils; forty years from that time until Jacob was given the blessing of the eldest son by his father Isaac and received God's blessing on his way to Haran;[9] twenty-one years from that time until he completed his toil in Haran and returned to Canaan with his family and wealth;[10] and forty years from the time Jacob returned to Canaan until his family entered Egypt at Joseph's invitation. In this way, the indemnity conditions which could not be restored horizontally were completed as extended vertical periods of fixed lengths.

Section 3

The Periods in the Age of the Providence of Restoration and Their Lengths

The Age of the Providence of Restoration, which was the age of image parallels, was to restore through indemnity the Age of the Providence to Lay the Foundation for Restoration, the age of symbolic parallels. Let us investigate the periods in this age and how their lengths were determined.

3.1 The Four-Hundred-Year Period of Slavery in Egypt

Noah laid the foundation of faith after fulfilling the forty days of the flood judgment for the purpose of separating Satan. When this foundation was shattered due to Ham's mistake, God tried to raise up Abraham to the same position as Noah by commanding him to make a symbolic offering while standing upon the foundation which had been laid through the intervening period of four hundred years. However, due to Abraham's mistake, this foundation was defiled by Satan. To recover this foundation of four hundred years, God had the Israelites undergo four hundred years of slavery in Egypt[11] and separate Satan once more. The period of slavery in Egypt was the image parallel to the period of sixteen hundred years from Adam to Noah in the age of

---

9. Gen. 27:1-29; 28:10-14
10. Gen. 31:41
11. Gen. 15:13; cf Foundation 3.1.2.1

3.2 The Four-Hundred-Year Period of the Judges

It is recorded that King Solomon began to build the Temple 480 years after the Exodus from Egypt, in the fourth year of his reign.[12] Since King Solomon's reign followed the forty-year reign of King Saul[13] and the forty-year reign of King David, we can deduce that there was a period of approximately four hundred years from the time the Israelites entered Canaan until the enthronement of King Saul. This was the period of the judges.

The Israelites under Moses were to secure the foundation of having separated Satan through their slavery in Egypt, thus restoring on the national level the foundation upon which Abraham had stood—the foundation of having separated Satan laid during the four hundred years from Noah to Abraham. However, after they entered Canaan under the leadership of Joshua, Moses' successor, they again turned faithless, allowing Satan to again defile this foundation of four hundred years. The Israelites needed to undergo another period for the separation of Satan before they could restore this foundation through indemnity. The period of the judges, which ran approximately four hundred years from the time the people entered Canaan until the enthronement of King Saul, was set up for this purpose.

The period of the judges was the image parallel to the period of the four hundred years from Noah to Abraham in the age of symbolic parallels. It was to restore that earlier period through parallel indemnity conditions.

3.3 The One-Hundred-and-Twenty-Year Period of the United Kingdom

The Age of the Providence of Restoration was set up to restore through indemnity the Age of the Providence to Lay the Foundation for Restoration. Therefore, Abraham, who commenced this providential age, was in the position of Adam; Moses was in the position of Noah; and King Saul was in the position of Abraham. Abraham was a transitional figure; he was responsible both to consummate the Age of the Providence to Lay the Foundation for Restoration and to begin the Age of the Providence of Restoration. Abraham was called to lay the family foundation for the Messiah as the basis for the national foundation

---

12. I Kings 6:1
13. Acts 13:21

for the Messiah. God had to lay the family foundation for the Messiah without fail in Abraham's day because it was His third attempt. Likewise, in King Saul's day, God was working to establish the national foundation for the Messiah for the third time. Hence, God again had to accomplish this providence without fail.

Due to his mistake in his symbolic offering, Abraham did not restore all at once the conditions inherited from Noah's course in the form of the various numerical periods necessary to restore the foundation of faith, specifically: 120 years, forty days, twenty-one days and forty days. Therefore, the horizontal restoration of these periods had to be extended vertically. They became successive indemnity periods of 120 years, forty years, twenty-one years and forty years in the generations of Abraham's family.

King Saul was to restore Abraham's position on the national level. By building the Temple, King Saul should have restored in a short time all the indemnity conditions in the form of numerical indemnity periods which had been set up to restore the foundation of faith in Moses' time. These included: 120 years (the three forty-year courses in Moses' life), forty days (the period of Moses' fasts), twenty-one days (the first national course to restore Canaan), and forty years (the wilderness course in the national course to restore Canaan). Nevertheless, King Saul was disobedient[14] and failed to fulfill God's Will. As in Abraham's time, the horizontal restoration of these indemnity periods had to be extended vertically into successive periods: the 120 years of the united kingdom, the four hundred years of the divided kingdoms of north and south, the 210 years of Israel's exile and return, and the four hundred years of preparation for the advent of the Messiah. After all these periods, the people of Israel were finally ready to receive the Messiah.

The period of the united kingdom was to restore the 120 years of Moses' life, during which he made three attempts to lay the foundation of faith for the national course to restore Canaan. Let us examine this parallel more closely. After the Israelites had endured four hundred years of slavery to separate Satan, Moses laid the foundation of faith through his forty years in the Pharaoh's palace. He then tried to lead the people into the land of Canaan, where he was to build the Temple. However, due to the people's faithlessness, this course was prolonged twice. Moses had to lay the foundation of faith anew through the forty-year course in the wilderness of Midian and again through the forty-year course of wandering in the wilderness. Likewise, Saul was enthroned as

---

14. I Sam. 15:11-23

the king of Israel after the Israelites had restored the four hundred years of slavery in Egypt through the four-hundred-year period of the judges. During the forty years of his reign, King Saul was to lay the foundation of faith by restoring through indemnity Moses' forty years of life in the Pharaoh's palace. He was then to build the Temple. Yet when King Saul became faithless, God's Will to build the Temple was prolonged through the two forty-year reigns of King David and King Solomon, thus constituting a total of 120 years for the period of the united kingdom.

This period was the image parallel to the period of 120 years in the age of symbolic parallels from the time Abraham left Haran until Jacob purchased the birthright from his brother. It was to restore that earlier period through parallel indemnity conditions. Just as the dispensation which began with Abraham was fulfilled after its prolongation through Isaac and Jacob, God's dispensation to build the Temple, which began with King Saul, was extended to King David and King Solomon before it was finally fulfilled.

3.4 THE FOUR-HUNDRED-YEAR PERIOD OF THE DIVIDED KINGDOMS OF NORTH AND SOUTH

Had King Saul accomplished the dispensation to build the Temple during the forty years of his reign, among the indemnity periods which he would have restored horizontally was Moses' forty-day fast, which had been carried out to recover the Word as revealed on the tablets of stone. Once King Saul lost faith, this indemnity period had to be restored as a vertical extension of horizontal restoration. This was the origin of the period of the divided kingdoms of north and south, which lasted nearly four hundred years. It began when the united kingdom was divided into Israel in the north and Judah in the south, and it lasted until the people of Judah were taken into exile in Babylon.

This period was the image parallel to the forty-year period in the age of symbolic parallels, from Jacob's purchase of the birthright from Esau until he received the blessings of Isaac and God[15] and went into Haran. It was to restore that earlier period through parallel indemnity conditions.

3.5 THE TWO-HUNDRED-AND-TEN-YEAR PERIOD OF ISRAEL'S EXILE AND RETURN

The people of the northern kingdom of Israel broke their covenant with God, and as a result, they were taken into captivity by the

---

15. Gen. 28:13

Assyrians. The people of the southern kingdom of Judah also sinned against God. As a result, they were taken into exile by the Babylonian king, Nebuchadnezzar. After they spent nearly seventy years as captives, Babylon fell to King Cyrus of Persia, who issued a royal decree liberating them. From that time, the Jewish people began a gradual return to Jerusalem and rebuilt the Temple. Ezra the scribe led the last group of returning Jews to Jerusalem, and Nehemiah rebuilt the city wall. Inspired by the prophecy of Malachi,[16] the people began preparations to receive the Messiah. This period came to an end approximately 210 years after the Jews were first taken into exile in Babylon and about 140 years after their liberation by the Persians. This was the period of Israel's exile and return.

Had King Saul accomplished the dispensation to build the Temple, one of the indemnity periods which he would have restored horizontally was the twenty-one-day period when Moses was meant to lead the Israelites from Egypt to Canaan in the first national course. After King Saul lost faith and this dispensation failed, this indemnity period had to be restored as a vertical extension of horizontal restoration. The 210-year period of Israel's exile and return was set up for this purpose.

This period was the image parallel to the twenty-one-year period in the age of symbolic parallels, which extended from the time Jacob received the blessing of the eldest son from Isaac until he returned to Canaan, and was to restore that earlier period through parallel indemnity conditions. It was to restore three seven-year periods: After arriving in Haran, Jacob worked seven years in order to marry Rachel but was given Leah; he worked seven more years for Rachel; he then worked seven years acquiring wealth before he returned to Canaan.[17]

3.6 THE FOUR-HUNDRED-YEAR PERIOD OF PREPARATION FOR THE ADVENT OF THE MESSIAH

After the Jewish people returned from exile to their homeland of Israel, they re-established their faith, rebuilt the city wall and, based on Malachi's prophecy, began as a nation to prepare for the Messiah. From that time until the birth of Jesus was a period of four hundred years, the period of preparation for the advent of the Messiah.

Had King Saul accomplished the dispensation to build the Temple, one of the indemnity conditions he would have restored horizontally through indemnity was the forty years of wandering in the wilderness

---

16. Mal. 4:5
17. Gen. 31:41

in the third national course. After King Saul lost faith and this dispensation failed, this indemnity period of forty years had to be restored as a vertical extension of horizontal restoration. The four-hundred-year period of preparation for the advent of the Messiah was set up for this purpose.

This period was the image parallel to the forty-year period in the age of symbolic parallels extending from the time Jacob returned to Canaan until his family entered Egypt at the invitation of his son Joseph. It was to restore that earlier period through parallel indemnity conditions.

Section 4

The Periods in the Age of the Prolongation of the Providence of Restoration and Their Lengths

The Age of the Prolongation of the Providence of Restoration has been to restore through substantial parallels the Age of the Providence of Restoration, the age of image parallels. As the periods of this age were to restore through indemnity the corresponding periods of the previous age, these periods proceeded in a parallel fashion, both in order and in length.

4.1 The Four-Hundred-Year Period of Persecution in the Roman Empire

Jesus came at the outset of the New Testament Age to complete the Will which had been entrusted to Abraham, the father of faith, who commenced the Old Testament Age. We recall that the Israelites had to endure a four-hundred-year period of slavery in Egypt to restore, on the national level, the foundation of faith which had been shattered due to Abraham's mistake in the symbolic offering. The early Christians underwent a comparable period of suffering to restore through indemnity the foundation of faith which had been destroyed due to the mistake of the Jewish people, who did not properly follow Jesus as the living sacrifice. This was the four-hundred-year period during which Christians were persecuted in the Roman Empire. The persecution abated by 313 A.D., when the Emperor Constantine formally recognized Christianity as a legal religion. In 392 A.D., the Emperor Theodosius I established Christianity as the state religion. This period was the substantial parallel to the Israelites' four-hundred-year period of slavery in Egypt, and its purpose was to restore that earlier period through parallel indemnity conditions.

4.2 THE FOUR-HUNDRED-YEAR PERIOD OF REGIONAL CHURCH LEADERSHIP

The next period in the Age of the Providence of Restoration was the four-hundred-year period of the judges, when judges led the Israelite tribes. Since the Age of the Prolongation of the Providence of Restoration has been the age of substantial parallels, it should contain a four-hundred-year period comparable to the period of the judges. What is called the period of regional church leadership began when Christianity was declared the state religion of the Roman Empire and ended with the enthronement of Charlemagne in 800 A.D. In this period, the people were led by regional church leaders—patriarchs, bishops and abbots—with multiple roles corresponding to the judges in Israel. This period was the substantial parallel to the four-hundred-year period of the judges, and its purpose was to restore that earlier period through parallel indemnity conditions.

4.3 THE ONE-HUNDRED-AND-TWENTY-YEAR PERIOD OF THE CHRISTIAN EMPIRE

When the people of Israel unified as a nation under the leadership of King Saul, they began the 120-year period of the united kingdom, which continued through the reigns of King David and King Solomon. The parallel 120-year period of the Christian empire, also called the Carolingian Empire, began with Charlemagne's enthronement as the emperor in 800 A.D. It ended in 919 A.D. when his royal line ceased in the eastern half of the realm and Henry I was elected king of the German lands. This period was the substantial parallel to the 120-year period of the united kingdom, and its purpose was to restore that earlier period through parallel indemnity conditions.

4.4 THE FOUR-HUNDRED-YEAR PERIOD OF THE DIVIDED KINGDOMS OF EAST AND WEST

Since the Temple's holiness was not properly upheld in the period of the united kingdom, the kingdom was eventually divided into two kingdoms: Israel in the north and Judah in the south. Thus began the four-hundred-year period of the divided kingdoms of north and south.

In the Age of the Prolongation of the Providence of Restoration, the Carolingian Empire was divided into two kingdoms: the Holy Roman Empire in the east and France in the west. Although when the Carolingian Empire was first divided, it was split into the kingdoms of the East Franks, the West Franks and Italy, Italy soon reverted to the rule of the East Franks and together these constituted the Holy Roman Empire, while the West Franks consolidated as the Kingdom of France. This four-hundred-year period of the divided kingdoms of east and west began with the division of the Christian empire in 919 and ended in 1309, when the papacy moved to Avignon, in what is now southern France. This period was the substantial parallel to the four-hundred-year period of the divided kingdoms of north and south, and its purpose was to restore that earlier period through parallel indemnity conditions.

4.5 The Two-Hundred-and-Ten-Year Period of Papal Exile and Return

During the period of the divided kingdoms of north and south, the kingdom of Israel in the north perished at the hands of the Assyrians because its people had fallen into corruption and idolatry. The kingdom of Judah in the south also became faithless and failed to uphold the holiness of the Temple; consequently, its people were taken into exile in Babylon, the satanic world. Over the next 210 years, they suffered in exile, returned to Israel, rebuilt the Temple, and renewed the covenant. The parallel period of papal exile and return also lasted approximately 210 years. It began in 1309 A.D. when, the papacy having become corrupt, Pope Clement V was forced to move the papacy from Rome to Avignon and live there subject to the kings of France. This period continued even after the papacy returned to Rome until the Protestant Reformation began in 1517. This period of 210 years was the substantial parallel to the 210-year period of Israel's exile and return, and its purpose was to restore that earlier period through parallel indemnity conditions.

4.6 The Four-Hundred-Year Period of Preparation for the Second Advent of the Messiah

After the Jewish people were liberated from their exile in Babylon and returned to Jerusalem, they reformed their religious and political life. Based on the prophecies of Malachi, they began preparations to receive the Messiah. After the four-hundred-year period of preparation for the advent of the Messiah, Jesus came to the Jewish people. To restore that period through indemnity in the Age of the Prolongation of the Providence of Restoration, we expect a parallel four-hundred-year period of preparation for the Second Advent of the Messiah. In fact, it began in 1517 with Martin Luther and the Protestant Reformation and has lasted until the eve of the Second Advent of Christ on the earth. As the substantial parallel to the four-hundred-year period of preparation for the advent of the Messiah, its purpose has been to restore that earlier period through parallel indemnity conditions.

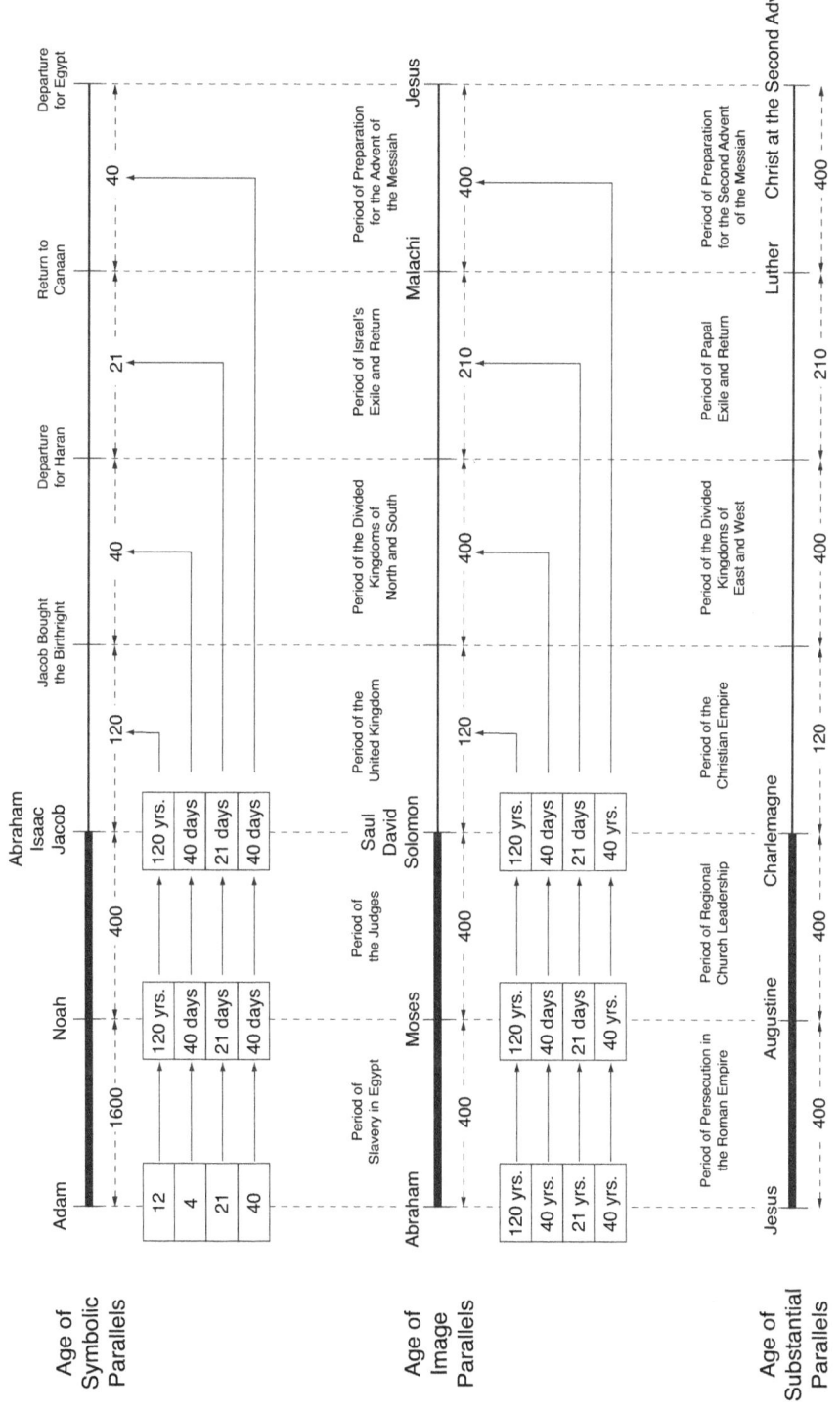

Chapter 4

The Parallels between the Two Ages in the Providence of Restoration

Since the ultimate purpose of the providence of restoration is to lay the foundation for the Messiah, if it is prolonged, the dispensations to restore this foundation must be repeated. We know that to establish the foundation for the Messiah, a central figure must make a symbolic offering acceptable to God by employing an object for the condition and passing through a required time period. In addition, he must lay the foundation of substance by making an acceptable substantial offering upon fulfilling the indemnity condition to remove the fallen nature. In the course of the providence, the repetition of dispensations to restore the foundation for the Messiah has meant, in effect, the repetition of dispensations to restore through indemnity the symbolic offering and the substantial offering. The historical record illuminates the parallels between providential periods caused by the repetition of dispensations to restore through indemnity the foundation for the Messiah. The Age of the Prolongation of the Providence of Restoration has been set up to restore the Age of the Providence of Restoration through parallel indemnity conditions of a substantial type. Let us examine the comparable characteristics of each providential period from this standpoint.

First, however, we need to identify what groups of people have had the central responsibility for God's providence and the historical sources which can shed light on their history. Human history consists of the histories of countless peoples. Nevertheless, God has specially chosen certain people to walk the model course of restoration to lay the foundation for the Messiah. God puts them at the center of His providence and guides them by His Principle. Their history, in turn, steers the course of human history as a whole. A nation or people entrusted with such a mission is called God's chosen people.

God's first chosen people consisted of the descendants of Abraham, Isaac and Jacob, who had established the family foundation for the Messiah. Therefore, the nation centrally responsible for God's providence in the Age of the Providence of Restoration was Israel. The Old Testament, which records the history of Israel, provides the source material with which to study the history of the providence in that age.

However, from the time that they rejected Jesus, the Jewish people lost their qualification to be centrally responsible for God's providence. Foreseeing this, Jesus uttered the parable of the vineyard, saying:

> The kingdom of God will be taken away from you and given to a nation producing the fruits of it. —*Matt. 21:43*

St. Paul said in anguish over his kinsmen, the Jewish people:

> For not all who are descended from Israel belong to Israel, and not all are children of Abraham because they are his descendants . . . it is not the children of the flesh who are the children of God, but the children of the promise are reckoned as descendants. —*Rom. 9:6-8*

Indeed, the people who became centrally responsible for the providence in the Age of the Prolongation of the Providence of Restoration were not the Jews, but rather the Christians. They assumed the mission to accomplish God's unfulfilled providence of restoration. Accordingly, the history of Christianity provides the source material for understanding providential history in this age. In this sense, the descendants of Abraham in the Old Testament Age may be referred to as the First Israel, and the Christians in the New Testament Age may be called the Second Israel.[1]

When we compare the Old Testament to the New Testament, the five books of the Law (Genesis to Deuteronomy), the twelve books of

---

1. Tit. 2:14; 1 Pet. 2:9-10

history (Joshua to Esther), the five books of poetry and wisdom (Job to the Song of Solomon) and the seventeen books of prophecy (Isaiah to Malachi) in the Old Testament correspond to the Gospels, Acts, the Letters of the Apostles and Revelation, respectively. However, while the books of history in the Old Testament record most of the two-thousand-year history of Israel, the Book of Acts records only the history of the earliest Christians in the generation after Jesus' death. To find historical records pertaining to God's work of restoration in the New Testament Age with a scope comparable to those found in the Old Testament, we must consult in addition the entire history of Christianity from Jesus' time to the present day. On this basis, we can compare the histories of the First and Second Israels and their impact on the character of each period in the two providential ages. Recognizing a pattern of parallel periods, we come to know more clearly that history has been shaped by the systematic and lawful providence of the living God.

Section 1

The Period of Slavery in Egypt and the Period of Persecution in the Roman Empire

After Jacob entered Egypt with his twelve sons and seventy kinsmen, their descendants suffered terrible abuse at the hands of the Egyptians for four hundred years. This was for the restoration of the four-hundred-year period from Noah to Abraham—a period for the separation of Satan—which had been defiled due to Abraham's mistake in his offering. The corresponding period of persecution in the Roman Empire was to restore this previous period through parallel indemnity conditions. Jesus' twelve apostles and seventy disciples were the first of many generations of Christians who suffered severe persecution in the Roman Empire over a period of four hundred years. By enduring this suffering, they were restoring through indemnity the four-hundred-year period of preparation for the advent of the Messiah—a period for the separation of Satan—which had been defiled due to the Jewish people's mistake in not honoring Jesus as a living sacrifice but leading him to the cross.

In the period of slavery in Egypt, the chosen people of the First Israel kept themselves pure by circumcision,[2] by making sacrifices[3] and, as they left Egypt, by keeping the Sabbath.[4] During the period of persecu-

---
2. Josh. 5:2-5
3. Exod. 5:3
4. Exod. 16:23

tion in the Roman Empire, the Christians as the Second Israel lived a life of purity by performing the sacraments of baptism and holy communion, offering themselves as sacrifices, and keeping the Sabbath. In both periods, the chosen people had to follow this way of pure faith to separate Satan, who was constantly assailing them due to the condition of previous mistakes by Abraham and the Jewish people.

At the end of Israel's slavery in Egypt, Moses brought the Pharaoh to his knees by the power of the three signs and ten plagues. He then led the Israelites out of Egypt and set out for the land of Canaan. Likewise, toward the end of the period of persecution in the Roman Empire, after Christians had drunk the cup of persecution to the fill, Jesus increased the numbers of believers by moving their hearts with his power and grace. By stirring the heart of Emperor Constantine, Jesus led him to recognize Christianity in 313 A.D. Jesus inspired Theodosius I in 392 A.D. to establish Christianity as the state religion. Christians thus restored Canaan spiritually inside the Roman Empire, the satanic world. In the Old Testament Age, God worked through the external indemnity conditions set by the Mosaic Law; likewise, God had Moses defeat the Pharaoh through the external power of miracles. In the New Testament Age, when God worked through the internal indemnity conditions of faith, He manifested His power internally by moving the hearts of people.

When the period of slavery in Egypt was over, Moses on Mt. Sinai received the Ten Commandments and God's Word revealed in the Law, which formed the core of the Old Testament Scriptures. By setting up and honoring the tablets of stone, the Ark of the Covenant and the Tabernacle, he paved the way for the Israelites to prepare for the coming of the Messiah. Likewise, at the conclusion of the period of persecution in the Roman Empire, Christians gathered the writings which had been left behind by the apostles and evangelists and established the canon of the New Testament. Based on these writings, they sought to realize God's ideals spiritually, ideals which had been enshrined in the Ten Commandments and the Tabernacle in the Old Testament Age. They built up churches and expanded their foundation to prepare for the Second Coming of Christ. After Jesus' ascension, the resurrected Jesus and the Holy Spirit guided Christians directly. Hence, God did not raise up any one person as the central figure responsible for His entire providence, as He had earlier.

Section 2

The Period of the Judges and the Period of Regional Church Leadership

Upon inheriting the mission of Moses, Joshua led the Israelites into the land of Canaan. For the next four hundred years, fifteen judges governed the Israelite tribes: thirteen judges from Othniel to Samson recorded in the Book of Judges, as well as Eli and Samuel. The judges filled the various responsibilities of prophet, priest and king, which became separate offices in the later periods. Israel in this period was a feudalistic society with no central political authority. In the New Testament Age, the period of regional church leadership was set up to restore the period of the judges through parallel indemnity conditions. In this period, regional church leaders—patriarchs, bishops and abbots—led Christian society. Like the judges of the Old Testament Age, they had duties similar to those of prophet, priest and king. As in the time of the judges, Christian society in this period was a feudalistic society under these local authorities.

In the age before Jesus, when God was working with the First Israel to establish a national foundation for the Messiah both spiritually and physically, politics, economy and religion tended to have a national focus. On the other hand, in the age after Jesus, Christians were building a spiritual kingdom under the leadership of Jesus, who stood upon the spiritual foundation for the Messiah. Their loyalty transcended national barriers, for they were serving the resurrected Jesus as the King of Kings. Therefore, the spiritual kingdom of Jesus was not confined to any one nation, but expanded to the far-flung corners of the globe.

The period of the judges began after the Israelites were liberated from slavery in Egypt and the younger generation united solidly under the leadership of Joshua and Caleb to enter the land of Canaan. They parceled out the territory among their clans and tribes. Settling in villages united around the judges, the people consolidated into a chosen nation and established a simple feudalistic society. Likewise, the period of regional church leadership in the Christian era began after the liberation of Christianity from the persecution of the Roman Empire, the satanic world. Christians spread the Gospel to the Germanic peoples, many of whom had migrated to Western Europe in the fourth century to escape the invading Huns. In their new land of Western Europe, God raised up the Germanic tribes as a new chosen people and established an early form of feudal society, which later matured into the feudalism of the Middle Ages.

As we discussed earlier, when the Israelites set out for Canaan, they first built the Tabernacle as the symbol of the Messiah and the object for the condition to decide who would stand in the position of Abel for the foundation of substance.[5] In the period of the judges, the Israelites should have exalted the Tabernacle and remained obedient to the direction of the judges. However, instead of destroying the seven Canaanite tribes, the Israelites lived among them and were influenced by their customs. They even took to worshipping their idols, thus bringing great confusion to their faith. Likewise, in the period of regional church leadership, the Christians were supposed to exalt the Church, which was the image of the Messiah, and follow the directions of its bishops and monastic leaders. The Church was the object for the condition to determine who would have the position of Abel. However, they became influenced by the religion and culture of the pagan Germanic tribes, which brought great confusion to the Christian faith.

Section 3

The Period of the United Kingdom and the Period of the Christian Empire

When the period of the judges came to a close and the First Israel entered the period of the united kingdom, the functions of the judge were apportioned to the offices of prophet, priest and king. The prophets received instructions directly from God, the priests kept charge over the Tabernacle and later the Temple, and the king governed the nation. Each carried on their distinct missions in guiding Israel to accomplish the goal of the providence of restoration. The purpose of the period of the Christian empire was to restore the period of the united kingdom through parallel indemnity conditions. Thus, when the period of regional church leadership came to a close, the missions of these leaders were apportioned to the offices of monastic leaders corresponding to the prophets, the pope corresponding to the high priest, and the emperor, who ruled the people. They were responsible to guide the Second Israel to accomplish the goal of the providence of restoration. In the previous period, the Christian Church had been divided into the five patriarchates of

---

5. cf. Moses and Jesus 2.2.2.3

Jerusalem, Antioch, Alexandria, Constantinople and Rome, with Rome dominant in the West. The pope, as the Roman patriarch was called, supervised all the bishops and abbots in Western Europe.

In the period of the united kingdom, the kings established the kingdom of Israel around the Temple, thereby manifesting the ideal of Moses' Tabernacle which was first conceived at the time of the Exodus. This was the image course for building the Kingdom of Heaven ruled by Jesus, which he would one day come to establish as the King of Kings.[6] Likewise, in the period of the Christian empire, Charlemagne's empire realized the ideal of the Christian state as set down in *The City of God* by St. Augustine—who lived when the Christians had just been liberated from the oppression of the Roman Empire, a time parallel to that of Moses. Once again, this was the image course for building the Kingdom of God, which Christ, as the King of Kings, will one day return to establish. Accordingly, in this period, the emperor and the pope were to realize the ideal Christian state by uniting wholeheartedly to follow the Will of God. The spiritual kingdom ruled by the pope, which had been founded upon the spiritual foundation for the Messiah, and the temporal kingdom ruled by the emperor should have united based on Christ's teachings. Had they done so, religion, politics and economy would have harmonized, and the foundation for the Second Advent of Christ would have been established at that time.

In the period of the united kingdom of Israel, the king was the central figure for restoring the foundation of faith. He was responsible to carry out the Word of God, which was given through the prophets. Before the king was anointed, the prophet and the high priest were to represent and teach the Word of God, and thus they stood in the position of Abel. Their mission, as required by the providence of restoration, was to restore the physical world from the position of the archangel, representing the spirit world. However, after they laid the foundation upon which the king could stand, and anointed and blessed him as the king, they were to take the role of Cain before him. The king was to rule his kingdom according to the guidance of the prophets, and the prophets were to obey the king as his subjects and counselors.

About eight hundred years after Abraham's descendants entered Egypt, by God's command the prophet Samuel anointed Saul as the first king of Israel.[7] King Saul stood upon the foundation of the four hundred years under the judges. Had he completed the forty years of his reign in accordance with God's desires, he would have stood in the

---

6. Isa. 9:6
7. I Sam. 8:19-22; 10:1-24

position of having restored through indemnity the four hundred years of slavery in Egypt and Moses' forty years in the Pharaoh's palace. Thereupon, King Saul would have fulfilled the dispensation of forty for the separation of Satan and laid the foundation of faith. If, upon this foundation, King Saul had built and exalted the Temple, the image of the Messiah, he would have then stood in the position Moses should have occupied had he not failed in the first national course to restore Canaan, but had built the Temple in Canaan and glorified it. If the Israelites had then stood upon this foundation of faith and faithfully followed King Saul as he honored the Temple, they would have laid the foundation of substance. The foundation for the Messiah would have been established at that time.

However, because King Saul disobeyed the commands of God given through the prophet Samuel,[8] he was in no position to build the Temple. Upon his failure, King Saul found himself in the same position as Moses after he had failed in the first national course to restore Canaan. As was the case with Moses, the providence of restoration through King Saul was extended. Forty years of King David's reign and forty years of King Solomon's reign would pass before the foundation of faith was laid and the Temple built. Furthermore, as we discussed earlier, King Saul was also in the position of Abraham. In the same manner that the Will entrusted to Abraham was finally brought to pass through Isaac and Jacob, God's Will to build the Temple through King Saul had to be continued through the reign of King David and was finally realized during the reign of King Solomon. Nevertheless, King Solomon left the position of Abel for the substantial offering when he fell into lust with his many foreign wives, who turned him away from God.[9] Hence, there was no way for Israel to establish the foundation of substance. The foundation for the Messiah, which should have been laid in the period of the united kingdom, was not realized.

In the period of the Christian empire, all the conditions pertaining to the united kingdom had to be restored through parallel conditions of indemnity. Once again, the central figure to restore the foundation of faith was the emperor. He was responsible to actualize the Christian ideals set forth by the leading monastics and the pope. The pope, for his part, stood in a position comparable to the high priest of Israel, who received God's commands through the prophets. He was responsible to lay the spiritual foundation upon which the emperor could realize the ideal Christian state. After crowning and blessing the emperor, the

---

8. I Sam. 15:1-23
9. I Kings 11:3-7

pope was to obey him as one of his subjects in temporal matters. The emperor, in turn, was to lift up and further the spiritual work of the papacy in his realm.

Pope Leo III crowned Charlemagne and blessed him as the first emperor of Christendom in 800 A.D. Charlemagne stood upon the foundation of the four-hundred-year period of regional church leadership, which restored through indemnity, in the form of substantial parallels, the four-hundred-year period of the judges. Therefore, like King Saul, he stood upon the foundation of a dispensation of forty for the separation of Satan. By faithfully living according to the teachings of Jesus in his work to realize the Christian ideal of the state, he was to establish the foundation of faith. Indeed, when Charlemagne was crowned emperor, he achieved this foundation. Had the Second Israel absolutely believed in and followed Charlemagne, the foundation of substance would have been laid, and thereby the foundation for the Messiah would have been established. In other words, the spiritual kingdom led by the pope and the earthly kingdom led by the emperor were to fully unite upon the existing spiritual foundation for the Messiah. Christ would then have returned upon this solid ground and built his Kingdom. However, the emperor did not remain obedient to God's Will and left the position of Abel for the substantial offering. Neither the foundation of substance nor the foundation for the Second Advent of the Messiah was established.

Section 4

The Period of the Divided Kingdoms of North and South and the Period of the Divided Kingdoms of East and West

Because King Solomon was led by his wives and concubines to worship idols, the united kingdom of Israel was divided upon his death, having lasted only three generations.[10] The kingdom of Israel in the north, which was founded by ten of the twelve tribes, was in the position of Cain, while the kingdom of Judah in the south, which was founded by the two remaining tribes, was in the position of Abel. This was how the period of the divided kingdoms of north and south began.

The Christian empire also began to divide in the third generation. Charlemagne's grandsons partitioned it into three kingdoms: the East

---

10. I Kings 11:5-13

Franks, the West Franks and Italy. The descendants of Charlemagne were in bitter and constant conflict with each other. The remnants of the Christian empire soon coalesced into two kingdoms, with Italy reverting to the rule of the East Franks. The kingdom of the East Franks flourished greatly under Otto I and came to be called the Holy Roman Empire. Claiming to be the heir of the Roman Empire, it ruled parts of Western Europe and sought to secure dominion over both politics and religion. The Holy Roman Empire stood in the position of Abel in relation to France, as the kingdom of the West Franks came to be called.

The northern kingdom of Israel was founded by Jeroboam, who had lived in exile in the days of King Solomon. It was ruled by nineteen kings over some 210 years. Through repeated assassinations, its short-lived royal families changed nine times; not one king was righteous in the sight of God. Nevertheless, God sent the prophet Elijah, who prevailed in the contest with 850 prophets of Baal and Asherah on Mt. Carmel when God sent down fire upon the altar.[11] Other prophets, including Elisha, Jonah, Hosea and Amos, spread the Word of God at the risk of their lives. Yet since the northern kingdom continued to worship foreign gods and did not repent, God had the Assyrians destroy them and took away their qualification as the chosen people forever.[12]

The southern kingdom of Judah was established by Solomon's son, Rehoboam. Its royal house continued in one dynastic line from David to Zedekiah, producing many righteous kings out of the twenty who ruled the kingdom for its nearly four hundred years of existence. Nevertheless, a succession of evil kings, combined with influence from the northern kingdom, led to much idolatry and corruption. Consequently, the people of the southern kingdom were taken into exile in Babylon.

In the period of the divided kingdoms of north and south, whenever the Israelites violated their covenant with God, straying from the ideal of the Temple, God sent many prophets—such as Elijah, Isaiah and Jeremiah—to admonish them and move them to repentance and internal reform. However, because the kings and the people did not heed the warnings of the prophets and did not repent, God chastised them externally by sending gentile nations such as Syria, Assyria and Babylon to attack them.

During the parallel period of the divided kingdoms of east and west, the papacy was corrupt. God sent prominent monks such as St. Thomas Aquinas and St. Francis of Assisi to admonish the papacy and promote internal reform in the Church. Since the papacy and the Church did not

---

11. I Kings 18:19-40
12. II Kings 17:7-23

repent, but sank further into corruption and immorality, God chastised them externally by letting their people fight the Muslims. This was the providential reason behind the Crusades. While Jerusalem and the Holy Land were under the protection of the Abbasid Caliphate, Christian pilgrims were received with hospitality. After the Caliphate collapsed and the Holy Land was conquered by the Seljuk Turks, cries of alarm went out that Christian pilgrims were being harassed. Outraged, the popes raised the Crusades to recover the Holy Land. There were eight Crusades, beginning in 1095 and continuing sporadically for about two hundred years. Despite some initial success, the Crusaders were defeated again and again.

The period of the divided kingdoms of north and south came to an end when gentile nations took the people of Israel and Judah into exile. They put an end to the monarchy in Israel. Likewise, at the close of the period of the divided kingdoms of east and west, the papacy had completely lost its prestige and credibility after the repeated defeats of the Crusades. Christianity thus lost its center of spiritual sovereignty. Moreover, since the lords and knights who had maintained feudal society were decimated by the Crusades, feudal society lost its political power and vigor. Since the papacy and the feudal lords had spent enormous funds to pursue these unsuccessful wars, they were left impoverished. Monarchic Christianity began to erode.

SECTION 5

THE PERIOD OF ISRAEL'S EXILE AND RETURN AND THE PERIOD OF THE PAPAL EXILE AND RETURN

By falling into faithlessness without repentance, the people of Israel failed to realize the ideal of God's nation founded upon the Temple. To make another attempt at fulfilling this Will, God had the people suffer hardships as exiles in Babylon. This was similar to when God had the Israelites suffer as slaves in Egypt to restore through indemnity Abraham's mistake in the symbolic offering.

In the period of the Christian empire, God worked through the pope and the emperor to establish a kingdom prepared for Christ at his Second Coming. God's intention was that ultimately they would bequeath the empire and the throne to the Messiah when he would come as the King of Kings and build God's kingdom[13] upon that foundation. Yet the emperors and popes became corrupt and did not repent. The popes did

---

13. Isa. 9:6; Luke 1:33

not lay the spiritual foundation upon which the emperors could stand as the central figures for the foundation of substance. Therefore, the foundation for the Second Advent of Christ was not established. To begin a new dispensation to restore this foundation, God allowed the popes to be taken into exile and suffer captivity.

In the earlier parallel period, nearly seventy years elapsed from the time King Nebuchadnezzar of Babylon took into captivity King Jehoiachin and his royal family, as well as prophets including Daniel and Ezekiel, priests, officials, craftsmen and many other Israelites, until the fall of Babylon and their liberation by the royal decree of King Cyrus.[14] It then took another 140 years for the exiles to return to their homeland in three waves, until they fully reformed themselves as a nation united around the Will of God as proclaimed in the messianic prophecies of Malachi. Henceforth, they began to prepare for the coming of the Messiah. In the period of papal exile and return, which was to restore this period through indemnity in the form of substantial parallels, Western Christianity had to walk a similar course.

The popes and priests, sunk in immorality, gradually lost the confidence of the people. The authority of the papacy sank even lower due to the repeated defeats of the Crusades. The end of the Crusades saw the gradual collapse of the feudal system in Europe and the emergence of modern nation-states. As the power of secular monarchies grew, the conflict between the popes and the kings escalated. In one such conflict, King Philip IV, "the Fair," of France imprisoned Pope Boniface VIII for a time. In 1309, Philip forced Pope Clement V to move the papacy from Rome to Avignon in southern France. For seventy years, successive popes lived there subject to the kings of France, until 1377 when Pope Gregory XI returned the papal residence to Rome.

After Gregory's death, the cardinals elected an Italian, the Archbishop of Bari, as Pope Urban VI. However, a group of cardinals, mostly Frenchmen, rejected him, elected another pope, Clement VII, and established a rival papacy in Avignon. The Great Schism continued into the next century. To resolve this impasse, the cardinals from both camps held a council in Pisa, Italy, in 1409, which dismissed both the Roman and Avignon popes and appointed Alexander V as the legitimate pope. The two popes, however, refused to resign, creating for a short time the spectacle of three contending popes. Shortly afterwards, cardinals, bishops, theologians, royalty and their envoys gathered for the General Council of Constance (1414-1417). It dismissed all three popes and elected Martin V as the new pope, effectively ending the Great Schism.

---

14. II Kings 24; 25; II Chron. 36; Jer. 29:10; 39:1-10

The Council of Constance insisted that the general councils of the Church had supreme authority, greater than that of the pope and with the power to elect or depose him, and directed that subsequent councils be held at regular intervals. Thus, it sought to reorganize the Roman church as a constitutional monarchy. However, in 1431, when delegates gathered for the next council, held in Basel, Switzerland, the pope tried to adjourn the meeting. The delegates refused to leave and carried on in the pope's absence, but to no effect; in 1449, they finally disbanded. The plan to institutionalize a constitutional monarchy within the Roman church came to naught, and the papacy recovered the authority it had lost in 1309.

The leaders of the conciliar movement in the fifteenth century had tried to reform the corrupt papacy by setting up a representative council composed of bishops and laymen and giving it supreme authority. Nevertheless, the papacy ended up reasserting its full authority, as it had not enjoyed since before its exile. Furthermore, these councils condemned more fundamental reforms as promoted by John Wycliffe (1330-1384) and Jan Hus (1373-1415), who was personally invited to attend the Council of Constance only to be burned at the stake. At that point, the die was cast for the outbreak of the Protestant Reformation.

This period of approximately 210 years ran from 1309, with the papacy's seventy years of exile in Avignon, through the Great Schism, the conciliar movement and the restoration of papal authority in the Roman church, to the eve of the Protestant Reformation spearheaded by Martin Luther in 1517. Its purpose was to restore through indemnity, in the form of substantial parallels, the 210-year period of Israel's exile and return—from Israel's seventy years of exile in Babylon through the stages of the returning to Israel and the rebuilding of the Temple, until the reform of politics and religion under the leadership of Ezra, Nehemiah and the prophet Malachi.

Section 6

The Period of Preparation for the Advent of the Messiah and the Period of Preparation for the Second Advent of the Messiah

Following the period of Israel's exile and return, another four hundred years elapsed before Jesus came. This was the period of preparation for the advent of the Messiah. Likewise, Christianity is to meet Christ at his Second Advent only after passing through four hundred years of the period of preparation for the Second Advent of the Messiah, which has followed the period of papal exile and return. It should restore through indemnity in the form of substantial parallels the period of preparation for the advent of the Messiah.

During the four thousand years of God's providence of restoration from Adam to Jesus, vertical indemnity conditions had accumulated due to Satan's repeated defilement of dispensations to restore the foundation of faith through periods of forty for the separation of Satan. The period of preparation for the advent of the Messiah was intended to be the final period of providential history in which all these conditions would be horizontally restored through indemnity. Likewise, the period of preparation for the Second Advent of the Messiah is intended to be the final period of providential history, when all the vertical indemnity conditions which have accumulated during the six-thousand-year history of the providence of restoration since Adam's day are horizontally restored.

Upon returning from the Babylonian exile, the Israelites established the foundation of faith by repenting of their past sin of idolatry, rebuilding the Temple[15] which had been destroyed by King Nebuchadnezzar, and reforming their faith based on the Mosaic Law under the guidance of Ezra the scribe.[16] They then began to prepare for the coming of the Messiah according to the word of the prophet Malachi. Likewise, after the papacy's return to Rome, medieval Christians established the foundation of faith by seeking to reform the Roman church; these efforts culminated in the Protestant Reformation led by Martin Luther. This movement pierced the gloom of medieval Europe with the light of the Gospel and pioneered new paths of faith.

One purpose of the period of preparation for the advent of the Messiah was to restore through indemnity in the form of image parallels the approximately forty years of Jacob's preparation to enter Egypt. This was the period in his life from his return to Canaan from Haran until he and his family entered Egypt. The period of preparation for the Second Advent of the Messiah is to restore this period through indemnity in the form of substantial parallels. Accordingly, Christians in this period have had to suffer tribulations and hardships as Jacob's family did until they met Joseph in Egypt, or as the Jews did before they met Jesus. Specifically, in the Age of the Providence of Restoration, people were justified before God by such external conditions as keeping the Mosaic Law and offering sacrifices. Therefore, during the period of preparation

---

15. Ezra 3:7-13; Ezra 6:1-15
16. Ezra 7:1-10; Neh. 8

for the advent of the Messiah, the First Israel had to suffer external hardships at the hands of the gentile nations of Persia, Greece, Egypt, Syria and Rome. During the Age of the Prolongation of the Providence of Restoration, Christians have been justified before God by internal conditions of prayer and faith according to the teachings of Jesus. Hence, in the period of preparation for the Second Advent of the Messiah, the Second Israel has had to walk a path of internal tribulations. The ideologies of Renaissance humanism and the Enlightenment, as well as the call for religious freedom which arose from the Reformation, have created a profusion of philosophies and theologies, causing great confusion in the Christian faith and turmoil in people's spiritual lives.

The period of preparation for the Second Advent of the Messiah has also been restoring, through parallel indemnity conditions of a substantial type, the internal preparations and external environment for the worldwide reception of the Messiah, which had first been set up during the four hundred years of the period of preparation for the advent of the Messiah.

In preparation for the First Coming of Christ, God sent the prophet Malachi to the chosen people 430 years beforehand to arouse in them a strong messianic expectation. At the same time, God encouraged the Jews to reform their religion and deepen their faith to make the internal preparations necessary to receive the Messiah. Meanwhile, among the world's peoples, God founded religions suited to their regions and cultures by which they could make the necessary internal preparations to receive the Messiah. In India, God established Buddhism through Gautama Buddha (565-485 B.C.) as a new development out of Hinduism. In Greece, God inspired Socrates (470-399 B.C.) and opened the brilliant age of classical Greek civilization. In the Far East, God raised up Confucius (552-479 B.C.), whose teachings of Confucianism established the standard of human ethics. Jesus was to come upon this worldwide foundation of preparation, and through his teachings he was to bring together Judaism, Hellenism, Buddhism and Confucianism. He was to unify all religions and civilizations into one worldwide civilization founded upon the Christian Gospel.

Since the Renaissance, God has been creating the religious, political and economic environment conducive to the work of Christ at his Second Coming. This has been the age to restore through indemnity, in the form of substantial parallels, the earlier period when God had set up the worldwide environment to prepare for the coming of Jesus. Beginning with the Renaissance, progress in virtually every field of human endeavor, including politics, economy, culture and science, has increased at a rapid rate. Today, these fields have reached their zenith and have created a global environment conducive to the work of Christ at his Second Coming. In Jesus' day, the Roman Empire ruled the vast domains around the Mediterranean Sea, integrated by an advanced and extensive transportation system reaching out in all directions. This was the center of a vast Hellenistic civilization founded on the Greek language. Thus, all the necessary preparations had been made for a swift transmission of the teachings of the Messiah from Israel, where Jesus lived, to Rome and the world. Similarly, in the present era of the Second Advent, the influence of the Western powers has expanded the democratic political sphere throughout the world. The rapid progress of transportation and communication has greatly bridged the gap between East and West, and the extensive contact among languages and cultures has brought the world much closer together. These developments characterize an environment in which the teachings of the returning Christ can freely and swiftly be conveyed to the hearts of all humankind. This will enable his teachings to bring rapid and profound changes all over the globe.

Section 7

The Providence of Restoration and the Progress of History

The Kingdom of Heaven on earth is a society whose structure is formed in the image of a perfect person.[17] Likewise, fallen society may be regarded as formed in the likeness of a fallen person. We can better understand the history of societies built by sinful humanity by examining the inner life of a fallen person.

A fallen person possesses both an original mind, which prompts him to pursue goodness, and an evil mind, which fills him with evil desires and rebels against the promptings of the original mind. Undeniably, the two minds are constantly at war with each other, inclining us toward shifting and conflicting behaviors. Since human society is composed of individuals who are constantly at war within themselves, interactions among them cannot help but be full of discord and conflict. Human history has consisted of people's conflict-ridden social relationships constantly changing with the course of time. Hence, it has necessarily unfolded in strife and warfare.

---

17. cf. Creation 3.2

Nevertheless, in the midst of the persistent fight between the original mind and the evil mind, people are ever striving to repel evil and follow the way of goodness. As they gain ground in their striving, their efforts bear fruit in righteous deeds. Because of the activity of the original mind within himself, even a fallen person can respond to God's providence of restoration and join in furthering the goal of goodness. Progress in history thus originates with individuals who, even amidst the vortex of good and evil, make determined efforts to reject evil and promote goodness. Therefore, the world toward which history is progressing is the Kingdom of Heaven, where the goal of goodness will be realized.

We must understand that conflicts and wars are interim phenomena to separate good from evil in the pursuit of this ultimate goal. Even though evil may triumph at times, God will use it to steer history toward the fulfillment of a greater good. In this respect, we can recognize that the progress of history toward goodness is driven by a process of constantly dividing good from evil according to God's providence of restoration.

Meanwhile, on the basis of his relationship of blood ties with the first human beings, Satan has worked through fallen people to realize, in advance of God, a perverted form of the ideal society which God intends to realize. As a result, in human history we witness the rise of unprincipled societies which are built upon twisted versions of the Principle. At the end of human history, before God can restore the Kingdom of Heaven on earth, Satan will have built an unprincipled world in a distorted image of the Kingdom: this is none other than the communist world. This is an instance of how Satan, who had a headstart in the course of history, has always mimicked God's plans in advance of God. In the course of the providence of restoration, a false likeness precedes the appearance of the true.[18] Jesus' prophecy that false Christs will appear before the Second Advent of Christ[19] can be elucidated by this aspect of the Principle.

7.1 THE PROGRESS OF HISTORY IN THE AGE OF THE PROVIDENCE OF RESTORATION

Some historians have held that the first society built by fallen people was a primitive collective society. From the viewpoint of God's providence, the primitive societies which fallen people built were cen-

---

18. cf. Preparation 3.2; Preparation 4.1
19. Matt. 24:23-24; cf. I John 2:18

tered on Satan. Though Satan may have tried to build a collective society where people shared their possessions with each other, it would still have been only a defective imitation of the society which God intends to build through people of perfect character: a society characterized by interdependence, mutual prosperity and universally shared values. Regardless of the form, this satanic primitive society could not have been free of struggle and division. If it had been, it would have perpetuated its existence forever without change, and God's providence of restoration could never have been fulfilled.

In reality, the two minds at war within a fallen person give rise to internal conflicts which manifest themselves through his actions and cause him to be in conflict with others. Therefore, it would have been impossible for a satanic primitive society pursuing the goal of collective living ever to maintain peace. As primitive societies evolved into larger-scale societies with different economic and social relations, these conflicts inevitably evolved in a corresponding manner. Due to the activity of the original mind calling people to respond to God's providence of restoration, divisions between relative good and evil surely arose in primitive societies under satanic sovereignty.

When we examine the course of social development guided by Satan, we find that clan societies arose out of the divisions between individuals in primitive societies. These societies have tended to expand in scope, with clan societies developing into feudalistic societies and then into monarchic societies by increasing their territory and power. Satan preempted this pattern ahead of God, because he understood God's plan to call good individuals out of the sinful world and have them build a good clan society, then expand to a good feudalistic society, and finally reach the stage of a good kingdom with territory and sovereignty sufficient for the Messiah to come and accomplish his work.

God called Abraham out of the sinful world to be the standard-bearer of goodness and blessed him with descendants who would uphold the Will of God. God raised up Abraham's descendants into the first Israelite clan society. They entered Egypt as a clan society, but by the time they left Egypt for Canaan, they had grown into a tribal society. Israelite society in the period of the judges was a feudalistic society. (A feudalistic society in this discussion refers to a society with a political system characterized by master-servant relationships of service and obedience and an economic system composed of self-sufficient units in small, isolated territories.) In the period of the judges, Israelite society had such characteristics. When the Israelites entered Canaan, a portion of land was allocated to each tribe. The judges who ruled these territories played a role similar to that of bishops and feudal lords in early medieval Europe.

It is the nature of a feudalistic society that its people espouse the beliefs of their lord and obey his commands. As long as the lord remains faithful to the Will of God, his people will follow him and stand on God's side. Living in a political system built on master-servant relationships and having a self-sufficient economy largely isolated from the outside world, they have considerable capacity to withstand Satan's invasion from outside. The main reason that a clan society develops into a feudalistic society is to bring property and people, which had belonged to Satan, back to God's side. By expanding the territory under God's sovereignty, they are better placed to ward off Satan's invasion. Understanding this divine providence, Satan tried to preserve his rule by preempting it and forming his own feudalistic societies many centuries earlier.

The providential purpose of the feudalistic society of early Israel was to lay a foundation for the establishment of a monarchic society with greater territory and more powerful sovereignty. The monarchic society amalgamated the smaller units of political and economic sovereignty secured by the earlier feudalistic society into a single territory with a large population, a strong economy and a well-defended sovereignty. This was done with the establishment of the united kingdom of Israel founded by King Saul.

Jesus was to come as the King of Kings.[20] God built the monarchic society in Israel to prepare a strong enough foundation for him to come as the Messiah and rule as King of Kings.

Long before this, Satan understood the providence to receive the Messiah behind the construction of the monarchy and had formed his own monarchic societies to block God's providence. Many centuries before the founding of the united kingdom of Israel, the first dynasty of Egypt had been founded, and pharaonic Egypt continued through some thirty dynasties. The ancient kingdom of Babylon had ruled all of Mesopotamia during the reign of King Hammurabi in the eighteenth century B.C., and the Hittites ruled supreme over the Near East in the region of Syria during the fourteenth century B.C. Even within the satanic world, there was constant warfare between relatively good kingdoms and relatively evil kingdoms, resulting in the separation of good from evil. This drive toward goodness is rooted in the original mind, which responds to the call of God's providence of restoration.

---

20. Rev. 11:15

Had King Solomon served God's Will until the end, he could have exercised his God-given political skills to unify the nations of the Near East. He could have assimilated the Egyptian, Minoan and Mesopotamian civilizations, which were weak at that time. He thus would have built a worldwide dominion to which the Messiah could come and realize God's sovereignty on earth. Unfortunately, Solomon fell into idolatry. Consequently, God had to begin a dispensation to dismantle this monarchic society which He had so painfully built up.

Since the kings of the united kingdom of Israel did not lay the foundation for the Messiah, nor complete the groundwork upon which God could restore His sovereignty, God eventually divided the kingdom into two: Israel in the north and Judah in the south. When they continued to transgress against God's Will, God let the northern kingdom of Israel be destroyed at the hands of the gentile nation of Assyria. The Assyrians in the eighth century B.C. had conquered the entire ancient Near East, including Egypt, to build the first world empire. The kingdom of Judah upheld God's Will for a time, but then rebelled against Him. Hence, God allowed it to fall into the hands of the neo-Babylonian Empire, which had supplanted Assyria as the second world empire.

After the fall of Judah, God kept the throne of Israel vacant and put the Jewish people under the control of successive gentile empires for most of the period leading up to the coming of the Messiah. Most notably, God placed them in the Hellenistic cultural sphere, which laid the ideological framework for democracy. God fashioned Israel's society in the form of democracy in order that when the Messiah came, he could be hailed as their king by the will of the people, who should have welcomed him wholeheartedly. However, the Jewish public did not so elevate Jesus. Without public support, he was crucified. Consequently, at the consummation of the providence which had begun two thousand years earlier with the calling of Abraham and his descendants out of the sinful world, its purpose was attained only spiritually.

7.2 THE PROGRESS OF HISTORY IN THE AGE OF THE PROLONGATION OF THE PROVIDENCE OF RESTORATION

7.2.1 THE PROVIDENCE OF RESTORATION AND THE HISTORY OF THE WEST

The Roman Empire, which had persecuted Christianity, finally knelt before the crucified Jesus in the fourth century and adopted Christianity as the state religion. Nevertheless, the original providential role of the Roman Empire, which had unified the ancient world around the

Mediterranean Sea, was to lay the foundation for Christ's kingdom on earth. Had the Jewish people believed in Jesus as the Messiah and united with him, the Roman Empire would have been won over by Jesus during his lifetime. Jesus would have been honored throughout the empire as the King of Kings. He would have established a worldwide dominion with Jerusalem as its capital. However, because the Jewish people disbelieved, Judea was destroyed and the Roman Empire was fated to decline. After a century of barbarian invasions, the Western Roman Empire came to an end in 476 A.D.

In this manner, the center of God's providence of restoration shifted from Judea, the land of God's bitter grief, to Western Europe, formerly the territory of the Western Roman Empire now occupied by the Germanic tribes. Accordingly, the spiritual providence of restoration based on Christianity has been conducted primarily in Western Europe. Only in Western Europe has the history of this era progressed strictly according to the pattern set by the providence of restoration.[21] The history of Christianity in Western Europe provides us with information about the events which shaped the Age of the Prolongation of the Providence of Restoration.

7.2.2 THE MUTUAL RELATIONS BETWEEN RELIGIOUS HISTORY, ECONOMIC HISTORY AND POLITICAL HISTORY

To enable human beings to rule both the spirit world and the physical world, God created them as the dual entities of spirit self and physical self.[22] Had human beings not fallen, their spirit self and physical self would have reached perfection together. Their spiritual intellect and physical intellect would have joined in complete harmony during earthly life. After human beings fell and became ignorant of both the spiritual and physical worlds, God worked to overcome spiritual ignorance through religion and physical ignorance through science.[23]

Religions have helped fallen people gradually overcome their spiritual ignorance by stimulating their latent original mind to activity. They have been teaching people to focus their lives on the invisible, causal world of God. Since not everyone feels an immediate need for religion, only a few exceptional people attain spiritual knowledge rapidly. For the vast majority, spiritual growth remains a slow process. We see this from the fact that even today, with religions widespread throughout the

---

21. Likewise, the course of historical development as discussed by the Marxist theory of historical materialism is also applicable only to the history of Western Europe.
22. cf. Creation 6.2
23. cf. Eschatology 5.1

world, people's spiritual level is often no better than that of people in ancient times.

On the other hand, everyone is familiar with the findings of science, which have greatly enhanced our knowledge of the physical world. Since science deals with practical matters, everyone feels a strong need for it. Thus, the increase in humankind's knowledge of the physical world has generally been widespread and rapid. Furthermore, while the objects of religious study are in the intangible, transcendent world of cause, scientific research examines tangible, material objects in the world of result. Hence, to this day religion and science remain theoretically irreconcilable. Moreover, because Satan, who holds sovereignty over the universe, attacks and corrupts people through their life in the world, religions teach one to deny the world. As such, religions cannot easily harmonize with science, which seeks to improve life in the world. We know that in the beginning, God created the outward physical body of human beings before imbuing them with their inner spirit.[24] The providence of restoration, which is a work of re-creation, follows the same pattern, from the external to the internal. From this providential perspective, it is evident that during their course of development, religion and science are often at variance, even in conflict.[25]

The same discord is found in the relationship between people's religious and economic life. Like science, economic activities deal with the practical world. Indeed, economic progress bears a close relationship to the development of science. Accordingly, religious history, based on the internal development of God's providence, and economic history, based on the external development of His providence, have taken divergent directions and have progressed at different rates. Therefore, to grasp the progress of the history of the West, which has followed the pattern set by God's providence of restoration, we must examine the history of Christianity and Western economic history separately.

As with the relationship between religion and science, religion and economy are related in that they are responsible for restoring the internal and external aspects of fallen people's lives. Although religion and economy, like religion and science, seem to develop at variance with each other, they are related in the life of society. Thus, there has been some mutual influence between the history of Christianity and economic history.

Religion and economy are integrated with our life in society through politics. Especially in Western Europe, politics has sought to connect

---

24. Gen. 2:7
25. cf. Preparation 1

economic development, which has closely followed the progress of science, with the path of Christianity, which has often lacked a clear sense of its providential direction. Western political history has pioneered a path through which to harmonize religion and economy. Therefore, to accurately grasp the progress of history as it moves toward the goal of the providence of restoration, we must also investigate separately the history of politics.

As an illustration of how the courses of religious, political and economic development have progressed separately, let us sketch the historical situation of Western Europe toward the end of the seventeenth century. With respect to the history of religion, democratic values had already taken root in the Christianity of this period. Christianity of a monarchic polity under the rule of the papacy had fragmented with the Protestant Reformation in 1517. The people of Europe, whose life of devotion in medieval times had been subject to the papal hierarchy, were gradually liberated to lead a Christian life based on their own reading of the Bible. With regard to the politics of this period, absolute monarchy was at its height. Economically, feudal society based on the manor system persisted in many parts of Europe. Thus, the same European society was becoming democratic with respect to religious life while remaining monarchic with respect to political life and feudal with respect to economic life.

We also should clarify why the development of history through most of the Old Testament Age was not characterized by this pattern of separate development. In ancient Israel, the progress of science was extremely slow. Hence, its economic life did not develop, and its society had little specialization. The people led a simple life under a social system in which religion was an integral part of their daily life. Bound by master-servant relationships and the strict code of the Mosaic Law, they had to obey their rulers in matters both political and religious. In that age, religion, politics and economy did not progress separately.

7.2.3 CLAN SOCIETY

Let us examine the progress of history in terms of religion, politics and economy during the New Testament Age. The inclination of the original mind to respond to God's providence of restoration generally brings about divisions in a society centered on Satan. Those who follow God's Will are singled out in this process and may gather to form a clan society on God's side. The birth of the Christian clan society followed this pattern. With the crucifixion of Jesus, the Jewish nation had fallen to Satan's side and God could not continue with His providence of restoration in that society under such circumstances. Consequently, God broke up that society, calling devout believers out of it to establish a Christian clan society.

In the Old Testament Age, Jacob's twelve sons led his seventy kinsmen to form the Israelite clan society and set out on the course of the providence. Similarly, in the New Testament Age, Jesus' twelve disciples led his seventy followers to form the Christian clan society and commence God's new providence. Christian clan society was composed of rudimentary communities with little or no structured political or economic system. In this period, religion, politics and economics did not progress independently.

Despite severe persecution, Christian clan society gradually prospered in the Roman Empire around the Mediterranean Sea and developed into a Christian tribal society. Battered by the mass migrations of peoples which began in the latter half of the fourth century, the Western Roman Empire fell by 476 A.D. Christian society expanded greatly as Christianity was brought to the Germanic peoples who migrated into this territory.

7.2.4 Feudalistic Society

With the progress of history, clan society developed into feudalistic society. A feudalistic society was born in Europe when, around the fall of the Roman Empire, imperial authority waned and the empire sank into chaos. In this society, religion, politics and economy would eventually divide and take separate paths.

In the early days of this feudalistic society, particularly among the newly-Christianized Germanic tribes, free peasants and warriors were ruled by local princes. Political power was diffused among many lords, each ruling over his territory in the absence of any national authority. Feudalistic society in Europe then gradually developed into a political system based on master-servant relationships at every level, as between lords of different ranks and their knights, and the self-sufficient economy of the manor system. After the fall of the Carolingian Empire, mature feudalism would spread everywhere in Europe. Land was divided into many manors, each ruled by a feudal lord. These lords were responsible for all aspects of life in their manors and had supreme judicial authority. Farmers traded their private land to the feudal lords or monasteries in exchange for military protection, and their land was returned to them as a fief. Vassal knights received manors from their feudal lords in return for service as their private soldiers. While a lower ranking knight might own only a single manor, each king or great lord possessed hundreds or thousands of such manors, which he distributed as fiefs to his vassals. The kings had limited power and were no more than great feudal lords.

Religious life in Europe during the period of regional church leadership developed along the same lines as the early feudalism of its political and economic life; hence it may be termed feudalistic Christianity. Patriarchs, archbishops and bishops assumed positions corresponding to major, medium and minor feudal lords. As a king was only one of the great feudal lords, the pope was only one of the five patriarchs. The political structure within the Roman Catholic church was founded upon strict hierarchical relationships between master and servant. A bishop or abbot had a social rank and power comparable to a secular feudal lord. Acting as the lord of his church estates, he could, if necessary, raise an army from the ranks of his vassals.

With respect to economic life, this period began with a time of transition from the slave society of ancient Rome to the manor system. Some of the land in this period began to be owned by a free peasantry. In terms of land tenure, people's status in this period could be classified into four grades: nobility, free peasantry, serfs and slaves.

In this way, out of the ashes of the Western Roman Empire, God raised a feudalistic society among the newly-Christianized Germanic peoples whom He had chosen to lead the providence. By strengthening small units under godly sovereignty in the spheres of religious, political and economic life, God laid the groundwork to establish a godly kingdom.

7.2.5 Monarchic Society and Imperialism

With the progress of history, feudalistic society developed into monarchic society. Politically, how did European monarchic society arise? The kingdoms built by the Germanic peoples in Western Europe were all short-lived, except for the Kingdom of the Franks. The Frankish kings of the Merovingian dynasty received Christianity and absorbed the heritage of Roman civilization to form a Germanic-Roman world in Western Europe. After the Merovingian kings lost power, Charles Martel became the effective ruler of the Franks. He expanded the kingdom by defeating the Moors, who had invaded from the southwest. His son, Pepin the Short, became the first Carolingian king and was the father of Charlemagne. Charlemagne thought highly of St. Augustine's vision of a Christian kingdom and made it the guiding principle of the realm. Charlemagne's empire unified western and central Europe, bringing stability to lands which had formerly been in turmoil due to massive migrations.

In the sphere of religion, monarchic Christianity, which followed feudalistic Christianity, was a spiritual kingdom which transcended national borders. It was established under the rule of the papacy and upon the spiritual foundation for the Messiah. In 800 A.D., Pope Leo III crowned Charlemagne emperor and gave him the Church's blessing. By this act, the pope passed on to him the central responsibility for the providence. The spiritual kingdom under the papacy and the Kingdom of the Franks under Charlemagne united and formed the Christian empire.

The period of the Christian empire was parallel to the period of the united kingdom of Israel in the Old Testament Age. In both cases, a monarchic society followed a feudalistic society for the purpose of consolidating a greater sovereignty, population and territory on God's side. It was explained earlier that the pope had been leading the Church from the position of archangel in order to pave the way for an earthly kingdom. But after crowning the emperor and giving him God's blessing, the pope was then to serve him from the position of Cain.[26] The emperor, in turn, was to uphold the teachings of the papacy and carry on political work to realize a kingdom fit to receive the Messiah. Had they thus built the Christian empire in full accordance with the Will of God, this period would have been the Last Days of human history, when the Messiah could have come. The new truth would have then appeared to resolve the problems of religion and science as an integrated human endeavor, guiding religion, politics and economy to progress in one unified direction based on God's ideal. On this basis, the foundation for the Second Advent of the Messiah was to have been established. Moreover, with the dawning of the period of the Christian empire, feudalism should have come to a complete end.

However, the popes and the emperors deviated from the Will of God. This made it impossible for them to realize Charlemagne's founding ideal. As a result, feudalistic society was not dismantled; on the contrary, it grew stronger over the next several centuries. Religion, politics and economy remained divided, with the spiritual kingdom ruled by the papacy coming into frequent conflict with earthly kingdoms ruled by kings.

The Christian empire failed to build a unified kingdom to which the Messiah could come. Charlemagne built his empire when the founda-

---

26. cf. Parallels 4

tion of early feudal society was ripe for consolidation into a strong monarchy. However, he never fully subjugated the vested powers of the feudal lords. Instead, the feudal system strengthened, with the Holy Roman Emperor reduced to just one of the great feudal lords.

The feudal system would dominate Europe until the rise of absolute monarchy in the seventeenth century. With the decline of feudalism at that time, the previously decentralized powers of the feudal lords came to be concentrated in the hands of kings of large nation-states. The kings came to command absolute power and justified it by the doctrine of the divine right of kings. Absolute monarchies flourished until the French Revolution in 1789.

In the sphere of religious history, what were some of the trends during the period when Christianity led by the papacy had a monarchic structure? The popes fell away from God's Will and became secularized; they were on the path of spiritual decline. Due to repeated defeats in the Crusades, the papacy lost its authority, and during its exile in Avignon, it was deprived of power and dignity. With the Protestant Reformation in 1517, Western Christianity ceased to be a unitary spiritual monarchy.

When we examine the progress of economic life, we find that feudal economic arrangements persisted even when political feudalism was being replaced by absolute monarchy. Capitalism was growing in the cities and towns, where manufacturers and merchants joined forces with the kings and fought against the constraining feudal system. New agricultural arrangements arose in the countryside, where independent farmers sought the aid of the king to resist the rule of the feudal lords. Still, neither of these economic developments could entirely displace feudalism, which continued until the French Revolution.

In the progress of economic history, feudalism was followed by capitalism, which was accompanied by the age of colonial expansion. As the consolidation of political sovereignty was the goal of absolute monarchy, monopolization of finances and capital was the goal of powerful capitalists. Capitalism arose concurrently with the rise of absolute monarchy in the seventeenth century and flourished during and after the Industrial Revolution. Capitalism's purpose in the providence was to promote the accumulation of capital and the centralization of economic activity to an extent impossible under feudalism; this was even more the case with imperialism.

The imperialist drive for colonial expansion which began in this period had, as its providential purpose, the establishment of a worldwide economic, political and religious foundation. This discussion focuses on European imperialism alone, because the course of God's providence of restoration was centered on Western Europe. Competition among the nations of Western Europe led to their scramble for colonies all over the globe before World War I. This enabled the entire world to progress into Western Christian civilization.

7.2.6 Democracy and Socialism

The age of monarchy gave way to the age of democracy. We recall that the purpose of monarchic society was to construct a kingdom which could support the Messiah and his reign. When this dispensation was not accomplished during the Christian empire, however, God began a process that would eventually tear down monarchic societies and raise up democracies in their place in order to commence a new providence for rebuilding a sovereign nation fit to receive the Messiah.

Democracy is based on the sovereignty of the people; it is government of, by and for the people. Its purpose is to destroy the political monopoly of monarchy, which had deviated from God's Will, and to establish a new political system capable of accomplishing the goal of the providence of restoration, namely, to receive and support the Messiah as the King of Kings.

How can democracy accomplish its purpose? With the flow of history, humankind's spirituality has become enlightened due to the merit of the age in the providence of restoration. People's original minds respond to the providence and seek religion, often without their knowing why. Eventually, people will come to receive Christianity, which God is raising to be the highest religion. In this way, the world today is converging to form a single civilization based on Christian ideals.

As history nears its consummation, the will of the people inclines toward Christian values. Democratic governments which abide by the will of the people also gradually become more Christian. Thus, when the Messiah returns to societies under the rule of democratic governments well-matured by the Christian spirit, he will be able to establish God's sovereignty upon the earth with the wholehearted support of the people. This will be the Kingdom of Heaven on earth. We need to understand that democracy was born to undermine satanic monopolies of power for the purpose of God's final providence to restore, by the will of the people, a heavenly sovereignty under the leadership of the returning Christ.

The democratic movements which rose against the absolute monarchies of the seventeenth and eighteenth centuries gave rise to revolutions in England, America and France. These revolutions destroyed monarchic societies and gave birth to today's democratic societies. The different forms taken by democracy according to the providential trends of Hebraism and Hellenism will be discussed in the next chapter.[27]

The progress of history in the religious sphere moved to the stage of democratic Christianity after monarchic Christianity was shattered by the Protestant Reformation of 1517. Through the Reformation, democratic forces within Christianity dismantled the spiritual kingdom over which the papacy had commanded sole authority. God's original desire was that the Christian empire unite with monarchic papal Christianity to build the kingdom to which the Messiah would come. However, when the popes failed in their responsibilities, the monarchic Christianity over which they had all authority had to be dismantled. This has been the mission of democratic Christianity, just as the mission of political democracy has been to destroy the absolutist sovereignty of secular monarchy. Accordingly, after the Protestant Reformation, the way was open for people to freely seek God through their own reading of the Bible, without the mediation of the priesthood. People were no longer subjected to the authority of others in their religious life, but could freely seek their own path of faith. Democratic Christianity has thus created a social environment which allows all people to seek freely for Christ at his return, regardless of the manner in which he may come.

Similarly, with the progress of economic history, socialist ideals arose which undermined imperialism and fostered a democratic form of economy. Although some historians have regarded World War I as a war fought by imperialist nations over colonies, in fact, soon after its conclusion the democratic spirit rose to prominence and began to undermine colonialist policy. At the end of World War II, the great powers began to divest themselves of their colonies and liberate the nations under their control. Upon the fall of imperialism, capitalism began to evolve into a form of economy which would foster equal and common prosperity.

It is only natural for the satanic realm, which reached its apogee in communism, to promote socialism. This is because Satan always attempts to realize, in advance of God, a defective imitation of the divine plan. God's plan is to develop a socialistic economy, although with a form and content utterly different from the state socialism that communism actually established.

According to God's ideal of creation, God confers upon each individual the same original value. Just as parents love all their children

---

27. cf. Preparation 3.1-3.2

equally, God desires to provide pleasant environments and living conditions equally to all His children. Moreover, in an ideal society, production, distribution and consumption should have the same organic relationship as exists between the functions of digestion, circulation and metabolism in the human body. Thus, there should not be destructive competition due to over-production, nor unfair distribution leading to excessive accumulation and consumption, which are contrary to the purpose of the public good. There should be sufficient production of necessary and useful goods, fair and efficient distribution of these goods, and reasonable consumption which is in harmony with the purpose of the whole. Just as the liver provides a reserve of nutrients for the human body, adequate reserves of capital should be maintained to ensure smooth operation of the entire economy.

Because human beings are created to live in an ideal society, they will inevitably pursue a socialistic ideal as they strive for freedom and democracy and further search into their original nature. This is particularly true at the consummation of providential history, when this ideal can actually be realized. As this natural desire springs forth from within, politics in democracy, which is shaped by the will of the people, will also move in that direction. Eventually, a socialistic society embodying God's ideal will be established. Early Christians lived according to this ideal in some respects by sharing all their goods in common.[28] Thomas More's *Utopia*, written in sixteenth-century England, and Robert Owen's humanistic socialism during the Industrial Revolution in England each expressed a vision of the socialist ideal. Catholic and Protestant socialist movements have also shared this vision, one example being Charles Kingsley's advocacy of Christian Socialism in England of the mid-nineteenth century. Their inclination toward socialism originated from the natural impulse of the original mind as it pursues the ideal of creation.

7.2.7 The Ideals of Interdependence, Mutual Prosperity and Universally Shared Values versus Communism

The merit of the age in God's providence of restoration has furthered the development of man's original nature, which had not been manifested due to Satan's grip on human life. Responding to the promptings of their inmost hearts, people everywhere have ardently aspired to the world of God's ideal where the purpose of creation is fulfilled. In seeking for a socialistic society on Heaven's side, their original mind has drawn them to the ideals of interdependence, mutu-

---

28. Acts 4:32-35

al prosperity and universally shared values. The world in which these ideals will finally be realized is none other than the Kingdom of Heaven on earth, under the leadership of the returning Christ.

Since Satan mimics God's providence in advance, the satanic side has advocated "scientific socialism" based on the theories of dialectical and historical materialism and has built the communist world. The theory of historical materialism asserts that human history began as a primitive collective society and will be consummated with the creation of an ideal communist society. The evident errors of this theory are due to the fact that it does not take into account the fundamental cause of historical progress. After creating human beings, God promised to realize the Kingdom of Heaven. However, because Satan had formed kinship relations with people before God did, God had to permit him to construct an unprincipled world through fallen people in a distorted imitation of the ideal society which God intends to accomplish on the earth. The communist world is this unprincipled world built by Satan.

Democracies of two types arose with the purpose of dismantling absolute monarchy and transferring sovereignty to the people. Likewise, movements to further the ideals of interdependence, mutual prosperity and universally shared values arose on God's side, while communism was born on Satan's side, in order to demolish economic systems which concentrated a society's wealth in the hands of a privileged few. Each of these movements has sought to establish a system which would distribute wealth more equally among people. The aspirations to socialism on both sides have arisen in their providential striving to realize a society based on a truly democratic economic system.

It was explained earlier that in the history of Western Europe as steered by the providence of restoration, the three aspects of religion, politics and economy have progressed separately through their own paths of development. How can they come together at one point at the consummation of providential history to lay the foundation for the Second Advent of Christ? A fundamental cause of this separate development was the divergence of religion and science, which are endeavors to overcome humanity's spiritual and physical ignorance. For the paths of religion, politics and economy to converge and realize God's ideal, a new expression of truth must emerge which can completely integrate religion and science. The religion founded upon this truth will lead all of humanity to become one with God in heart. Such people will build an economy in accordance with the divine ideal. These will be the foundations for a new political order which can realize the ideal of creation. This will be the messianic kingdom built on the principles of interdependence, mutual prosperity and universally shared values.

Chart 3: The Progress of History as Guided by the Providence of Restoration

The Age to Lay the Foundation for the Providence of Restoration

Adam — 1600 — Noah — 400 — Abraham — 120 — Jacob — 40 — Joseph — 21 — [40]

The Age of the Providence of Restoration

Abraham → Jesus

Period of Slavery in Egypt	Period of the Judges	Period of the United Kingdom	Period of the Divided Kingdoms of North and South	Period of Israel's Exile and Return	Period of Preparation for the Advent of the Messiah
400	400	120	400	210	400
Israelite Clan Society	Feudalistic Israelite Society	Monarchic Israelite Society	Monarchic Israelite Society		Democratic Israelite Society

The Age of the Prolongation of the Providence of Restoration

Jesus → Christ at the Second Advent

Religious History

Period of Persecution under the Roman Empire	Period of Regional Church Leadership	Period of the Christian Empire	Period of the Divided Kingdoms of East and West	Period of Papal Exile and Return	Period of Preparation for the Second Advent of the Messiah
400	400	120	400	210	400
Christian Clan Society	Feudalistic Christianity	Monarchic Christianity	Monarchic Christianity		Democratic Christianity

Political History

| Christian Clan Society | Feudalistic Society | Christian Monarchy | Feudalism | | Absolute Monarchy (1600) / French Revolution (1789) / Democracy |

Economic History

| Christian Clan Society | The Manor System (Feudalism) | | | | Industrial Revolution / Capitalism / Imperialism / Socialistic Economy |

Chapter 5

The Period of Preparation for the Second Advent of the Messiah

The period of preparation for the Second Advent of the Messiah was the four-hundred-year period from the Protestant Reformation in 1517 to the end of World War I in 1918. The character of this period was already summarized in comparison with the parallel period of preparation for the advent of the Messiah, but a more detailed examination will be made here. With respect to the providence of restoration, this period is divided into three periods: the period of the Reformation, the period of religious and ideological conflicts, and the period of the maturation of politics, economy and ideology.

Section 1
The Period of the Reformation (1517-1648)

The 130-year period of the Reformation began in 1517, when Martin Luther raised the banner of the Protestant Reformation in Germany, and lasted until the wars of religion were settled by the Treaty of Westphalia in 1648. The character of this period was shaped by the Renaissance and the Reformation, both products of medieval feudal society. When the purpose of God's providence through medieval society was not fulfilled, the direction of providential history shifted and God worked to establish anew the foundation for the Second Advent of the Messiah through the Renaissance and the Reformation. Therefore, we cannot understand the nature of this period without studying these two events.

Let us begin by looking back at medieval society and examining what influences it exerted upon the original nature of the people of that age which led them to embark upon the Renaissance and the Protestant Reformation. In the late Middle Ages, man's original mind was repressed, its free development blocked by the social environment of feudalism and the secularization and corruption of the Roman church. Faith is the path each person must walk in search of God. Faith should be nurtured through a direct vertical relationship between God and each individual. Yet in that age, the papacy and the clergy, with their rituals and dogmas, constrained the people's devotional life. Moreover, the rigid social stratification of feudalism did not allow for religious freedom. Meanwhile, religious offices were bought and sold. Bishops and priests often exploited their offices to lead lives of luxury and decadence. As a consequence, the papacy lost its sanctity and became no different than other institutions of worldly power. It lost the ability to guide the spiritual lives of the people. In this way, the social environment of the late Middle Ages blocked the path through which the original nature of the people could be restored. Fettered by such circumstances, medieval Europeans were prompted by the impulses of their innermost hearts to break down their social environment to open the way for the restoration of their original nature.

Our original nature may be divided into two aspects: internal and external. Let us examine this with reference to the Principle of Creation. As the substantial object partners to God in image, we resonate with His dual characteristics and bear the likeness of His original internal nature and original external form. The give and take between our internal nature and external form is the basis upon which we exist and thrive. Accordingly, our original nature seeks to fulfill two types of desires: internal and external. When God conducts the providence to restore us, He accommodates these two pursuits of our original nature.

God created the physical self of the first humans before creating their spiritual self.[1] Accordingly, in the providence of restoration, God

---

1. Gen. 2:7

recreates us by restoring first what is external and then what is internal. It was explained earlier[2] that we fallen people can make the substantial offering, which is internal, only after successfully completing the symbolic offering, which is external. After these are achieved, we establish the foundation for the Messiah, which is even more internal.

The process of restoring fallen people's relationship to God has also progressed from external to internal. God first restored people to the position of servant of servants[3] in the period prior to the Old Testament Age by having them offer sacrifices. Next, He restored people to the position of servants[4] in the Old Testament Age through the Mosaic Law. In the New Testament Age, God has restored us to the position of adopted children[5] through our faith. Finally, in the Completed Testament Age, He will restore us to the position of true children through heart.[6]

In the same way, God first worked to restore our external social environment through science and then worked to restore our spirituality through religion. In the order of creation, angels, who are external, were created before people, who are internal. In restoration, God first raises up the angelic world, which is external, and mobilizes it for restoring the external, physical world centering on the human body and then the internal, spirit world centering on the human spirit.

Medieval Europeans were to restore their original God-given nature by first severing their ties to Satan, who had defiled the society when the papacy failed its internal responsibility to restore the foundation of faith and sank into immorality. As people pursued the recovery of the internal and external aspects of their original nature, the thought of the age branched out into two movements to recover the heritage of the past, which we distinguish in relative terms as Abel-type and Cain-type. The Cain-type movement began as a revival of Hellenism, the culture and philosophy of ancient Greece and Rome. It gave rise to the Renaissance,[7] whose core value was humanism. The Abel-type movement began as a revival of the Hebraic heritage of Israel and the early Christian Church. It gave rise to the Protestant Reformation, whose core value was faith in God.

The trends of Hebraism and Hellenism had formed long ago and had encountered each other several times in the course of prior history. From 2000 B.C., the Minoan civilization flourished on the island of Crete, succeeded by the Mycenaean civilization on the Greek mainland. By the

---

2. cf. Foundation 1.3
3. Gen. 9:25
4. Lev. 25:55
5. Rom. 8:23
6. cf. Moses and Jesus 3.3.2
7. "Renaissance" is a French word meaning rebirth.

eleventh century, these civilizations had created a Cain-type Hellenic civilization, whose guiding ideology was humanism. Around the same time in the Near East, the Abel-type Hebraic civilization was born, with Jewish monotheism as its guiding ideology. This was the period of the united kingdom. Had the kings of Israel in that period laid the foundation for the Messiah and received him, this flourishing Hebraic civilization could have assimilated the waning Hellenic civilization to form one worldwide civilization. However, when the kings failed to fulfill the Will of God, this dispensation was not accomplished. Instead, after the Jews were taken into exile in Babylon, they returned only to be put under subjection to the Greeks in 333 B.C. and then to Rome in 63 B.C. Thus, during the centuries leading up to and including Jesus' time, Hebraism was placed under the dominion of Hellenism.

Had the Jewish people honored Jesus and united under him, the Roman Empire would have become the messianic kingdom under the reign of Christ. Hebraism then would have assimilated Hellenism to form one worldwide Hebraic civilization. Instead, when Jesus was rejected and this providence was frustrated, Hebraism remained under subjection to Hellenism. In 313 A.D., Emperor Constantine officially recognized Christianity by the Edict of Milan. From that time on, Hebraism gradually began to overcome Hellenism. By the beginning of the eighth century, it had formed two civilizations: Eastern Orthodoxy and Roman Catholic Christianity.

Had the popes and emperors who were responsible for restoring the foundation of faith in the Carolingian period not become faithless, the foundation for the Second Advent of the Messiah would have been established at that time. Hebraism would have completely assimilated Hellenism to form one worldwide civilization. Instead, their faithlessness and immorality allowed Satan to corrupt the guiding medieval ideology, which was founded upon Hebraism. As a consequence, God had to conduct a new dispensation for the separation of Satan. Just as God had divided fallen Adam into Cain and Abel to separate Satan, God divided the prevailing ideology of the Middle Ages into two trends of thought: the movements to revive Cain-type Hellenism and Abel-type Hebraism. These bore fruit in the Renaissance and the Reformation, respectively.

The Hellenic trend of thought, revived by the humanism of the Renaissance, soon took a dominant position over the Hebraic trend. This period was thus to restore through parallel indemnity conditions that phase in the period of preparation for the advent of the Messiah when the Jewish people were under the dominion of the Greeks and

Hebraism was under subjection to Hellenism. We recall that only by Cain submitting to Abel could Satan be separated from Adam, thereby laying the foundation of substance necessary for receiving the Messiah in Adam's family. Likewise, only by Cain-type Hellenism submitting to Abel-type Hebraism could Satan be separated from the prevailing spirit of the age. Then the foundation of substance necessary for receiving Christ at the Second Advent could be established worldwide.

1.1 THE RENAISSANCE

It was explained above that the Renaissance grew out of the external pursuits of the original nature. What values were the medieval people pursuing? Why and how did they pursue these values?

According to the Principle of Creation, we are created to attain perfection by fulfilling our given responsibility of our own free will, without God's direct assistance. We are then to attain oneness with God and acquire true autonomy. Therefore, it is the calling of our original nature to pursue freedom and autonomy. A person of perfect character understands the Will of God and puts it into practice through his own insight and reason, without the need to rely on revelations from God. Hence, it is only natural that we pursue reason and understanding. We also are endowed with the God-given right to master the natural world, to tame and cultivate it in order to create a pleasant living environment, by investigating the hidden laws of nature through science. Hence, we value the natural world, pursue science, and esteem the practical life.

In medieval feudal society, the original human nature had long been repressed. Hence, people were all the more ardent in their pursuit of these values, which arose from the external promptings of their original nature. They began to probe into the classical heritage of Hellenism, which they imported from the Muslims as a result of expanded contacts with the East after the Crusades. The classical Greeks and Romans had pursued the external aspirations of the original human nature. They valued freedom, autonomy, reason, the natural world and the practical life. They developed the sciences to a considerable degree. Since these were in full accord with the desire of the original nature in medieval man, the movement to revive the ancient heritage of Hellenism caught fire. Renaissance humanism thus rose to prominence.

The Renaissance came to life in fourteenth-century Italy, which was the center of the study of the classical Hellenic heritage. Though it began as a movement imitating the thought and life of ancient Greece and Rome, it soon developed into a wider movement which transformed the medieval way of life. It expanded beyond the sphere of culture to encompass every aspect of society, including politics, economic life and religion. In fact, it became the external driving force for the construction of the modern world.

1.2　THE REFORMATION

The providence of restoration centering on the medieval papacy did not bear fruit due to the secularization and decadence of the Church leadership. Consequently, as the people advocated humanism, they also rebelled against the ritualism and rules of the Church which were constraining their free devotion. They fought against the stratified feudal system and papal authority which deprived them of autonomy. They protested against the medieval view that faith required unquestioning obedience to the dictates of the Church in all areas of life, which denied them the right to worship God according to the dictates of conscience based on their own reading of the Bible. They also questioned the otherworldly and ascetic monastic ideal which devalued the natural world, science and the practical affairs of life. Out of these grievances, many medieval Christians revolted against the rule of the papacy.

Accordingly, as medieval Europeans sought to realize the external aspirations of their original nature, they also began to pursue its repressed internal aspirations. They called for the revival of the spirit of early Christianity, when believers zealously lived for the Will of God, guided by the words of Jesus and the apostles. This medieval movement to revive Hebraism began with John Wycliffe (1324-1384), a professor of theology at Oxford University, who translated the Bible into English. He asserted that neither the papacy nor the priesthood could determine the standard of faith, but only the Bible itself. Demonstrating that many of the dogmas, ceremonies and rules of the Church had no basis in Scripture, he denounced the priesthood for its decadence, exploitation of the people and abuse of power.

The Protestant Reformation thus had roots in fourteenth-century England, when papal dignity was at a low point. Similar movements for reform also arose in fifteenth-century Bohemia and Italy, but they were crushed and their leaders executed. To raise funds to build St. Peter's Basilica, Pope Leo X began selling indulgences, which Catholic doctrine affirmed would remit the penalty for sin due in the next life. When this indulgence was proclaimed in Germany in 1517, a movement to protest this abuse ignited a fuse which exploded in the Protestant Reformation under the leadership of Martin Luther (1483-1546), a professor of biblical theology at the University of Wittenberg. The flames of the Reformation grew strong and soon spread to Switzerland under the leadership of Huldrych Zwingli (1484-1531), to France as led by John Calvin (1509-1564), and into such nations as England and the Netherlands.

The wars of religion which swirled around the Protestant movements continued for more than one hundred years until 1648, when the Treaty of Westphalia ended the Thirty Years' War. Protestantism triumphed in Northern Europe, while among the peoples of Southern Europe the Roman Catholic church solidified its influence.

The Thirty Years' War between Protestants and Catholics was fought on the soil of Germany. However, this conflict was not simply a religious war. More than that, it was a civil and political conflict to decide the fate of the German states. The Treaty of Westphalia, which concluded this war, was both a religious settlement which established an accommodation between the Protestants and Catholics and a political settlement which resolved international territorial disputes among such nations as Austria, France, Sweden and Spain.

Section 2

The Period of Religious and Ideological Conflicts (1648-1789)

The period of religious and ideological conflicts refers to the 140 years beginning with the secure establishment of Protestantism at the Treaty of Westphalia in 1648 and ending with the French Revolution in 1789. As modern people continued to pursue the internal and external desires flowing from their original nature, they could not avoid divisions in theology and disputes among philosophies which arose as they exercised freedom of faith and thought.

As previously discussed, God has worked His providence of restoration throughout the course of history by repeatedly separating those representing Abel from those representing Cain, from the individual level to the world level. In the Last Days, this fallen world is divided into the Cain-type communist world and the Abel-type democratic world. Just as the foundation of substance could have been laid in Adam's family had Cain submitted to Abel and obeyed him, in the Last Days the Cain-type world is to submit to the Abel-type world to establish the worldwide foundation of substance. This is necessary before we can receive Christ at the Second Advent and realize the unified world.

For this to happen, the two views of life which would later mature into these two worlds had to be developed in this period.

2.1 THE CAIN-TYPE VIEW OF LIFE

The pursuit of the external aspects of the original nature first aroused a movement to revive the ancient heritage of Hellenism and gave birth to the humanism of the Renaissance. Renaissance humanism opposed medieval culture by elevating the dignity of human beings and the value of the natural world over devotion to God and religious dedication. The medieval mind had prized obedience to God while belittling the natural world and regarding the human body as base and even sinful. The Renaissance established a new perspective on life, one which exalted the value of human beings and nature and sought to understand them through reason and experience, logic and experiment. Spurred by the progress of natural science, this view of life gave rise to two major schools of modern philosophy: rationalism, based on the deductive method and empiricism, based on the inductive method.

Rationalism, founded by the French philosopher Rene Descartes (1596-1650), maintained that the investigation of truth can be founded only on man's innate reason. After doubting every truth received from history and tradition, Descartes was left with only his reason, as expressed in the proposition, "I think; therefore, I am." From this first principle, he used the deductive method to affirm knowledge about the external world. Although Descartes accepted and even tried to prove the existence of God based on reason, later rationalists ended up doubting or even denying God's existence.

The English philosopher Francis Bacon (1561-1626) founded empiricism, which held that truth can be investigated only through one's experience. This school asserted that the human mind is like a blank sheet of paper *(tabula rasa)*. It held that to attain new knowledge, one must erase all prejudices and try to comprehend the truth through experience and observation of the external world. Rationalism, which valued human reason while turning away from God, and empiricism, which prized human experience and experimental science, both did away with mysticism and superstition. Whether by using reason or empirical observation to guide human life, they both tended to divorce human beings and the natural world from God.

The Renaissance launched these two currents of thought, which were rooted in humanism. Instead of facilitating the internal inclination to seek God, it gave birth to a view of life which encouraged people to follow only external pursuits. This blocked their path to God and led them toward Satan's realm. For this reason, it is called the Cain-type view of life. By the turn of the eighteenth century, the Cain-type view of life had broken down the verities enshrined by history and tradition. All matters in human life came to be judged by reason or empirical observation. Anything deemed irrational or other-worldly, including belief in the God of the Bible, was thoroughly discredited. People's energies were narrowly directed toward the practical life. Such was the ideology of the Enlightenment, which developed out of the two trends of empiricism and rationalism. The Enlightenment was the driving force behind the French Revolution.

Representative of this Cain-type view of life was deism, founded by the English philosopher Edward Herbert (1583-1648). Deism propounded a theology rooted entirely in human reason. Deists rejected the notion that there could be any harmony between revelation and reason, a traditional view held since the time of Thomas Aquinas. They limited God to a Creator who set the universe in motion and left it to run of its own accord according to the laws of nature which He had set up. They denied that people had any need of divine revelation or miracles.

In the beginning of the nineteenth century, the German philosopher Georg W.F. Hegel (1770-1831) made a comprehensive synthesis of eighteenth-century idealism. However, many of the followers of Hegel were influenced by the atheism and materialism of the French Enlightenment and propounded the school of left-wing Hegelianism, which turned the logic of Hegel's dialectic on its head. David F. Strauss (1808-1874), a left-Hegelian, wrote *The Life of Jesus*, which denied the Bible's accounts of Jesus' miracles as fabrications by his credulous followers. Ludwig Feuerbach (1804-1872) argued in *The Essence of Christianity* that God was nothing other than the projection of people's inward psychological nature. Their arguments became foundational for modern atheism and materialism.

Karl Marx (1818-1883) and Friedrich Engels (1820-1895) systematized the logic of the left-wing Hegelians as dialectical materialism. They were influenced by Strauss and Feuerbach and also by French socialism. They combined dialectical materialism with atheism and socialism to create the ideology of communism. In this way, the Cain-type view of life, which budded after the Renaissance and grew through the Enlightenment into atheism and materialism, matured into the godless ideology of Marxism, which became the cornerstone of the communist world of today.

2.2 THE ABEL-TYPE VIEW OF LIFE

Some people regard the progress of history from the medieval to the modern world as a process which has alienated people from God and religion. This is because they view history according to the Cain-type view of life. The original nature, however, not only pursues external values; it also seeks internal values. As medieval people were prompted by their original nature to pursue internal values, a movement arose to revive Hebraism which bore fruit in the Protestant Reformation. The Reformation spawned philosophies and religious teachings which developed a multi-dimensional view of life seeking to realize the God-given, original nature of human beings. We call this the Abel-type view of life. Even as the Cain-type view of life led away from God and faith, the Abel-type view of life guided modern people to seek God in a deeper and more thoughtful way.

The German philosopher Immanuel Kant (1724-1804) analyzed philosophically the internal and external pursuits of the original nature, thus pioneering the Abel-type view of life in the philosophical sphere.[8] In his Critical Philosophy, he assimilated the conflicting theories of empiricism and rationalism. According to Kant, our various sensations occur by contact with external objects. These alone may give us the contents of cognition but cannot actualize the cognition itself. To have full cognition, one must possess certain forms of intuition and thought (which are *a priori* and transcendental) with which to unify the various contents (which are *a posteriori* and experiential) through a synthetic judgment. These forms of intuition and thought are the very subjectivity of the self. Therefore, cognition is actualized when the various sensations coming from external objects are integrated and unified with one's subjective forms by the spontaneous action of thinking and understanding. Thus, Kant overturned empiricism, which held that cognition is determined by external objects, and established a new theory that cognition is governed by the subjective mind. Kant's philosophy was succeeded by a number of idealist philosophers: Johann Fichte (1762-1814), Friedrich Schelling (1775-1854) and Hegel. Hegel, in particular, pioneered a new philosophy based on the Hegelian dialectic. Their idealism solidified the Abel-type view of life in the field of philosophy.

In the religious sphere, new movements emerged which opposed the prevailing influence of rationalism in religion and stressed the

---

8. Kant's ethical theory may illustrate this point even more clearly. Kant believed that neither reason nor observation could provide a sound basis for knowledge of God. He argued that we can best apprehend the reality of God through the moral law, which operates within the conscience of every person. Thus, he gave philosophical grounding for the Abel-type view of life.—Ed.

importance of religious zeal and the inner life. They valued mystical experience over doctrines and rituals. For example, Pietism appeared in Germany under the leadership of Philip Spener (1635-1705). This movement had a strong conservative bent and adhered to the traditional faith while simultaneously emphasizing mystical experience.

Pietism spread to England and flourished among the faithful there, giving rise to new church movements including Methodism, founded by the Wesley brothers (John, 1703-1791, and Charles, 1707-1788). Their work brought about a great revival in England, which had been in a state of spiritual stagnation.

George Fox (1624-1691), the English mystic who founded the Quakers, asserted that Christ is the inner light which illuminates the souls of believers. He insisted that unless one first receives the Holy Spirit, joins in mystical union with Jesus and experiences Christ's inner light, he cannot understand the true meaning of the Bible. The Quakers endured severe persecution in England but eventually prospered in America.

Emanuel Swedenborg (1688-1772) was a renowned scientist whose spiritual senses were awakened; he began a systematic investigation of the spirit world and discovered many of its secrets. Although his research was long ignored by theologians, recently, as increasing numbers of people have communicated with the spirit world, its value is gradually being recognized. In these diverse ways, the Abel-type view of life was maturing to form the democratic world of today.

SECTION 3

THE PERIOD OF MATURATION OF POLITICS, ECONOMY AND IDEOLOGY (1789-1918)

The religious and philosophical conflicts in the previous period coalesced into the Cain-type and Abel-type views of life. At the outset of this new period—the period of maturation of politics, economy and ideology—the two views of life matured, taking their separate paths. As they matured, they founded two different forms of society with distinct social structures: a Cain-type society and an Abel-type society. At the same time, politics, economy and ideology (the sphere of religion and philosophy) progressed to the stage just prior to the transition into the ideal world. This period lasted from the French Revolution, through the Industrial Revolution, to the end of the First World War.

3.1 Democracy

The earlier discussion of democracy in the context of the progress of history was limited to the social changes which led to its emergence.[9] Here, we will examine the internal developments behind the rise of today's democracy, specifically the ideological tides on which it rose out of the swells and eddies of history.

In the period of the Christian empire of the ninth century, God had intended that the spiritual kingdom ruled by the papacy and the earthly kingdom ruled by the emperor unite to form a Christian monarchic society as a foundation for the messianic kingdom. This would have established the foundation for the Messiah. A strong messianic kingdom would have brought an early end to feudalism in Europe. Yet because this providence was not realized, feudalism persisted, while Europe's political, religious and economic histories took separate paths of development. The political power of the feudal lords began to wane after the Crusades, declined further during the Renaissance and the Reformation, and became feeble by the time of the Enlightenment. By the seventeenth century, the feudal lords had yielded much of their political power to the kings, who built centralized nation-states and ruled them as absolute monarchs. The kings justified their supreme power by the doctrine of the divine right of kings.

The social causes of the rise of absolute monarchy included, first, the rise of new citizen classes which allied themselves with the kings to fight the feudal lords. Second, in the economic sphere, there arose a need for powerful states with mercantilist economic policies which could protect and control trade to further their national economic interests. The powerful foundation of a nation-state was needed to overcome feudalism and dominate an economy based on trade.

The rise of absolute monarchy is also connected with the progress of providential history, which requires that feudalistic society consolidate into monarchy. However, after God's providence to establish His Kingdom in the Carolingian period failed because the popes and emperors at that time did not unite, the ensuing feudal society under papal rule became corrupt. Developing according to the course which Satan had preempted, it gave birth to monarchic societies on Satan's side.

Let us now examine the ideological trends behind the demise of absolute monarchy with reference to the providence of restoration, which was headed toward the rise of the communist world based on the Cain-type view of life and the democratic world based on the Abel-type

---

9. cf. Parallels 7.2

view of life. Since medieval feudal society ran counter to both Hebraism and Hellenism, these two ideologies worked in tandem to tear it down as they established societies built upon the Cain-type and Abel-type views of life. Similarly, the absolute monarchies which followed the Protestant Reformation deprived people of freedom of faith, which was a value propounded by democratic Christianity. Absolute monarchy thus ran counter to the goal of the Abel-type view of life. Moreover, the vestiges of feudalism in that society constrained the progress of the citizen class as advocated by leading atheists and materialists, thereby countering the goal of the Cain-type view of life. Therefore, these two views of life worked in tandem to tear down absolute monarchy. They established Cain-type and Abel-type democracies, which would eventually mature into the communist world and the democratic world.

3.1.1 Cain-Type Democracy

Cain-type democracy arose out of the French Revolution. France at the time of the French Revolution was in the grip of the Enlightenment. The thought of the Enlightenment was rooted in the Cain-type view of life and was deviating into atheism and materialism. Swayed by the Enlightenment, French citizens were awakened to the flaws of absolute monarchy. There was also a widespread desire to tear down the remnants of the feudal system, which was still entrenched in the society.

The French Revolution was ignited in 1789 by popular calls for democracy from a citizenry schooled in the Enlightenment. They sought to overthrow the power of the ruling class, eradicate the remnants of feudalism, and establish freedom and equality for ordinary citizens, the Third Estate. The French Revolution established democracy with the proclamation of the Declaration of the Rights of Man. Nonetheless, the democracy born out of the French Revolution was a Cain-type democracy. Although it destroyed absolutism, it sought to firmly secure the Cain-type view of life. The leading thinkers behind the French Revolution were Enlightenment figures such as Denis Diderot (1713-1784) and Jean Le Rond D'Alembert (1717-1783), who adhered to atheism or materialism. Furthermore, despite its ideals of individual freedom and equality, the actual course of French democracy in the years of the revolution and afterward tended toward totalitarianism.

In this way, those espousing the Cain-type view of life championed the Enlightenment and gave rise to the French Revolution, thus establishing Cain-type democracy. It completely blocked the inclination of the human spirit to seek for God. As it continued to develop with its sole focus on the external aspects of life, it would later be systematized into Marxism in Germany and Leninism in Russia, eventually forming the communist world.

3.1.2 ABEL-TYPE DEMOCRACY

From their very origins, the democracies which emerged in England and the United States were different from the democracy born out of the French Revolution. The latter was a Cain-type democracy founded by atheists and materialists, who were raised in the Cain-type view of life, as they attempted to dismantle absolutism and feudalism. The English and American democracies, on the other hand, were founded by sincere Christians, the fruits of the Abel-type view of life, and were born out of their victorious fight with absolutism to win religious freedom. Hence, these are Abel-type democracies.

Let us examine how Abel-type democracy was established in England and the United States. In England, James I (r. 1603-1625) strengthened absolute monarchy and the state church while persecuting Puritans and other dissenting Christians, many of whom fled to other European nations or to the American continent in search of religious freedom. His son Charles I (r. 1625-1649) was met with rebellion by the Presbyterians of Scotland, who rallied around the National Covenant in 1640. The Puritans, who formed the core membership of the English Parliament, then launched the Puritan Revolution in 1642 which soon came under the leadership of Oliver Cromwell.

Later, after Charles II (r. 1660-1685) restored absolute monarchy and strengthened the Anglican church against all other Christians, and his brother James II (r. 1685-1688) declared himself a Catholic, Protestant leaders invited William of Orange (r. 1688-1702), his son-in-law, who was at that time Stadtholder of the Netherlands, to intervene. In 1688, William landed in England with his troops to defend religious freedom and civil rights. Upon his enthronement, William approved the Declaration of Rights offered to him by the Parliament, which recognized the Parliament's independent rights. This became foundational for the English constitutional monarchy. Since the revolution of 1688 was accomplished without bloodshed, it came to be known as the Glorious Revolution.

Although there were external causes of these English revolutions, such as the citizens' desire for political freedom from the ruling class including the nobility and the Anglican priesthood, the more internal cause was the drive to gain religious freedom.

Many Puritans and dissenting Christians who had been persecuted in England emigrated to the American continent to obtain religious freedom. They founded an independent nation in 1776 and established American democracy. Born out of the Abel-type view of life, Abel-type democracy has developed from these beginnings into the democratic world of today.

3.2 THE SIGNIFICANCE OF THE SEPARATION OF POWERS

The concept of the separation of powers into three branches of government was advocated by Montesquieu (1689-1755), a leading thinker of the Enlightenment. It sought to prevent the concentration of political power in the hands of a single individual or institution, as was the case with political absolutism. The idea was proclaimed in the Declaration of the Rights of Man during the French Revolution.

From the beginning, the separation of powers was to be characteristic of the political structure of the ideal society which God has been working to realize. Yet here again, as we observe throughout the course of the providence, Satan was defectively mimicking an aspect of the Principle ahead of its realization by God. Let us then briefly examine the political structure of the ideal world.

The universe, as we have seen, is patterned after the structure of a perfect human being. By the same token, the ideal world to be built by fully mature people is also to resemble the structure and functions of a perfect individual.[10] By analogy with the human body, whose organs function in accordance with the subtle commands of the brain, all the institutions of the ideal global society are to abide by the desires of God. Just as the commands of the brain are transmitted to every part of the body through the peripheral nervous system branching out from the spinal cord, in the ideal world God's guidance is conveyed to the entire society through Christ, who corresponds to the spinal cord, and God-loving leaders, who correspond to the peripheral nervous system. The peripheral nervous system branching out from the spinal cord corresponds to a nation's political parties. Thus, in the ideal world, people of God led by Christ will form organizations analogous to today's political parties.

In the human body, the lungs, heart and stomach maintain harmonious interaction in accord with the directions of the brain, transmitted through the spinal cord and the peripheral nervous system. By analogy, the three branches of government in the ideal world—the legislative,

---

10. cf. Creation 1.1; 1.2; 3.2

judicial and executive branches—will interact in harmonious and principled relationships when they follow God's guidance as conveyed through Christ and people of God. Just as the four limbs of the body move according to the commands of the brain for the welfare of the individual as a whole, the economic institutions of the ideal world, corresponding to the limbs, will uphold the desire of God and promote the welfare of the entire world. Just as the liver stores nourishment for the entire body, in the ideal world there will always be a certain reserve to be tapped as needed for the public good.

Since every part of the human body has a vertical relationship with the brain, horizontal relationships are naturally established between the different organs to form an integrated organism. Likewise, in the ideal world, because people's horizontal relationships with each other are rooted in their vertical relationship with God, they will form one integrated and interdependent society in which they share all their joys and sorrows. In this society, to hurt someone else will be experienced as hurting one's own self. Hence, its citizens simply will not want to commit crime.

Let us now examine how, in the providence of restoration, God has been working to restore this ideal social structure. In the course of Western history, there was a time when the functions of the three branches of government and the political parties were concentrated in one individual, the king. This was modified from time to time when the king dominated the government, while the Church under the leadership of the papacy played a role similar to that of a political party. The political system underwent a fundamental change at the time of the French and American Revolutions when the government was divided into the three branches—legislative, judicial and executive—and political parties took on distinct roles. With the establishment of constitutional democracy, the framework for the ideal political system was set up.

Thus, political systems have changed over the course of history because fallen human society was being restored to the ideal society, the structure and functions of which will be patterned after a perfected individual. Today's democracies, characterized by the three separate branches of government and a proliferation of political parties, resemble the structure of a healthy human body to some extent. Nevertheless, because of the Fall, today's democracies in fact bear more of a likeness to the body of a sick or injured person. They cannot fully display their original qualities and functions in their full potential. Since the political parties are ignorant of the Will of God, they may be compared to a nervous system which is unable to transmit directions from the brain.

Since constitutions are not written in accordance with the Word of God, the three branches of government currently function like internal organs which cannot sense or respond to the commands of the brain because the peripheral nerves have been severed. They lack order and harmony, and suffer continual conflicts among themselves.

Therefore, Christ at the Second Advent, by restoring people's vertical relationship with God, will remedy the illness of the present political system that it may reflect God's design. This will unleash society's true potential.

3.3 The Significance of the Industrial Revolution

God's ideal of creation cannot be fulfilled merely by forming a world without sin. God blessed human beings to have dominion over the universe.[11] We are to seek for the hidden laws of nature and advance science and technology to create a pleasant living environment. Religion and science have shouldered their respective responsibilities for helping fallen people overcome the internal and external aspects of their ignorance. Therefore, in the Last Days of history, we can expect not only the emergence of a truth which can guide people to completely alleviate their spiritual ignorance; we may also expect the progress of science to solve all the mysteries of the physical universe.[12] Together, they will bring human society to the stage just prior to the realization of the ideal world. Thus, we can understand that the Industrial Revolution which began in England arose out of God's providence to restore the living environment to one suitable for the ideal world.

The economic structure of the ideal society also resembles the structure of a healthy human body. Production, distribution and consumption should have an organic, interdependent relationship such as that which exists between the digestive, circulatory and metabolic systems. There should not be destructive competition due to overproduction; nor should there be excessive accumulation or overconsumption due to unfair distribution, which would be contrary to the welfare of all people. There should be adequate production of necessary and useful goods, fair distribution to supply what is sufficient for people's needs, and reasonable consumption in harmony with the purpose of the whole.

The mass production born of the Industrial Revolution led England to claim vast colonies as sources of raw materials and markets for goods. In so doing, the Industrial Revolution opened up a vast territo-

---

11. Gen. 1:28
12. cf. Eschatology 4.3

ry for the propagation of the Gospel. Accordingly, it contributed to both the internal and external aspects of the providence of restoration.

3.4 THE RISE OF THE GREAT POWERS

We have seen how after the Renaissance, the unitary worldview of medieval Europe was divided into Cain- and Abel-type views of life. These gave rise to two types of political revolutions and founded two types of democracies, both of which were greatly strengthened as a result of the Industrial Revolution. The two types of democracies were on the course to form the democratic and the communist worlds.

Following the Industrial Revolution, spurred by the rapid progress of science, industrialization created economies characterized by overproduction. The great powers of Europe, which felt an urgent need to pioneer new lands as markets for their products and as sources of raw materials for their factories, grew strong as they competed with each other in the scramble for colonies. Thus, two factors—the two trends in ideology and the course of economic development following the progress of science—caused the later political division of the world into two blocs: the democratic world and the communist world.

3.5 RELIGIOUS REFORMS AND POLITICAL AND INDUSTRIAL REVOLUTIONS SINCE THE RENAISSANCE

The Cain-type movement which began with the revival of Hellenism overthrew the medieval world and gave birth to the humanism of the Renaissance. As this movement developed further, moving in Satan's direction, it gave birth to the Enlightenment, which may be regarded as the second renaissance in the current of ideology. Enlightenment thought further matured in the satanic direction, giving birth to historical materialism, which is the core of communist ideology. This may be regarded as the third renaissance.

Since the satanic side mimics in advance the providence of God, we may expect that God's providence calls for three stages of revolution to take place in each of the three spheres of religion, politics and economy. In the sphere of religion, the first reformation took place under Martin Luther's leadership after the first renaissance. A second reformation was launched after the second renaissance by the spiritual movements led by people such as the Wesley brothers, Fox and Swedenborg. From our examination of the progress of history, it is evident that a third reformation will occur following the third renaissance. Indeed, the state of today's Christianity desperately calls for such a reformation.

In the political sphere, we can surmise that reform also is taking place in three stages. First, medieval feudal society collapsed under the weight of the first renaissance and the first reformation. Next, absolute monarchy was destroyed by the forces unleashed by the second renaissance and the second reformation. Finally, the communist world was formed by the political revolutions brought on by the third renaissance. Through the coming third religious reformation, the democratic world on God's side will triumph in the ideological war and bring the communist world on Satan's side to its knees. Then the two worlds will unite into one Kingdom of Heaven on earth under God.

The economic changes which follow the religious and political reforms have been progressing in three industrial revolutions. The first Industrial Revolution originated in England and was based on the steam engine. A century later, the second Industrial Revolution took place in many advanced nations based on electricity and the gasoline engine. The third Industrial Revolution will flower by safely tapping the power of the atom; it will construct a pleasant living environment for the ideal world. In the centuries of preparation prior to the Second Advent of the Messiah, the three stages of revolutions in the three spheres of religion, politics and industry, which followed the three renaissances, have been a necessary course for the construction of the ideal world, as required by the principle of development through three stages.

Section 4

The World Wars

4.1 The Providential Causes of the World Wars

Wars break out due to such factors as conflicts of political and economic interests and clashes of ideology. Yet these are merely external causes. There are also internal causes of wars, just as there are internal and external motives for every human action. Human actions are decided by the free will of the individual, who is trying both to respond externally to the situation with which he is confronted and to follow his internal tendency toward the Will of God and the advancement of His providence of restoration. Therefore, the good or evil of a human action should not be judged only by external motives. The same can be said of the world wars, which have resulted from the worldwide collision between the actions of numerous individuals arising from their free will. Accordingly, we cannot grasp the providential significance of the world wars by focusing only on conflicts of political and economic interests, ideological clashes and other such external causes.

What are the internal, providential causes of the world wars? First, the world wars have resulted from Satan's last desperate struggle to preserve his sovereignty. Since the Fall of the first human ancestors, Satan has been building defective, unprincipled imitations of God's ideal world. Aiming to restore the ideal world of His Principle, God has been in pursuit, gradually expanding His dominion by reclaiming it from the unprincipled world under Satan's bondage.[13] Accordingly, in the course of the providence of restoration, a false representation of the ideal appears before the emergence of its true manifestation. The biblical prophecy that the antichrist will appear before the return of Christ is an illustration of this truth.

Human history under Satan's evil sovereignty will end with the Second Advent of Christ. Then it will be transformed into the history of humanity abiding in the realm of God's good sovereignty. At that time, Satan will put up a last-ditch fight. When the Israelites were about to leave Egypt in the national course to restore Canaan, Satan worked through the Pharaoh to wage a bitter struggle to keep them in bondage. By virtue of this, God's side was entitled to strike him with three supernatural signs. Similarly, in the Last Days, Satan has been putting up his last struggle to undermine God's side as it has prepared itself to embark upon the worldwide course to restore Canaan. God's three counterattacks to Satan's aggressions have manifested themselves as the three world wars.

Second, the three world wars have occurred in order to fulfill the worldwide indemnity conditions to restore the three great blessings. Upon creating human beings, God gave them three blessings: to reach individual perfection, multiply as an ideal family and have dominion over the creation.[14] By fulfilling these blessings, our first ancestors were to build the Kingdom of Heaven on the earth. Since God Himself created human beings and blessed them, He did not annul these blessings just because they fell. God had to allow fallen people to build an unprincipled world that has imitated the three blessings, though defectively, under Satan's leadership. Accordingly, at the consummation of human history, unprincipled worlds have emerged which have realized defectively the outward form of the three blessings: an individual championing Satan's causes, multiplication of satanic children, and the conquest of the world under Satan's domination. To fulfill the worldwide indem-

---

13. cf. Parallels 7.1
14. Gen. 1:28

nity conditions to restore God's three great blessings, three world conflicts must break out by which God can prevail over these satanic worlds through the three stages of formation, growth and completion.

Third, the three world wars have occurred so that all humanity may overcome on the world level the three temptations by which Satan tempted Jesus. As Jesus' disciples, Christians are to follow the course of their Teacher and overcome the three temptations which he confronted in the wilderness as individuals, families, nations and at the world level.

Fourth, the world wars have taken place to fulfill the worldwide indemnity condition to restore God's sovereignty. Had the first human beings not fallen but reached perfection by passing through the three stages of the growing period, they would have realized the world of God's sovereignty. Similarly, worldwide restoration must pass through three stages. The restoration of this world requires that it first be divided into Cain-type and Abel-type worlds, and that there be three final wars in which the heavenly, Abel-type world prevails over the satanic, Cain-type world. This is a condition to restore through worldwide indemnity Cain's murder of Abel. After that, the world of God's sovereignty can be established. Accordingly, the world wars are the final global conflicts in human history, restoring horizontally through indemnity the purpose of all the wars that have been waged for the restoration of God's sovereignty in the vertical course of the providence.

4.2 The First World War

4.2.1 Summary of the Providence in the First World War

Absolute monarchy had come to an end as a consequence of the Cain-type and Abel-type democratic revolutions, which had arisen out of the Cain-type and Abel-type views of life. The Industrial Revolution which followed cleared away the remnants of feudalism and led to the ascendancy of capitalism. This was followed by the age of imperialism.

In the political sphere, the First World War was a conflict between Abel-type democracies, which pursued the goal of the providence of restoration, and authoritarian states where Cain-type democratic ideals were thriving and which stood in opposition to the goals of the providence of restoration. It was fought between the imperialist nations on God's side and the imperialist nations on Satan's side. In terms of economic interests, this war was a conflict between more established and newly industrializing capitalist nations over colonies. In the sphere of religion and ideology, the Cain-type nations included Turkey, a Muslim nation persecuting Christianity, and its allies, Germany and Austria-Hungary. They fought the Abel-type nations of Great Britain, the United States, France and Russia, which generally upheld Christianity. At the conclusion of the First World War, the Abel-type democracies had gained victory at the formation stage.

4.2.2 What Decides God's Side and Satan's Side?

The question of which nations are on God's side and which are on Satan's side is decided based on the direction of God's providence of restoration. Those who are in line with the direction of God's providence or are acting in concert with that direction, even indirectly, are on the side of God, while those who take an opposing position are on the side of Satan. Therefore, whether or not an individual or nation belongs to God's side or Satan's side is not always in agreement with the judgment of our common sense or conscience. For example, someone who is ignorant of God's providence may judge that Moses' killing of the Egyptian taskmaster was evil. Yet, it may be regarded as a good act because it was in line with God's providence. Likewise, the Israelites invaded the land of Canaan and killed many Canaanites seemingly without much justification. To someone ignorant of God's providence, their action might seem evil and cruel; nevertheless, it was just in the sight of God. Even if there were more good-hearted people among the Canaanites than among the Israelites, at that time the Canaanites collectively belonged to Satan's side, while the Israelites collectively belonged to God's side.

Let us further investigate this concept in the sphere of religion. Since the goal of every religion is goodness, every one of them belongs to God's side. However, when a religion obstructs the path of another religion which stands closer to the center of God's providence, it will find itself standing on Satan's side. A religion is given a mission for its age, but if, after its time of responsibility has passed, it becomes an obstacle to an emerging religion which comes with a new mission for the next age, then it stands on the side of Satan. Before the coming of Jesus, Judaism and its believers stood on God's side. However, when they persecuted Jesus, who came with a new mission—which among other things would have fulfilled the purpose of Judaism—they moved to the side of Satan, irrespective of how faithfully they had served God in the past.

In the modern world, systems which espouse the Abel-type view of life belong to God's side while those which espouse the Cain-type view of life stand on Satan's side. For example, no matter how ethical and sacrificial a materialistic thought rooted in the Cain-type view of life may appear from a humanistic perspective, it still belongs to Satan's side. For this reason, the communist world can be judged to be the satanic world. On the other hand, since the democratic world, which grants religious freedom, is based on the Abel-type view of life, it may be judged to be on God's side.

Christianity was established as the central religion with the ultimate mission to fulfill the goals of all religions.[15] Hence, any nation which persecutes Christianity or obstructs its progress, either directly or indirectly, stands on Satan's side. In the First World War, the Allied Powers led by Great Britain, the United States, France and Russia were Christian nations; moreover, they had been fighting to liberate the Christians under persecution in Turkey. Thus, they stood on God's side. On the other hand, Germany and Austria-Hungary, the leading Central Powers, supported Turkey, a Muslim nation which persecuted Christianity. Therefore, together with Turkey, they stood on Satan's side.

4.2.3 THE PROVIDENTIAL CAUSES BEHIND THE FIRST WORLD WAR

What were the providential, internal causes of the First World War? The First World War had to take place, first, to fulfill the worldwide indemnity condition to restore God's three great blessings at the formation stage. Satan has been constructing in advance a defective imitation of God's ideal world, which was to have been established by Adam. Hence, there should appear at the end of history an unprincipled world which has realized a distorted, outward form of the three blessings at the formation stage, led by an antitype of Adam on Satan's side. God's side should then prevail over this unprincipled world to fulfill the indemnity condition.

In fact, Kaiser Wilhelm II (1859-1941) of Germany, who launched the First World War, was this antitype of Adam on Satan's side. He was in the formation-stage likeness of one who has attained individual perfection. He displayed the form of having fulfilled the blessing of multiplying children by advocating Pan-Germanism, and displayed a form of dominion over the creation by implementing his policy of world hegemony. In this manner, the Kaiser realized an unprincipled world completing a satanic imitation of the three great blessings at the formation stage. The First World War was to fulfill the worldwide formation-stage indemnity condition to restore, in the future, the world where the three

---

15. cf. Eschatology 2.3

great blessings will actually be completed centering on God.

Second, the First World War took place in order to have people on God's side collectively overcome Jesus' first temptation on the world level. In light of the meaning of Jesus' three temptations, we can recognize that God's side had to prevail in the First World War to fulfill the indemnity condition to restore God's first blessing worldwide. By prevailing in his first temptation in the wilderness, Jesus recovered himself, symbolized by the rock, and laid the foundation to restore perfection of individual character. Likewise, by prevailing in the First World War, God's side not only was to defeat Satan's world and its center, it also was to build God's world and lay the foundation for its own center, Christ at the Second Coming. This was to be the basis upon which the returning Christ could be born and perfect his individual character.

Third, the First World War took place in order to lay the formation-stage foundation for the restoration of God's sovereignty. Democracy arose to bring an end to authoritarian monarchic regimes and as the final political system with the mission to restore God's sovereignty.[16] In the First World War, God's side was responsible to be victorious and expand its political territory to Christianize the world. By thus establishing a vast and firm political and economic foundation, it would secure the formation-stage foundation for the democratic world and, at the same time, the formation-stage foundation to restore God's sovereignty.

4.2.4 The Providential Results of the First World War

The victory of the Allied Powers in the First World War fulfilled the formation-stage indemnity condition to restore God's three great blessings worldwide. By overcoming Jesus' first temptation on the worldwide level, they fulfilled the indemnity condition to restore God's first blessing worldwide. The victory of democracy also established the formation-stage foundation for the restoration of God's sovereignty. With the defeat of the satanic world and its ruler, the Kaiser, the world on God's side won the formation-stage victory and laid the foundation for the birth of the returning Christ, who is destined to be the Lord of God's world.

Contemporaneous with this, communism was established in Russia. Stalin soon rose to power as the antitype of Christ at the Second Advent on Satan's side. Since Christ comes with the ideals of the Kingdom of Heaven on earth—interdependence, mutual prosperity and universally shared values—the satanic side tries to realize these ideals in advance by building an imitation of the Kingdom of Heaven on earth, led by the

---

16. cf. Parallels 7.2.6

satanic counterpart to Christ at the Second Advent.

In conclusion, with the victory of God's side in the First World War, the foundation was laid for the Second Advent of the Messiah. From that time, the formation stage of the dispensation of the Second Advent commenced.

4.3 THE SECOND WORLD WAR

4.3.1 SUMMARY OF THE PROVIDENCE IN THE SECOND WORLD WAR

The spiritual origin of modern democracy lies in the people's striving to realize the values of the Abel-type view of life. Democracy follows the internal and external aspirations of the original human nature and will certainly develop in the direction of God's ideal world. Fascism, on the other hand, constrains people from following the aspirations of their original nature. In the Second World War, democracy, while standing upon the formation stage victory attained in the First World War, defeated fascism and secured victory at the growth stage.

4.3.2 THE NATURE OF FASCISM

When economic depression overwhelmed the world in the 1930s, some nations tried to break out of it by adopting fascism. This was the road taken by Germany, Japan and Italy, which felt isolated and beset by adversity.

What, then, is fascism? Fascism denies the fundamental values of modern democracy, including respect for the individual and his basic rights, freedoms of speech, the press and association, and the parliamentary system. Race or nationality is the ultimate value, to be upheld by a strong nation-state. Individuals and institutions exist only for the benefit of the state. Under fascism, individuals cannot claim freedom as their inviolable right; they are to sacrifice their freedom in their duty to serve the state. The guiding political principle of fascism holds that all power and authority should be entrusted in one supreme leader rather than distributed among people. The personal will of the leader dictates the governing ideology for the entire nation. Mussolini in Italy, Hitler in Germany, and the leaders of Japan's militaristic government were dictators of the fascist type.

4.3.3 The Nations on God's Side and the Nations on Satan's Side in the Second World War

In the Second World War, an alliance of the democratic nations of the United States, Great Britain and France led the nations on God's side. Satan's side was the alliance of the fascist nations: Germany, Japan and Italy. What determined that the former stood on God's side and the latter on Satan's side? The Allies stood on God's side because their political systems were democracies, the political system for the final stage in the providence of restoration founded upon the Abel-type view of life. The Axis Powers, on the other hand, stood on Satan's side because they upheld fascism, which was anti-democratic and stemmed from the Cain-type view of life. Moreover, the Allies and Axis Powers were separated into God's side and Satan's side because the former nations supported Christianity while the latter opposed and persecuted Christianity.

Germany, the leader of the Axis Powers, deprived people of their basic freedoms, and its ideological oppression denied them their religious freedom. Furthermore, Hitler massacred six million Jews. After concluding a concordat with the pope, Hitler attempted to subordinate the churches under the control of cooperative bishops while corrupting Christianity into a nationalistic neo-paganism based on primitive Germanic religion. In protest, some Protestants and Catholics put up bitter resistance.

Japanese militarists during the Second World War forced every church in Korea to install a *kamidana*, an altar for the Japanese Shinto gods, and compelled Korean Christians to worship at Shinto shrines. Those Christians who did not comply were imprisoned or killed. Korean Christians who had fled to Manchuria in search of religious freedom were brutally massacred. These measures against Korean Christianity were intensified toward the end of the war.

Italy supported Germany's cause as one of the Axis Powers. Against the general thrust of God's providence, Mussolini promoted Catholicism as the state religion with the selfish intention to use it for unifying the people under his fascist regime. On these grounds, Germany, Japan and Italy during the war may be classified as the nations on Satan's side.

4.3.4 The Providential Roles of the Three Nations on God's Side and Satan's Side

One purpose behind the Second World War was to fulfill the worldwide condition of indemnity at the growth stage to restore God's three great blessings, as was meant to occur at the time of Jesus. In the beginning, it was due to the Fall of Adam, Eve and the Archangel that God's three great blessings were not realized. Therefore, in the restoration of the three blessings, there necessarily have to be three actors taking these respective roles. Thus, God spiritually restored the three blessings in the providence of spiritual salvation through the joint efforts of the resurrected Jesus as the second Adam, the Holy Spirit representing Eve,[17] and angels. Accordingly, during the Second World War, the three nations on God's side representing Adam, Eve and the Archangel led the fight against the three nations on Satan's side, which also represented Adam, Eve and the Archangel. The victory of the nations on God's side would make a growth-stage indemnity condition for the restoration of the three great blessings. Satan, who was aware of this providence, took the lead by mustering the three nations representing Adam, Eve and the Archangel on his side and had them attack the three nations on God's side.

The United States, as a masculine type of nation, represented Adam on God's side. Great Britain, as a feminine type of nation, represented Eve on God's side. France, as a mixed type of nation, represented the Archangel on God's side. On Satan's side, Germany, as a masculine type of nation, represented Adam; Japan, as a feminine type of nation, represented Eve; and Italy, as a mixed type of nation, represented the Archangel. In the First World War, the United States, Great Britain and France had represented at the formation stage these three positions on God's side, while Germany, Austria and Turkey took these positions on Satan's side.

The Soviet Union, a nation on Satan's side, participated in the Second World War on God's side. How was it possible? When medieval society could not fulfill its providential purpose, it became a hindrance to both God's side and Satan's side, which then divided and began developing along paths leading to the maturation of the democratic world and the communist world. The Cain-type and Abel-type views of life worked in tandem to break down medieval feudal society and later, absolute monarchy and imperialism. Just as God's providence progresses while riding on the currents of its time, Satan's effort to build an unprincipled imitation of the ideal world is also bound to the currents of its time. When the prevailing social order obstructs the formation of new societies, including those furthering Satan's goals, Satan joins in the fight to destroy it.

In a similar fashion, fascism had become an obstacle to both Satan's side and God's side. Because the providence of restoration through indemnity required that God temporarily permit Satan's side to form the

---

17. cf. Christology 4.1

communist world, the Soviet Union in. the Second World War was allowed to join forces with the nations on God's side to destroy fascism, in order that it might quickly build up its communist state. Nevertheless, as soon as the Second World War was over, the communist world and the democratic world separated like oil and water.

4.3.5 The Providential Causes behind the Second World War

The internal, providential causes behind the Second World War were as follows: First, the war broke out to fulfill the worldwide indemnity condition at the growth stage to restore God's three great blessings. The ideal world where God's three blessings are fulfilled, which could not be realized by Adam due to the Fall, was to have been realized by Jesus, whom God sent as the Second Adam. Yet this ideal was realized only spiritually because Jesus died on the cross. Since Satan tries to realize in advance a defective imitation of the ideal world, at the consummation of history, there will surely emerge an unprincipled world which has realized defectively the outward form of the three great blessings at the growth stage under the leadership of a satanic antitype of Jesus. God's side must prevail over this world and thereby fulfill the worldwide indemnity condition at the growth stage required for the restoration of the ideal world, where the three great blessings are fully realized centering on God.

Hitler was the satanic antitype of Jesus. Though his will was totally contrary to Jesus', certain aspects of Hitler's life mimicked in a perverted manner some of the events in Jesus' life: his grandiose vision, his single life and the disappearance of his corpse are examples. Hitler was also the satanic antitype of perfected Adam at the growth stage. He made a travesty of the blessing of the multiplication of children by advocating the purity of the German people as the master race and mimicked the blessing of dominion over the creation by his policy of world conquest. In this manner, Hitler realized an unprincipled world with a satanic form of the three blessings, fulfilled at the growth stage. By prevailing in the Second World War, God's side was to fulfill the worldwide indemnity condition at the growth stage to restore the ideal world of God's three blessings.

The second providential cause behind the war was to have the people on God's side overcome Jesus' second temptation on the world level. In light of the meaning of Jesus' three temptations, we can recognize that God's side had to prevail in the Second World War to fulfill the indemnity condition to restore worldwide God's second blessing.

As Jesus laid the foundation for the restoration of children by overcoming the second temptation in the wilderness, God's side was to lay the worldwide growth-stage foundation for democracy by triumphing in the Second World War.

The third providential cause behind the war was to lay the growth-stage foundation for the restoration of God's sovereignty. By the victory of God's side in the First World War, the democratic world had secured its formation-stage foundation. Working to build the Cain-type world, Satan's side also benefited from the collapse of Czarist absolutism during the First World War and laid the formation-stage foundation for the communist world. During the Second World War, the communist world and the democratic world built their separate growth-stage foundations before parting company at the conclusion of the war. Building this growth-stage foundation for the democratic world restored the growth-stage foundation of God's sovereignty.

4.3.6 The Providential Results of the Second World War

The victory of God's side in the Second World War fulfilled the growth-stage indemnity condition to restore God's three great blessings worldwide. Having the significance of overcoming Jesus' second temptation on the world level, the victory fulfilled the indemnity condition to restore God's second blessing worldwide. Finally, by laying the growth-stage foundation for the democratic world, it established the growth-stage foundation to restore God's sovereignty.

While Hitler was the antitype of Jesus on Satan's side, Stalin was the antitype of the Second Advent of Christ on Satan's side. The fact that Hitler and his nation were destroyed, while Stalin and his foundation of worldwide communism grew strong, indicated that the time for building the spiritual kingdom under the leadership of the resurrected Jesus had passed, and the age for building a new heaven and new earth[18] under the leadership of Christ at the Second Advent had begun.

At the conclusion of the Second World War, the growth stage of the dispensation of the Second Advent commenced. Many Christians began receiving revelations about the return of Jesus, and God's spiritual works began occurring throughout the world. Since then, the established churches have become increasingly confused, divided and secularized; they have been gradually losing the heart of their spiritual life. These are phenomena of the Last Days, occurring on account of God's final providence to unify all religions through the new, ultimate expression of the truth.

---

18. Rev. 21:1-7

4.4 THE THIRD WORLD WAR

4.4.1 IS THE THIRD WORLD WAR INEVITABLE?

We know that because God gave the first human ancestors the blessing to rule the universe, when Satan works through fallen people to create an unprincipled imitation of the world where this blessing is fulfilled, God has to allow it. On the heels of Satan, God conducts His providence to claim back Satan's world and its fruits. At the consummation of human history, Satan's side and God's side will strive until they each attain sovereignty over a world. This is why the democratic world and the communist world stand confronting each other. Consequently, it became inevitable that there be world wars, first to divide and then to unify these two worlds.

The First and Second World Wars had the providential purpose of dividing the globe into the communist world and the democratic world. Afterward, yet another war must take place to bring about their unification. This conflict is the Third World War. It is inevitable that the Third World War take place; however, there are two possible ways it may be fought.

One way to bring Satan's side to surrender is through armed conflict. However, at the conclusion of the conflict, there should come an ideal world in which all humanity is to rejoice together. This can never be built merely by defeating enemies in battle. Afterward, they must be brought to submission internally, that everyone may be reconciled and rejoice sincerely from the bottom of their hearts. To accomplish this, there must come a perfect ideology which can satisfy the desires of the original nature of all people.

The other way this war may be fought is as a wholly internal, ideological conflict, without the outbreak of armed hostilities, to bring Satan's world to submission and unification in a short time. People are rational beings. Therefore, a perfect, unified world can be established only when people submit to one another and participate in unification through a profound reawakening.

By which of these two ways will the Third World War actually be fought? It depends upon success or failure in carrying out the human portion of responsibility.

From where will the ideology essential to the resolution of this conflict and the establishment of the new world come? It surely cannot come out of the communist world, rooted in the Cain-type view of life, since the Cain-type view of life opposes the internal aspirations of the original human nature. Rather, this ideology must arise out of the democratic world, which is rooted in the Abel-type view of life. Nonetheless, it is a fact of history that no conventional ideology among those prevailing in the democratic world can effectively defeat communist ideology. Therefore, a hitherto unknown ideology will emerge from within the democratic world.

For the new ideology to be born, there must first arise a new expression of the truth. This new truth is the essence of the Abel-type view of life and the core of democracy. As has been the case in the past, when the new expression of truth appears, it may contradict the old expressions of truth in which many people have believed. Hence, even the democratic world will be divided into two camps which, like Cain and Abel, will be pitted against each other. When the new truth secures a victorious foundation in the democratic world and then conquers communist ideology, the unification of the world will be achieved based on the one truth.

Satan knew God's plan to unify the world through the one truth and presented a false imitation of the truth in order to unify humanity centering on himself. This false truth is dialectical materialism. Dialectical materialism denies the existence of any spiritual reality, setting up an explanation of the universe based on a wholly materialistic logic. In denying the existence of God, it also denies the existence of Satan. Thus, in promoting dialectical materialism, Satan was effectively denying his own reality, even risking his own demise. Satan understood what would unfold at the close of human history and knew well that he would surely perish. Accepting that this was not the time to be worshipped, he rose in a monstrous denial of God, even at the sacrifice of himself. This is the spiritual root of dialectical materialism. As long as the democratic world lacks the truth which can overturn this evil doctrine, it will always be vulnerable and on the defensive. For this reason, someone on God's side must proclaim the perfect truth.

4.4.2 Summary of the Providence in the Third World War

The Third World War is the final conflict in the providence of restoration. Through this war, God intends that the democratic world bring the communist world to submission and build the ideal world. Leading up to the First World War, the nations on God's side had expanded their political and economic dominion by claiming colonies throughout the world, to be used by God for His providence. At the conclusion of the war, these nations laid the worldwide formation-stage foundation for democracy. Through the Second World War, they laid the worldwide growth-stage foundation for democracy, thereby firmly consolidating the democratic world. During the Third World War, God's side is to found the perfect Abel-type view of life based on the new truth and complete the worldwide completion-stage foundation for democracy. God's side is then to guide all of humanity into one unified world. In summary, the Third World War is the last great war at the close of history, when God's side restores horizontally through indemnity all that was lost to Satan throughout the three stages of the prolonged providence.

4.4.3 The Providential Causes behind the Third World War

As was explained above, whether the Third World War is waged by force of arms or as an ideological conflict depends upon the responsibility of the people who are serving the providence of God. Regardless, it is inescapable that this worldwide conflict take place.

What are the internal, providential causes behind the Third World War? First, the war has to take place to fulfill the worldwide indemnity condition at the completion stage to restore God's three great blessings. When Jesus could accomplish the providence of restoration only spiritually due to the disbelief of the people, it became necessary that he return and restore the world of God's ideal both spiritually and physically. Yet, since Satan realizes in advance a defective form of God's ideal, at the consummation of history there will emerge an unprincipled world with the pretense of having restored the three great blessings under the leadership of a satanic antitype of Christ at the Second Advent. By prevailing over this satanic world, God's side is responsible to fulfill the worldwide indemnity condition at the completion stage to restore the ideal world in which the three great blessings are fulfilled centering on God.

Stalin was the satanic antitype of Christ at the Second Advent. He was idolized as a perfect human being. By advocating the solidarity of farmers and workers in opposition to the democratic world, he mimicked the blessing of the multiplication of children, and by his policy of worldwide communist domination, he achieved the outward semblance of the blessing of dominion over the creation. Stalin thus created a vast communist world which realized defectively the outward form of the three great blessings. We must understand that the communist world is the unprincipled and flawed imitation of the world of God's ideal, which will be characterized by interdependence, mutual prosperity and universally shared values founded in God.

Second, the Third World War has to take place to have the people on God's side overcome Jesus' third temptation on the world level. In light of the meaning of Jesus' three temptations, we recognize that God's side must prevail in the Third World War to fulfill the indemnity condition to restore worldwide God's third blessing. As Jesus established the foundation to restore dominion over the creation by overcoming the third temptation in the wilderness, God's side must win in the Third World War to restore human beings' dominion over the entire universe.

Third, the Third World War has to take place to lay the completion-stage foundation for the restoration of God's sovereignty. God's side must be victorious in the war to destroy the communist world and return all sovereignty to God. Then the ideal world will be established based upon the principles of heaven and earth.

4.4.4 The Providential Results of the Third World War

Long ago, God intended to conclude His providence of restoration in Adam's family by working through Cain and Abel. Instead, Cain murdered Abel, commencing the sinful history of humanity. God began the dispensation of dividing good and evil to restore the failure in Adam's family on the individual level and developed it through the levels of family, clan, society, people and nation. The time has come when God conducts this dispensation on the world level. God intends to restore through indemnity the entire providence, which was prolonged to the third stage, by winning victory in the three world wars, which belong to the final chapter of providential history.

In the beginning, the first human ancestors lost their connection of heart to God when they fell prey to the tempting words of Satan. Through the internal, spiritual fall and the external, physical fall, they inherited the lineage of Satan. Therefore, the providence of restoration can be completed only after fallen people restore their heart toward God through God's life-giving Word, are saved both spiritually and physically, and inherit God's lineage.[19]

The victories of God's side in the three world wars will fully restore through indemnity all these aspects of the providence of restoration. They will make possible the realization of God's ideal world, for which God has labored with unremitting tears over the centuries of human misery since the Fall.

---

19. cf. Moses and Jesus 3.3.2

Chapter 6

The Second Advent

Jesus clearly foretold of his return.[1] Yet he added that no one knew of the day and hour of his return, not the angels, not even himself.[2] Hence, it has been commonly thought unwise to speculate about the date, place and manner of the Second Advent.

Nevertheless, we can deduce from the words of Jesus, "But of that day and hour no one knows . . . but the Father only,"[3] and the verse, "Surely the Lord God does nothing, without revealing his secret to his servants the prophets,"[4] that God, who knows the day and hour, will surely reveal all secrets about the Second Advent to His prophets before He carries out His work.

Although Jesus said that the Lord will come like a thief,[5] it is also written that for those in the light, the Lord will not come covertly, like a thief.[6] When we reflect upon the events at Jesus' First Coming, we realize that he came like a thief to the priests and scribes who were in darkness, but to the family of John the Baptist, which was in the light, God plainly revealed Jesus' birth beforehand. When Jesus was born, God divulged this secret to the three wise men, Simeon, Anna and the shepherds. Jesus said:

> But take heed to yourselves lest your hearts be weighed down with dissipation and drunkenness and cares of this life, and that day come upon

---

1. Matt. 16:27
2. Matt. 24:36
3. Ibid.
4. Amos 3:7
5. Rev. 3:3

you suddenly like a snare; for it will come upon all who dwell upon the face of the whole earth. But watch at all times, praying that you may have strength to escape all these things that will take place, and to stand before the Son of man. —*Luke 21:34-36*

Thus, Jesus strongly suggested that the secret of the time, place and manner of his return will be revealed to the faithful people who are vigilant, that they may prepare for the day of the Second Advent.

In the providence of restoration, God always revealed to His prophets what He would do before He carried it out. The flood judgment in Noah's day, the destruction of Sodom and Gomorrah, and the birth of Jesus are only a few examples. Accordingly, regarding the Second Advent of the Lord, God will certainly give prophecies to those faithful believers who are in the light and have ears to hear and eyes to see. As it is written:

And in the last days it shall be, God declares, that I will pour out my Spirit upon all flesh, and your sons and your daughters shall prophesy, and your young men shall see visions, and your old men shall dream dreams. —*Acts 2:17*

SECTION 1

WHEN WILL CHRIST RETURN?

We call the time of Christ's Second Advent the Last Days. As it was already explained, we are living in the Last Days today.[7] We can thus understand that today is truly the time of Christ's return. From the standpoint of providential history, Jesus came at the conclusion of the two-thousand-year-long Old Testament Age, the Age of the Providence of Restoration. The Principle of Restoration through Indemnity leads us to infer that Christ is to return at the end of the two-thousand-year-long New Testament Age, the Age of the Prolongation of the Providence of Restoration, which has been restoring the previous age through substantial parallel conditions of indemnity.

As was discussed in detail with reference to the First World War, soon after the defeat of Germany and the Kaiser (the antitype of Adam on Satan's side), Stalin (the antitype of Christ at the Second Advent on Satan's side) rose to power and built up the communist world.[8] This

---

6. I Thess. 5:4
7. cf. Eschatology 4
8. cf. Preparation 4.2.4

meant that the time was drawing nigh when Christ would return and restore through indemnity the ideal world characterized by interdependence, mutual prosperity and universally shared values. We can thus conclude that the period of the Second Advent began soon after the end of the First World War.

SECTION 2

IN WHAT MANNER WILL CHRIST RETURN?

2.1 PERSPECTIVES ON THE BIBLE

God reveals well in advance all the essential matters of His Will in parables and symbols, in order that people living in any age can understand the demands of the providence for their time and for the future according to the level of their intellect and spirituality. The fact that God used parables and symbols in the Bible has inevitably resulted in many divergent interpretations. This is a major reason why the churches have become divided. In interpreting the Bible, therefore, the most important matter is to find the right perspective.

For example, consider John the Baptist. For two thousand years we read the Bible with the preconception that John completed his given mission; therefore, its passages appear to support this. But when we re-examined the Bible more closely from a different standpoint, we could clearly recognize that John the Baptist in fact did not complete his mission.[9]

Until today many of us have read the Bible with the preconceived notion that Jesus will come on the clouds with signs and wonders. This is based on such words of Jesus as:

> They will see the Son of man coming on the clouds of heaven with power and great glory; and he will send out his angels with a loud trumpet call, and they will gather his elect from the four winds. —*Matt. 24:30-31*

If we adhere closely to a literal interpretation, the biblical evidence indeed seems to point in that direction. However, the idea that Christ will return on the clouds is totally unacceptable to the scientific mind of the modern age. We find it necessary to probe more deeply into the Bible from another standpoint to grasp the true meaning of such verses.

This new perspective is suggested by our earlier investigation of the biblical passages concerning John the Baptist. The prophet Malachi had

---

9. cf. Messiah 2.3

foretold that Elijah would return before the coming of the Messiah.[10] As they eagerly awaited that day, many Jews believed that Elijah, who had ascended to heaven, would come down from heaven in the same way he had ascended. Contrary to their expectation, however, Jesus boldly claimed that John the Baptist, the son of Zechariah, was Elijah.[11] If we believe Jesus' testimony, the return of Elijah was never meant to take place in the miraculous manner many Jewish people expected. In fact, it occurred through the birth of a child. In like manner, many Christians to the present day believe that Jesus will return on the clouds. However, what we have learned about the actual return of Elijah suggests another possibility: that Christ's return may be fulfilled through the birth of a child, just as at the First Coming. From this new perspective, let us closely re-examine the biblical verses concerning the Second Coming.

At the First Coming of Jesus, many of the learned men of Israel thought that the Messiah would be born in Bethlehem as a descendant of King David.[12] Yet there were undoubtedly many other Jews who expected the Messiah to come on the clouds. This belief was based on their reading of the prophecy of Daniel, "I saw in the night visions, and behold, with the clouds of heaven there came one like a son of man,"[13] and other prophecies of supernatural events in the Last Days.[14] Therefore, the Pharisees and Sadducees questioned Jesus, demanding that he show them a sign from heaven as proof that he was the Messiah.[15] Without any of the supernatural signs from heaven foretold in the Bible, they could not readily accept him as the long-awaited Messiah. The belief that the Messiah should come supernaturally persisted after the death of Jesus, even among some heterodox Christians who believed that he had not come in a body of flesh. The apostle John condemned those believers as antichrists:

> For many deceivers have gone out into the world, men who will not acknowledge the coming of Jesus Christ in the flesh; such a one is the deceiver and the antichrist. —*II John 7*

Many Christians assert that the prophecy in Daniel concerns the Second Advent of Christ. However, in the Old Testament Age, God was working to fulfill the entire purpose of the providence of restoration with the coming of Jesus, as the Bible attests: "For all the prophets and

---

10. Mal. 4:5
11. Matt. 11:14
12. Matt. 2:5-6; Micah 5:2
13. Dan. 7:13
14. e.g., Joel 2:30-31
15. Matt. 16:1-4; Mark 8:11-12

the law prophesied until John,"[16] and "For Christ is the end of the law, that every one who has faith may be justified."[17] Thus, before Jesus himself began speaking about his return, no one ever even imagined a Second Advent. It is obvious that no Jew at the time thought this verse in Daniel referred to anything other than what they believed to be the first and only coming of the Messiah.

Contrary to the expectations of many faithful Jews who believed on biblical grounds that the Messiah would come on the clouds with signs and portents in the heavens, Jesus was born on the earth as a child in a lowly family. Hence, we should re-examine the Bible from the perspective that the Second Advent of Christ may not take place in a miraculous way. It may, in fact, take place in the same manner as the First Advent.

2.2 Christ Will Return as a Child on the Earth

Jesus made a number of predictions foretelling what would happen to the Lord at his return:

> But first he must suffer many things and be rejected by this generation.
> —*Luke 17:25*

If Jesus were to return literally on the clouds of heaven with power and great glory and with the trumpets of angels,[18] would he not readily be accepted and honored, even by this sin-ridden world? Returning in such a manner, there is no way he would ever suffer persecution or rejection.

Why, then, did Jesus foretell that he would face such a miserable situation upon his return? The Jews of his day were eagerly looking forward to the day when Elijah would come down from heaven. He was supposed to come before the Messiah as his herald, as Malachi had prophesied.[19] Instead, before the people had heard any news of Elijah's return, Jesus, a man of lowly birth, came like a thief, claiming to be the Messiah. Therefore, they despised Jesus and persecuted him.[20] As Jesus reflected upon his situation, he foresaw that at the Second Advent, the Christians awaiting his return would once more fix their gaze upon the sky. Hence, they would be likely to persecute Christ at the Second Advent when he is born in the flesh and appears unexpectedly, like a thief. They would condemn him as a heretic, just as Jesus was condemned. That is why he

---

16. Matt. 11:13
17. Rom. 10:4
18. Matt. 24:30-31
19. Mal. 4:5
20. cf. Messiah 2.2

foretold that the Lord would suffer and be rejected by his generation. This prophecy can be fulfilled only if Christ returns in the flesh; it cannot possibly come true if he comes on the clouds.

Jesus said:

> I tell you, he will vindicate them speedily. Nevertheless, when the Son of man comes, will he find faith on earth? —*Luke 18:8*

As the world enters the Last Days, increasing numbers of Christians are striving to develop stronger faith. How can they all fall into faithlessness at the Second Advent of the Lord if he literally comes on the clouds of heaven amidst the sounds of angels' trumpets and the glory of God? This prophecy also cannot be fulfilled if Christ returns in a supernatural manner.

In Jesus' day, many Jews thought the Messiah would be born in Bethlehem and emerge as their king,[21] but only after Elijah had returned from heaven. Contrary to this expectation, before Elijah had appeared, a carpenter's son from Nazareth stepped forward and presented himself as the Messiah. It is thus understandable that Jesus could not find any believer among the Jews faithful and zealous enough to follow him even to the point of death. Jesus grieved over this situation and lamented that something similar might happen upon his return. He foresaw that at the Second Advent, the believers would be looking only toward heaven, thinking that Christ will return on the clouds in glory. Therefore, when Christ does in fact return to the earth as a man of humble origins, he may not find any faith, as was the case in Jesus' day. This prophecy in Luke can never be fulfilled unless the returning Christ is born on the earth.

Some scholars interpret this verse to mean that the tribulations in the Last Days will be so severe as to cause all believers to become faithless. Yet in the course of the providence, no tribulation, no matter how bitter, has effectively blocked the way of the faithful. How much less so in the Last Days, when faithful Christians are eager to pass through the last gate to Heaven! It is the universal nature of faith that the greater our trials and tribulations, the more zealously we seek God's salvation.

Jesus once said:

> On that day many will say to me, "Lord, Lord, did we not prophesy in your name, and cast out demons in your name, and do many mighty

---

21. Matt. 2:6

> works in your name?" And then will I declare to them, "I never knew you; depart from me, you evildoers." —*Matt. 7:22-23*

If a Christian is so faithful as to perform miracles in the name of the Lord, then how much more ardently would he believe in and serve the Lord when he comes on the clouds in great glory? Wouldn't Jesus then receive him warmly? Why, then, did Jesus speak as if he would reject such faithful Christians upon his return? If the returning Christ rejects such devout believers, who in the Last Days can possibly be saved? This prophecy also cannot be fulfilled if Jesus comes on the clouds.

In Jesus' day, there must have been many Jews whose faith was so ardent that they could perform miracles in God's name. Yet, since they believed that Elijah himself would descend from heaven before the Messiah came, it was hard for them to accept that Elijah was present among them as John the Baptist—all the more so because of John's denial.[22] Hence, they did not accept Jesus as the Messiah and ostracized him from the community. Consequently, Jesus had to abandon them in tears. In like manner, at the Second Advent of Christ, those Christians who expect his miraculous and glorious appearance will almost certainly reject him if he comes in the flesh of humble birth. No matter how faithful they may be, the Lord will be left with no choice but to abandon them because they will have transgressed against God.

The series of prophecies concerning the Last Days in Luke, Chapter 17, cannot possibly be fulfilled if Christ returns in a supernatural manner. These verses can be explained only on the premise that Christ will return by being born on the earth. Let us examine each of them closely.

> The kingdom of God is not coming with signs to be observed.
> —*Luke 17:20*

If the Lord comes on the clouds or in some miraculous way, the Kingdom of God will arrive in a manner conspicuous to everyone. Even at the First Advent, the Kingdom of God had already arrived on the earth with the birth of Jesus. Yet the Jewish people could not see it, for since they were still waiting for the return of Elijah from heaven, they could not believe in Jesus. Likewise, at the Second Advent, although the Kingdom of God will dawn upon the earth with the birth of Christ, Christians who believe that he will come on the clouds accompanied by supernatural events will disbelieve in the Lord and thus not see the Kingdom of God.

---

22. John 1:21

> Behold, the kingdom of God is within you. —*Luke 17:21*[23]

In Jesus' day, those who believed in and followed him had already partaken of the Kingdom of Heaven in their hearts. Likewise, at Christ's Second Advent, because he will be born on the earth, the Kingdom of Heaven will be realized first in the hearts of those who believe in him and follow him. When these individuals increase in number to form societies and nations, the Kingdom of Heaven within will gradually be manifested in the world as an outward, visible reality. Accordingly, Jesus meant that the promised Kingdom of Heaven will not be realized in an instant, as it would if Christ were to return on the clouds.

> You will desire to see one of the days of the Son of man, and you will not see it. —*Luke 17:22*

If the Lord comes on the clouds with the sounds of angels' trumpets, everyone will be able to see him. Who, then, would desire to see the day of the Son of man and not see it? Yet Jesus foretold that the people will not see the day. At Jesus' First Advent, the day of the Son of man dawned upon the earth with his birth, yet the disbelieving Jews could not see the day. Likewise, at the Second Advent of Christ, the day of the Son of man will have dawned with his birth on earth. Yet many Christians will not be able to see the day because, convinced as they are that he will come in a miraculous way, they will not believe in him or follow him even after encountering him. Even though the day of the Son of man will have already come, they will not be able to see it.

> And they will say to you, "Lo, there!" or "Lo, here!" Do not go, do not follow them. —*Luke 17:23*

As was discussed earlier,[24] in the Last Days Christians who have attained a certain spiritual level may receive the revelation that they are the Lord. Not understanding the basis in the Principle for such a revelation, they are likely to proclaim themselves to be the Messiah and thus become antichrists before the Lord to come. Therefore, Jesus spoke these words as a warning not to be misled or confused by such people.

> As the lightning flashes and lights up the sky from one side to the other, so will the Son of man be in his day. —*Luke 17:24*

---

23. KJV
24. cf. Resurrection 2.2.6

When Jesus was born, the news of the birth of the King of the Jews reached King Herod and troubled all of Jerusalem.[25] At the Second Advent, advances in transportation and communication will allow the news of the Second Advent to travel to the far-flung corners of the globe, East and West, with lightning speed.

> As it was in the days of Noah, so will it be in the days of the Son of man.
> —Luke 17:26 [26]

When Noah knew that the flood judgment was imminent, he called the people to enter his ark.[27] Yet they did not heed his words, and all were drowned. Similarly in the Last Days, Christ will return in the flesh and call to the people to enter the ark of truth. Yet Christians who stubbornly fix their gaze upon the sky, expecting to see miraculous signs of the Lord's appearance, will not heed the words of truth proclaimed from the earth. Instead, they will reject the Lord as a heretic. Heedless as the people of Noah's day, they will have failed to serve God's providential Will.

> Whoever seeks to gain his life will lose it, but whoever loses his life will preserve it. —Luke 17:33

Would anyone have to risk his life to follow the Lord if he comes on the clouds with the sounds of angels' trumpets? Because Jesus returns through a physical birth, he will appear to be a heretic to Christians who expect him to come in a miraculous way. Hence, those who follow him must be ready to face even death. The verse means that if the people believe in and follow him at the risk of their lives, they will live. If on the other hand, swayed by worldly circumstances, they turn against him and retreat from him to save their own skins, death will befall them.

> Where the body is, there the eagles will be gathered together.
> —Luke 17:37

Thus Jesus answered a query about the place of the Second Advent. We recall that birds of prey descended upon the dove and pigeon which had not been properly divided on Abraham's altar.[28] This taught us that Satan is always looking for an opportunity to claim what is not sancti-

---

25. Matt. 2:2-3
26. Luke 17:25 was discussed previously.
27. II Pet. 2:5
28. Gen. 15:11

fied. We can thus understand the meaning of Jesus' enigmatic reply: just as vultures gather around a carcass to eat it, and devils gather around those who are spiritually dead to claim them, the Lord, who is the source of life, will come to a place of abundant spiritual life. Jesus meant by these words that the Lord will appear among the faithful believers. At Christ's Second Advent, people of ardent faith will gather together in one place with the assistance of many spirits.[29] This will be the place of life where the Lord will appear. Jesus was born among the chosen people, who worshipped God most faithfully. In particular, he revealed himself as the Messiah to those who had the faith to follow him and become his disciples.

Since Christ will be born on the earth at his Second Advent, it is written: "She brought forth a male child, one who is to rule all the nations with a rod of iron, but her child was caught up to God and to his throne."[30] The rod of iron here signifies the Word of God, with which the Lord will judge the sinful world and restore the Kingdom of Heaven on earth. It was earlier explained in detail[31] that judgment by fire is judgment by the Word.[32] Hence, the Word of Jesus, which will be our judge on the Last Day,[33] is the same Word by which heaven and earth will be cast into the fire of judgment,[34] and is the very breath of the Lord's mouth by which he will slay the lawless one.[35] The Word Jesus speaks is also called "the breath of his lips" and "the rod of his mouth."[36] It is symbolized by the rod of iron, as it is written, "He shall rule them with a rod of iron, as when earthen pots are broken in pieces."[37]

The verse speaks of a male child, who is born of a woman and is caught up to God and to His throne. Who, then, is born of a woman as someone worthy to sit on God's throne and rule all the nations with the Word of God? He can be none other than Christ at the Second Advent, who will be born on the earth, rule as the King of Kings and build the Kingdom of Heaven on earth.[38] At the beginning of the Gospel of Matthew, there is a record of the four adulterous women in Jesus' lineage.[39] This shows that the Savior of humankind is to be born as a sinless man out of a sinful lineage to save all the descendants of sinful lineages. Many Christians have interpreted the woman in the above verse as the Church.[40] They drew this interpretation based on

---

29. cf. Resurrection 2.3.2.2; 3.1; 3.2
30. Rev. 12:5
31. cf. Eschatology 3.2.2
32. Jer. 23:29
33. John 12:48
34. II Pet. 3:7
35. II Thess. 2:8
36. Isa. 11:4
37. Rev. 2:27
38. Rev. 19:16
39. Matt. 1:3, 5, 6
40. "The rest of her offspring" (Rev. 12:17) should be taken to signify the adopted children of God. (Rom. 8:23)

the premise that Christ at the Second Advent would come on the clouds.

Some Christians believe that the Second Advent of Christ occurs whenever Jesus comes to dwell within the hearts of people[41] through the descent of the Holy Spirit.[42] Jesus has been dwelling within the hearts of faithful believers ever since his resurrection and the Holy Spirit's descent at Pentecost.[43] If this were truly the Second Advent, then it already took place two thousand years ago.

Moreover, some denominations teach that Jesus will return as a spirit. However, immediately after his resurrection from the tomb on the third day, Jesus appeared before his disciples with the same appearance as he had during his earthly life. Ever since that time, he has freely visited and taught many Christians who have attained a high spiritual level. Thus, this sort of Second Coming also first took place two thousand years ago. If these were correct understandings, then we would have no reason to anticipate the historical Second Advent and look forward to it as the day which will fulfill our most cherished hopes.

Even though Jesus' disciples had frequent encounters with the resurrected Jesus who appeared to them in spirit, they still awaited his Second Advent. We can deduce that they were not anticipating the Second Advent to be Jesus' return as a spirit. For example, when Jesus appeared in a vision to the apostle John, he said to him, "Surely I am coming soon," to which John replied, "Amen. Come, Lord Jesus!"[44] Here, Jesus and John both clearly distinguished Jesus' spiritual appearances from the Second Advent. This shows that Christ at his Second Advent will not come as a spirit. He will be born as a child on the earth, just as at the First Advent.

There are several reasons in the Principle why Christ must return as an earthly man. God created both the incorporeal world and the corporeal world. Then God created human beings with the aspects of both spirit and flesh, intending for them to rule over the two worlds in fulfillment of His blessings.[45] Due to Adam's Fall, human beings lost the qualification to be lords of the two worlds. Consequently, the creation was deprived of its true masters and has been lamenting and longing for the appearance of the children of God who can truly rule it.[46] Jesus, the perfected Adam, came as the perfect Lord of the two worlds.[47] By engrafting all believers with himself[48] and bringing them into oneness with him, he intended to make them qualified to be the lords of the universe.

---

41. John 14:20
42. Acts 8:15-17
43. Acts 2:4
44. Rev. 22:20
45. cf. Creation 6.3
46. Rom. 8:19-22
47. I Cor. 15:27
48. Rom. 11:17

Nevertheless, when the Jews turned against Jesus, God had to commit his body to the cross as a ransom for the redemption of humanity. Since Jesus' physical body was delivered into the hands of Satan, physical salvation was left unaccomplished. Jesus ascended from this earthly world with the promise that he would return and complete the salvation which he had realized only spiritually.[49] In the meantime, there has not been even one person on the earth who has attained perfection both spiritually and physically, ruled the spiritual and physical worlds, and brought them into harmony. This is the reason Christ cannot return only in a spiritual body. As at the First Advent, he must come as a human being and grow to perfection in both spirit and flesh. Then, by engrafting all humanity with himself both spiritually and physically, he is to guide them to perfection both in spirit and flesh and make them qualified to be the lords of both the spiritual and physical worlds.

Jesus was originally supposed to restore the Kingdom of Heaven on earth. He was to become the True Parent of restored humanity and the king of God's earthly kingdom.[50] However, due to the people's disbelief, he could not accomplish this original Will of God, but went to the cross promising to return at a later time and surely fulfill it. Accordingly, at the Second Advent, Christ is again responsible to build the Kingdom of Heaven on earth and there become the True Parent and king of all humanity. This is another reason why, as at his First Coming, Christ at his Second Coming must be born on the earth.

The redemption of sins is possible only through an earthly life.[51] To redeem our sins on the earth, Christ must come as a man on the earth. The salvation which Jesus provided through his crucifixion, however, is limited to the spiritual dimension. It does not resolve the original sin, which is transmitted through our physical bodies and remains active within us. Therefore, Christ must come again to provide complete salvation to humanity, including physical salvation. He certainly cannot achieve this if he comes only as a spirit. He must come in a physical body, as at his First Coming.

We have thus clarified that Christ's Second Advent will not be a spiritual coming, but a physical coming similar to the First Advent. Even supposing that Christ were to come back in spirit, it would be perplexing that the spirit, transcendent of time and space and perceptible only to the spiritual senses, would ride on clouds composed of matter. On the other hand, if the Second Advent were to occur through Christ's

---

49. cf. Messiah 1.4
50. Isa. 9:6; Luke 1:31-33
51. cf. Creation 6.3.2

sudden appearance in the flesh, riding on the clouds, how could he stay aloft? Where would he reside prior to his appearance? Some people may object to such questions, arguing that for the omnipotent God nothing is impossible. However, God cannot ignore His own laws and principles. God does not and need not work His providence in violation of His own Principle by having Christ, who should return in flesh no different from our own, reside in outer space and then return borne on clouds. In conclusion, we have demonstrated beyond any doubt that the Second Advent of Christ will take place through his physical birth on the earth.

2.3 WHAT IS THE MEANING OF THE VERSE THAT CHRIST WILL RETURN ON THE CLOUDS?

Since Christ's return will take place through his birth on earth, what can be the meaning of the biblical prophecies that he will come on the clouds? To probe into this matter, we must first investigate what the clouds represent. The following passage is typical:

> Behold, he is coming with the clouds, and every eye will see him, every one who pierced him; and all the tribes of the earth will wail on account of him. Even so. Amen. —*Rev. 1:7*

According to this verse, everyone should be able to see Christ when he returns. When St. Stephen was martyred, only he and those faithful Christians whose spiritual senses were open were able to see Jesus sitting at the right hand of God.[52] Likewise, if Jesus is to descend from the spirit world as a spirit, then only those believers whose spiritual senses are open will be able to see him; thus not every eye would see Christ when he comes again. The biblical prophecy that everyone will see the Lord can be fulfilled only if he returns in the flesh. Since a body of flesh cannot ride on the clouds, the clouds in the verse must symbolize something else.

In the same passage, it is also written that even those who pierced Jesus will see his return. Those who pierced Jesus were Roman soldiers. However, those Roman soldiers will not be able to see the Lord at his return. To behold the returning Lord, those soldiers must be resurrected; but according to the Bible, those who will be resurrected at Christ's return are only those faithful Christians who participate in the first resurrection. The rest of the spirits will be resurrected only after the passage of "a thousand years" in the Kingdom.[53] Therefore, "every one who

---
52. Acts 7:55
53. Rev. 20:4-5

pierced him" must be a metaphor describing some other group of people, not the Roman soldiers. In fact, it refers to those Christians alive at the time of the Second Advent who hold fast to the belief that Jesus will return on the clouds. When Christ returns to the earth through a humble birth contrary to their expectation, they will not recognize him but will persecute him. If "every one who pierced him" is a metaphor, then the clouds in the same verse should also be metaphorical.

What do the clouds actually symbolize? Clouds are formed by the evaporation of impure water from the earth. In the Bible, water often symbolizes fallen people.[54] We may deduce that clouds symbolize devout Christians whose hearts dwell in heaven and not on the earth because they have been reborn and raised from their fallen state. The Bible and other sacred scriptures also use the symbolism of clouds to indicate the multitudes.[55] We sometimes find this figure of speech used in casual conversation. In Moses' course, the pillar of cloud which guided the Israelites by day represented Jesus, who was to come as the leader of Israel; the pillar of fire by night represented the Holy Spirit who, as Jesus' counterpart, would guide Israel by the fire of inspiration. We can conclude that Jesus' coming on the clouds signifies that he will emerge from among a group of reborn believers to become the leader of Christians, the Second Israel. Recall that when Jesus was asked about the place of his return, he replied, "Where the body is, there the eagles will be gathered together."[56] Jesus meant by this that he will return to the place where faithful believers have gathered, which basically signifies the same thing as the biblical prophecy that Christ will return on the clouds.

When we interpret the clouds metaphorically in this way, it is evident that at his First Coming Jesus himself symbolically came down from Heaven on the clouds. It is written, "The first man was from the earth, a man of dust; the second man is from heaven,"[57] and "No one has ascended into heaven but he who descended from heaven, the Son of man."[58] Even though Jesus was born on the earth, from the standpoint of the providence and with regard to his true value, he indeed came from Heaven. This is also the true meaning of the prophecy in Daniel[59] which foretold that Jesus would come on the clouds.

---

54. Rev. 17:15; Ps. 144:7
55. Heb. 12:1; cf. Ezek. 38:9
56. Luke 17:37
57. I Cor. 15:47
58. John 3:13
59. Dan. 7:13

2.4 Why Did Jesus Say that the Lord Will Come on the Clouds?

There are two reasons why Jesus prophesied that the Lord will return on the clouds. First, it was to prevent the delusions of antichrists from creating confusion among believers. If Jesus revealed plainly that he would return through a physical birth, then it would have been impossible to prevent false messiahs from causing great confusion. Since Jesus emerged as the Messiah from a humble background, anyone from any social stratum with a certain level of spirituality could claim to be his Second Advent and dazzle the world with a great delusion. Fortunately, since most Christians have expected Christ to return on the clouds and have fixed their gaze upon the sky, this turmoil has been largely avoided. Now, however, since the time is full, the truth that Christ will return through a physical birth must be revealed.

Second, it was to encourage Christians who were walking a difficult path of faith. There are other occasions when Jesus gave paradoxical words to encourage his followers to accomplish God's Will as rapidly as possible. For example, he said, "Truly, I say to you, you will not have gone through all the towns of Israel, before the Son of man comes."[60] This led his disciples to believe that the Second Advent would take place in the near future. When Jesus told Peter of his approaching martyrdom, Peter asked him what would become of the disciple John. Jesus replied, "If it is my will that he remain until I come, what is that to you?"[61] Jesus also said, "Truly, I say to you, there are some standing here who will not taste death before they see the Son of man coming in his kingdom."[62] These sayings led the disciples to think they would meet the returning Jesus in their lifetime.

The hope of Jesus' imminent return inflamed the zeal of his disciples and gave them the strength to overcome persecution by Judaism and the Roman Empire. Encouraged by the ardent hope of the Second Advent, they were filled with the Holy Spirit[63] and established the early Christian Church, even amidst great adversity. Jesus wanted to inspire and encourage his disciples, who would be carrying a heavy cross. For this reason, he prophesied that he would come on the clouds in the power and glory of God and accomplish everything at lightning speed.

---

60. Matt. 10:23
61. John 21:22
62. Matt. 16:28
63. Acts 2:1-4

Section 3
Where Will Christ Return?

If Christ comes again as a man born on the earth, he will certainly be born among a people who are chosen by God in accordance with His predestination. Where is the place God has chosen for Christ's return? Who are the people chosen to receive him?

3.1 Will Christ Return among the Jewish People?

Some Christians expect that Christ will come again among the Jewish people, based on several passages from the Bible: "And I heard the number of the sealed, a 144,000 sealed, out of every tribe of the sons of Israel,"[64] and "Truly, I say to you, you will not have gone through all the towns of Israel, before the Son of man comes."[65] However, to interpret these verses in this way is to misunderstand God's providence.

On this matter, Jesus uttered the parable of the vineyard:

> "Hear another parable. There was a householder who planted a vineyard, and set a hedge around it, and dug a wine press in it, and built a tower, and let it out to tenants, and went into another country. When the season of fruit drew near, he sent his servants to the tenants, to get his fruit; and the tenants took his servants and beat one, killed another, and stoned another. Again he sent other servants, more than the first; and they did the same to them. Afterward he sent his son to them, saying, 'They will respect my son.' But when the tenants saw the son, they said to themselves, 'This is the heir; come, let us kill him and have his inheritance.' And they took him and cast him out of the vineyard, and killed him. When therefore the owner of the vineyard comes, what will he do to those tenants?" They said to him, "He will put those wretches to a miserable death, and let out the vineyard to other tenants who will give him the fruits in their seasons." Jesus said to them . . . "Therefore I tell you, the kingdom of God will be taken away from you and given to a nation producing the fruits of it." —*Matt. 21:33-43*

In this parable, the householder represents God, the vineyard represents God's work, the tenants entrusted with the work represent the Jewish people, the servants represent the prophets, the son of the householder represents Jesus, and the other tenants who harvest the fruits represent some other nation which can receive Christ at the Second Advent and realize God's Will. By this parable, Jesus conveyed that he will not

---
64. Rev. 7:4
65. Matt. 10:23; cf. Matt. 16:28

come again to the people who persecuted him. God will take away the mission previously entrusted to them and give it to another people who can produce its fruits upon Christ's return.

Why, then, does the Bible seem to portray Christ as returning to Israel? To answer this question, we must first inquire as to the meaning of Israel. "Israel" means the one who has prevailed. Jacob received this name upon defeating the angel who wrestled with him at the ford of Jabbok.[66] Jacob wrestled with the angel to secure the position of Abel for the foundation of substance. By successfully securing the position of Abel and making the substantial offering, Jacob established the family foundation for the Messiah. His descendants, who inherited the responsibility for God's providence upon this foundation, are called Israel or the chosen people. The term "Israel" thus signifies the people of God who have triumphed through their faith and does not necessarily apply to everyone who comes out of Jacob's lineage. Thus, John the Baptist said to the Jews, "Do not presume to say to yourselves, 'We have Abraham as our father'; for I tell you, God is able from these stones to raise up children to Abraham."[67] Moreover, St. Paul said, "For he is not a real Jew who is one outwardly, nor is true circumcision something external and physical. He is a Jew who is one inwardly, and real circumcision is a matter of the heart, spiritual and not literal,"[68] and "not all who are descended from Israel belong to Israel."[69] They reproached those Jews who boasted that they were the chosen people based only on their lineal connection to Abraham, even though they were not in fact living according to the Will of God.

It can be said that the descendants of Jacob were Israel at the time of their departure from Egypt under Moses' leadership, but they no longer were when they turned against God in the wilderness. Therefore, God swept them away in the wilderness and led only the younger generation into Canaan; these God regarded as the true Israel. Of the descendants of Abraham who entered the land of Canaan, the ten tribes of the northern kingdom of Israel, who transgressed against God, perished because they lost their qualification as God's chosen people. Only the two tribes of the southern kingdom of Judah, who continued to uphold the Will of God, remained the chosen people who could eventually receive Jesus. Nevertheless, when they led Jesus to the cross, they also lost their qualification to be the people centrally responsible for God's providence.

---

66. Gen. 32:28
67. Matt. 3:9
68. Rom. 2:28-29
69. Rom. 9:6

Who became the chosen people after Jesus' crucifixion? They were none other than the Christians who inherited the faith of Abraham and took on the mission which Abraham's descendants did not complete. St. Paul wrote, "Through their trespass salvation has come to the Gentiles, so as to make Israel jealous,"[70] testifying that the center of God's providence of restoration had shifted from the Jews to the Gentiles.[71] Therefore, the chosen people who should lay the foundation for Christ at the Second Advent are not the descendants of Abraham, but rather the Christians who have inherited the faith of Abraham.

3.2 Christ Will Return to a Nation in the East

As Jesus explained through the parable of the vineyard,[72] when the Jewish people, like the tenants in the parable who killed the son of their master, led Jesus to the cross, they lost their providential mission. Which nation, then, will inherit the work of God and bear its fruits? The Bible suggests that this nation is in the East.

The Book of Revelation describes the opening of a scroll sealed with seven seals:

> And I saw in the right hand of him who was seated on the throne a scroll written within and on the back, sealed with seven seals; and I saw a strong angel proclaiming with a loud voice, "Who is worthy to open the scroll and break its seals?" And no one in heaven or on earth or under the earth was able to open the scroll or to look into it, and I wept much that no one was found worthy to open the scroll or to look into it. Then one of the elders said to me, "Weep not; lo, the Lion of the tribe of Judah, the Root of David, has conquered, so that he can open the scroll and its seven seals." —*Rev. 5:1-5*

The Lion of the tribe of Judah signifies Christ; it is he who will open the seven seals in the Last Days. After six of the seals are opened:

> Then I saw another angel ascend from the rising of the sun, with the seal of the living God, and he called with a loud voice . . . saying, "Do not harm the earth or the sea or the trees, till we have sealed the servants of our God upon their foreheads." And I heard the number of the sealed, a hundred and forty-four thousand. —*Rev. 7:2-4*

---

70. Rom. 11:11
71. Acts 13:46
72. Matt. 21:33-43

This indicates that the seal of the living God will be placed on the foreheads of the 144,000 in the East, where the sun rises. These chosen ones will accompany the Lamb at his return.[73] We can thus infer that the nation which will inherit the work of God and bear its fruit for the sake of the Second Advent is in the East. There Christ will be born and received by the 144,000 elect of God. Which among the nations of the East is chosen to receive the Lord?

3.3 The Nation in the East is Korea

Since ancient times, the nations in the East have traditionally been considered to be the three nations of Korea, Japan and China. Among them, Japan throughout its history has worshipped the sun goddess, Amaterasu-omi-kami. Japan entered the period of the Second Advent as a fascist nation and severely persecuted Korean Christianity.[74] China at the time of the Second Advent was a hotbed of communism and would become a communist nation. Thus, both nations belonged to Satan's side. Korea, then, is the nation in the East where Christ will return. Let us examine from the viewpoint of the Principle the various ways in which Korea has become qualified to receive Christ at the Second Advent. As the nation to which the Messiah returns, Korea had to meet the following qualifications.

3.3.1 A National Condition of Indemnity

For Korea to become a nation fit to receive the Messiah, it had to fulfill a national dispensation of forty for the separation of Satan for the cosmic-level restoration of Canaan. Why was Korea given this condition of indemnity? If Christ returns to Korea, the Korean people are destined to become the Third Israel. In the Old Testament Age, the descendants of Abraham who upheld God's Will and endured persecution in Egypt were the First Israel. The Christians, who were persecuted as heretics by the Jews as they honored the resurrected Jesus and carried on the providence of restoration, became the Second Israel. Christ at his return is likely to be similarly condemned as a heretic by the Christians of his time, in accordance with the prophecy that he will suffer and be rejected by his generation,[75] as was Noah in his days. If so, God will have to abandon the Christians who are persecuting Christ, just as He abandoned the Jews who rejected Jesus.[76] Then the Korean people, who will

---

73. Rev. 14:1
74. cf. Preparation 4.3.3
75. Luke 17:25
76. Matt. 7:23

attend the returning Christ and support him to complete the third chapter of God's providence, will become the Third Israel.

The First Israel suffered four hundred years in Egypt. This was to fulfill a dispensation of forty for the separation of Satan as required to set out on the national course to restore Canaan. The Second Israel had to prevail over the four hundred years of persecution in the Roman Empire to fulfill a dispensation of forty for the separation of Satan, as required to commence the worldwide course for the restoration of Canaan. As the Third Israel, the Korean people had also to suffer under a nation on Satan's side for a period which fulfills the number forty. Thereby, they could fulfill a dispensation of forty for the separation of Satan as required to commence the cosmic-level course to restore Canaan. This was the forty-year period during which Korea suffered untold hardships as a colony of Japan.

Korea was an early objective of Japan's imperialist policy. The Ŭlsa Treaty of Protection, concluded in 1905 by Hirohumi Ito of Japan and Wan-yong Lee of Korea,[77] imposed on Korea the status of a Japanese protectorate. All of Korea's diplomatic rights were given over to the care of the Foreign Affairs Ministry of Japan. Japan stationed a governor-general and appointed military officials in every district to control all of Korea's domestic affairs. In a short time, Japan had forced its will upon the Korean people, dictating their politics, diplomacy and economic affairs.

Japan forcibly annexed Korea in 1910. The Japanese committed atrocities against the Korean people, imprisoning and executing many patriots and depriving the people of their freedom. When a movement for independence broke out on March 1, 1919, the Japanese killed thousands of civilians in every part of the peninsula. At the time of the great Kanto earthquake in 1923, the Japanese made scapegoats of innocent Koreans living in Tokyo and massacred many of them. Meanwhile, many Koreans who could no longer endure Japanese oppression gave up their homes and fled to the wilderness of Manchuria in pursuit of freedom. There they endured untold hardships and gave their hearts and souls for the independence of their homeland. The Japanese military searched from village to village for these loyal Koreans. In some villages, they herded young and old alike into a building and set it on fire, burning them alive. Japan continued such tyranny right up to the day of its fall.

The Koreans who were killed in the March 1 independence movement and in the wilderness of Manchuria were predominantly Christians. Toward the end of its colonial rule, Japan embarked on a notorious policy to stamp out independent Christianity in Korea.

---

77. A pro-Japanese Minister of Education

Christians were forced to worship at Shinto shrines; those who did not comply were imprisoned or executed. When Emperor Hirohito of Japan surrendered at the end of World War II, the Korean people were finally liberated from their bondage.

The Korean people suffered for forty years, from the Ŭlsa Treaty of Protection of 1905 to their liberation in 1945. Their suffering paralleled the hardships of the First Israel in Egypt and the Second Israel in the Roman Empire. Korea's independence movement was led mainly by Christians, both at home and abroad; it was the Christians who suffered the most under Japan's tyranny.

3.3.2 God's Front Line and Satan's Front Line

In the Last Days, the world is divided into the democratic world and the communist world. Because he had given Adam the blessing of dominion, God had to give Satan a free rein to create through Adam's descendants an unprincipled world. God has had to follow in pursuit, working to restore the unprincipled world to His side. When Christ returns to restore this fallen world to its original state as created by God, he will surely work to save the communist world. No doubt the nation to which he returns will play the central role in this dispensation. Korea, the nation where Christ will return, is the place most dear to God and most abhorred by Satan. It is the front line for both God and Satan, a place where the forces of democracy and the forces of communism collide. This line of confrontation is Korea's thirty-eighth parallel, which was drawn to fulfill the providence of God.

At the point of confrontation between God and Satan, a sacrifice must be offered as the condition to determine the outcome of their struggle. The Korean people were this sacrifice, placed on this front line of battle to be offered for the sake of the restoration of the universe. Therefore, God divided the Korean nation, just as Abraham's sacrifices were supposed to be divided. This is the reason behind the division of Korea by the thirty-eighth parallel, which split it into two nations: one Cain-type and the other Abel-type.

The thirty-eighth parallel is the front line of battle between democracy and communism. At the same time, it is the front line of battle between God and Satan. The Korean War, which raged across the thirty-eighth parallel, was not merely a civil war; it was a conflict between the democratic world and the communist world. Moreover, it was a conflict between God and Satan. Because this war had worldwide significance for the accomplishment of the providence of restoration, the armed forces of the member states of the United Nations were mobilized for the first time. Even though the participating nations may not have understood this providential significance, they were acting in line with God's Will for the liberation of the spiritual fatherland.

At the fall of the first human ancestors, God's side and Satan's side parted ways from a single point. Life and death, good and evil, love and hate, happiness and sorrow, fortune and misfortune, all have divided from a single point and come into continual conflict with each other in human history. These divided realities consolidated separately into the Cain-type and Abel-type worlds, which eventually matured to form the democratic world and the communist world. When these two worlds came into global conflict, it was centered on the Korean peninsula. Religions, ideologies, political forces and economic systems all came into conflict and caused great confusion in Korean society, which then had worldwide impact. This is because phenomena which took place in the spirit world unfolded as physical reality in Korea, the central providential nation, and were magnified worldwide. This outbreak of social and ideological chaos was a clear sign that a new world order was fast approaching. As Jesus once said, "As soon as its branch becomes tender and puts forth its leaves, you know that summer is near."[78]

When the disciples asked Jesus of the place of his return, he said, "Where the body is, there the eagles will be gathered."[79] Eternal life and eternal death collide in Korea, the front line of the battle between God and Satan. Devils, symbolized by the eagles, gather in this land in search of the spiritually dead, while the returning Lord comes to this land in search of the people of abundant life.

3.3.3 THE OBJECT PARTNER OF GOD'S HEART

To become the object partners of God's Heart, we must first walk a path of blood, sweat and tears. Ever since human beings fell under the dominion of Satan and came to oppose God, God has been grieving with the heart of a parent who lost his children. God has labored continually in the sinful world to save immoral and wretched human beings who are nonetheless His children. Moreover, in His efforts to recover His rebellious children, time and time again God had to let the most righteous and beloved ones be sacrificed to the satanic world, even delivering Jesus, His only begotten Son, to the cross. God has been

---

78. Matt. 24:32
79. Luke 17:37

grieving in this way every day since the human Fall.[80] Accordingly, an individual, family or nation who is fighting the satanic world for the sake of God's Will cannot avoid the path of blood, sweat and tears. How can we, as loyal and faithful children, be comfortable and complacent and still expect to remain the object partners of our Heavenly Father, who is suffering in deep agony?

The nation which can receive the Messiah should become the object partner of God's Heart by demonstrating filial piety. That is why it must walk a path of blood, sweat and tears. Both the First Israel and the Second Israel walked a path of suffering. The Korean people, the Third Israel, have done likewise. Their miserable history was the path required of the chosen people of God. One can never be certain what great blessings such a path of affliction may eventually bring.

The nation qualified to stand as the object partner of God's Heart must be a people of goodness. The Korean people, a homogeneous race with a four-thousand-year history, rarely invaded other nations. Even during the Kokuryo and Silla periods, when they boasted impressive military might, they used their forces only to thwart invaders. Considering that a fundamental nature of Satan is to aggressively encroach upon others, it is clear that the Korean people are qualified to stand on God's side. God's strategy is to claim victory after His side has been attacked first. Although countless prophets and saints have been sacrificed in the course of history, and even Jesus died on the cross, time and again God claimed victory in the end. Although Satan's side was the aggressor in the First and Second World Wars, in the end victory was won by the nations on God's side. Similarly, the Korean people have been invaded numerous times by foreign powers. God's true intention in having them endure these tribulations was to have them stand on His side and secure the final victory.

The Korean people are by nature endowed with a religious character. Their religious inclination has led them to strive always for that which transcends physical reality and is of more profound value. From ancient times, when their culture was still primitive, the Korean people have evinced a strong desire to worship God. They did not have a high regard for religions which superstitiously deified nature or strove for happiness in temporal life. They have always revered the virtues of loyalty, filial piety and chastity. Their fondness for folk tales which express these virtues, such as "The Tale of Shim-ch'ŏng" and "The Tale of Ch'unhyang," stems from this powerful underpinning of their culture.

---

80. Gen. 6:6

3.3.4 Messianic Prophecies

The Korean people have long cherished a messianic hope, nurtured by the clear testimonies of their prophets. The First Israel believed in the testimonies of its prophets[81] that the Messiah would come as their king, establish the Kingdom and bring them salvation. The Second Israel was able to endure an arduous path of faith due in part to their hope in the return of Christ. Similarly, the Korean people, the Third Israel, have believed in the prophecy that the Righteous King will appear and found a glorious and everlasting kingdom in their land. Clinging to this hope, they found the strength to endure their afflictions. This messianic idea among the Korean people was revealed through the *Chŏnggamnok,* a book of prophecy written in the fourteenth century at the beginning of the Yi dynasty.

Because this prophecy foretold that a new king would emerge, the ruling class tried to suppress it. The Japanese colonial regime tried to stamp out this notion by burning the book and oppressing its believers. After Christianity became widely accepted, the idea was ridiculed as superstition. Nevertheless, this messianic hope still lives on, deeply ingrained in the soul of the Korean people. The hoped-for Righteous King foretold in the *Chŏnggamnok* has the appellation Chŏngdoryŏng (the one who comes with the true Word of God). In fact, this is a Korean prophecy of the Christ who is to return to Korea. Even before the introduction of Christianity to Korea, God had revealed through the *Chŏnggamnok* that the Messiah would come to that land. Today, scholars affirm that many passages of this book of prophecy coincide with the prophecies in the Bible.

Furthermore, among the faithful of every religion in Korea are those who have received revelations that the founders of their religions will return to Korea. We learned through our study of the progress of cultural spheres[82] that all religions are converging toward one religion. God's desire is for Christianity of the Last Days to become this final religion which can assume the responsibility of completing the goals of the many religions in history. The returning Christ, who comes as the center of Christianity, will attain the purposes which the founders of religions strove to accomplish. Therefore, with respect to his mission, Christ at his return may be regarded as the second coming of the founder of every religion.[83] When the second comings of the founders of the vari-

---

81. Mal. 4:2-5; Isa. 60:1-22
82. cf. Eschatology 4.2
83. cf. Resurrection 2.4

ous religions appear in Korea in fulfillment of the diverse revelations, they will not come as different individuals. One person, Christ at the Second Advent, will come as the fulfillment of all these revelations. The Lord whose coming has been revealed to believers in various religions, including the Maitreya Buddha in Buddhism, the True Man in Confucianism, the returning Ch'oe Su-un who founded the religion of Ch'ŏndogyo, and the coming of Chŏngdoryŏng in the *Chŏnggamnok*, will be none other than Christ at the Second Advent.

Finally, we witness revelations and signs being given to spiritually attuned Christians testifying to the Second Coming of Christ in Korea; they are sprouting in profusion like mushrooms after a rain. God's promise that He will pour out His spirit upon all flesh[84] is being fulfilled among the Korean people. As devout Christians make contact with spirits from various levels of the spirit world, from the lower realms to Paradise, many are receiving clear revelations that the Lord will come to Korea. However, the current leadership of the Korean Christian churches is fast asleep. Spiritually ignorant, they go about their ministries oblivious to these signs of the times. This is similar to what happened in Jesus' time. The priests, rabbis and scribes, who should have been the first to recognize the birth of the Messiah, remained entirely ignorant of it because they were spiritually blind. The astrologers and shepherds who received revelations were the ones who knew of Jesus' birth.

Jesus said, "I thank thee, Father, Lord of heaven and earth, that thou hast hidden these things from the wise and understanding, and revealed them to babes."[85] He was lamenting over the spiritual ignorance of the Jewish leadership of his time, while on the other hand, he was grateful that God bestowed grace upon pure and uneducated believers by revealing His providence to them. In today's Korean Christianity, at a time parallel to Jesus' day, similar phenomena are taking place, albeit in more complex ways. Through pure and innocent lay believers, God has been revealing many heavenly secrets concerning the Last Days. However, because they would be chastised as heretics if they were to proclaim them in public, they are keeping these truths to themselves. Meanwhile, like the priests, rabbis and scribes of Jesus' time, many Christian clergy take pride in their knowledge of the Bible and their ability to interpret it. They take pleasure in the reverence they receive from their followers; they are content to carry on the imposing duties of their offices; yet, to God's grief, they are entirely ignorant of God's providence in the Last Days.

---

84. Acts 2:17
85. Matt. 11:25

3.3.5 THE CULMINATION OF ALL CIVILIZATIONS

Spiritual and material civilization, built upon religion and science—the quests to overcome the two aspects of human ignorance—must be brought into harmony. Only then can we resolve the fundamental problems of human life and realize the world of God's ideal.[86] In the world Christ comes to realize, science will be highly developed. It will be a society with the highest level of civilization, one in which all civilizations which have developed through the vertical course of providential history will be restored horizontally under the leadership of the Lord. Therefore, the spiritual and material aspects of civilization developing from religion and science, which have flourished all over the world, will be embraced and harmonized in Korea as guided by the new truth. Then they will bear fruit in the ideal world of God's deepest desire.

First, the essences of all civilizations which developed on the land should bear fruit in Korea. The ancient continental civilizations which arose in Egypt and Mesopotamia bequeathed their fruits to the peninsular civilizations of Greece, Rome and Iberia, and thence to the island civilization of Great Britain. This island civilization passed on its culture to the United States, a continental civilization. Then the direction was reversed, with the United States passing on its culture to the island civilization of Japan. Now these fruits are to be harvested in the peninsular civilization of Korea, where Christ is to be born.

Next, the essences of civilizations born on the shores of rivers and seas should bear fruit in the Pacific civilization to which Korea belongs. The river civilizations which arose on the shores of the Nile, Tigris and Euphrates Rivers passed on their cultures to the civilizations in the vicinity of the Mediterranean Sea: Greece, Rome, Spain and Portugal. These bequeathed their fruits to the civilizations on the Atlantic Ocean: notably, Great Britain and the United States. All these fruits will be harvested in the civilization of the Pacific Ocean, which links together the United States, Japan and Korea.

Last, civilizations born out of different climate zones should bear fruit in Korea. In the round of the seasons, living things begin their life and multiplication in spring, flourish in summer, bear fruit in autumn, and store their reserves in winter. The cycle of spring, summer, autumn and winter is repeated not only year by year, but also day by day: morning corresponds to spring, afternoon to summer, evening to autumn, and night to winter. The four phases of human life—childhood, youth, middle age, and old age—also fit this pattern. Human history, too, unfolds

---

86. cf. Eschatology 5.1

according to the seasons, because an aspect of God's Principle underlying His creation is the harmonious, seasonal circle of life.

God created Adam and Eve in the springtime of human history. Accordingly, history was supposed to begin from the temperate-zone civilization of Eden. Then, in its summer season, it should have moved to a tropical civilization; in autumn, to a cool-zone civilization; and it should have reached its culmination in a frigid-zone civilization analogous to the winter season. However, due to the Fall, human beings were degraded to the level of savages. Instead of building a temperate-zone civilization, they prematurely came to live in the tropical zones as primitive men. On the continent of Africa, they built the tropic-zone civilization of Egypt. This continental civilization passed on its culture to the peninsulas and islands where cool-zone civilizations developed. They bequeathed their fruits to the frigid-zone civilization of the Soviet Union. Now this current is to culminate in the formation of the temperate-zone civilization of the new Eden. This should certainly take place in Korea, where all civilizations are to bear fruit.

SECTION 4

PARALLELS BETWEEN JESUS' DAY AND TODAY

The period of the Second Advent is parallel to the time of Jesus. The situations unfolding in Christianity today are similar to those which took place in Judaism at Jesus' time. Let us examine some of these parallels.

Today's Christianity, like the Judaism of Jesus' day, adheres too rigidly to institutional authority and ceremonies, while internally it is corrupt. At the time of Jesus, many priests and scribes had become enslaved to ritualism and legalism, and their spiritual life was corrupt. Therefore, Jews with sincere faith flocked to Jesus, that accused heretic, to slake their spiritual thirst. Similarly, in today's Christianity, many leading clergymen and priests are captive to their authorities and enamored of their rituals while their spirits grow dimmer each day. Hence, devout Christians are wandering about the mountains and plains in search of the true path. They are seeking new leaders who can guide them out of this spiritual wilderness and show them the way to the inner light.

Christian leaders today, like the Jewish leaders of Jesus day, will probably be the first to persecute Christ at the Second Advent. Jesus came to found a new era which would fulfill the words of the Old Testament proclaimed by the prophets. He did not limit himself to repeating the words of the Old Testament, but gave new words of truth fit for the new era. The Jewish priests and scribes criticized Jesus' words and deeds based on their narrow understanding of the Old Testament Scriptures. Their mistaken judgment led them to deliver Jesus to the cross.

Similarly, the purpose of Christ at the Second Advent is to build a new heaven and a new earth[87] upon the foundation of the spiritual salvation which had been laid by Christianity in the New Testament Age. When he returns, he will not merely repeat the words of the New Testament given two thousand years ago, but will surely add new words of truth necessary for the founding of a new heaven and a new earth. However, those Christians of today whose minds are narrowly attached to the letter of the New Testament will criticize the words and deeds of Christ at his return based on their narrow understanding of the Scriptures. Therefore, it can be expected that they will brand the Lord a heretic and persecute him. This is why Jesus foretold that at the Second Advent, Christ would first suffer many things and be rejected by his generation.[88]

When people receive revelations about Christ at the Second Advent or hear his words, they will respond in ways similar to the way the Jews in Jesus' day responded. God did not reveal the news of the birth of Jesus to the priests and scribes, but to gentile astrologers and pure-hearted shepherds. This is like the case of a father who, due to the ignorance of his own children, has to confide in his step-child. Likewise, God may well reveal the news of the return of Christ first to lay people, to marginal spiritual groups and churches which the mainstream treats with disdain, or to conscientious non-believers. Only later may the news reach the mainstream Christian clergy who are unthinkingly keeping to their conventional ways of faith. In Jesus' day, those who sincerely received the Gospel were not the Jewish leaders, but simple common folk and Gentiles. Likewise, at Christ's return, simple Christians and non-Christians will accept the Lord's words before the Christian leadership, which regards itself as God's elect. This is the meaning of Jesus' parable of the marriage feast. When the invited guests, the leading men of the community, declined the king's invitation:

> He said to his servants, "The wedding is ready, but those invited were not worthy. Go therefore to the thoroughfares, and invite to the marriage feast as many as you find." And those servants went out into the streets and gathered all whom they found, both bad and good; so the wedding hall was filled with guests. —*Matt. 22:8-10*

---

87. Rev. 21:1-4
88. Luke 17:25

Both in Jesus' day and at the Second Advent, many devout believers who set out on the path of faith with the hope of entering Heaven may actually find themselves in hell. In Jesus' day, because the priests and scribes had the responsibility to guide God's chosen people, they should have been the first to recognize that the Messiah had come and should have led the Jewish people to him. To help them fulfill their mission, Jesus took the initiative; he visited the Temple and taught them the Gospel before teaching anyone else.[89] However, when they did not receive him, Jesus had no choice but to search the shores of Galilee and take disciples from among the fishermen there. He had to minister to the dregs of society and associate with sinners, tax collectors and prostitutes. Eventually, the priests and scribes persecuted him to the point where he had to accept the fate of the cross. They committed this murder, believing that they had done a righteous deed by eliminating a dangerous heretic and blasphemer. Then they continued on with their customary clerical duties for the rest of their lives, reciting the Holy Scriptures, paying their tithes, and making sacrifices at the Temple, all with the assurance that they were headed toward Heaven. Instead, after they passed on, they found themselves most unexpectedly in hell. Ironically, the very path upon which they had set out to reach Heaven had led them astray.

Recognizing that similar events may occur in the Last Days, each of us should seriously examine ourselves. Many Christians today are dashing on a path which they believe leads to Heaven. Yet if they take a wrong step, their path may actually lead them to hell. This is why Jesus once said that he will rebuke many devout believers in the Last Days, even those whose dedication is so strong that they can cast out demons and perform miracles in his name: "I never knew you; depart from me, you evildoers."[90]

In truth, no one faces a more precarious situation than believers who live in such a transition period of history as exists today. No matter how much faith we have demonstrated in our lives, if we, like the Jewish leaders of Jesus' day, take the wrong step of turning against the returning Christ, all our efforts will have been in vain. Of these people, Daniel had said, "Many shall purify themselves, and make themselves white, and be refined; but the wicked shall do wickedly; and none of the wicked shall understand; but those who are wise shall understand."[91]

---

89. Luke 2:42-47
90. Matt. 7:23
91. Dan. 12:10

Section 5

The Chaotic Profusion of Languages and the Necessity for Their Unification

If human beings had not fallen, we would have formed one global family, which may be likened to a body whose members are all interlinked with each other with God as their head. Then all would have shared a common language; there never would have risen a profusion of tongues unintelligible to one another. The reason various languages arose and prevented free communication between peoples is that, once their vertical relationship with God was severed at the Fall, all horizontal relationships between people were also cut off. Humanity then splintered, dispersed to different geographical locations, and formed isolated communities.

There is also a biblical account giving spiritual insight into the confusion of languages. This is the story of the Tower of Babel.[92] Noah's descendants had shared a common language. One day, the descendants of Noah's second son Ham, who had sinned against God, built the Tower of Babel to exalt themselves even above God, thus furthering the will of Satan. When the descendants of Shem and Japheth, who stood on God's side, helped with the construction, God brought such confusion to their languages that they could no longer communicate with each other to further the will of Satan.

As children of the same parents, having the same feelings of joy, anger, sorrow and pleasure, if we cannot share our deepest feelings with one another because we speak different languages, it is the greatest of misfortunes. Our languages therefore must be unified if we are to realize the ideal world of one global family which can honor Christ at the Second Advent as our True Parent. As expressed in the account of the building of the Tower of Babel, chaos was brought to our languages when we exalted the will of Satan. The principle of restoration through indemnity requires that we participate in the construction of God's tower and the glorification of God's Will as the way to unify all languages.

Based upon which language will all languages be unified? The answer to this question is obvious. Children should learn the language of their parents. If Christ does indeed return to the land of Korea, then he will certainly use the Korean language, which will then become the mother tongue for all humanity. Eventually, all people should speak the

---
92. Gen. 11:1-9

True Parents' language as their mother tongue. All of humanity will become one people and use one language, thus establishing one global nation under God.

Index

Aaron, 230, 238-239, 244-246, 256, 261, 281
Abel, 156, 160-161, 176, 180, 182, 190-203, 209-214, 217-221, 229, 232-236, 241, 265, 275-276, 292, 301, 350-353, 367, 377, 379
  position of, 161, 192-194, 203, 205, 207, 217-219, 221, 225, 227, 231, 233, 235, 237, 241, 253, 268, 270, 276, 279-280, 318-322, 397
Abel-type democracy, 360-361, 371
Abel-type view of life, 356-357, 359-361, 368-369, 371-372, 377-378
Abimelech of Gerar, 214
Abraham, 42, 62-63, 107, 114, 117, 139, 149, 156, 167-168, 178, 180, 182-186, 199, 201, 206-223, 230, 232, 234, 242, 247, 264, 275, 284, 291-295, 299-305, 307, 314-316, 319-320, 323, 330, 332, 389, 397-399, 401
Abraham's family, 63, 182, 185, 206, 212, 214-215, 220-221, 230, 294, 302, 304
absolute, 2, 7, 21, 36-37, 41, 50, 67, 70-71, 77, 81, 113, 154-161, 197, 199, 215, 247, 257, 259, 265, 286-287, 290
accusation, 266
Adam, 16, 19, 30, 32, 34, 38-39, 41-44, 47, 53-57, 59, 63-69, 72-75, 80-81, 87-88, 94, 96, 98, 101, 118, 120, 135-137, 139, 141-143, 156-158, 161, 163, 165-166, 169-172, 175-176, 178-186, 189-200, 202-211, 213-214, 218-222, 232-234, 239, 245, 249, 255, 266, 274-275, 282-284, 287, 291-296, 298-303, 326, 350-351, 353, 369, 373-374, 379, 382, 391, 401, 407
  first, 178, 202
  perfect, 44, 47, 55, 57, 64-65, 88, 165, 195, 202, 255, 270, 274, 374, 391
  restored, 207, 245, 249, 255, 270
  second, 156, 171-172, 178, 199, 202-203, 239, 249, 255, 266, 274, 287, 292, 373-374
  third, 202-203
Adam's family, 139, 161, 176, 181, 189-190, 192, 194-198, 200, 203-205, 208-209, 211, 214, 219-221, 232, 284, 292-294, 301, 351, 353, 379
adopted children, 284-285, 390
Africa, 407
age of image parallels, 186, 290, 302, 305, 307
age of substantial parallels, 187, 290, 307-308
age of symbolic parallels, 186, 290, 302-303, 305-307
Age of the Prolongation of the Providence for Restoration, 185, 290, 307-310, 313-314, 327, 332-333, 382
Age of the Providence of Restoration, 138, 185, 231-233, 245, 290-291, 302-303, 307-310, 313-314, 326-327, 329, 332-333, 382
Age of the Providence to Lay the Foundation of Restoration, 185, 232-233, 245, 290-291, 302-303
Alexander V, 324
all things, 18, 20-21, 28-30, 34, 37, 39, 41, 43-47, 77-78, 81, 96, 154, 167-168, 171, 180, 187, 194-196, 203, 208, 240-241, 269, 274, 292, 382 -see also natural world
Allied Powers, 368, 370, 372
altar, 210, 213-214, 246, 262, 293, 322, 372, 389
Amalekites, 100, 244, 266
Amaterasu-omi-kami, 399
America, 85, 340, 357
American Revolution, 362
Amos, 322
angel, 44, 48, 58-64, 67-69, 71, 73, 75-76, 114, 117-118, 120, 125, 147, 168, 178, 186, 215, 219, 222, 227, 241, 266, 269, 274-275, 349, 373, 381, 383, 385-386, 388-389, 397-398
anger, 245, 249, 254-255, 257, 272, 410
animals, 16, 18, 22, 29, 31, 35, 40, 42, 102, 200, 223
Anna, 114, 381
antichrist, 142, 366, 384, 388, 395
antitype, 369-370, 374-375, 378, 382
anxiety, 48, 71, 106, 108, 137
apostle, 119, 127, 315-316, 352, 384, 391
Aquinas, Thomas, 322, 355
Archangel, 63-68, 72-73, 79, 93, 186, 190-194, 197, 201, 209, 227-228, 235, 239, 284, 373
  position of, 63, 65, 319, 338
Ark of the Covenant, 180, 192, 244-248, 253, 257, 261, 263-264, 266, 269, 276, 280-281, 316
artist, 16, 33, 35
Assyria, 100, 306, 309, 322, 332
atheism, 2, 355, 359
Atlantic Ocean, 406
atom, 16, 18, 22, 27, 29, 365
attendance, 125,129, 140, 146, 151, 158, 187, 247, 275, 325, 400
attitude, 54, 103, 106, 130-131, 257
atonement, 11, 246
Augustine, 319, 337
Austria, 353, 368-369, 373
authority, 62, 70-71, 78, 105, 178, 228, 259, 317, 324-325, 336, 339, 341, 352, 371, 407
Avignon, 297, 309, 324-325, 339
Axis Powers, 372

Baal, 123, 267, 322
Babylon, 297, 305-306, 309, 322-325, 331, 350
Babylonian exile, 306, 326
Bacon, Francis, 354
baptism, 177, 270, 316
Basel, Council of, 325
beauty, 10, 27, 29-30, 35, 37-39, 44-45, 102, 153, 160
Beelzebul, 107, 116, 125
belief, 6, 11, 42, 53, 115, 120, 123, 130, 166, 355, 384, 394
Bethlehem, 384, 386
Bible, 8, 10-11, 16, 40-42, 53-55, 79, 87-94, 104-105,

413

107, 114, 119-122, 130-133, 142-147, 153-154, 165-167, 181, 225, 231, 243, 284, 297, 335, 341, 352, 355, 357, 383-385, 394, 398, 404-405
birthright, 161, 191, 218-219, 222, 227, 295, 302, 305
bishops, 308, 317-319, 324-325, 331, 337, 348, 372
blessing, 59, 62-63, 81, 87, 141, 161, 179, 207, 219, 228-229, 286, 302, 305-306, 320, 338, 369, 391, 401, 403
  first, 33-34, 39, 96-98, 179, 192, 273, 275, 370, 376
  second, 34, 39, 67, 97-99, 274-275, 374-375
  third, 34-36, 39, 101-102, 275, 379
  three, 32-33, 39, 83, 88-89, 96, 171-172, 195, 199, 272, 276, 366-367, 369-370, 373-375, 378
blood of death, 211-212, 240
blood relationship, 72, 329 -see also lineage
body, 2-6, 17-19, 23, 26-37, 39, 42, 45-49, 58, 73, 80-81, 118-119, 130, 136-137, 145, 149, 163-164, 167, 169, 177, 193-194, 203-205, 228, 231, 246, 256-258, 267, 273, 275, 278, 281, 296, 334, 342, 349, 354, 361-363, 384, 389-394, 402, 410
Bohemia, 352
bondage, 39, 51, 88, 200, 243, 295, 366, 401
Boniface VIII, 324
Book of Changes, 20-21
brain, 81, 361-363
Bride, 172, 239, 244-249, 261, 272, 284
  of Jesus, 239, 245, 247-248, 261
  of Christ, 245
brides, 122, 170, 210, 274
bronze serpent, 116-117, 258, 266
Buddha, 3, 149-150, 164, 327, 405
Buddhism, 85, 150, 327, 405
butterfly, 135

Cain, 156, 160-161, 176, 180, 182, 190-194, 196-198, 201, 203, 209-220, 229, 233-237, 241, 265, 275-276, 280, 292, 301, 319, 321, 338, 350-353, 367, 377, 379
Cain-type democracy, 359-360
Cain-type view of life, 354-356, 358-360, 368-369, 372, 376
Caleb, 251-252, 256, 259, 264-265, 317
Caliphate, 85, 323
Calvin, John, 161, 353
Canaan, 42, 100, 116, 120, 158, 178, 191, 201, 207-208, 219-222, 227-243, 246, 283, 292-298, 302, 307, 316-318, 320, 326, 330, 368, 397
  course to restore, 215, 226-228, 231, 234, 243, 246, 249, 254, 257-263, 267-272, 275, 283, 292, 295, 297-298, 304, 306, 320, 366, 399-400
Canaanites, 237, 251, 368
Capitalism, 339, 341, 367
Carolingian, 85, 308-309, 336-337, 350, 358
Catholic, 337, 342, 350, 352-353, 360, 372
cause and result, 5, 17, 19-20, 22, 33
central figure, 107, 150, 157, 159, 178, 180, 190, 196-199, 203, 206, 217-221, 225, 229-234, 267, 283, 285, 290-295, 299-301, 313, 316, 319-320
central nation, 157, 402
Central Powers, 369
Ch'ondogyo, 405
Charlemagne, 295, 308, 319, 321-322, 337-338
Charles I, 360
Charles II, 360

Charles Martel, 337
cherubim, 55, 247, 281
child, 1, 11, 113, 117, 125, 169, 221, 231-235, 268-269, 276, 279, 284, 384-385, 390-391
China, 84-85, 399
Chongdoryong, 150, 404-405
Chonggamnok, 404-405
chosen people, 61, 90, 111, 114, 116-117, 121, 158-159, 178, 182, 202, 216, 222, 228, 234, 240, 267, 278, 284, 314-315, 317, 322, 327, 390, 396-398, 403, 409
Christ, 11, 24, 44, 56, 61-62, 70-72, 79, 88, 90-99, 103, 106, 111, 114, 119, 121, 125, 127, 137, 140-146, 150-154, 166, 169-172, 184-187, 202-203, 244-245, 255-256, 260, 263, 273, 278, 281-286, 292, 310, 316, 319, 321-328, 333, 340-343, 350-353, 357, 361-366, 370-371, 375, 378, 382-410 -see also Jesus, Second Advent, cross, Bride
Christian empire, 295, 308-309, 318-323, 338, 340-341, 358
Christianity, 2, 4-5, 10-11, 24, 53, 85-86, 99, 105, 113, 147, 150-151, 178, 185, 286, 307-308, 314-317, 323-325, 332-341, 350, 352, 355, 359, 364, 368-372, 399-400, 404-408
Christians, 5, 7, 11, 53-56, 79, 89-90, 95-96, 107, 114, 117-123, 140, 143, 145, 167, 183, 234, 273, 278, 281-286, 307, 314-319, 326-327, 342, 352, 360-361, 367, 369, 372, 375, 384-396, 398-401, 405-409
church, 134, 169, 308, 317-318, 321-322, 325-326, 337-338, 348-349, 352-353, 357, 360, 362, 372, 390, 395
circular motion, 26-27, 32
circumcision, 61, 240, 315, 397
civilization, 61, 327-328, 337, 340, 349-350, 406-407
clan society, 100, 286, 330-331, 335-336, 379
Clement V, 309, 324
Clement VII, 324
clouds, 79, 94, 124, 248, 383-389, 391-395
cognition, 103-104, 356
collective sin, 72, 117
colonies, 8, 87, 340-341, 363-364, 367, 377
commandment, 43, 65-67, 75, 120, 154, 158, 179, 208, 227, 260
common base, 22-24, 26-27, 38, 64-67, 69, 72, 76, 145, 147, 204
communism, 5, 8, 87, 341-343, 355, 370, 375, 399, 401
communist world, 85-87, 100, 329, 343, 353, 355, 358-360, 364-365, 369, 373-379, 382, 399, 401-402
competition, 340, 342, 363
Completed Testament, 140, 184-185
Completed Testament Age, 184, 210, 349
completion stage, 41, 49, 184, 210, 212, 214, 290, 297, 378
conciliar movement, 325
condition-see indemnity condition; object for the condition
conflict, 8, 57, 70-71, 84, 86-88, 98-100, 107, 142-143, 322, 324, 328-330, 334, 338, 347, 353, 357, 363, 365-367, 376-378, 401-402
Confucianism, 85, 327, 405
Confucius, 149, 327
conscience, 1, 9, 23, 50-51, 64-65, 108, 352, 356, 368

conscientious people, 50, 147, 151, 176, 408
Constance, Council of, 324-325
Constantine, 307, 316, 350
Constantinople, 319
contradiction, 2, 6-7
corporeal world, 45-46, 391
cosmos, 30, 34, 45-47, 155, 164-166, 199-201, 204, 209, 246, 286
course to restore Canaan-see Canaan
covenant, 180, 192, 244-248, 253, 257, 261, 263-264, 266, 269, 276, 280-281, 305, 309, 316, 322, 360
creativity, 27
creatorship, 44, 67, 78
Crete, 349
crime, 58-59, 61, 69, 74, 88, 362
Cromwell, Oliver, 360
cross, 11, 44, 90, 105, 112-119, 121-123, 130, 140-146, 158, 168, 177-178, 183, 187, 202, 229, 236, 249, 258, 269, 278, 285, 287, 315, 374, 392, 395-398, 402-403, 408-409 -see also Jesus
Crusades, 323-324, 339, 351, 358
cultural spheres, 84-86, 88, 98-99, 102, 150, 332
culture, 8, 10, 318, 327, 349, 352, 354, 403, 406-407
Cyrus, 306, 324

D'Alembert, Jean Le Rond, 359
Daniel, 324, 384-385, 409
David, 106, 117, 201, 292, 303, 305, 308, 320, 322, 384, 398
Day of Atonement, 246
death, 1, 3, 6-8, 49-50, 54, 92-93, 96, 113-119, 125, 133-137, 139-140, 146, 166, 211-212, 216, 228-231, 240-241, 258, 260, 277, 283, 315, 321, 324, 384, 386, 389, 395-396, 402
Declaration of Rights, 360
Declaration of the Rights of Man, 359, 361
deism, 355
democracy, 8, 86-87, 100, 332, 340-342, 358-362, 364, 367-368, 370-372, 375, 377-378, 401
  Cain-type, 359-360
  Abel-type, 359-360
democratic, 8, 86-87, 97, 100, 282-283, 328, 335, 340-341, 343, 353, 357-359, 361, 364-365, 367, 369-370, 372-378, 401-402
democratic world, 8, 86, 100, 353, 357-359, 361, 364-365, 369-370, 373-378, 401-402
Descartes, Rene, 354
desires, 1-3, 6, 36-37, 48-49, 51, 53, 59-64, 70-76, 81, 84, 89, 121-122, 191, 194, 208, 268, 319, 328, 341-342, 351, 353, 348, 359-362, 376, 388, 403-406
Devil, 57, 59, 68-69, 147, 228, 244, 284
devils, 12, 390, 402
dialectical materialism, 343, 355, 377 -see also historical materialism
Diderot, Denis, 359
direct dominion, 44-45, 67, 82, 136, 296, 298
disciples, 12, 42, 66, 83-84, 96, 105, 108, 112, 114, 118, 122-129, 144-145, 168, 238, 262, 277-280, 283-286, 293, 315, 336, 367, 390-391, 395, 402, 409
dispensation of forty for the separation of Satan, 232, 234-235, 237, 250-251, 268, 271, 275-276, 279, 320-321, 399-400
dispensation to start, 235, 237, 241-242, 253-254, 256, 259, 261, 268-269, 276, 280, 283, 285

divided kingdoms, 304-305, 308-309, 321-323
divine nature, 15-16, 34, 80, 82-83, 112-113, 164-167
divine spirit, 49, 140-141, 144, 146, 150, 168
doctrines, 6, 11, 70, 107-108, 131, 150, 154, 169, 357
Dominic, 322
dominion, 29-30, 32, 35, 39, 43-44, 62, 67, 73, 77-78, 81, 88, 101-102, 134, 136, 142, 175, 193, 195, 209, 212, 218-222, 240, 266, 272-275, 281, 322, 332-333, 350, 363, 366, 369, 374, 377-379, 401-402
dove, 42, 178, 201-203, 208-212, 297-298, 301, 389
dual characteristics, 15-22, 24-34, 38, 41, 45, 47-48, 163-165, 170-172, 283, 294, 296, 298, 348
dual purposes, 33

eagles, 389, 394, 402
East Asian philosophy, 20-21
Eastern Orthodoxy, 350
economy, 317, 319, 327, 331, 333-336, 338-343, 347, 357-358, 364
Eden, 55-58, 87-88, 165-166, 234, 247, 255, 407
Edict of Milan, 350
Egypt, 94, 120, 182, 191, 201, 208-222, 228-251, 254-269, 275, 299-308, 315-320, 323, 326-327, 330-332, 366, 397, 399-401, 406-407
electricity, 365
elements, 16, 18, 22, 27, 29-30, 35, 46-49, 61, 64-65, 70, 79, 91, 98, 144, 165, 167
Eli, 317
Elijah, 46, 93, 122-124, 126-128, 130, 145, 149, 201, 267, 270, 322, 384-387
Elisha, 322
embodiment, 28, 197, 295-299
Emmaus, 279
emotion, 8, 29, 37
emperors, 321, 323-324, 338, 350, 358
empiricism, 354-356
energy, 18, 21-22, 24, 28-29, 31
Engels, Friedrich, 355
engraft, 55-56, 165, 169, 276-280, 284-285, 391-392
Enlightenment, 3, 327, 355, 358-359, 361, 364
environment, 3, 29, 76, 81, 102, 220, 282, 327-328, 341, 348-349, 351, 363, 365
envy, 72-73
Ephraim and Manasseh, 192
equal, 5, 8, 78, 87, 97, 125, 161, 166, 177, 341
equality, 97, 359
Esau, 153, 160-161, 192, 217-219, 222, 227, 295, 302, 305
eternal life, 6, 23, 36, 48, 92, 115, 134-136, 154, 166, 255, 402
ethics, 100, 102, 327
Euphrates, 406
Europe, 4, 85, 317, 319, 322, 324, 326, 331, 333-340, 343, 348-349, 352-353, 358, 360, 364
Eve, 16, 19, 30, 32, 34, 38-42, 44, 53-69, 72-76, 80-81, 87, 94-98, 101, 136-137, 141-143, 156-158, 163, 169-176, 186, 190-193, 195, 197, 201, 204, 209, 229, 239, 245, 249, 258, 283, 295-299, 310, 325, 373, 407
evil mind, 1-2, 7, 49, 51, 53, 84, 328-329
evil spirits, 69, 71, 147-148, 151
evolution, 85
exile; Israel, 304-306, 309, 323, 325
  papal, 309, 323-324, 326

Exodus, 42, 257, 261, 275, 303, 319
external form, 17-21, 27-29, 31-37, 41, 47, 49-50, 74, 167, 348
Ezekiel, 324
Ezra, 306, 325-326

failure, 56, 73, 111, 116, 130, 156, 178, 189-190, 197, 203-207, 212-216, 223, 236-237, 241, 252-253, 263, 269, 277-278, 294, 300-301, 320, 376, 379
faith, 9, 23, 44, 54, 66-67, 75, 89-90, 95, 112-113, 116-122, 125-126, 131, 133, 138-146, 150, 157, 163, 172, 177, 184, 186, 192, 199, 206-209, 213-216, 223, 226, 242, 247, 254, 256-269, 273-287, 305-307, 316, 318, 326-327, 341, 348, 352-359, 385-387, 390, 395-398, 404, 407-409 -see also foundation of faith
faithlessness, 126, 128, 155, 190, 198, 203, 234, 247, 249, 252, 254-258, 263, 267, 272-273, 276-277, 281, 304, 323, 350, 386
Fall, 2, 9-10, 23, 34, 42-43, 47, 50,53-89, 94-99, 101-104, 111, 116, 118, 135-137, 141-143, 153-155, 163, 165, 172, 175-176, 180-181, 189-197, 199, 204-205, 210, 212, 228, 232, 235, 238-239, 247, 252, 255, 258, 266, 272, 274, 283-287, 295-299, 324, 332, 336, 341, 362, 366, 373-374, 379, 386, 391, 400-403, 407, 410
  course of, 104, 190
  motivation of, 62
  physical, 63-65, 68, 72, 136, 190, 379
  spiritual, 57, 63-65, 68, 71-72, 190, 379, 402
fallen Adam, 55-56, 65, 67, 139, 172, 179, 189, 191, 194, 196-197, 255, 350
fallen nature, 72-74, 181, 192-194, 196-197, 203, 217-219, 222, 225, 227-228, 233, 235-237, 241-242, 248-250, 252, 254, 259, 268-270, 274, 276, 279-280, 283, 290-291, 301, 313
fallen people, 7, 11, 23, 37, 44, 47, 55, 60, 72-76, 83-84, 87, 96-97, 102-104, 107, 112, 118, 137-138, 141, 157-163, 168-172, 176, 179-183, 186-190, 198, 220, 225, 238, 240, 245, 248, 264, 273, 284, 300, 309, 329, 333-334, 343, 349, 363, 366, 376, 379, 394
false Christs, 329
Far East, 85, 327
Fascism, 371-374
fast, 201, 244, 248-250, 257, 271-272, 275-278, 296, 298, 305, 394, 402, 405
father of faith, 139, 182, 199, 206-207, 209, 213, 223, 284, 307
fear, 54, 71, 75, 89, 106, 127, 137, 215, 236, 251, 259, 262, 269
female, 16, 18, 22, 31, 239
femininity, 19-20
feudalistic society, 317, 330-331, 336-338, 358
Feuerbach, Ludwig, 355
Fichte, Johann G., 356
fidelity, 38, 216, 234
fig tree, 96
filial piety, 38, 403
First Advent, 95, 107, 144, 151, 282, 285, 327, 381, 384-385, 387-388, 391-392, 394, 408
first blessing, 33-34, 39, 96-98, 179, 192, 273, 370, 376
First Cause, 18, 21, 136, 193
First Coming -see First Advent
First Israel, 282, 286, 314-315, 317-319, 327, 331, 399-401, 403-404
first resurrection, 143, 147, 393
firstborn, 191-192, 207, 218, 235, 241, 263
flood, 42, 89, 182, 198-201, 204, 206-207, 211-213, 232, 275, 296-297, 300-302, 382, 389
force of the Principle, 66
forefathers, 148, 231, 293
foreshadow, 202, 239, 262, 297
form spirit, 49, 81, 93, 139, 145-146, 184
formation stage, 41, 49, 139, 183-184, 186, 209-210, 212, 214, 290, 297, 368-371, 375, 373, 377
fornication, 58, 61
forty, 200-201, 207, 234, 275, 297-300, 400
forty days, 178, 200-201, 207, 211, 227-228, 232, 244-245, 248, 250-252, 257, 271-272, 277, 285, 293, 296, 298, 300-302, 304
forty years, 178, 201, 207, 232, 234-237, 252-254, 259-263, 266, 268, 275, 279, 298-302-307, 319-320, 326, 401
foundation of faith, 179-182, 189-192, 194-203, 206, 208, 217, 220, 230-237, 241, 248-253, 257, 259, 263, 271, 275-279, 282-285, 290-299, 301-307, 319-321, 326, 349-350
foundation of substance, 179, 181, 189, 192, 194-198, 203-206, 217-220, 225, 230, 233-237, 242, 247-254, 259, 264, 268-270, 276-280, 283-285, 290-291, 295-299, 313, 318-321, 324, 351, 353, 397
foundation for restoration, 185, 189, 232-233, 245, 290-291, 295-296, 298-300, 302-303, 313-314, 370, 375, 379
foundation for the Tabernacle, 248-254, 257, 259-260, 263-264, 276-277, 280
foundation for the Messiah, 179, 182-186, 189, 194-198, 206, 214-217, 220-222, 230-233, 249, 263-264, 269-270, 276-277, 280-286, 290-291, 294, 301, 303-304, 313-314, 317-321, 332, 338, 349-350, 358, 397
  family, 156, 182, 185, 189, 194-198, 206, 220-221, 264, 284-286, 294, 303-304, 314, 397
  national, 182-183, 185, 220, 222, 233, 264, 303-304, 317
  spiritual, 280-281, 285, 317, 319, 321, 338
  worldwide, 183, 185
  cosmic, 185
four, 25, 200, 296-298
four hundred years, 213, 218, 221, 234, 247, 264, 268, 299, 302-303, 305-310, 315, 321, 347
four position foundation, 21, 24-28, 30-39, 41, 44-45, 49, 66-69, 164, 171-172, 194, 200, 239, 275-276, 283, 292, 295-298, 300
Fox, George, 357
France, 85, 309, 322, 324, 340, 353, 359, 368-369, 372-373
Francis of Assisi, 322
Franks, 309, 322, 337-338
free will, 69, 74-75, 80, 351, 365
freedom, 69, 74-76, 97, 327, 342, 348, 351, 353, 359-361, 369, 371-372, 400
French Revolution, 76, 339, 353, 355, 357, 359-361
fruit of the tree of the knowledge of good and evil, 10, 53-54, 57, 59-60, 75, 120, 136-137, 179, 193

Galilee, 128, 229, 280, 409
Garden of Eden -see Eden
generations, 65, 117, 138, 144, 182, 199-200, 206-207,

210, 213-214, 222, 228, 290-291, 293-294, 298-301, 304, 315, 321
Gentiles, 100, 263, 268, 286, 322-323, 327, 332, 390, 398, 408
Germanic, 317-318, 333, 336-337, 372
Germany, 347, 352-353, 357, 360, 368-369, 371-373, 382
Gethsemane, 42, 258
Gilgal, 261-262
give and take action, 21-24, 26-28, 31-32, 34, 36, 38, 46, 48-51, 64-65, 69, 72, 76, 144
global nation, 411
global village, 103
Glorious Revolution, 360
God; absolute, 36, 41, 71, 77, 81, 154-160, 199, 215, 247, 290
  centered, 27, 30, 35, 44, 49, 69, 89, 164, 172, 181, 199, 335
  Creator, 10, 21, 43, 77, 167, 176, 186, 274, 355
  faith in, 9, 75, 180, 190, 215, 230, 235, 265, 348-349
  Father, 19, 117, 168, 182, 222, 302, 397
  First Cause, 18
  Heart of, 8, 10, 34, 44-45, 76, 80-81, 101-102, 112-113, 138, 164, 168, 178, 181, 187, 196, 206, 235, 241, 257, 379, 402-403
  omnipotent, 10, 76, 81, 393
  omnipresence, 31
  omniscient, 10, 76, 159
  Origin, 9, 24, 41, 256
  Will -see Will
  Word -see Word of God
God's grief, 333, 405
God's side, 100, 176, 182-183, 189, 192, 215, 221, 231, 235, 241, 269, 331, 335-336, 338, 343, 365-379, 402-403, 410
golden calf, 229, 245, 249, 256, 265
good and evil, 2-3, 7-8, 10, 38-39, 42, 48, 53-57, 59-60, 69-71, 75, 101, 106, 120, 136-137, 157, 171, 179, 190, 193, 197, 211-212, 262, 329-331, 379, 402
good spirits, 71, 147
goodness, 1-4, 6-7, 9-10, 25, 30, 32, 37, 39-40, 42, 44-45, 48-51, 53, 60, 70-71, 81-82, 84, 86, 89, 98-100, 136, 147, 151, 155, 190-191, 193-194, 211, 218-219, 235, 238, 328-331, 368, 403
Gospel, 21, 104, 121, 127-129, 140, 154, 180, 315, 317, 326-327, 364, 390, 408-409
governance, 31, 43, 67, 102, 137
grace, 44, 48, 92, 95, 113, 128, 157, 160, 177, 242-243, 253-254, 266, 276, 281, 316, 405
Great Britain, 368-369, 372-373, 406
Great Schism, 324-325
Great Powers, 8, 87, 341, 364, 369
Greece, 268, 327, 349-351, 406
Gregory XI, 324
growing period, 40-43, 77-78, 81, 138, 179, 181, 200, 209, 228, 290, 295-298, 367
growth stage, 41, 43, 49, 101, 139-142, 145, 175, 183-184, 186, 209-214, 290, 297, 371-375, 378
guilty conscience, 64-65

Ham, 89, 182, 199, 203-207, 213, 218-219, 221, 284, 300-302, 410
Hammurabi, 331
happiness, 1, 3, 6, 64, 66, 87, 153, 402-403

Haran, 207-208, 215, 219, 222, 228-229, 236, 240, 242, 253, 297, 302, 305-306, 326
harmony, 5, 9, 18-19, 21, 23-24, 26, 30, 36-39, 41, 46-47, 50, 70, 74, 80, 97, 112, 143, 167, 172, 296, 333, 342, 355, 361-363, 392, 406-407
Heart of God -see God
heaven, 5, 9, 11-12, 24, 50, 57-62, 79, 84, 88, 91, 94-97, 100, 103, 106-108, 112, 123, 128-129, 138, 147-149, 164, 170, 182-186, 198, 201-206, 215-216, 243-246, 256, 263, 267-268, 274, 297, 342, 375, 379, 383-387, 390, 394, 398, 405, 408-409
 -see also Kingdom of Heaven
heavenly law, 9, 72, 86, 248
Hebraism, 341, 349-352, 356, 359
Hegel, G.W.F., 355-356
hell, 9, 50, 58, 60, 69, 77, 82, 89, 111, 117, 137, 151, 169, 171, 176, 409
Hellenism, 327-328, 332, 341, 349-351, 354, 359, 364
Henry I, 308
Herbert, Edward, 355
heretic, 283, 385, 389, 399, 407-409
Herod, 229, 231, 389
Hinduism, 85, 327
Hirohito, 401
historical materialism, 333, 343, 364
Hitler, 371-372, 374-375
Hittites, 331
Holy Communion, 177, 316
Holy Land, 323
Holy Place, 246, 256, 281
Holy Roman Empire, 309, 322
Holy Spirit, 42, 56, 80, 94-95, 99, 105, 126-127, 137, 145, 163, 169-172, 177, 186, 239-240, 243-244, 246, 280-281, 316, 357, 373, 391, 394
hope, 12, 55, 61, 65, 87, 89, 112, 116, 128, 141, 143, 170, 202, 395, 404, 409
horizontally, 17, 19-20, 22, 24, 81-82, 97, 142-143, 187, 210, 219, 228, 290, 292-294, 299, 301-302, 304-307, 326, 362, 367, 378, 406, 410
humanism, 327, 349-352, 354, 364
human society, 64, 68, 70-71, 73, 86, 136, 328, 351, 362-363
humility, 205
Huns, 317
Hur, 244
Hus, Jan, 325

I Ching -see Book of Changes
ideal world, 5, 32, 36, 61, 73, 87-90, 97, 151, 229, 342, 352, 357, 361-363, 365-366, 369, 371, 373-374, 376-379, 383, 406, 410
idealism, 8, 355-356
ideology, 8, 87, 100-101, 106, 332, 347, 350, 353, 355, 357-358, 364-367, 371-372, 376-378, 402
idols, 229, 318, 321
ignorance, 2-3, 6-10, 50, 71, 76, 79, 84, 86, 96, 99, 103-105, 114-116, 123, 126, 128, 130, 333, 343, 363, 405-406, 408
image, 18-20, 28, 32, 34-35, 45, 62, 77, 97, 171, 186, 212, 246, 248, 283, 290, 302-303, 305-307, 318-320, 328-329, 348
  course, 226, 267, 319
imitation, 330, 341, 343, 369-370, 373-374, 376-378
immaturity, 42, 55, 60, 64, 66-68, 75, 78, 81-82, 295
imperialism, 337, 339, 341, 367, 373

incarnation, 92, 95, 104, 123, 167, 179-180, 202, 230, 273-274, 283
incorporeal world, 27, 45-46, 48, 391
indemnity
    condition, 121, 148, 177-181, 189, 192-205, 208-210, 214, 217-228, 233, 235-237, 240-242, 248-255, 259, 268-270, 276, 279-280, 283, 290-291, 301, 313, 367-375, 378-379, 399
    condition to remove the fallen nature, 181, 192-197, 203, 217-219, 222, 225-228, 233-237, 241-242, 248-254, 259, 268-270, 276, 279-280, 283, 290-291, 301, 313
    restoration through, 99, 176-177, 184-185, 193, 207, 214, 229, 279, 292-295, 301, 373, 382, 410
India, 85, 327
indirect dominion, 43-44, 77
individual embodiment of truth, 28, 297
individual perfection, 33-34, 36, 80-81, 96-98, 164, 272-273, 366, 369-370
Industrial Revolution, 339, 342, 357, 363-365, 367
inherit, 43-44, 56, 67, 77-78, 123, 130, 149, 191, 206-207, 219, 221, 230, 234-235, 247, 260, 265, 278, 292, 317, 379, 398-399
instinct, 47
intellect, 2, 6, 8, 11, 29, 37, 73, 75, 103-104, 142, 183-184, 333, 383
interdependence, 330, 342-344, 370, 378, 383
internal nature, 17-21, 27-29, 31-37, 41, 47, 49-50, 74, 167, 348, 356
Isaac, 42, 160, 178, 180, 182, 213-218, 220-223, 225, 232, 242, 292, 294, 301-302, 305-306, 314, 320
Isaac's family, 182, 217, 221-222, 225
Isaiah, 83, 118-120, 315, 322
Ishmael, 217, 220
Islam, 85 -see also Muslim
Israel, 90, 92, 96, 111, 114, 117, 123, 185, 222, 227, 234, 236, 239, 243, 251, 254, 259-260, 264, 293, 297, 304-306, 308-309, 314-323, 325, 327-328, 331-332, 335, 338, 349-350, 384, 394-398
    First, 282, 286, 314-315, 317-319, 327, 331, 399-401, 403-404
    Second, 234, 278, 282, 286, 314, 316, 318, 321, 327, 394, 399-401, 403-404
    Third, 282, 286, 399-400, 403-404
Israelites, 55, 61, 63, 100, 116, 120, 145, 178, 191, 201, 211, 213, 215, 226-227, 229, 231-238, 240-265, 267-269, 272, 275-278, 297, 302-308, 316-318, 320, 322-324, 326, 330, 366, 368, 394
Italy, 85, 309, 322, 324, 351-352, 371-373

Jabbok, 219, 227, 397
Jacob, 63, 94, 117, 144, 153, 160-161, 180, 182, 192, 208, 213, 215, 217-223, 225-229, 231, 236, 240, 242, 253, 262, 266-267, 285, 292-295, 297, 301-302, 305-307, 314-315, 320, 326, 336, 397
Jacob's course, 144, 221, 223-227, 236, 240, 242, 293
Jacob's family, 182, 221-222, 225, 229, 326
James I, 360
James II, 360
Japan, 371-373, 399-401, 406
Jehoiachin, 324
Jeremiah, 322
Jericho, 260-264
Jeroboam, 322
Jerusalem, 93, 115, 124, 202, 246, 306, 309, 319, 323, 333, 389
Jesus, 4-7, 11-12, 23-24, 42-50, 54-60, 66-69, 72, 83-84, 88-96, 99, 101, 104-108, 111-134, 137-142, 144-151, 154-158, 163-172, 176-186, 194, 197, 201-203, 208-210, 215, 222, 225-234, 238-250, 255-287, 291-293, 296, 299, 306-309, 314-321, 325-336, 350, 352, 355, 357, 367-375, 378, 381-409
    birth of, 123, 231, 306, 382, 385, 387, 389, 405, 408
    course of, 222, 226, 231, 234, 239, 246, 260, 278-279, 282, 287, 319, 403
    crucifixion, 42, 44, 72, 113-115, 119, 121, 130, 139, 144, 146, 185, 246, 262, 279-281, 335, 392, 398 -see also cross
    mission, 122, 128-130, 140, 260, 265, 278, 286, 409
    Savior, 11, 47, 111-113, 171, 176, 238, 390
    second Adam, 156, 171, 178, 202, 239, 255, 266, 274, 287, 292, 373
    Son of God, 11, 23, 151, 226, 271, 273, 284
    temptation, 273-275, 370, 374-375, 379
    resurrection, 42, 137, 139, 168, 170, 201, 279-280, 285
Jesus' course, 208-209, 215, 225-228, 231, 234, 237, 239, 242-243, 260, 266-267, 271, 277-278, 282, 285-287, 403
Jewish people, 72, 95, 107, 114-115 , 117, 120, 123-128, 130, 146, 156-158, 183, 197, 202-203, 234, 249, 255, 267-283, 286, 306-309, 314-316, 326-327, 332-333, 350, 372, 384-389, 392, 396-399, 398, 407-409
Job, 68-69, 315
John the Baptist, 60, 112, 114, 122-131, 142, 145, 149, 180, 209-210, 228, 234, 265, 267-273, 275-280, 282, 284-287, 381, 383-384, 387, 397
Jonah, 201, 322
Jordan, 42, 126, 209, 228-229, 260-262, 264, 270
Joseph, 94, 219, 221, 231, 302, 307, 326
Joshua, 42, 156, 228, 244, 251-252, 256-257, 259-265, 277-278, 282-283, 303, 315, 317
joy, 1, 3, 6, 8, 30, 32-37, 39, 48, 70, 74, 80-83, 89, 164, 215, 410
joy of God, 8, 33-34, 74, 80
Judah, 106, 305-306, 308-309, 321-323, 332, 397-398
Judaism, 327, 368, 395, 407
Judas Iscariot, 69, 156, 158, 262, 277, 280, 286-287
Judea, 114, 125, 269, 333
judges, 92, 262, 303, 305, 308, 317-319, 321, 330
judgment, 24, 50, 58, 90-92, 107, 129, 134, 137, 148, 155, 176, 198-201, 204, 206-207, 211, 213, 261, 275, 296, 300-302, 356, 368, 382, 389-390, 408
justice, 97, 117
justification, 139-140, 368

Kadesh-barnea, 158, 252-254, 259
Kaiser, 369-370, 382
Kant, Immanuel, 356
Kingdom of Heaven, 9, 32-33, 36, 69-70, 81, 84, 112, 118, 125, 129, 140-141, 146-147, 150, 265-266, 286, 319, 329, 343, 388
    on earth, 9-10, 36, 49-50, 55, 70, 81, 84, 89-90, 94, 111-113, 116, 118, 140, 147, 165, 169-170, 172, 202, 227, 263, 277, 282, 284, 328-329, 340, 343, 365-366, 370, 388, 390, 392

in heaven, 36, 49, 81, 83, 113, 129, 134, 140-141, 146, 210, 258, 277, 286, 388
kings, 11, 106, 180, 263, 292-293, 309, 319-322, 324, 332, 337-339, 350, 358
King of Kings, 231, 263, 317, 319, 323, 331, 333, 340, 390
Kingsley, Charles, 342
Korea, 372, 399-407, 410
Korean Christians, 372, 405
Korean War, 401

Laban, 219, 222, 228, 240, 242, 253
Lamb, 210, 216, 239, 241, 399
languages, 328, 410
Last Days, 56, 69, 79, 86-108, 122, 141-142, 145, 149, 151, 165, 198, 286, 338, 353, 363, 366, 375, 382, 384, 386-389, 398, 401, 404-405, 409
law, 1-2, 9, 72, 83, 86, 104, 124, 139, 193, 248, 356 -see also Mosaic Law
lay people, 144, 184, 277, 398, 408
League of Nations, 102
Leah, 219, 221, 231, 306
Leo III, 321, 338
Leo X, 352
Levites, 125, 191, 268
liberation, 306, 317, 324, 401-402
life elements, 48, 61, 144
life spirit, 49-50, 135-136, 139, 145, 147, 171, 273
light, 1, 7, 9, 11-12, 20, 40, 73-74, 79, 94-95, 127, 149, 165, 168, 202, 240-241, 314, 326, 357, 370, 374, 379, 381-382, 407
likeness, 19, 32, 41, 62, 163-164, 292, 328-329, 348, 362, 369
lineage, 54, 60-61, 65, 68, 72, 118-119, 137, 159, 176, 199, 205, 216, 229, 234, 284-285, 379, 390, 397 -see also blood relationship
literal, 10, 40, 54, 79, 90-91, 93, 133, 146, 232, 383, 385-386, 397
liver, 342, 362
living sacrifice, 183, 307, 315
living spirit elements, 48-49
Logos, 170-171
Lot, 63, 207, 209
love, 4-5, 9, 23-24, 29-30, 35, 38-39, 44-45, 49-50, 54, 59-60, 63-70, 73-76, 88, 97-103, 125, 128, 134, 136, 160-161, 171, 177-178, 190-193, 201, 219-220, 235-236, 268-269, 273, 283, 341, 402
and beauty, 35, 37-39, 44-45
brotherly, 9, 103
conjugal, 38, 64, 67
loyalty, 38, 206, 215-216, 234, 253, 259, 317, 403
Lucifer, 63-64, 68, 73, 76
lust, 58, 320
Luther, Martin, 310, 325-326, 347, 364

Maitreya Buddha, 149-150, 405
Malachi, 90-91, 122-124, 126, 268, 306, 309, 315, 324-327, 383, 385
male, 16, 18, 22, 31, 240, 390
Manchuria, 372, 400
manna, 227-228, 243, 246, 251, 261-262, 266, 281
manor system, 335-337
martyrdom, 178, 395
Marx, 355
Marxism, 85, 333, 355, 360 -see also dialectical materialism
Mary, 117-118, 120, 229
masculinity, 16, 19-20
materialism, 5, 8, 85, 333, 343, 355, 359, 364, 377
matter, 16, 28-29, 42, 44, 66, 75, 111, 113, 118, 124, 129, 160, 164-165, 182, 277, 283, 291, 369, 383, 386-387, 392-393, 396-397, 409
Matthias, 156, 280, 286
maturation of politics, economy and ideology, 347, 357
maturity, 60, 64, 67-68, 77, 80-81, 142, 175, 298-300 -see also perfection
mediator, 23, 46, 166, 193, 219
medieval, 4, 326, 331, 335, 348-356, 359, 364-365, 373
Mediterranean Sea, 328, 333, 336, 406
mercy seat, 247, 281
merit of the age, 76, 97, 104, 138-140, 148, 184, 340, 342
Mesopotamia, 331, 406
Messiah, 6, 89, 93, 95, 111-117, 120-129, 140-141, 146, 157, 175, 179-183, 189, 194, 198, 206, 220-229, 233, 244-250, 264-273, 276-278, 284-285, 291, 304-309, 316-318, 323-333, 338-341, 350, 371, 384-390, 395, 399, 403-405, 409 -see also Christ; Second Advent; foundation for the Messiah
  purpose of, 119, 310
  mission, 115-116, 140-141
messianic, 111, 327
  kingdom, 338, 344, 350, 358
  prophecies, 324, 404
  spiritual, 280-281, 285, 317
Methodism, 357
Michael, 228
microcosm, 34, 47, 165
Midian, 236-237, 252, 259, 266, 276, 298-299, 304
Middle Ages, 318, 348, 350 -see also medieval
Middle East, 85
midway position, 71, 176, 189
mind, 1-7, 17-19, 23, 27-39, 45, 47-53, 64, 71, 74-76, 80, 84, 97, 119, 128, 136, 163-164, 167, 193-194, 256, 296, 328-335, 342, 348, 354, 356, 383
Minoan civilization, 349
miracles, 6, 114-115, 125, 128, 234, 238, 240-241, 249, 254, 265, 269, 280, 283, 316, 355, 387, 409
Miriam, 239
mistake, 117, 143, 178, 182, 185, 206, 209, 211-213, 217-222, 230, 232, 234, 247, 255, 263, 284, 287, 292, 294, 300-302, 304, 307, 315, 323
Moab, 258
modern, 5, 7, 18, 40, 85-87, 90, 96, 102, 104, 113, 125, 133, 324, 352-356, 368, 371, 383
model course, 208-209, 221-222, 225-228, 231, 242, 264, 266-267, 314
molecules, 16, 18, 22, 29
monarchic society, 331-332, 337-338, 340, 358
monarchy, 100, 323, 325, 331, 335, 339-341, 343, 358-360, 365, 367, 373
monastic, 318, 352
Montesquieu, 361
moon, 79, 94-95
Moon, Sun Myung, 12
More, Thomas, 342
Moriah, 215, 242

Mosaic Law, 107, 120, 145, 180, 256, 316, 326, 335, 349
Moses, 42, 46, 93, 104, 107, 120, 123, 144, 149, 156, 158, 178, 180, 201, 207-208, 213, 215, 222, 225-273, 275-283, 291-293, 295-296, 298, 300, 303-306, 316-320, 368, 394, 397
Moses' family, 144, 208, 229, 248
motion, 26-28, 32, 292, 355
motivation of the Fall, 62, 64
multiplication of life, 31
murder, 194, 284, 367, 409
Muslim, 323, 351, 368-369
Mussolini, 371-372
mutual prosperity, 330, 342-344, 370, 378, 383
Mycenaean, 349

nakedness, 59, 203-205
national course, 215, 221, 234-237, 241-243, 248, 250, 252-254, 257, 259-261, 263-264, 267-268, 271-272, 276-279, 281-283, 298, 304, 306-307, 320, 366, 400
national condition of indemnity, 399
natural world, 3, 10, 16, 29-30, 34-36, 38-39, 42, 45, 67, 81, 101-102, 166-167, 180, 195, 200, 209, 214, 275, 296, 351-352, 354 -see also all things
Near East, 331-332, 350
Nebuchadnezzar, 306, 324, 326
Nehemiah, 306, 325
Netherlands, 85, 353, 360
new age, 107-108, 141, 146, 180, 184, 209, 232, 295, 297, 307, 314-317, 335-336, 349, 368, 375, 382, 408
new heaven and new earth, 88, 91, 95, 107, 408
New Testament, 104, 314, 316, 408
New Testament Age, 107, 141, 146, 180, 184, 209, 295, 297, 307, 314-317, 335-336, 349, 382, 408
New Testament Word, 95, 139, 180, 183-185
new truth, 6-12, 87, 103-108, 140, 143, 338, 343, 375, 377-378, 406, 408
Nicodemus, 169-170
Nile, 239, 406
nine, 298
Nineveh, 201
Noah, 42, 89-91, 101, 107, 144, 156-157, 180, 182, 198-214, 218-221, 228, 232, 275, 284, 291-304, 315, 382, 389, 399, 410
Noah's ark, 42, 182, 200, 275, 298
Noah's family, 89, 156, 182, 198-201, 203-207, 209, 211-212, 214, 219, 221, 293-294, 300
non-believers, 408
non-religious people, 151
number, 25, 40-42, 144, 200-201, 207, 211, 213, 216, 228, 234, 248, 252, 275, 290-292, 295-300, 356, 385, 388, 396, 398, 400
numerical period of indemnity, 180, 200, 290-291, 294-295, 299, 301, 304
nutrients, 22, 35, 342

obedience, 54, 70, 127, 166, 178, 199, 205, 207, 215, 232-233, 237, 241, 245, 249, 251, 254, 263, 268, 283, 318, 321, 330, 352, 354
object for the condition, 180, 190, 199-200, 208-210, 232-233, 290-291, 295, 313, 318
object of faith, 66, 199, 247, 250, 290
object partner, 5, 17, 20-24, 28, 30-39, 44-48, 69, 80-84, 91, 164-167, 170-172, 195, 204-205, 212, 283, 285, 292, 294-295, 297, 348, 402-403
offering, 23, 42, 104, 178, 180, 190, 192, 194, 197-198, 201, 210, 213-216, 219, 223, 242, 247, 270, 275-276, 293-294, 315-316, 320-321, 323, 326, 349
  substantial, 195-198, 203, 205, 207, 210, 217-221, 233, 291-292, 301, 313, 349, 397
  symbolic, 182-183, 185, 195-196, 199, 203, 207-218, 220-221, 230, 232-233, 291-292, 294, 301-302, 304, 307, 313, 323, 349
Old Testament, 93, 107-108, 139, 146, 180, 256, 314-316, 407-408
Old Testament Age, 55-56, 93, 104, 107, 120, 141, 145-146, 180, 183-186, 209, 232, 256, 269, 284-285, 295, 297, 307, 314, 316-317, 335-336, 338, 349, 382, 384, 399
Old Testament Word, 95, 180, 183-185 -see also Mosaic Law
olive tree, 55, 149, 169, 284
144,000, 144, 396, 399
120 years, 199, 205, 295, 301-302, 304-305
oneness, 23-27, 30, 34, 37-38, 44, 65, 80, 113, 164, 167, 172, 210, 216, 280, 284, 294, 296, 351, 391
oppression, 117, 212, 237, 268, 319, 372, 400
oriental medicine, 21
origin-division-union action, 24-25, 31, 41, 171, 292
original mind, 1-4, 6-7, 30, 49-51, 53, 71, 74-76, 84, 97, 328-331, 333, 335, 342, 348
original sin, 11, 54-56, 61, 72, 88, 112-113, 118-119, 143-144, 147, 168-172, 175-176, 179, 181, 233, 277, 284-285, 392
original nature, 18-21, 23, 31, 33, 35-36, 41, 68, 73, 75-76, 100, 113, 178, 181, 228, 233, 277, 342, 348-349, 351-354, 356, 371, 376-377
original value, 36-37, 80, 97, 134, 163, 169, 341
Owen, Robert, 342
ownership, 43, 180

Pacific civilization, 406
papacy, 309, 321-326, 335, 338-339, 341, 348-349, 352, 358, 362
papal exile, 309, 323-324, 326
parable of the vineyard, 63, 314, 396, 398
parable of the marriage feast, 408
parables, 104-105, 383
Paradise, 12, 42, 62, 93, 140-141, 145-147, 150-151, 176, 405
parallel periods, 101, 289-291, 299, 307, 310, 315
parallels
  image, 186, 290, 302, 307, 326
  substantial, 187, 290, 307-308, 314, 321, 324-327
  symbolic, 186, 290, 302-303, 305-307
parent, 1, 9, 30, 54, 103, 113, 169-170, 233, 235, 268, 276, 283, 402
Parliament, 360
Passover, 262
patriarchs, 308, 317, 337
Paul, 1, 15, 18, 30, 47, 60, 68, 113, 119, 153, 160, 244, 285, 314, 397-398
Pentecost, 56, 280, 391
Pepin, 337
perfection, 5, 10, 19, 30, 33-38, 41-44, 49-50, 55, 65, 67, 73-74, 77, 80-81, 96-98, 101-102, 120, 135, 138, 144, 147, 151, 163-167, 176, 255, 272-273, 295-297, 333, 351, 366-370, 392

persecution, 4, 117, 307, 315-317, 336, 357, 369, 385, 395, 399-400
Persia, 268, 306, 327
Peter, 42, 50, 62, 69, 96, 121, 130, 147, 271, 286, 352, 395
Pharaoh, 208-209, 230-231, 234-238, 240-243, 266, 268-269, 298, 304-305, 316, 320, 366
Pharisees, 60, 115, 384
Philip IV, 324
Philistines, 210, 236, 242
philosopher, 4, 354-356
philosophy, 20-21, 70, 98, 100, 102, 106, 349, 354, 356-357
physical body, 46-47, 136-137, 334, 392
physical fall, 63-65, 68, 72, 136, 190, 379
physical mind, 47-48, 50-51
physical salvation, 118-119, 121, 171, 280, 392
physical self, 47-50, 63, 104, 134, 138, 144, 149, 164, 333, 348
physical world, 30, 46-47, 103, 135, 164-165, 246, 273, 319, 333-334, 349, 402
Pietism, 357
pillar of fire, 243, 261, 394
Pisa, 324
planets, 23, 26
plants, 16, 18, 22, 29, 31, 35, 40, 42
political parties, 361-362
politics, 317, 319, 322, 325, 327, 333-336, 338, 342-343, 347, 352, 357, 364-365, 400
pope, 318-325, 337-341, 350, 358, 372
Portugal, 85, 406
power of love, 64-67, 75-76
power of the Principle, 65-67, 371
prayer, 42, 108, 113, 116, 121, 145, 154, 157, 201, 269, 327
predestination, 69, 90, 153-161, 197, 203, 205, 213, 215, 222-223, 286, 290, 396
 of God's Will, 155-156, 197, 205, 286
 of human beings, 155, 158, 206
preparation for the advent of the messiah, 268, 304, 306-307, 309-310, 315, 325-327, 347, 350
preparation for the second advent of the messiah, 309-310, 325-327, 347
priesthood, 341, 352, 360
priests, 72, 125, 129, 246, 259, 261, 263, 268-269, 277, 317-320, 324, 348, 381, 405, 407-409
primitive, 81, 86, 102, 329-330, 343, 372, 403, 407
Principle, 25-27, 43, 64-66, 69, 71, 74-78, 83, 88, 120, 140-143, 149-150, 154, 170, 175-176, 190-192, 211-215, 225, 230, 273-274, 291-298, 314, 329, 338, 354, 361, 365-366, 371, 388, 391, 393, 399, 407
 autonomy and governance, 43
 of Creation, 11, 15, 20-21, 49, 62, 66-67, 77-78, 83, 112, 135-138, 144, 156, 164-167, 171, 186, 190, 195, 200, 275, 292, 295, 348, 351
 of Restoration, 44, 175-176, 187, 193, 207, 214, 229, 279, 382, 410
progress of history, 75, 86, 106, 328-337, 339, 341, 356, 358, 364
prolongation, 44, 69, 90, 139, 157, 185, 213, 216, 220, 222, 232, 234, 242, 249, 251-252, 264, 270, 282, 290-294, 299, 301-314, 327, 332-333, 378-379, 382
promise, 5, 83, 91, 114, 178, 202, 216, 234, 240, 314, 392, 405
prophecy, 11, 69, 90-91, 93-95, 117, 119-121, 123-124, 126, 133, 141-142, 145, 201, 221, 256, 269, 306, 309, 315, 324, 329, 366, 382, 384, 386-387, 393-394, 399, 404
prophet, 24, 80, 90, 98-99, 111, 114-115, 118, 122-123, 129-130, 138, 186-187, 201, 225-226, 230, 233, 267-269, 293, 317-320, 322, 324-327, 381-384, 396, 403-404, 407
Protestant, 309-310, 325-326, 335, 339, 341-342, 347-349, 352-353, 356, 359-360, 372
providence
 of restoration, 10, 23, 42-44, 50, 57, 69-70, 76, 79, 82-92, 96-107, 111-113, 117, 136, 138, 141-161, 165, 168, 175, 177, 181-189, 194-199, 205-208, 211, 215, 220-233, 244-245, 255, 264-267, 275, 278, 280-298, 300-310, 313-314, 318-320, 326-336, 340-343, 347-353, 358, 362-368, 372-373, 377-379, 382, 384, 398-401
 of resurrection, 138-140, 144, 184
 of salvation, 8, 44, 56, 82-84, 121, 157, 159, 283, 373
providential history, 86-88, 99, 143, 270, 283, 289, 291-293, 299, 301, 314, 326, 335, 342-343, 348, 358, 379, 382, 406
Puritans, 360-361
purity, 81, 316, 374
purpose of creation, 10, 19, 25, 27, 30-33, 36, 38-45, 50, 59, 64, 70-75, 79-83, 99, 101, 111-112, 135, 137, 143-144, 155-156, 163-171, 175, 179-181, 195, 198, 206, 272, 275, 282-283, 292-299, 342

quail, 227, 243, 266
Quakers, 357

race, 2, 9, 247, 371, 374, 403
Rachel, 219, 221, 231, 306
Rameses, 243
rationalism, 354-356
raven, 201, 205, 212
Rebecca, 160
rebirth, 11, 88, 94, 163, 166, 168-172, 179, 239, 279-280, 284, 349
reciprocal relationship, 17-18, 22-23, 47, 49, 164, 170, 204
re-creation, 159
Red Sea, 229, 234, 236, 242-243, 246-247, 249, 253, 261, 269
redemption by the cross, 11, 113, 118-119, 146, 177, 258
Reformation, 4, 297, 309-310, 325-327, 335, 339, 341, 347-350, 352, 356, 358-359, 364-365
regional church leadership, 308, 317-318, 321, 337
Rehoboam, 322
reincarnation, 149-150
relationship, 5, 16-24, 28-29, 33-38, 45, 47-50, 55, 58-65, 72, 74, 80, 135, 138, 142, 161-164, 167-170, 191-195, 204, 240, 266, 270, 284-285, 329, 334, 342, 348-349, 362-363, 410
relative, 37, 70-71, 190, 330, 349
religion and science, 3, 6-7, 86-88, 105, 333-334, 338, 343, 363, 406
religion, 3-8, 24, 61, 70, 84-88, 98-105, 147, 150-151, 178, 307-308, 316-319, 322-340, 343, 347, 349, 352-357, 363-369, 372, 375, 402-406

religious and ideological conflicts, 347, 353
religious history, 333-334, 339, 341
Renaissance, 85, 327, 348-351, 354-355, 358, 364-365
repentance, 84, 112, 126, 136, 151, 236, 251, 266, 322-323
Rephidim, 244, 250-251, 256-257, 259
representation, 226, 246, 248, 254, 256, 267, 366
resemble, 20, 27, 32, 40, 361-362
responsibility, 43-44, 49, 67, 69, 72-78, 83, 89-90, 101, 120-121, 138-144, 155-161, 167, 178-179, 186-187, 197-198, 203-206, 213-223, 226, 230, 249, 262-266, 271-272, 286-293, 314, 338, 349, 351, 368, 376, 378, 397, 404, 409
restoration
   providence of, 10, 23, 42-44, 50, 57, 69-70, 76, 79, 82-92, 96-107, 111-113, 117, 136, 138, 141-151, 154-161, 165, 168, 175, 177, 181-189, 194, 196-199, 205-208, 211, 215, 220-226, 229-233, 244-245, 255, 264-267, 275, 278, 280-286, 289-295, 298-314, 318-320, 326-336, 340-353, 358-368, 372-373, 377-384, 398-401
   through indemnity, 99, 176-177, 184-185, 193, 207, 214, 229, 279, 292-295, 301, 373, 382, 410
resurrection, 42, 44, 93, 133-140, 143-151, 177, 184, 216, 393
   first, 143, 147, 393
   Jesus, 42, 119, 137, 139, 168, 170, 177, 201, 243, 250, 258, 278-280, 285 ,391
   meaning of, 133, 136
   returning, 144-151
revelations, 142-143, 145, 351, 375, 404-405, 408
reverse, 73, 244
revival, 4, 7, 136, 349, 352, 357, 364
revolutions, 70-71, 76, 340, 360, 362, 364-365, 367
Righteous King, 322, 404
righteousness, 38, 40, 71, 91, 117, 127, 130, 166
rise and fall of nations, 84-85, 98-99, 153
risk, 59, 227, 322, 389
rock; at Rephidim, 250-251, 256, 259
   Christ, 244-245, 256
   Moses struck twice, 254-259, 265, 267, 271-272
rod of iron, 229, 243, 390
Roman Empire, 4, 269, 283, 307-309, 315-319, 322, 328, 332-333, 336-337, 350, 395, 400-401
   persecution under, 4, 307, 315-317, 400
Rome, 85, 268, 309, 319, 324, 326-328, 337, 349-351, 406
Russia, 360, 368-370

sabbath, 124, 315-316
sacrament, 177, 316
sacrifice, 23-24, 42, 113, 134, 176, 178, 180, 183-185, 190, 192, 195, 197, 199, 209-214, 216-217, 223, 242, 245, 246, 275, 293, 307, 315-316, 326, 349, 371, 377, 401, 409
Sadducees, 384
saints, 4, 12, 56, 62, 88, 93-94, 98-99, 107, 133, 144-146, 187, 403
salvation, 4-5, 8-9, 11, 44, 56, 82-84, 90, 108, 111-113, 117-122, 124, 139, 153, 157, 159, 163, 171, 177, 197, 211, 225, 240, 246, 248, 250, 256, 258, 279-281, 283, 373, 386, 392, 398, 404, 408
   physical, 118-119, 121, 171, 280, 392
   providence of, 8, 44, 56, 82-84, 121, 157, 159, 283, 373

spiritual, 90, 118-119, 121-122, 139, 246, 258, 280, 373, 408
Samaria, 128
Samson, 210, 317
Samuel, 317, 319-320
sanctification, 61
Sarah, 207-209, 214
Satan, 23, 39, 44, 51, 53, 57-61, 68-77, 82-91, 94, 97-100, 118-123, 134, 136-137, 144, 155, 168, 172-218, 225-232, 235, 238-240, 243, 248, 253-258, 263, 266-267, 271-281, 287, 295-298, 329-335, 341-343, 350, 355, 358, 361, 364-379, 392, 401-403, 410
   claimed, 87, 144, 182, 191, 207, 212, 232, 237, 241, 299
   defiled, 180, 200, 216, 218, 227-228, 232, 238, 248, 251, 253, 256, 263, 271, 295-296, 299-300, 302, 349
   invaded, 200, 217, 223, 249, 251-252, 257, 259, 263, 270-271, 301
   lineage of, 60, 65, 68, 137, 284-285, 379
   separation of, 100, 175-176, 201, 213-217, 221, 228-237, 242-245, 248-253, 263, 267-268, 271-272, 275-276, 279, 281, 285, 293, 302-304, 315-316, 320-321, 326, 350-351, 399-400
   subjugate, 226, 266-267
   submission, 69, 222, 225-227, 229, 266-267
Satan's side, 100, 176, 192, 215, 219, 221, 231, 241, 331, 336, 343, 358, 365, 367-370, 372-373, 375-376, 382, 399-400, 402-403
Satan's sovereignty, 68, 100, 366
Saul, 100, 155, 201, 292, 303-308, 319-321, 331
Schelling, Friedrich, 356
science, 3-4, 6-7, 10, 18, 28, 40, 81, 86-88, 102-103, 105, 182, 295, 327, 333-335, 338, 343, 349, 351-352, 354, 363-364, 406
Scotland, 360
scriptures, 6-7, 11, 92-93, 108, 115, 122-123, 126, 133, 316, 352, 394, 408-409
second Adam, 39, 98, 156, 171-172, 178-179, 196, 199, 202-203, 239, 249, 255, 266, 274, 287, 292, 373-374
second blessing, 34, 39, 67, 97-99, 274, 374-375
Second Coming, 56, 61, 71-72, 90, 95, 107, 111, 116, 118, 121-123, 130, 140-146, 149-151, 157, 183-187, 202, 210, 229, 260, 262, 278, 281-283, 286, 291-292, 309-310, 316, 319-329, 338, 343, 347-348, 350-351, 353, 363-366, 370-371, 375, 378, 381-411
second Eve, 39, 170-172, 191, 239, 249, 310
second self, 39, 167
Second Israel, 234, 278, 282, 286, 314, 316, 318, 321, 327, 394, 399-401, 403-404
secular, 324, 337, 341
selfishness, 71
sensibility, 32, 46, 102, 107
serpent, 57-59, 61-62, 116-117, 238, 258, 266, 277
separation of Satan- see Satan
servant, 62-64, 260, 284, 337, 349
serve, 9, 58, 98, 119, 127, 129-130, 140, 143, 153, 160, 190, 200, 222, 229, 231, 233, 260, 262, 274, 285, 338, 371, 387, 389
Seth, 156, 197-199
seven, 100, 106, 201-202, 219, 229, 263, 296-297, 306, 318, 398

seventy, 229, 244, 285, 293, 306, 315, 324-325, 336
sexual, 5, 58-65, 72, 191, 204, 240
shame, 59, 204-205
Shem, 203, 218-219, 410
Shim-ch'ong, 403
Shinto, 372, 401
signs, 90, 96-98, 101, 115, 125, 128, 234, 238-241, 247, 249, 252-254, 261, 265-266, 269, 276, 280, 283, 316, 366, 383-385, 387, 389, 402, 405
Simon, 114, 381
sin, 2, 5, 9, 11, 36, 49, 53-58, 61, 65, 72, 74, 80-83, 112-113, 119, 136, 148, 151, 155, 191-194, 202-206, 210-213, 221, 229, 234-235, 239-240, 243-244, 247, 255, 260, 279, 326, 352, 363, 392
   collective, 72, 117
   inherited, 54, 72
   original, 11, 54-56, 61, 72, 88, 112-113, 118-119, 143-144, 147, 168-172, 175-176, 179, 181, 233, 277, 284-285, 392
   root of, 53, 61, 72, 229
sinless, 11, 74, 81, 83, 94, 112, 170, 284, 390
Sinai, 236, 244-245, 248-250, 316
six days, 40-41, 43, 248, 263, 398
sixteen hundred years, 199, 205, 207, 299-300, 302
slavery in Egypt, 201, 212, 232, 234, 275, 299, 302-303, 305, 307-308, 315-317, 320
socialism, 340-343, 355
Socrates, 327
Sodom and Gomorrah, 58, 382
solar system, 23, 26
Solomon, 123, 201, 275, 292, 303, 305, 308, 315, 320-322, 332
sovereignty, 68, 71, 82, 84-85, 88-91, 94, 98-101, 106-107, 211-212, 264, 323, 330-332, 334, 337-341, 343, 366-367, 370, 375-376, 379
Soviet Union, 85, 373-374, 407
Spain, 85, 353, 406
Spener, Philip, 357
spherical, 25-28, 30-31, 292
spiral, 101, 289
spirit body, 48, 145, 349
spirit mind, 48-51, 136
spirit self, 47-50, 63, 103-104, 135, 148-149, 164, 333
spirit world, 9, 12, 30, 36, 46-49, 62, 69, 81-82, 93, 123, 134-136, 139-142, 145-147, 164-165, 168, 176, 273, 285, 319, 333, 349, 357, 393, 402, 405
spirits, 46, 50, 62-63, 69, 71, 93, 108, 134-135, 139-141, 144-151, 168, 171, 273, 390, 393, 405, 407
spiritual course, 104, 215, 228, 243, 258, 260, 277-279, 281, 285
spiritual communication, 142
spiritual experience, 71, 104
spiritual fall, 57, 63-65, 68, 71-72, 190, 379, 402
spiritual life, 6, 375, 390, 407
spiritual phenomena, 71, 97, 141, 375
spiritual salvation, 90, 118-119, 121-122, 139, 246, 258, 280, 373, 408
spiritual senses, 45, 48, 146, 357, 392-393
spirituality, 96, 98, 102-104, 142, 183-184, 340, 349, 383, 395
spy mission, 178, 251-252, 259-260, 263-264, 275, 277, 296, 298, 300
staff, 229, 238, 243, 246, 254, 261, 281
Stalin, 370, 375, 378, 382
stars falling, 94

Stephen, 114, 393
Strauss, D. F., 355
structure, 17, 23, 27, 35, 45-48, 73, 328, 337, 339, 361-363
struggle, 1, 7-8, 84, 97, 219, 222, 330, 366, 401
subject, 18-19, 22, 26, 30, 38-39, 66, 81, 84, 309, 324, 335
subject partner, 5, 17-28, 30-33, 37-39, 44, 46-48, 65, 83, 91, 170, 297
Succoth, 243
suffering, 5, 12, 72, 82-83, 120-121, 148, 208, 219-220, 240, 271, 282, 307, 315, 401, 403
sun, 12, 23, 26, 79, 94-95, 211, 398-399
Sweden, 353
Swedenborg, Emanuel, 357
Switzerland, 325, 353
symbol, 20, 28, 35, 54, 57, 94, 104-105, 195, 229, 239, 243, 245-246, 248, 255, 277, 290, 318, 383
symbolic course, 226, 267
symbolic foundation, 182, 195, 232, 291, 302
symbolic offering -see offering
Syria, 268, 322, 327, 331

Tabernacle, 114, 244-254, 257, 259-260, 263-264, 266, 269, 275-277, 280-281, 316, 318-319
tablets of stone, 244-251, 253, 255-257, 259, 261, 266-267, 269, 272-273, 276, 280, 305, 316
Tao, 20
Taoism, 85
Temple, 80, 114, 125, 129, 137, 164, 180, 246, 248-250, 262, 267, 271, 273-276, 278, 292, 303-306, 308-309, 318-320, 322-323, 325, 409
   ideal of, 123, 281, 319, 322
   Jesus as, 123, 169, 262, 273-274, 281
temptation, 64-65, 75, 101, 143, 273, 275, 379
ten, 200, 298-300
Ten Commandments, 72, 120, 244-245, 254-255, 276, 316
ten generations, 182, 199-200, 206-207, 213, 298-300
ten plagues, 238-241, 253-254, 261, 266, 276, 316
Terah, 207
Theodosius I, 316
theologians, 62, 324, 357
theology, 169, 352-353, 355
thief, 141, 381, 385
third Adam, 101, 202-203
third blessing, 34-36, 39, 101-102, 275, 379
Third Estate, 359
Third Israel, 282, 286, 399-400, 403-404
Third World War, 370, 375-379
Thirty Years War, 353
thirty-eighth parallel, 401
three, 25, 41-42, 211, 213, 228, 292, 296-297
three days, 42, 215, 228, 240, 242-243, 261-262, 266, 278
three great blessings, 32-33, 83, 88-89, 96, 171-172, 195, 199, 272, 276, 366-370, 373-375, 378
three manifestations of grace, 253-254, 276
three object purpose, 24-25, 28, 31, 39, 41, 66, 171, 283, 292, 295, 297
three signs, 238-239, 241, 253-254, 261, 266, 276, 316, 366
three stages of growth, 41, 367
three temptations, 42, 271-272, 275, 277, 367, 370, 374, 379

tomb, 5, 42, 93, 145-146, 215, 228, 391
tower of Babel, 410
tradition, 70, 107, 150, 231, 354-355
Transfiguration, 46, 93, 123
tree of knowledge of good and evil, 10, 42, 53-57, 59-60, 75, 120, 136-137, 171, 179, 193
tree of life, 54-56, 87-88, 149, 165-166, 171, 247, 255, 281
Trinity, 11, 42, 62, 163, 169, 171-172, 244, 296-297
True Father, 88, 170-171, 239, 280
True Man, 150, 405
True Mother, 103, 170-171, 239, 280, 411
True Parents, 36, 94, 99, 169, 171-172, 239, 280, 282-283, 411
trumpet, 79, 93, 263, 383, 385-386, 388-389
truth, 2-12, 20, 23-24, 28, 30, 37, 49, 63, 66, 71, 75-76, 87, 92, 95, 103-108, 116, 119-122, 127, 131, 140, 143, 164, 208, 270, 273, 297, 343, 354, 363, 366, 377, 389, 395, 409
Turkey, 368-369, 373
twelve, 25, 94, 123, 144, 228, 251, 260-262, 280, 285-286, 293, 295, 299, 301, 315, 321, 336
twenty-one years, 219, 236, 240, 297, 302, 304
two thousand years, 4, 11, 104, 115, 139, 182-186, 222, 281-282, 315, 332, 383, 391, 408
210 years, 297, 304, 306, 309, 322, 325

Ulsa Treaty of Protection, 400-401
unaccomplished, 90, 144, 156, 187, 211, 280, 392
unfulfilled, 55, 121, 178, 182, 282, 290, 293, 314
unification, 85, 87, 376-377, 410
of religions, 150
of Christianity, 105, 150-151
unify, 7, 327, 332, 356, 375-377, 410
unique, 7, 20, 104, 143, 155, 164-166
unite, 23, 27, 38-39, 44, 46, 49, 172, 262, 280, 299, 321, 341, 358, 365
united kingdom, 123, 295, 303-305, 308, 318-321, 331-332, 338, 350
United Nations, 8, 87, 102, 368, 372, 402
United States, 87, 360, 368-369, 372-373, 402, 406
unity, 8, 11, 16, 200, 298-300
universal prime energy, 21-22, 24
universally shared values, 330, 342-344, 370, 378, 383
universe, 3-4, 10, 12, 15-23, 27-42, 45-47, 57, 59, 62, 64, 67-68, 78, 102, 104, 141-142, 164-167, 191, 201, 204, 211-212, 218, 294-296, 334, 355, 361, 363, 376-379, 391, 401
unprincipled, 64-67, 75-77, 88, 190-191, 196, 200, 274, 329, 343, 366, 369, 373-374, 376, 378, 401
Urban VI, 324
Utopia, 342

value, 29, 36-37, 45, 77, 80, 97, 134, 163-166, 168-169, 177, 256, 341, 349, 351, 354, 357, 359, 371, 394, 403
vertical indemnity conditions, 187, 292-294, 299, 301, 326

vertical, 17, 19-20, 22, 24, 81-82, 97, 142, 144, 169, 187, 210, 219, 228, 290, 292-294, 299, 301-302, 304-305, 307, 326, 348, 362-363, 367, 406, 410
victory, 144, 196, 216, 218-219, 231, 244, 264, 273, 275, 294, 368, 370-371, 373, 375, 379, 403
vine, 55, 118, 169
virtue, 9, 11, 18, 26, 43, 50, 61, 146, 257, 366, 403
vitality elements, 48-49, 144
void, 9, 20, 40

war, 1, 8, 87, 119, 236, 328, 330, 341, 353, 365, 401
causes of, 369
water, 20, 24, 29, 35, 40, 46-47, 83, 101, 126, 177, 201-202, 205, 229, 234, 239, 243-244, 250-251, 254-257, 259, 261-262, 266, 283, 374, 394
wealth, 3, 100, 128, 209, 219, 227, 241, 302, 306, 343
Wesley, 357, 364
Westphalia, Treaty of, 347, 353
wife, 23, 25, 30, 34, 38, 64, 67, 125, 172, 195, 207-210, 214, 221, 231, 240, 283, 296, 320-321
wilderness, 114, 116, 120, 125-130, 178, 201, 207, 227-228, 234-238, 242-247, 250-254, 257-279, 287, 298-306, 367, 370, 375, 379, 397, 400, 407
Will; human, 11, 29, 37, 45, 53, 69, 71, 76, 89, 155, 160, 363, 371
of God, 37, 44-45, 57-58, 62, 70-71, 80, 89-90, 112-117, 120-121, 127, 134, 139, 142-144, 149-151, 155-161, 165, 168, 178, 182, 187, 193, 197-202, 205, 211, 215-217, 222-223, 229, 235, 240-247, 265, 270, 282-286, 291-294, 301-305, 314, 319-324, 329-335, 338-342, 351, 362, 365, 389, 392-403, 410
of Heaven, 36, 49, 58, 81, 89, 113, 138, 148-149, 202, 243, 329, 340, 365, 388
William of Orange, 360
wisdom, 64-65, 127, 130, 222, 238, 292, 315
womb, 117, 128, 153, 160, 192, 218
Word of God, 21, 30, 43, 67, 69, 74, 92, 104, 111, 133, 180, 190, 232, 243, 245, 247, 250, 273, 283, 319, 322, 363, 390, 404
World War I, 87, 340-341, 347, 357, 367-378, 382-383
World War II, 8, 87, 341, 370-375, 378, 401
World Wars, 365-367, 376, 379, 403 -see also Third World War
worldwide course to restore Canaan, 215, 228, 234, 240-243, 267-271, 275-282, 366
worship, 122, 137, 178, 244, 272-275, 321-322, 352, 372, 401, 403
Wycliffe, John, 325, 352

yang and yin, 16-21, 47-48, 170, 243
Yi Dynasty, 402

Zechariah, 125, 127, 269, 384
Zedekiah, 322
Zipporah, 240
Zoroastrians, 151
Zwingli, Huldrych, 353

www.ingramcontent.com/pod-product-compliance
Lightning Source LLC
Chambersburg PA
CBHW040323300426

44112CB00021B/2856